BOWEN'S

ATLAS

1918

BOWEN'S

Michigan State Atlas

CONTAINING

A Separate Map of Each County, Showing Section, Township and Range Lines, Railroad and Interurban Lines, Churches and School Houses and Public Highways, With a Historical Sketch of Each County

---

IMPROVED ROADS SHOWN IN COLORS

Also Containing Maps of Michigan, the United States and the World, and the Official Soil Map of Michigan; Population of Townships, Cities and Villages and Geographical and Other Tables of Value

---

1916

B. F. BOWEN & CO., Inc.

INDIANAPOLIS

FOREWORD

When Elwood Haynes drove his first little automobile down the streets of Kokomo, Indiana, he did not realize that within the next score of years this invention of his would revolutionize highway transportation in the whole world. There is no gainsaying the fact that the automobile has been the direct cause of the building of more miles of good roads in the United States during the past twenty years than all other agencies put together. In Michigan alone the automobile tax for 1915, all of which was applied to road construction, amounted to $1,500,000. It is estimated that 1,650 miles of roads will be built in the state in 1916, at an estimated cost of $3,271,000. Thus it may be seen that the automobile is responsible for more than one-third of the money to be expended on the roads this year.

Good roads are a necessary concomitant of good civilization. It has been said that when a community pulls itself out of the mire of bad roads and builds highways that are usable in all kinds of weather, it is on the road to a better and happier existence. With good roads, isolation ceases, social life takes on a new aspect, educational and religious affairs are benefited and, in short, every phase of the community's life is raised to a higher standard. It is a law of human nature that some good things have to be forced on people; not one man out of a hundred would take out life insurance were it not forced upon him; many a farmer who has objected to paying for good roads has lived to see the benefit of the expenditure and enjoy the road to which he had so vigorously objected.

Fortunately the country is awake as never before to the actual value in dollars and cents of good highways. The federal government has recently passed the Bankhead Act, which provides for an appropriation to all states that have a centralized direction of road improvements. Forty-three of the states have qualified to receive federal aid, only the states of Indiana, South Carolina, Georgia, Mississippi and Texas not having highway commissions under the direction of the state Legislature. The government proposes to extend aid to the various states in proportion to their road mileage and the amount set aside by the state itself.

Michigan is pre-eminently a state of automobiles and the many beautiful highways threading the state in every direction have been constructed in a large measure with the tax on the automobile. Within the past year the Dixie Highway has aroused new interest in good roads and this is especially true since the Highway in Michigan follows the shores of Lakes Huron and Michigan around the lower peninsula. This road, when completed, has a length of 3,989 miles. It will traverse eight states, touch four state capitals, one hundred and ten county seats and pass through one hundred and forty-four counties. The Highway has an eastern and western division and runs from Mackinaw, Michigan, through the states of Michigan, Indiana, Ohio, Kentucky, Tennessee, Georgia and Florida.

More people are using the highways today than ever before. It is a long step from the blazed trail and corduroy roads of our grandfathers to the macadamized, brick or cement roads of today. People of today have more leisure and more inclination to travel than did the early settlers of our state. With the building of good roads in all directions, it has become possible to go from one end of the state to the other in a day or two. At the present time the farmer in his automobile can travel farther in one day than it was possible for him to travel in a week under conditions as they existed fifty years ago.

Every person who travels the highways of the state feels the need of an accurate guide to the roads. In no other way is it possible to tour the state without a useless expenditure of time and money, not to say patience. A good automobile guide is as essential as good gasoline. It is confidently believed that Bowen's Automobile and Sportsmen's Guide is the best publication of its kind which has ever been offered to the traveling public of Michigan. Each county map has been submitted to competent local authorities for verification, special attention having been given to the delineation of the main traveled thoroughfares. State and county officials have extended the company every courtesy in the effort to make this work accurate in every detail. Especial credit is due the State Highway Commission, Good Roads Association, Wolverine Auto Club, Detroit Automobile Dealers' Association and the different commercial clubs of the state. All of these organizations have taken a hearty interest in the preparation of the Guide. A large number of the automobile factories have also co-operated in various ways with the company. The historical sketch which accompanies each county map was furnished by Hon. A. C. Carton, of the Public Domain Commission.

The Bowen Guide is the first serious attempt to prepare a publication of this magnitude in the state. The company has been engaged in the preparation of the maps and the collection of data for the past year. During this time its representatives have visited every county in the state in their efforts to make the publication as nearly accurate as possible. Finally, the company wishes to thank the many thousands of persons who have made this publication possible.

THE PUBLISHERS.

CONTENTS

Business directory 6, 7
Automobile and Sportsmen's Guide, adv. 8
Dort Motor Co., Detroit, adv. 9
Wayne Hotel, Detroit, adv. 10
Charlevoix Hotel, Detroit, adv. 11
D. & C. Navigation Co., adv. 12
Tuller Hotel, Detroit, adv. 13
Index to key map 14
Instructions as to use of maps 14
Key map, state of Michigan 15
A. B. Higman, Benton Harbor, adv. 16
Berrien county, sketch 16
Berrien county, map 17
Cass county, sketch 18
Cass county, map 19
St. Joseph county, sketch 20
St. Joseph county, map 21
Branch county, sketch 22
Branch county, map 23
Hillsdale county, sketch 24
Hillsdale county, map 25
Lenawee county, sketch 26
Lenawee county, map 27
Monroe county, sketch 28
Monroe county, map 29
Wayne county, sketch 30
East and West Michigan Pikes 30a
Wolverine Highway 30a
Fifty- and Ninety-mile Pleasure Trips from Detroit 30b
Wayne county, map 31
Washtenaw county, sketch 32
Washtenaw county, map 33
Buell Auto Co., Jackson, adv. 34
American Oil Co., Jackson, adv. 34
Jackson county, sketch 34
Jackson county, map 35
Calhoun county, sketch 36
Calhoun county, map 37
Kalamazoo county, sketch 38
Kalamazoo county, map 39
VanBuren county, sketch 40
VanBuren county, map 41
Allegan county, sketch 42
Allegan county, map 43
Barry county, sketch 44
Barry county, map 45
J. A. Fritz, Charlotte, adv. 46
Eaton county, sketch 46
Eaton county, map 47
Dyer-Jenison-Barry Co., Lansing, adv. 48
Bates & Edmonds Motor Co., Lansing, adv. 48
Michigan Karlsbad Sanitarium, Lansing, adv. 48
Ingham county, sketch 48
Ingham county, map 49
Livingston county, sketch 50
Livingston county, map 51
Oakland county, sketch 52
Oakland county, map 53
Macomb county, sketch 54
Macomb county, map 55
St. Clair county, sketch 56
St. Clair county, map 57
Lapeer county, sketch 58
Lapeer county, map 59
L. D. Gillett, Flint, adv. 60
Guaranty Title & Mortg Co., Flint, adv. 60
Oak Grove Hospital, Flint, adv. 60
Allen & Burchy, Flint, adv. 60
Genesee county, sketch 60
Genesee county, map 61
Shiawassee county, sketch 62
Shiawassee county, map 63
Clinton county, sketch 64
Clinton county, map 65
Ionia county, sketch 66
Ionia county, map 67
Kent county, sketch 68
Kent county, map 69
Ottawa county, sketch 70
Ottawa county, map 71
Muskegon county, sketch 72
Muskegon county, map 73
Montcalm county, sketch 74
Montcalm county, map 75
Gratiot county, sketch 76
Gratiot county, map 77
Saginaw county, sketch 78
Saginaw county, map 79
Tuscola county, sketch 80
Tuscola county, map 81
Sanilac county, sketch 82
Sanilac county, map 83
Huron county, sketch 84
Huron county, map 85
Bay county, sketch 86
Bay county, map 87
Midland county, sketch 88
Midland county, map 89
Isabella county, sketch 90
Isabella county, map 91
Mecosta county, sketch 92
Mecosta county, map 93
Newaygo county, sketch 94
Newaygo county, map 95
Oceana county, sketch 96
Oceana county, map 97
Mason county, sketch 98
Mason county, map 99
Lake county, sketch 100
Lake county, map 101
Osceola county, sketch 102
Osceola county, map 103
Clare county, sketch 104
Clare county, map 105
Gladwin county, sketch 106
Gladwin county, map 107
Arenac county, sketch 108
Arenac county, map 109
Iosco county, sketch 110
Iosco county, map 111
Ogenaw county, sketch 112
Ogenaw county, map 113
Roscommon county, sketch 114
Roscommon county, map 115
Missaukee county, sketch 116
Missaukee county, map 117
Wexford county, sketch 118
Wexford county, map 119
Manistee county, sketch 120
Manistee county, map 121
Benzie county, sketch 122
Benzie county, map 123
Grand Traverse county, sketch 124
Grand Traverse county, map 125
Kalkaska county, sketch 126
Kalkaska county, map 127
Crawford county, sketch 128
Crawford county, map 129
Oscoda county, sketch 130
Oscoda county, map 131
Alcona county, sketch 132
Alcona county, map 133
Alpena county, sketch 134
Alpena county, map 135
Montgomery county, sketch 136
Montgomery county, map 137
Otsego county, sketch 138
Otsego county, map 139
Antrim county, sketch 140
Antrim county, map 141
Leelanau county, sketch 142
Leelanau county, map 143
Charlevoix county, sketch 144
Charlevoix county, map 145
Emmet county, sketch 146
Emmet county, map 147
Cheboygan county, sketch 148
Cheboygan county, map 149
Presque Isle county, sketch 150
Presque Isle county, map 151
Mackinac county, sketch 152
Mackinac county, map 153
Chippewa county, sketch 154
Chippewa county, map 155
Luce county, sketch 156
Luce county, map 157
Schoolcraft county, sketch 158
Schoolcraft county, map 159
Alger county, sketch 160
Alger county, map 161
Delta county, sketch 162
Delta county, map 163
Menominee county, sketch 164
Menominee county, map 165
Dickinson county, sketch 166
Dickinson county, map 167
Marquette county, sketch 168
Marquette county, map 169
Iron county, sketch 170
Iron county, map 171
Gogebic county, sketch 172
Gogebic county, map 173
Ontonagon county, sketch 174
Ontonagon county, map 175
Houghton county, sketch 176
Houghton county, map 177
Baraga county, sketch 178
Baraga county, map 179
Keweenaw county, sketch 180
Keweenaw county, map 181
Population of townships, cities and villages 182
Geological survey maps, between 182b and 183
Agricultural Statistics, United States 183
Population of counties, cities and towns 184–187
Michigan, map 190–189
Populations and altitudes, United States 190–194
United States, map 192–193
Armies of the world 195
Navies of the world 195
Militia of the United States 195
Governments of the world 195
Time, difference of, between Washington and places named 195
Army of the United States 195
World, map of 196–197
Geographical tables 198

DIRECTORY
OF
Hotels, Garages, Automobile and Accessory Dealers, Banks, Real Estate, Etc.

ADRIAN.
City Garage.
New Adrian Hotel.
Raymond, S. W., Garage.

ALGONAC.
Mullikin, C. A., Drugs.

ALLEGON.
Burrill Tripp Company, Merchants.
First National Bank.
Stein, John C., Real Estate.
Updike, T. L., Real Estate.
Vahue, Robert L., Book Store.
Weeks & Montague, Allegan County Real Estate and Abstract Office.

ALMA.
Brunner, W. Alex, Drugs.
First State Bank.
Hopkins, D. E., Wright Hotel.
Look Patterson Drug Company.
M. L. Perrigo, Studebaker Salesroom and Garage.
McKenzie, J., Cigars.
Republic Motor Truck Company.
Wyant, A. C., Garage.

ALMONT.
Wolverine Garage.

ALPENA.
Alpena County Savings Bank.
Alpena National Bank.
Reynolds, Charles, Garage.

ANN ARBOR.
Ann Arbor Savings Bank.
Brooks, Charles L., Real Estate.
Farmers & Mechanics Bank.
Overland Garage Company.
Weber, George, Book Store.

BAD AXE.
Bad Axe Auto Company, Garage.
Clark & McCaren Company, Grocery.
Dunlay Garage Company.
Misses Skinner, Book Store.
Schaffer, E. F., Transfer Line.

BATTLE CREEK.
Central National Bank.
Cushman Auto Sales Company, Garage, Ford Agency and Accessories.
Fischer, E. C., Manager Fischer Company.
Hoffmaster, B. F., Battle Creek Taxi Company.
Williams, Arthur B.

BAY CITY.
Ames, G. W., Real Estate.
Bay City Tire Supply Company, Tire Repairing.
Central Auto Company, Garage.
Crotty, H., Camera Supplies.
Farmers Auto and Machinery Company.
First National Bank.
Jenison Hardware Company.
Lewis Manufacturing Company.
McKerlie, D. K., Garage.
Peterson, Arthur F., Garage.
W. T. Foley & Company, Drugs.
Werler Auto Company, Garage.
Wilton & Mack, Books, Etc.

BEAVERTON.
Nickham, William C., Garage.

BENTON HARBOR.
Berrien County Bank.
Downell, Frank T., Drugs and Books.
Higman, Arthur B., Real Estate and Loans.
Messner, A. F., Garage.

BERRIEN SPRINGS.
Miller, George, Garage.

BIG RAPIDS.
Bertram, L. F., Auto Garage.

BIRCH RUN.
Dodge, E. M., Garage.
Reid, Claude, Garage.

BLISSFIELD.
Ries, Daniel, Hotel.

BRIGHTON.
W. O. Pitkin & Son, Garage.

BROWN CITY.
Sheppard, S. T., Drugs.

BUCHANAN.
Kelling, M. J., Cigar Store.

CADILLAC.
Van Liew, George, Real Estate.

CAPAC.
Bolton, R. E.
Bueeen & Mitchell.
Capac Garage.
Capac Savings Bank.

CARO.
Lawrence, B. E., Sporting Goods.
H. S. Myers & Company, Garage.
B. A. Smith & Company, Garage.

CARSON CITY.
Ralph, F., Garage.

CASEVILLE.
R. L. Hubbard & Company, Bankers.

CASS CITY.
Reushler, J. A., Garage.
Treadgold's Drug Store.

CASSOPOLIS.
Central Drug Store, W. D. Hopkins Propr.

CERESCO.
Ulrich Motor Sales Co., Oakland Agency.

CHARLEVOIX.
Charlevoix States Savings Bank.

CHARLOTTE.
Beard, F. E., Books and Stationery.
Collins Drug Store.
Fritz, J. A., Garage.
Smith, J. M. C., Banker.

CHEBOYGAN.
Cheboygan Auto Sales Company.
Cheboygan State Bank.
First National Bank.

CLARE.
Clare County Savings Bank.
Ehrlich, Con, Salesman.
J. T. Brown & Sons, Garage.
Mussell, Mrs. A. E., Drugs.

CLINTON.
B. O. Randall & Company, Drugs.
Lancaster, George W., Garage.
Williams, Fred H., Hotel.

CLIO.
Clio State Bank.

COLDWATER.
Reed, F. J., Bookseller and Stationer.
Standard Garage.

CORUNNA.
Yaklin, W. N., Garage, King Agency.

DAVISON.
Vilas, A. L., Garage.

DETROIT.
A. L. A. Tire Company, Inc.
American Indemnity Company.
Auto Equipment Company.
Auto Supply Company.
Banner Realty Company.
Bemb-Robinson Company, Hudson Motor Cars.
Buick Motor Company.
Burton, C. M., Abstracter.
Chalmers Motor Company.
Charlevoix Hotel.
Chesbrough, Frank P., Real Estate.
Cunningham Auto Company, Maxwell Cars.
Cunningham's Drug Store.
D. & C. Navigation Company.
Denby, Edwin, Attorney.
Dennen's Book Shop.
Detroit Auto Hardware Company.
Detroit Life Insurance Company.
Detroit Trust Company.
Devlin Company, The, Automobiles.
Dort Motor Company.
Down Town Garage.
Doxtator, Charles H., Real Estate.
Drake, George A., & Company, Stationery, Printing, Office Furniture.
Earle, Horatio S., Farm and Road Machinery.
Equitable Life Insurance Company.
Pasquelle, L. J., Real Estate.
Fighe, M. J., Real Estate.
Ford Motor Company.
Fromley, Wilson & Company, Real Estate.
General Sales Company.
Goebel Brewing Company.
Gordon Auto Sales Company.
Grusser Motor Company, Hupmobile Distributors, G. Edward Biel, Mngr.
Hannan Real Estate Company.
Hayes, J. H., Wayne Hotel.
Hilton, Hart & Garrett Company, Printers.
Hines, Edward F., Printing.
Hines, Edward N. (Speaker-Hines Printing Co.
Holden, James S., Real Estate.
Hotel Charlevoix.
Hurst Garage Company.
Hyde, O. F., Company, Real Estate.
Interstate Fire Insurance Company.
John Hancock Life Insurance Company.
Judson Bradway, Real Estate.
King, Grinnison Realty Company.
Lambrecht, Kelly & Company, Real Estate.
Leland, Thad E., Real Estate.
Logan, J. H., Real Estate.
Lyon, Edward F., Company, Automobile Springs, Axle Parts.
McCandless Brothers, Wholesale Lumber.
Manufacturers and Traders Casualty Company.
Marchant, S. A., Real Estate.
Merchants Realty Company.
Michigan Mutual Life Insurance Company.
Michigan Workmen's Compensation Mutual Insurance Company.
Moss, W. E., & Company, Bankers.
Muir Lynn Realty Company.
Northern Assurance Company.
Ohio & Michigan Coal Company.
Ohio State Life Insurance Company.
Oldsmobile Company.
Paige Detroit Motor Company.
Peoples State Bank.
Piser, Walter C., Real Estate.
Radford, Block Company, Distributors Oakland and Marmon Cars.
Richmond & Backus Co., The, Stationers, General Printers, Blank Book Manufacturers, Office Furniture.
Robinson, L. J., & Company, Chalmers Motor Cars, Distributors for Michigan.
Schmidt, Herman A., Automobile Manufacturer.
Service Garage.
Sheehan, John V., Company, Books.
Slocum, James, Real Estate.
Speaker-Hines Printing Co.
Standart Brothers, Ltd., Wholesale Hardware and Sporting Goods.
Stomfeltz, Lovely & Company, Real Estate.
Studebaker Corporation.
Thompson, J. Walter, Company, Advertising.
Tuller Hotel.
Union Trust Company, Real Estate Department.
United States Auto Supply Company.
Waldelich Ross Realty Company.
Warren, Cady, Ladd & Hill, Attorneys.
Watkins & Radcliffe, Dealers and Jobbers, Automobile Accessories.
Wayne County and Home Savings Bank.
Wayne Hotel.
Wetmore, Quinn & Company, Paige and Saxon Cars.
Wilson & Smith, Real Estate.
Winton Company, Automobiles.
Wolverine Auto Club.

DURAND.
Durand Drug Company.

EAST LANSING.
Terrien, F. F., Salesman.

EATON RAPIDS.
Ferguson, R. G., Garage.
Graham, F. A., Druggist.

EAU CLAIRE.
Ward, Walter H., Drugs.

ELSIE.
Sheldon & Son, Garage.

ESCANABA.
Delta Title, Land and Loan Company, Abstracters.

EVART.
Postal Hardware Company, Garage.

FARWELL.
Burton, William, Pharmacist.

FENTON.
Davis, J. Frank.
Enders, M. P.
Fenton Elevator Company.
Fenton State Bank.

FLINT.
Abraham Foss Company, Sporting Goods.
Aldrich, Isaac N., Real Estate, Loans and Insurance, Representing The Merrill Corporation of Chicago.
Allen & Burchy, Real Estate.
Allen & Curtis, Architects.
Beach, Allen J., Insurance.
Buick Motor Company, Automobiles.
Carlton, M. E., Company, Books, Etc.
Central Drug Store.
Chevrolet Motor Company.
Crescent Company, Sporting Goods.
Dort Motor Car Company.
Farm Realty Company.
Flint Garage.
Flint Land Company.
Ford Sales Company, Ford Cars and Accessories.
Genesee County Abstract Company.
Gillett, L. D., Overland and Willys-Knight Sales Agency.
Guaranty Title & Mortgage Co.
Hawley Hotel.
Hetchley-Babb, Real Estate.
Home Realty Company.
Hotel Bryant.
Industrial Savings Bank.
Lewis Manufacturing Company.
Martin & Zimmerman Drug Company.
Marvel Carburetor Company.
Mercer, John W.
Monroe Motor Company.
National Bank of Flint.
Oak Grove Hospital.
Paige Sales Company.
Paterson, W. A., & Company, Carriage Manufacturers.
Patterson Auto Sales Company.
Ralston Land Company.
Union Trust & Savings Company.
Van Vleet, Jared, Real Estate.
Wood, George, Drugs.
Woolfit & Macomber, Insurance and Real Estate.

FLUSHING.
Cameron, R. T., Drugs.

FOWLER.
Weber, Louis, Garage.

FOWLERVILLE.
Sprague, Lee C., Garage.

FRANKENMUTH.
State Bank.

GALIEN.
Standard Garage, Louis J. Norris, Propr.

GLADWIN.
Morris, Robert, Garage.

GRAND HAVEN.

Perry, J. J., Merchant.

GRAND LEDGE.

Stuart, D. C., & Son, Garage.

GRAND RAPIDS.

Charles Franklin Company.
Dowling, George E., Cadillac Salesman.
Fizsch Auto Supply Company.
Fourth National Bank.
Grand Rapids Trust Company.
Hass Realty Company.
Jenkins, J. C., Rigard Agency.
Kridler & Son.
Michigan Trust Company.
Peoples Savings Bank.
Preferred Life Insurance Company.
Service Garage Company.

HASTINGS.

Skinner Garage Company.
Colgrove, P. T., President Good Roads Association.

HOLLAND.

Brink, Henry R., Book Store.
Peoples Garage, Lievense Bros., Props.
Ven Hunzin, Thomas W., Garage.

HOWELL.

Dean, Bert, Sprague Garage.

HUDSON.

Harrington, H. C., Garage.

IMLAY CITY.

Holden, T. F., Drugs.

IONIA.

Smith, Smith & McEween, Druggists.
Collar & Hullberger, Garage.
Miller & Ashe, Garage.
National Bank of Ionia.
Marshall Wright Lumber Company.
Branch Auto Sales Co.

ITHACA.

Goodwin, T. A., Drugs.
Barken Garage.

JACKSON.

American Fork & Hoe Company, Manufacturers.
American Oil Company.
American Sewer Pipe Company.
American Top Company.
Briscoe Motor Sales Company, West Pearl Street.
Buell Auto Company.
Central Auto and Supply Company, Garage.
Haynes Wheel Company.
Isbell & Company, Grain and Seeds.
Jackson Auto Company, Jackson Automobiles.
Jackson Cushion Spring Company.
Jackson Rim Company.
Jackson State Savings Bank.
Lewis-Allen Company, Automobiles, Supplies, Storage, Repairing.
Lewis Spring & Axle Company.
McLaughlin, Ward & Company, Elevator.
Mutual Motors Company, Automobile Factory.
Shenf, E. J., Seedman.
Sparks, Withington Company, "Safety First" Sound Sparton.
Stockbridge Elevator Company, Elevator.
United States Land and Investment Company, Real Estate.

JONESVILLE.

Saxton, E. H., Druggist.

KALAMAZOO.

First National Bank.
Harlow, W. O., Automobiles.
Home Savings Bank.
Kalamazoo Auto Company.
Kalamazoo Auto Sales Company, Overland Automobiles.
Kalamazoo Storage Battery Company.
Thompson, R. C., Sporting Goods.

LAKEVIEW.

Lape, Curt P., Hotel.

LANSING.

Bailey, The J. W., Company, Real Estate.
Bates & Edmonds, Engineers.
Bennett Buick Auto Company.
Brooks, E. H., Abstracter.
Butler Block Pharmacy.
Campbell & Darling, Drugs.
Crotty Brothers, Book Dealers.
Downey Hotel.
Dyer-Jenison-Barry Company, Ltd., Real Estate and Bonds.
Emery, A. M., Bookdealer.
Goodell, George M., Insurance.
Hedges & Gibson, Drugs and Books.
Houghton, F. W., Drugs.
Huntington, A. D., Cigar Stand.
Ivory Brothers, Drugs.
Kerns, W. G., Hotel Wentworth.
Lansing Garage Sales Company, Garage.
Lansing State Savings Bank.
Larabee, J. H., Leather and Sporting Goods.
Michigan Karlsbad Sanitarium.
Price, Glenn W., Cigar Stand.
Prudden, W. K., & Company, Manufacturers.
Reo Motor Company.
Robinson Drug Company.
Roger Leather Goods Company.
Shiffer, C. B., Druggist.
Sturgis, Amos D., Druggist.
Tracy Auto Tire Repair Company.
Wentworth Hotel.

LAPEER.

England, C., Garage.
First National Bank.
Gardiner, J. N., Drugs.

LAWRENCE.

Thomas & Sons, Garage.

LESLIE.

St. Clair Bros., Garage.

LOWELL.

Gregory, Percy, Garage, Agency Buick and Studebaker Cars.
Lowell State Bank.
Marr, D. G., Banker.
Smith Garage.

MANISTIQUE.

Hoppins, C. M., Garage.
Putnam, A., Drugs.

MARLETTE.

Burke, O. E., Garage.

MARSHALL.

Commercial Savings Bank.
Green, Grove, Drugs.
Ulrich Motor Sales Company, Garage, Oakland Agency.

MASON.

Farmers Bank.
Hazelton Bros., Garage.
Whitmore, P. D., Real Estate.

MIDDLETON.

Hull, Ray, Garage.

MIDLAND.

Main Garage.

MILAN.

Milan Garage and Sales Company.

MONROE.

First National Bank.
Monroe Garage, Gasoline, Repairs, Accessories, Storage.
Monroe Overland Company.

MT. CLEMENS.

Mt. Clemens Garage and Motor Sales Company.

MT. MORRIS.

Bank of Mt. Morris.

MT. PLEASANT.

Battles Automobile Company, Garage.
Ellsman & Ervay Garage, Automobiles and Accessories, Repairing.
Johnson's Garage.
Myers & Miller, Real Estate.
Park Hotel.

MORENCI.

First National Bank.

MUSKEGON.

Barcus, W. W., Inc., Real Estate.
Bowman & Van Dam, Real Estate Investments and Resort Property.
Boyd, J. F., Cigars.
Boyd's Book and Stationery Store.
Erme Ter Veen, Cigars.
Gibney, C. N., Stationery and News.
Hathaway, F. E., Cigars.
Knizenga & Whipple, Books.
Muskegon Abstract Company.
Union National Bank.

NEWBERRY.

Campbell, D., Hotel.
Sweney, C. H., & C. A. Kuntison, Garage.

NORTH BRANCH.

Dee, M. B., Druggist.

NORTH LANSING.

Ward & Searlett Company, Garage.

ONAWAY.

Onaway State Savings Bank.
Onaway Wood Rim Company.

OVID.

Smith, G. F., & Son, Garage.

OWOSSO.

Hartshorn Auto Company.
Owosso Savings Bank.

PETOSKEY.

Golden, Roy A., Garage.
Northern Auto Company, Garage.

PIGEON.

Diebel Auto Company.
Harder, H. B., Garage.

PINCONNING.

Walworth, C., Garage.

PLAINWELL.

Travis, F. D., Garage and Automobiles.

PONTIAC.

Oakland County Savings Bank.
Pontiac Savings Bank.
Waldron, E. P., Real Estate.

PORT AUSTIN.

Allen, Dan, Garage.
Cartwright, G. Russell, Ford Cars.

PORT HURON.

Barkell, William, Taxis.
Beard, Campbell & Co., Hardware.
Commercial Bank.
First National Exchange Bank.
Harrington Hotel.
Kaill, Lee, Drugs.
MacTaggart, David, Books.
Moore, Alex, Representing Duluth Steamship Agency.
Pettis Garage.
St. Clair County Savings Bank.
Unger, H. T., Sporting Goods.
Yakom, Geo. E., Garage.

PORTLAND.

Curtis, A. A., Garage.
Divine, L. E., & Son, Hotel.
Sayer, C. H., Garage.

ROMEO.

Ostrander, F. L., Garage.

ROSEBUSH.

Matteson, F. C., General Merchandise.

SAGINAW.

Appleby, B. G., & Co., Real Estate, Bonds, Investments and Loans.
Appleby, B. G., Stocks, Bonds and Public Utility Operator.
Banister, J. L., Drugs.
Bless Bros., Automobiles, Accessories.
Culver-Deisler Company, Drugs.
Eastman & Range, Garage.
Electric Vehicle Company.
Kelsey & Son, F. J., Books.
Owens, Harry, Central Wholesale Company.
Russell, Everett M., Electrical Repairs.
Saginaw Cadillac Company.
Second National Bank.
Simons Sales Company, Overland Agency.
Swinton & Company, Stationery and Books.
Tire Service Company.
Wisner Edgar, News Stand.

ST. CHARLES.

Hartley, Peter A.

ST. CLAIR.

Commercial Savings Bank.
Heythaler, A. W., Garage.
Hart & Scott, Real Estate.
St. Clair Delivery System, Moving Van.

ST. JOHNS.

St. Johns National Bank.
Smith, A. T., Garage.
William G. Moss Auto Company, Studebaker and Maxwell Agency.

ST. LOUIS.

Burlingame & Son, Garage.

SALINE.

Gaylord, George E., Square Deal Garage.

SHEPHERD.

Shepherd Auto Company, Garage.

SHERIDAN.

Russell, A. N., Automobiles.

SOUTH HAVEN.

Griffin & Wheaton, Garage.
Reusch, Henry, Book Store.

SOUTH LANSING.

D. & A. Sales Company.

STANDISH.

Ireland, L., Garage.

STANTON.

Main Street Garage.

TECUMSEH.

Barrett Bros., Hotel.
Gaston, George W., Jeweler.
Pulver, B. J., Drugs.
Tecumseh Co-operative Association, Hardware.
Tecumseh Garage.
Tecumseh State Savings Bank.

THREE OAKS.

Three Oaks Auto Sales Company.

THREE RIVERS.

Schoonmaker, F. L., Cigars.

TRAVERSE CITY.

DeWitt, W. L., Lumber.
First National Bank.
Gorde's Garage.
Hamilton, Frank, Merchant.
Oberlin, J. P., Hotel.
West Michigan Garage.

UNION CITY.

Union City National Bank.

VASSAR.

Caro Vulcanizing Works, Tire Repairing.
Grant, William, Garage.
Melvin, Carl, Hotel.
State Savings Bank of Vassar.

VICKSBURG.

Farmers State Bank.
First National Bank.

WATERVLIET.

Olson, John B., Jr., Garage.

WAYNE.

O'Brien, W. J., Drugs.

WELLS.

The I. Stephenson Frisbie Co., Manufacturers.

WEST BRANCH.

Rosebeck, B., Garage.
Yeo, N. M., Abstract Company.

WEST SAGINAW.

Krogmann, H. G., Repairs.

WILLIAMSTON.

Gorsline Bros., Furniture and Ford Cars.
Hotel Glaser.

YALE.

Percy, N. B., Garage.
Harrington, J. W., Hotel.
First National Bank.

YPSILANTI.

First National Bank.

ZEELAND.

Karsten, H. H., & Bro., Garage.

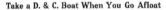

ALPHABETICAL LIST OF COUNTIES, WITH KEY NUMBER

133 Alcona
161 Alger
43 Allegan
135 Alpena
141 Antrim
109 Arenac
179 Baraga
45 Barry
87 Bay
123 Benzie
17 Berrien
23 Branch
37 Calhoun
19 Cass
145 Charlevoix
149 Cheboygan
155 Chippewa
105 Clare
65 Clinton
129 Crawford
163 Delta
167 Dickinson
47 Eaton
147 Emmet
61 Genesee
107 Gladwin
173 Gogebic
125 Grand Traverse
77 Gratiot
25 Hillsdale
177 Houghton
85 Huron
49 Ingham
67 Ionia
111 Iosco
171 Iron
91 Isabella
35 Jackson
39 Kalamazoo
127 Kalkaska
69 Kent
181 Keweenaw
101 Lake
59 Lapeer
143 Leelanau
27 Lenawee
51 Livingston
157 Luce
153 Mackinac
55 Macomb
121 Manistee
169 Marquette
99 Mason
93 Mecosta
165 Menominee
89 Midland
117 Missaukee
29 Monroe
75 Montcalm
137 Montmorency
73 Muskegon
95 Newaygo
53 Oakland
97 Oceana
113 Ogemaw
175 Ontonagon
103 Osceola
131 Oscoda
139 Otsego
71 Ottawa
151 Presque Isle
115 Roscommon
79 Saginaw
83 Sanilac
159 Schoolcraft
63 Shiawassee
57 St. Clair
21 St. Joseph
81 Tuscola
41 Van Buren
33 Washtenaw
31 Wayne
119 Wexford

COUNTIES IN NUMERICAL ORDER ACCORDING TO KEY NUMBERS

17 Berrien
19 Cass
21 St. Joseph
23 Branch
25 Hillsdale
27 Lenawee
29 Monroe
31 Wayne
33 Washtenaw
35 Jackson
37 Calhoun
39 Kalamazoo
41 Van Buren
43 Allegan
45 Barry
47 Eaton
49 Ingham
51 Livingston
53 Oakland
55 Macomb
57 St. Clair
59 Lapeer
61 Genesee
63 Shiawassee
65 Clinton
67 Ionia
69 Kent
71 Ottawa
73 Muskegon
75 Montcalm
77 Gratiot
79 Saginaw
81 Tuscola
83 Sanilac
85 Huron
87 Bay
89 Midland
91 Isabella
93 Mecosta
95 Newaygo
97 Oceana
99 Mason
101 Lake
103 Osceola
105 Clare
107 Gladwin
109 Arenac
111 Iosco
113 Ogemaw
115 Roscommon
117 Missaukee
119 Wexford
121 Manistee
123 Benzie
125 Grand Traverse
127 Kalkaska
129 Crawford
131 Oscoda
133 Alcona
135 Alpena
137 Montmorency
139 Otsego
141 Antrim
143 Leelanau
145 Charlevoix
147 Emmet
149 Cheboygan
151 Presque Isle
153 Mackinac
155 Chippewa
157 Luce
159 Schoolcraft
161 Alger
163 Delta
165 Menominee
167 Dickinson
169 Marquette
171 Iron
173 Gogebic
175 Ontonagon
177 Houghton
179 Baraga
181 Keweenaw

EXPLANATION

White Face Figures on the margin of the sectional county maps indicate the page number of the adjoining county.

Automobile Routes are indicated by red lines, the heavy lines indicating the trunk lines or main highways, while improved roads are indicated by lighter red lines. Black parallel lines indicate ordinary roads.

Red Letters along county boundaries show connecting point of roads, which will enable the traveler, at a glance, to connect with the same road in the adjoining county. For example, if the traveler leaves Newaygo county, Page 95, on road marked "U," he will enter the adjoining county, Mecosta, Page 93, on road marked with the same letter.

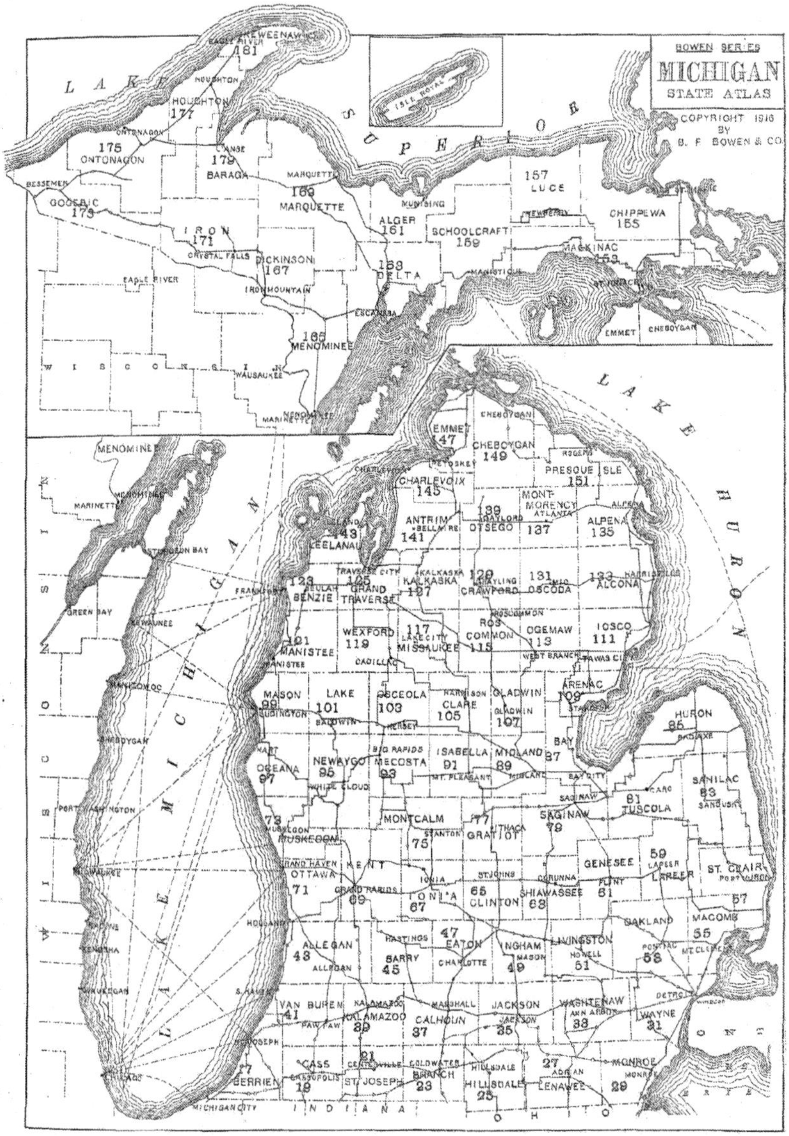
BOWEN SERIES
MICHIGAN
STATE ATLAS
COPYRIGHT 1916
BY
B. F. BOWEN & CO.
LAKE SUPERIOR
ISLE ROYAL
LAKE MICHIGAN
LAKE HURON
WISCONSIN
INDIANA
OHIO
KEWEENAW 181
HOUGHTON 177
175 ONTONAGON
179 BARAGA
GOGEBIC 173
IRON 171
169 MARQUETTE
ALGER 161
SCHOOLCRAFT 159
157 LUCE
CHIPPEWA 155
MACKINAC 153
DICKINSON 167
163 DELTA
165 MENOMINEE
EMMET 147
CHEBOYGAN 149
PRESQUE ISLE 151
CHARLEVOIX 145
MONTMORENCY
139 OTSEGO
ANTRIM 141
137
ALPENA 135
143 LEELANAU
123 BENZIE
125 GRAND TRAVERSE
KALKASKA 127
129 CRAWFORD
131 OSCODA
133 ALCONA
121 MANISTEE
WEXFORD 119
117 MISSAUKEE
ROSCOMMON 115
OGEMAW 113
IOSCO 111
MASON 99
LAKE 101
OSCEOLA 103
CLARE 105
GLADWIN 107
ARENAC 109
HURON 85
OCEANA 97
NEWAYGO 95
MECOSTA 93
ISABELLA 91
MIDLAND 89
BAY 87
SANILAC 83
TUSCOLA 81
73 MUSKEGON
MONTCALM 75
77 GRATIOT
SAGINAW 79
GENESEE 59
LAPEER
ST. CLAIR 57
OTTAWA 71
KENT 69
IONIA 67
65 CLINTON
SHIAWASSEE 63
61
OAKLAND
MACOMB 55
ALLEGAN 43
BARRY 45
47 EATON
INGHAM 49
LIVINGSTON 51
53
VAN BUREN 41
KALAMAZOO 39
CALHOUN 37
JACKSON 35
WASHTENAW 33
WAYNE 31
27 BERRIEN
CASS 19
21 ST. JOSEPH
BRANCH 23
HILLSDALE 25
27 LENAWEE
MONROE 29

BERRIEN COUNTY.

Berrien county was laid out and organized in 1829 and was named in honor of Attorney-General John M. Berrien. This county is located in the extreme southwest corner of the Lower Peninsula in what is known as the heart of Michigan's original fruit belt. It is bounded on the north by Van Buren county, on the east by Van Buren and Cass counties, on the south by Indiana and on the west by Lake Michigan. This county has a total land area of 362,981.63 acres, of which 332,826 acres are devoted to splendid farms. The county has a population of about 53,622 (1910 census). In 1911, a valuation of $65,105,048 was placed on all taxable lands by the state board of tax commissioners. The school system is equal to that of any in the state, there being in all 169 schools, requiring the services of 365 teachers, with an enrollment last year of 10,837 students. All parts of the county are equipped with good telegraph, telephone and rural mail service. There are 18 banks and 18 newspapers, five of which are published daily.

St. Joseph is the county seat and has a population of about 6,000. It is beautifully located on the east shore of Lake Michigan at the mouth of the St. Joseph river and on the Pere Marquette and Michigan Central Railroads, 63 miles by water from Chicago and 90 miles from Milwaukee. The natural advantages of convenient transportation routes by rail or by water, the added attraction of a beautiful and exceptionally healthful location, the interest centering in scenic environs, fishing, boating and other amusements, have made this one of the most popular summer resorts in the state. It is lighted by electricity, has broad, shaded, well paved streets, water works, fire department, sanitary sewerage system, two banks, first-class hotels, trolley system, public library, churches of the Catholic, Church of God, Congregational, Episcopal, German, Baptist, German Evangelical, German Lutheran, German United Evangelical, Methodist and Swedish Lutheran denominations, public school system. Large quantities of fruit that grow in this section are shipped from St. Joseph. Two daily and three weekly newspapers are published. Some of the city's important industrial establishments are basket and fruit package factories, knit goods factory, iron works, sash and door factory, paper-mill, flour and planing-mills, door, map, air rifle, electrical machinery, boiler and washing machine factories. It is connected with Benton Harbor, one mile distant, by electric railway.

Benton Harbor, the largest city in the county, has a population of about 10,000. It is 63 miles by water from Chicago, 90 miles by rail, and 84 miles from Milwaukee and is on the Pere Marquette and Michigan Central Railroads, near the the confluence of the Paw Paw and St. Joseph rivers, one mile inland from the mouth of the latter on Lake Michigan and connected therewith by a ship canal of sufficient depth to receive the largest lake steamers and affording one of the best harbors on the shore. It is the center of a great fruit-growing district and one of the most important fruit shipping ports on the lake.

The city is lighted by electricity and gas, has water works, an efficient fire department, police department, electric street railway, wide, shaded and well paved streets, excellent sewerage, handsome churches of many denominations, fine school system, public library, opera house, three banks, first class hotels, four wholesale fruit houses and three progressive newspapers, two of which are published daily and one weekly. Eastman Springs, a well-known health resort, is located one mile east and is connected by car line. The city's principal manufacturing industries include one of the largest book binding and loose-leaf plants in the world, malleable foundry plants, metal sectional furniture factory, lumber-mills, saw and planing-mills, box and fruit package factories, wagon and buggy factory, pickle, cider and vinegar works, ornamental stamping works, metal and iron company, flour and feed-mills, garment factory, cigar factories, also manufactories of saw-filing machinery, brooms, gas engines, tents and awnings, etc.

Other principal towns of the county are Berrien Springs, Buchanan, Coloma, Watervliet, Three Oaks, New Buffalo, Niles and Eau Claire. The principal transportation facilities are the Michigan Central, Pere Marquette, Southern Michigan (electric), the Graham & Morton Transportation Company, Benton Transit Company, and the Benton Harbor & St. Joseph Railway.

BENTON HARBOR.

A. B. Mignan, Real Estate and Loans.

Berrien County Bank.

BERRIEN COUNTY

MICHIGAN

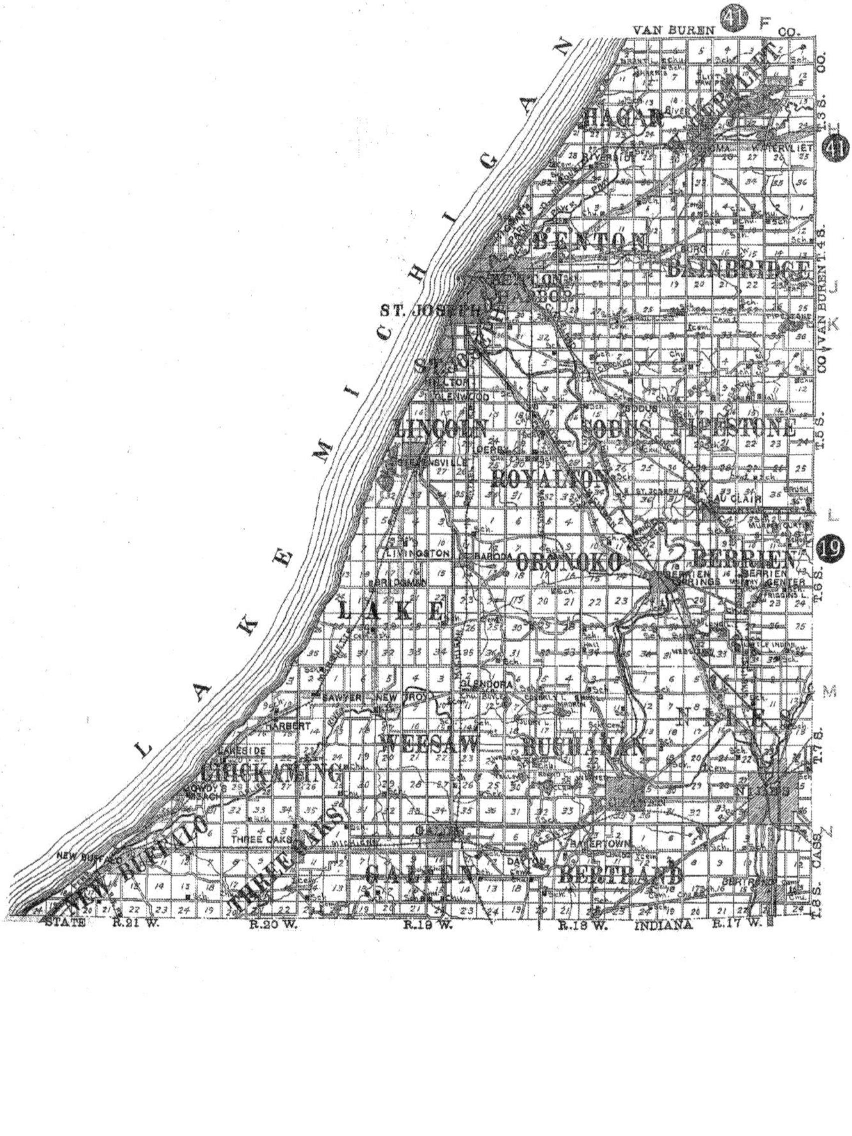

CASS COUNTY.

In 1829, the county of Cass was laid out and organized, and was named in honor of Louis Cass, then territorial governor. The county is located in the southwestern part of the Lower Peninsula. It is bounded on the north by Van Buren county, on the east by St. Joseph county, on the south by Indiana and on the west by Berrien county. The 1910 census gives Cass county a population of 20,624. The total land area comprises 316,303.00 acres. Of this number, 295,433 acres are devoted to farms, which are wonderfully productive, and in 1911 the state board of tax commissioners placed a valuation of $24,517,091 on all taxable lands. The school system is equal to that of any of the larger counties, there being 114 schools, attended by 4,008 children and requiring 170 teachers. Telephone, telegraph and rural mail service can be found in every community throughout the county. There are 10 banks, 1 daily and 5 weekly newspapers.

Cassopolis is the judicial seat of the county and has a population of about 1,500. It is located on the Michigan Central and Grand Trunk Railroads, 14 miles northeast of Niles and 89 miles southwest of Jackson. The town is lighted by electricity, has water works, a fire department, handsome court house, opera house, two banks, churches of the Baptist, Methodist, Presbyterian, African Methodist, Episcopal and African Baptist denominations, excellent educational advantages, and two weekly newspapers.

Among the other thriving communities of the county are Dowagiac, Marcellus and Vandalia. Dowagiac is an enterprising city of 5,088 inhabitants (1910 census), and is located on the Michigan Central and Benton Harbor & St. Joseph Railways, and on a branch of the Dowagiac river. It is 10 miles northwest of Cassopolis. The city is situated in the heart of one of the finest agricultural districts in the state, is well laid out with wide, well-paved and shaded streets, is lighted by electricity, has municipally-owned water works, fire department, opera house, 3 banks, 3 newspapers, churches of the Congregational, Christian, Catholic, Baptist, Disciples and Methodist denominations, a public school system on a plane with any site of its size in the state, public library and a ladies library. Among the leading industries are manufactories of stoves and furnaces, carriages, wagons, auto carriages, grain seeders, flour, cigars, carriage tops, leather novelties, sash doors, lumber, axles, cabinets, brooms, tanks, oils, etc.

Marcellus has a population of about 1,100 and is a station on the Grand Trunk Railway, 14 miles northwest of Cassopolis; has Baptist, Evangelical, Methodist and United Brethren churches, public hall, water works, electric lighting plant, two banks and a newspaper. The Michigan Central, Grand Trunk Railways and the Benton Harbor & St. Joseph Electric Railway are the principal transportation facilities of the county.

CASS COUNTY

MICHIGAN

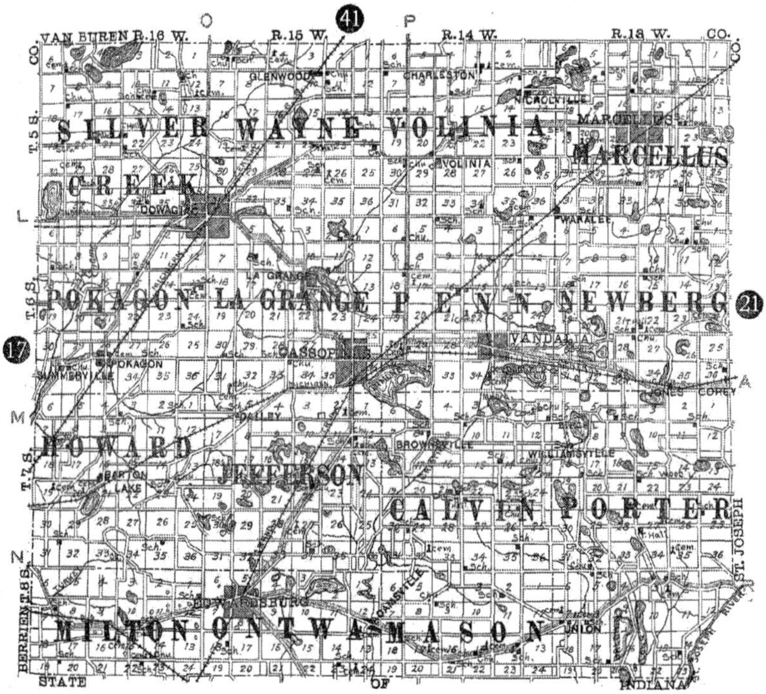

ST. JOSEPH COUNTY.

This county was laid out and organized in 1829 and takes its name from the river which flows through it and the river in turn was so called in honor of the patron saint of New France. St. Joseph county is located in the extreme southern part of the Lower Peninsula. It is bounded on the north by Kalamazoo county, on the east by Branch county, on the south by Indiana, and on the west by Cass county. The total land area is 319,794.45 acres, of which nearly 301,000 acres are in farms which rank among the best in the state. The population is 25,499 (1910 census). The valuation of taxable property, as estimated by the state board of tax commissioners in 1911, is $29,009,846. There are 128 schools, furnishing positions for 227 teachers, and a total enrollment of 4,729 students. The county has thirteen banks, one daily and eight weekly newspapers. First class telegraph, telephone and rural mail service is found in every community.

Centerville, the judicial seat of the county, has a population of about 700. It is located on the Michigan Central Railroad and on the Prairie river, sixty-four miles southwest of Jackson and one hundred and forty-one from Detroit. It has Baptist, Lutheran, Methodist and Presbyterian churches, electric light, water works, fire department, a bank and a weekly newspaper.

Sturgis, one of the largest cities of the county, has about 4,500 inhabitants. It is located in the heart of one of the richest and most productive sections of the state, at the intersection of the Grand Rapids & Indiana and the Lake Shore & Michigan Southern Railways, thirteen miles southeast of Centerville, eighty-five from Grand Rapids. It owns and operates its own electric light, power and water plant, has a fire department, sanitary sewerage system, broad streets, churches of many denominations, a public library, two banks and two live newspapers. The manufactures embrace furniture, children's go-carts, steel tanks, shears, stair rods, brass goods, plumbers' goods, reels, corn poppers, doors, blinds, medicines, woodenware, etc.

Other towns of the county are Burr Oak, Colon, Constantine, Mendon, Three Rivers, and White Pigeon. Three Rivers, with a population of about 5,000, is located at the junction of the Portage, Rock and St. Joseph rivers, hence the name, and is a station on the Michigan Central Railroad, and the Lake Shore and Michigan Southern Railway, six miles west of Centerville. The location of the city is unique in itself and each of the three streams have wide sweeping bends and are bordered with rich farm lands and woods. The city has broad, well paved and beautifully shaded streets, is lighted by electricity, has water works, sewerage system, fire department, several churches, a $30,000 union high school, a commercial college, a public library, four ward schools, an opera house, first class hotels, two banks, a daily newspaper, etc. Each of the rivers offer excellent water power facilities and each is harnessed by a mammoth cement dam. The principal manufactures embrace interurban cars, hand cars, observation cars and railroad velocipedes, sweaters, wool undergarments, paper, rattan furniture, brass goods, farm implements, electrical supplies, castings, etc. There is also a pork packing establishment, two robe tanneries and one of the largest strawberry nurseries in the world. The transportation facilities of the county are the Michigan Central, Lake Shore & Michigan Southern, Grand Rapids & Indiana and the Grand Trunk Railroads.

ST. JOSEPH COUNTY

MICHIGAN

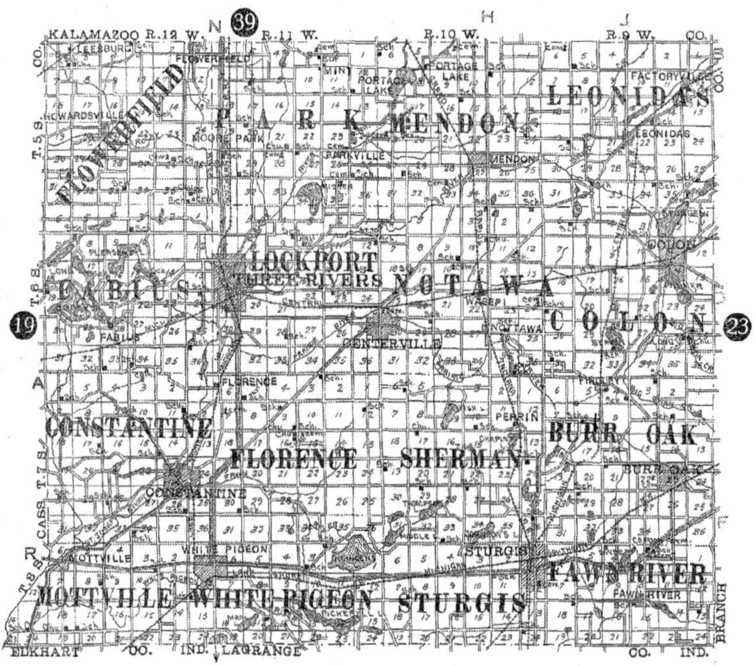

BRANCH COUNTY.

Branch county was laid out and organized in 1829 and was named in honor of Secretary of Navy John Branch. It is located in the middle of the lower tier of counties in the Lower Peninsula and is bounded on the north by Calhoun county, on the east by Hillsdale county, on the south by Indiana and on the west by St. Joseph county. The entire population is 25,605 (1910 census). The total land area is 320,719.92 acres, of which about 307,000 acres are in farms. In 1911, the state board of tax commissioners placed a valuation of $33,297,585 on all taxable lands. There are 131 schools, an enrollment of 4,856 scholars, requiring the services of 211 teachers. The county has nine banks, one daily and six newspapers. Good telegraph, telephone and rural mail service can be found in every locality.

The capital city of Branch is Coldwater, a city of about 6,000 inhabitants. It is located on the Lake Shore & Michigan Southern Railway, 43 miles southwest of Jackson and 65 miles south of Lansing. The name "Coldwater" is an interpretation of the Indian word applied to the beautiful group of lakes in the vicinity. The city has wide and well-laid-out streets, is lighted by electricity, has good sewerage system, municipal water works and electric lighting plant, fire department, a $12,000 public library, three banks, opera house, hospital, a $50,000 post-office, public hall, good hotels, one weekly and two daily newspapers.

The various industries include a foundry, creamery, gas, light and fuel plant, planing-mills, machine shop, brass works, flour-mill, carriage factory, cement plant and manufactories of ladders, cigars, gasoline engines, lawn furniture, wooden novelties, medicine, castings, etc. Four public schools, churches of the leading denominations, the State Public School, consisting of 18 buildings and occupying 160 acres, is located in Coldwater. The surrounding country is a rich and productive agricultural section.

The other principal towns are Bronson, Sherwood, Union City and Quincy. Transportation facilities of the county are Lake Shore & Michigan Southern and the Michigan Central Railroads.

BRANCH COUNTY

MICHIGAN

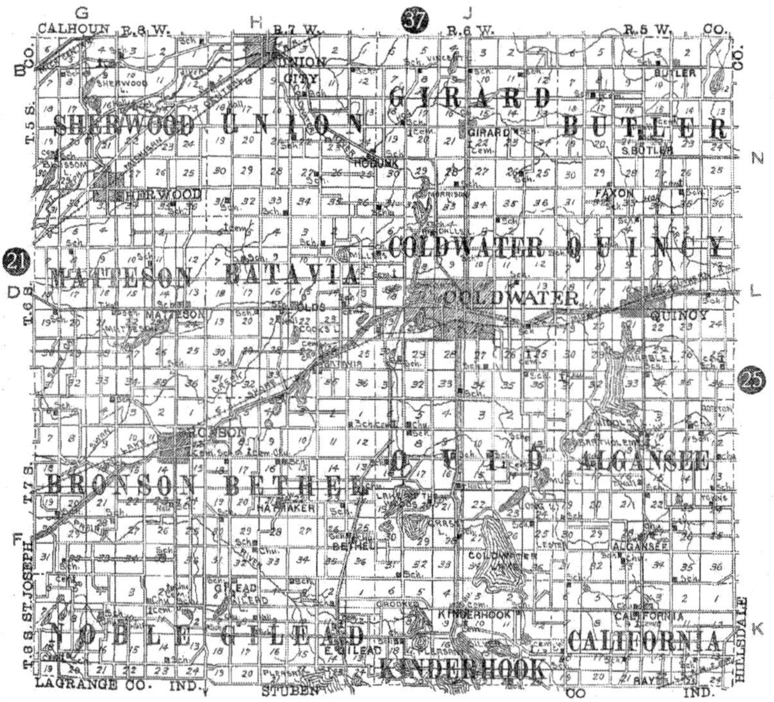

HILLSDALE COUNTY.

Hillsdale county was laid out in 1829, and was organized in 1835. The county was well named and describes in a word the condition of the surrounding country. It is located in the central part of the southern tier of counties, in the Southern Peninsula, and is bounded on the north by Calhoun and Jackson counties, on the east by Lenawee county, on the south by Indiana and on the west by Branch county and Indiana. This county has a total land area of 386,067.50 acres. Of this number, about 375,000 acres are devoted to farms, which are wonderfully productive. The population is 29,673 (federal census 1910). In 1911, the state board of tax commissioners placed a valuation of $34,090,892 on all taxable lands. The school system is equal to that of any of the larger counties. There are 171 schools, requiring the services of 273 teachers, and last year's records show an enrollment of 5,928 students. The county has 12 banks, 1 daily and 9 weekly newspapers. Good telegraph, telephone, and rural mail service is found throughout the county.

Hillsdale is the judicial seat and the largest city of the county. It has a population of about 5,000. It is located on the St. Joseph river and on the Lake Shore & Michigan Southern Railroad, 29 miles south of Jackson and 91 southwest of Detroit. The city is lighted by electricity and gas, has water works, wide and well shaded streets, good fire department, sanitary sewerage system, first-class hotels, opera house, three banks and a daily newspaper. There are churches of the Adventist, Baptist, Episcopal, Free Will Baptist, Lutheran, Methodist, Presbyterian, Universalist, and Catholic denominations, an up-to-date public school system, public library, a postoffice building costing about $65,000, city hall costing about $45,000. This is the home of Hillsdale College, situated upon one of the most sightly spots in the state. There are a number of prosperous industrial enterprises, including planing-mills, flouring-mills, gasoline engine works, glove and mitten factories, gas plant, shoe factory, truck and wagon works, wheel works, screen door works, door rail and door hanger factory, creamery, tannery, handle factory, etc.

Other enterprising towns include Camden, Jonesville, Litchfield, Montgomery, North Adams and Reading, the largest of which are Jonesville, population 1,400, and Reading, population 1,100. Jonesville is located on the St. Joseph river and on the Lake Shore & Michigan Southern Railroad, four and one-half half miles west of Hillsdale and twenty-five miles from Jackson. It is lighted by electricity, has water works, good educational facilities, a public library, a theater, a public hall, a bank and two weekly newspapers. There are churches of several denominations. Reading is located on the Lake Shore & Michigan Railway, ten miles southwest of Hillsdale and thirty-six miles from Jackson. It is supported by a rich agricultural section and is an important shipping point for wheat, corn, wool, fruit and produce. Has Baptist, Free Will Baptist, Methodist and Presbyterian churches, a graded public school, opera house, a bank, tanneries, a robe factory, flour and saw-mills, chair factory, feed and grist-mill and a weekly newspaper. The principal transportation facilities of the county are the Lake Shore & Michigan Southern and the Cincinnati Northern Railroads.

HILLSDALE COUNTY

MICHIGAN

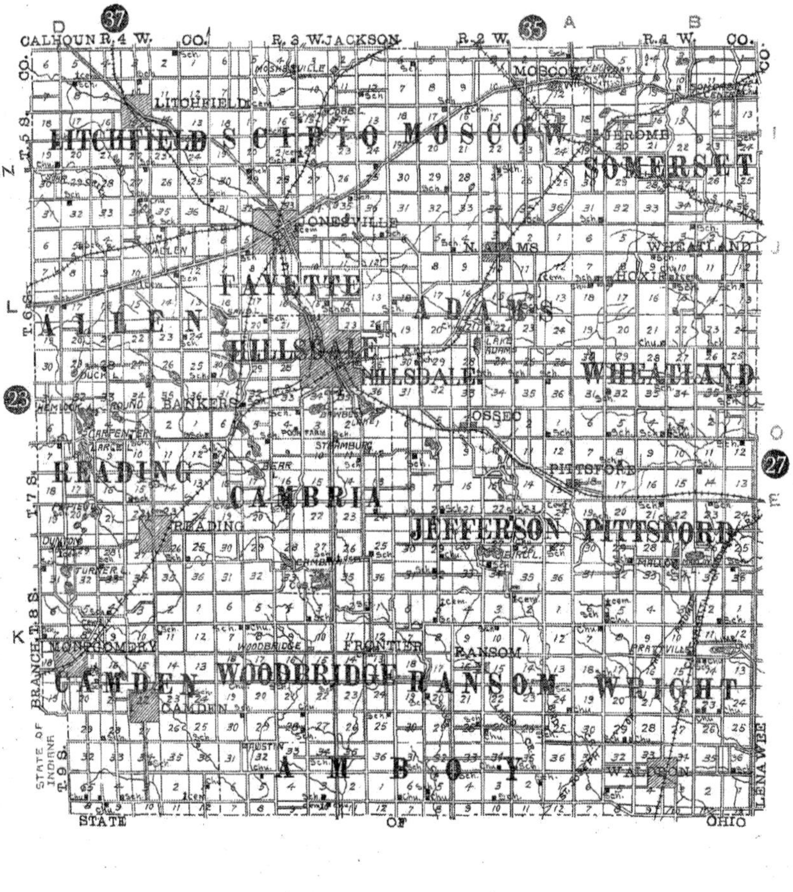

LENAWEE COUNTY.

Lenawee county was laid out in 1822 and was organized in 1826. The name is of Indian derivation from the Delaware Indian word "Leno," meaning man. It is located in the extreme southern part of the Lower Peninsula and is bounded on the north by Jackson and Washtenaw counties, on the east by Monroe county, on the south by Ohio, and on the west by Hillsdale county. The total land area is 486,677.51 acres, of which about 463,000 acres are devoted to farms which are wonderfully productive. The population is 47,907 (1910 census). In 1911, the state tax commissioners placed a valuation of $58,227,881 on all taxable lands in the county. The school system is equal in every respect to that of the other counties. There are 208 schools, 8,721 children in attendance, requiring 351 teachers. There are twenty-two banks, two daily and eight weekly newspapers. Excellent telegraph, telephone and rural mail service is found in every community.

Adrian is the judicial seat of the county, also the largest city, having about 11,000 inhabitants. It is located on the south branch of the river Raisin and on the Detroit, Toledo & Ironton, Lake Shore & Michigan Southern, and the Wabash Railroads, 33 miles northwest of Toledo, 58 southwest of Detroit and 83 south of Lansing. The city is noted for its beautiful shade trees and its wide pleasant avenues. It is lighted by electricity, with good police and fire departments, a fine system of water works, five parks, a $51,000 postoffice, a $40,000 Young Men's Christian Association, a $36,000 public library, a high school erected at a cost of about $100,000. Adrian College, an institution controlled by the Methodist Protestant denomination, and the State Industrial Home for Girls are located here. There are about seventeen churches, representing the leading denominations. The school facilities of Adrian are among the best in the state and include several public schools and four parochial schools. Adrian has five banks, an opera house, first-class hotels and two daily newspapers.

Adrian is one of the largest producers of wire fence in the country. In addition to this great industry there are furniture factories, basket and veneer works, a large condensed milk factory, two large knitting mills, flour mills, brick and tile machinery manufactory, carriage works, handle factory, planing-mills, granite and marble works, foundry and machine shops, steel casting works, boiler works, bicycle and machinery works, manufactories of screen doors, steel posts, pumps, cheese, cigars, razor strops, cement blocks, gloves, etc. Large quantities of grain, live stock, dairy produce, pork, lard, fruit, etc., are shipped. There are numerous large nurseries located near the city.

Tecumseh, another prosperous city, has a population of about 3,000. It is located on the River Raisin and on the Lake Shore & Michigan Southern, the Detroit, Toledo & Ironton Railways, and the Detroit, Toledo & Monroe Short Line Railway, 9 miles north of Adrian, 33 from Jackson and 59 from Detroit. The town is beautifully laid out with wide, well-paved and shaded streets, owns and operates its own electric light plant and water works, has a fine sewerage system, an efficient fire department, churches of the leading denominations, a high school and three ward school buildings, good hotels, an opera house, two banks and two newspapers. Among the more prominent industries are two flouring-mills, brick and tile machinery and clay crusher manufactory, planing-mill, a foundry, wire fence factory, manufactories of building material, engines, castings, boilers, brick and tile, macaroni, carriages, wagons, etc. Tecumseh is the trade center for one of the richest agricultural sections in the state, and an important industry is that of celery growing.

Other important towns are Addison, Blissfield (population, 1,550), Britton, Clayton, Clinton (population, 1,200), Deerfield, Hudson (population, 2,300), Morenci (population, 1,600), Onsted and Cement City. The principal transportation facilities of the county include the Lake Shore & Michigan Southern, Wabash, Detroit, Toledo & Ironton and the Cincinnati Northern Railways, and the Detroit, Toledo & Short Line (electric).

LENAWEE COUNTY

MICHIGAN

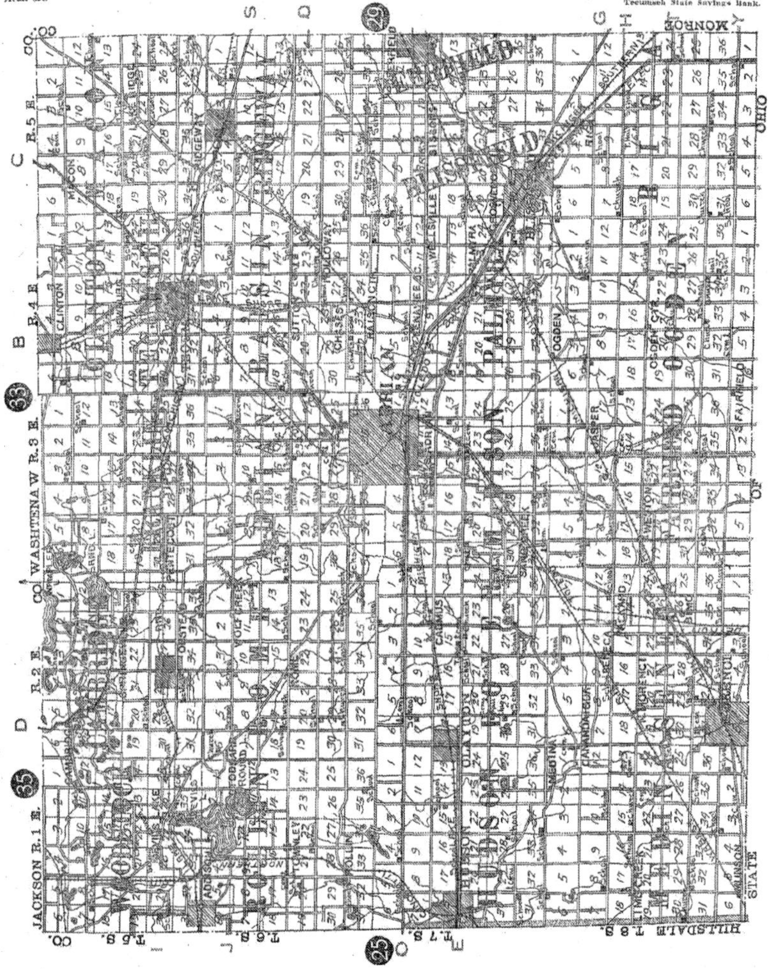

MONROE COUNTY.

Monroe county was laid out in 1817, organized in 1822, and was named in honor of President Monroe. This county is located in the extreme southeastern part of the Lower Peninsula. It is bounded on the north by Washtenaw and Wayne counties, on the east by Lake Erie, on the south by Ohio and on the west by Lenawee county. The total land area is 356,292.52 acres, about 333,000 acres of which are in splendid farms. The population is 32,917 (1910 census). The valuation of taxable property, as estimated by the state board of tax commissioners in 1911, is $33,363,252. There are 145 schools, furnishing positions for 199 teachers, and an enrollment of 6,287 students. The county has thirteen banks and ten weekly newspapers, also good telegraph, telephone and rural mail service.

Monroe, the second oldest city in the state and the judicial seat of Monroe county, has a population of about 7,500. It is situated on the River Raisin, about three miles above its mouth on Lake Erie, and is a station on the Lake Shore & Michigan Southern, Michigan Central and Pere Marquette Railroads, 35 miles southwest of Detroit and 25 from Toledo, Ohio. The Detroit United Railway (electric) connects Detroit, Toledo and Monroe. The city is lighted by electricity, has good water works system, a well-equipped fire department, good sewerage system, churches of the leading denominations, a fine high school building and several ward schools. There is also a Catholic orphan asylum for girls, a convent, the St. Mary's Academy, and St. Mary's College, a handsome public library, a court house costing about $40,000, three newspapers, etc.

The manufactures include flour, lumber, sash, doors and blinds, furniture frames, glass, paper boxes, cordage, beer, wine, pumps, cigars, butter, cheese, agricultural implements, paper, carriages, wagons, etc. Within the past few years the beef industry has developed wonderfully, the people of the county giving special attention to rearing fine beef cattle, also the well-known Percheron horses. The land in the neighborhood is fertile, and grain, grass, fruit, grapes and berries are grown in large quantities. Monroe is also noted for its extensive nurseries.

Dundee has a population of about 1,100, and is located on the River Raisin, and on the Ann Arbor, Detroit, Toledo & Ironton and the Lake Shore & Michigan Southern Railways, 15 miles west of Monroe, 22 northwest of Toledo, Ohio, and 48 southwest of Detroit. The town is lighted by electricity, has Congregational, Baptist, German Lutheran and Methodist churches, good educational advantages, two banks and a weekly newspaper.

Other towns are Maybee and Petersburg. The principal transportation facilities of the county are the Detroit & Toledo Shore Line, Michigan Central, Lake Shore & Michigan Southern, Pere Marquette, Detroit, Toledo & Ironton, Ann Arbor, Wabash and the Toledo, Ann Arbor & Jackson Railways.

MONROE COUNTY

MICHIGAN

MONROE.

Monroe Overland Co., Distributors Federal Tires.
Monroe Garage.
First National Bank.

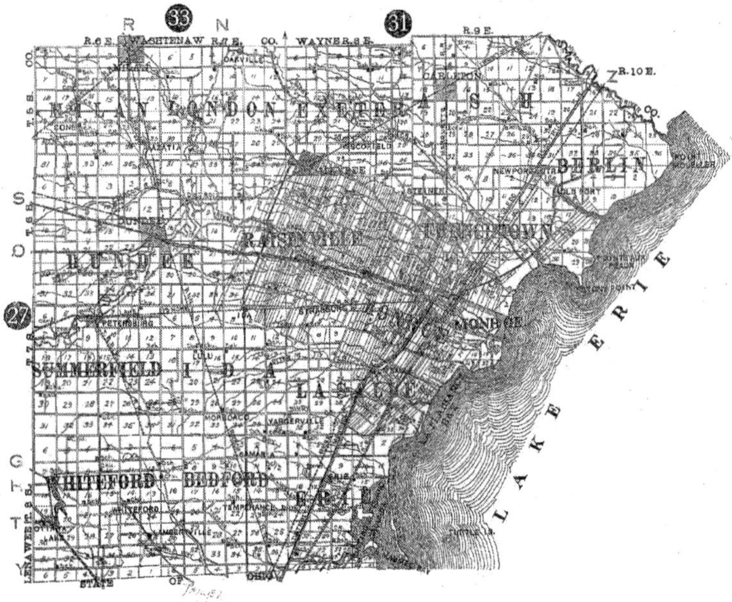

WAYNE COUNTY.

In 1796, Secretary Sargent, acting governor, instituted the county of Wayne. It originally included all the Lower Peninsula and a large section of Indiana and Ohio and a strip along the west shore of Lake Michigan (for the purpose of including the settlement of Green Bay), and the east part of the Upper Peninsula. For a name they selected that of "Mad" Anthony Wayne—a conquering hero then in their midst. The present county of Wayne is located in about the southeast corner of the Lower Peninsula. It is bounded on the north by Oakland and Macomb counties, on the east by the St. Clair river and Lake St. Clair, on the south by the St. Clair river and Monroe county, and on the west by Washtenaw county. The total land area is 367,638.57 acres. Of this number about 317,000 acres are in fine farms. The population is 531,590 (1910 census). The valuation of taxable property as estimated by the state board of tax commissioners in 1911, is $685,918,145. There are 254 schools with a total enrollment of 91,615 students, requiring the services of 2,214 teachers. The county has thirty banks, eight daily newspapers and forty-three weekly newspapers. Telephone, telegraph and rural mail service is found in every locality throughout the county.

Detroit, the largest city in the state and the county seat of Wayne county, has a population of over 500,000. The city has an area of 41.44 square miles, 202 miles of public sewers, 480 miles of lateral sewers, 400 miles of paved streets, 31 parks and parkways with a combined acreage of 1,244, a water works plant with a daily capacity of about 177,000,000 gallons, a municipally owned electric light plant, fire and police departments which rank among the best in the country, ninety-eight public school buildings, a beautiful public library, many churches representing nearly every denomination, a Y. M. C. A. building erected at a cost of about $750,000, many banks, newspapers, etc. From a standpoint of beauty, there are few cities that can compare with it, and situated on the pathway of the commerce of the Great Lakes, Detroit does not watch it all go by, by any means. Cases, boxes, bales, barrels, bags and packages, will be found destined for every civilized land and bound for all points along the chain of the inland seas.

An important aid to Detroit's commerce and traffic is the tunnel beneath the river, completed and opened in 1910 by the Michigan Central Railroad, at a cost of approximately $10,000,000. As an engineering feat, it takes rank with the famous undertakings of the world. A few of the principal manufacturing interests of the city are automobiles and auto parts, clothing, boots and shoes, car building and repairing, cigars, food products, stoves and other heating apparatus, soda ash and other alkaline products, printing, furniture and numerous other industries.

Wyandotte has a population of about 10,000. It is located on the Detroit river and on the Detroit & Toledo Shore Line, the Detroit, Toledo & Ironton, the Lake Shore & Michigan Southern and the Michigan Central Railroads, and the Detroit United Electric Railway, twelve miles from Detroit, and forty-seven from Toledo. The city has municipally owned water and electric light plants, paved streets, fire department, a public library, churches of the leading denominations, a central school building, two ward schools and six parochial schools, two banks and two weekly newspapers. This city possesses some of the largest manufacturing plants in the state. Among the more prominent industries are three salt manufacturing plants, a ship building company, chemical manufactory, cement factory, rug and fur factory, foundries, trunk factory, a sheet metal works, etc.

Other enterprising cities and towns of the county are Belleville, population 500; Dearborn, population 1,000; Ford City, population 1,800; Grosse Pointe (suburb of Detroit), Hamtramck, population 4,000; Highland Park (suburb of Detroit), River Rouge, population 4,500; St. Clair Heights, population 1,800; Trenton, population 1,225; Plymouth, population 2,000, and Wayne, population 1,500. These towns are surrounded by a thickly settled and rich agricultural district and ship large quantities of grain, hay, straw, fruit, potatoes and farm produce of all kinds.

The principal transportation facilities of the county are the Detroit, Toledo & Ironton Railroad, Pere Marquette Railroad, Wabash Railroad, Detroit & Toledo Shore Line, Lake Shore & Michigan Southern Railroad, Michigan Central Railroad, Detroit, Monroe & Toledo Short Line Railroad, Grand Trunk, Canadian Pacific, Detroit United Railway (electric), Northern Steamship Company, Erie & Western Transportation Company (Anchor Line), Detroit & Buffalo Steamboat Company, E. M. Railway & Navigation Company, Detroit & Cleveland Navigation Company, and other boat lines.

EAST AND WEST MICHIGAN PIKES AND WOLVERINE HIGHWAY.

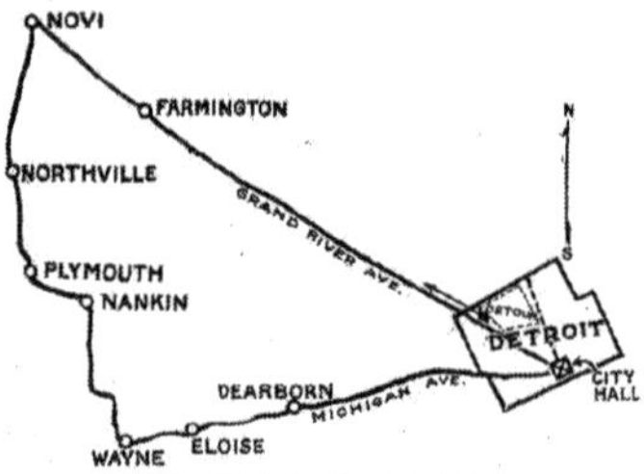

A FIFTY-MILE, ONE-DAY TRIP.

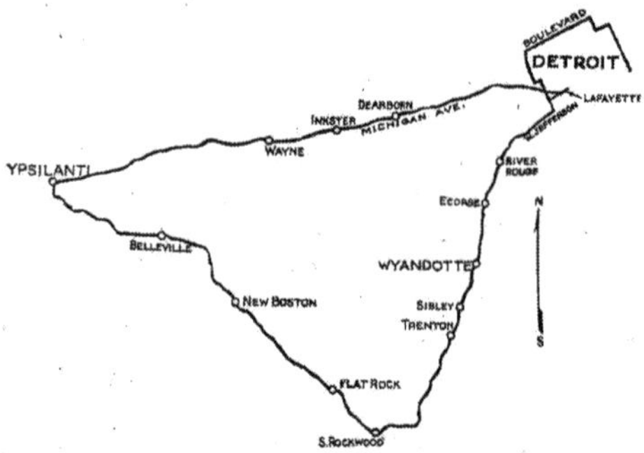

DETROIT-YPSILANTI NINETY-MILE TRIP.

WAYNE COUNTY

MICHIGAN

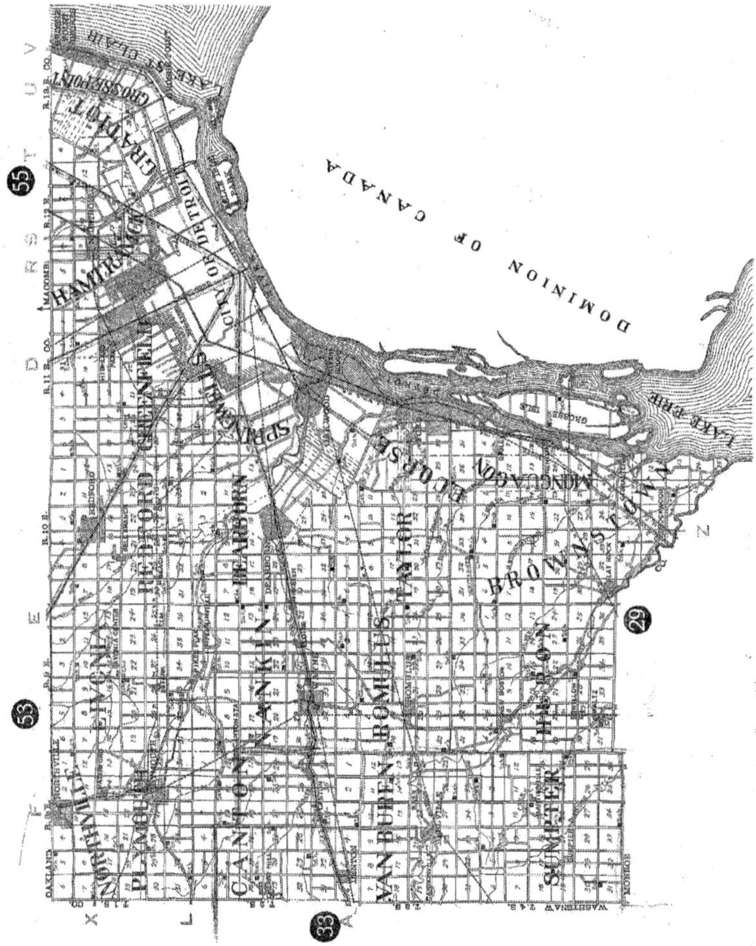

WASHTENAW COUNTY.

Washtenaw county was laid out in 1822, and was organized in 1826. This county was part of the region lying west of the Detroit district commonly called by the Chippewa Indians "Washtenong," meaning a river that extends far off, referring to the Grand river. It is located in the southeastern part of the Lower Peninsula and is bounded on the north by Livingston and Oakland counties, on the east by Wayne county, on the south by Lenawee and Monroe counties, and on the west by Jackson county. The total land area is 454,047.24 acres. Of this number about 428,000 acres are in splendid farms. The population is 44,714 (1910 census). The valuation of taxable property, as estimated by the state board of tax commissioners in 1911, is $54,719,685. The county has a fine school system. There are 174 schools, a total enrollment of 7,818 students, requiring the services of 341 teachers. The county has sixteen banks, three daily and sixteen weekly newspapers. Good telegraph, telephone and rural mail service is found throughout the county.

Ann Arbor, the capital city of the county, has a population estimated at about 16,000. This city is, of course, most widely known as the seat of Michigan's great State University. It is situated on the Huron river, on the main line of the Michigan Central Railroad, on the Ann Arbor Railroad, and on the Detroit United Railway (electric), thirty-eight miles from Detroit. The city is lighted with electricity and a large well established gas company also furnishes light and fuel gas, has a good sewerage system, a court house erected at a cost of about $75,000, well equipped fire department, a $45,000 Y. M. C. A. building, an excellent public school system including one of the finest high school buildings in the state erected at a cost of about $300,000, a beautiful new auditorium, first class hotels, 200 acres of parks and boulevards, a beautiful public library, churches of many denominations, five banks, two daily newspapers, etc. The industrial institutions include manufactories of pianos, organs, furniture, agricultural implements, lamps, ladders, automobile attachments, hay baling machines, flour, corsets, skirts, waists, baking powder, carriages, wagons, brick, tile, cement building block, beer, boilers, engines, sash, doors and blinds, knitted goods, trusses, beet sugar machinery, pumps, etc.

Ypsilanti, the second largest town in the county, has a population of about 6,230. It is located on the Lake Shore & Michigan Southern Railroad, the Michigan Central Railroad, and the Detroit United Railway (electric), twenty-nine miles southwest of Detroit and eight southeast of Ann Arbor. It is lighted by electricity, and has an excellent system of public water supply, has churches of the leading denominations, excellent schools, a ladies' library, an opera house, a business college, first class hotels, two banks and a daily newspaper. Ypsilanti is the seat of the State Normal College. The manufacturing interests include paper mills, foundries and machine shops, flour mills, knitting mills, a creamery, novelty works and manufactories of carriages, wagons, buggy bodies, rubber tire setters, flour mill and elevator machinery, bean pickers, underwear, farm implements, axe handles, sash, doors, blinds, dress stays, etc.

Other important towns of the county are Chelsea, Dexter, Manchester, and Saline. Chelsea is located on the Michigan Central Railroad, and on the Detroit, Jackson & Chicago Railway, fourteen miles west of Ann Arbor and fifty-four from Detroit. It has a municipal electric light plant and water works system, churches of the leading denominations, excellent educational advantages, two banks and two weekly newspapers. The country contributory to Chelsea is very fertile and is one of the best wheat raising districts in the state. The principal shipments are cereals, wool, fruit, berries and live stock. The principal transportation facilities of the county are the Pere Marquette Railroad, the Michigan Central Railroad, Ann Arbor Railroad, Lake Shore & Michigan Southern Railroad, Wabash Railroad and the Detroit United Railway (electric).

WASHTENAW COUNTY

MICHIGAN

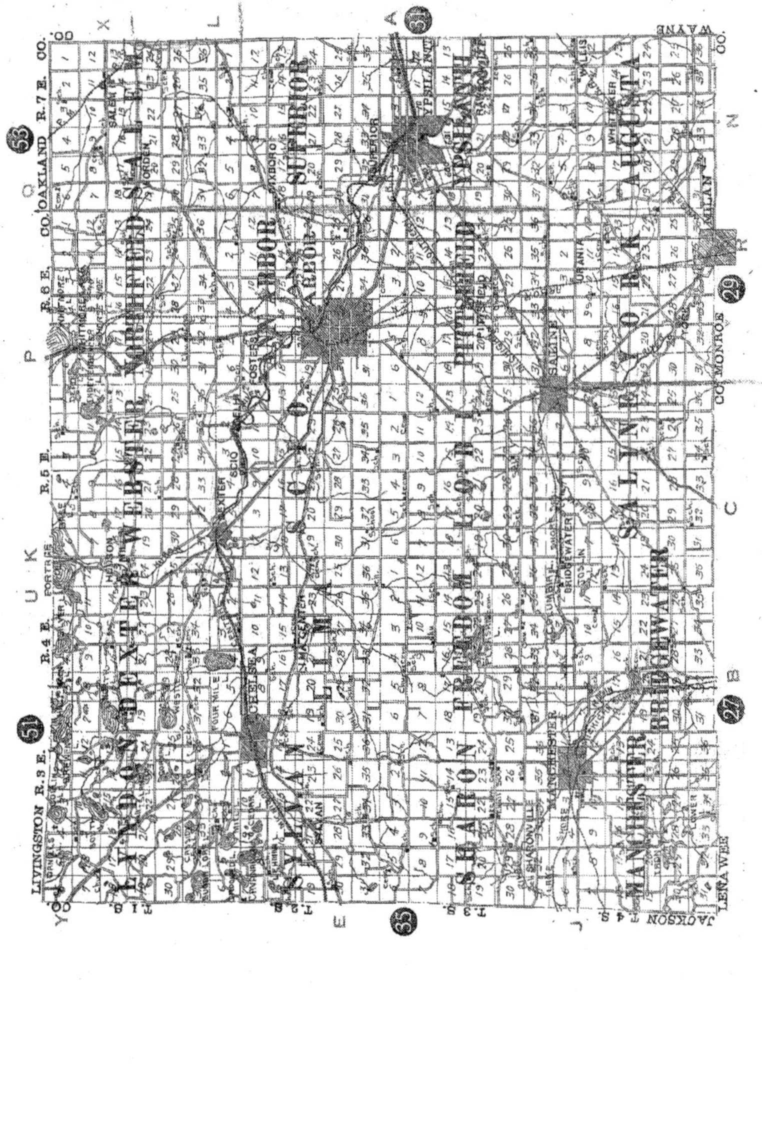

JACKSON COUNTY.

Jackson county was laid out in 1829 and was organized in 1832, being named in honor of President Andrew Jackson. It is located in the south central part of the Lower Peninsula, and is bounded on the north by Eaton and Ingham counties, on the east by Washtenaw county, on the south by Hillsdale and Lenawee counties and on the west by Calhoun county. The total land area of the county is 458,452.12 acres. Of this number, about 423,006 acres are in splendid farms. The population is 53,426 (1910 census). The valuation of taxable property, as estimated by the state board of tax commissioners in 1911, is $53,728,298. The county has 172 schools, attended by 8,331 students, requiring 345 teachers. There are thirteen banks, two daily and eight weekly newspapers. All parts of the county are provided with telephone, telegraph and rural mail service.

Jackson is the largest city, also the judicial seat of the county. It is located on Grand river and on the Michigan Central, Lake Shore & Michigan Southern, Grand Trunk, Cincinnati Northern Railways, also the Michigan United Traction and the Detroit United Railway (electric). The Michigan Central car shops are located here. The city has an area of nine square miles, ten miles of paving, fifty-four miles of public sewers, six public parks, comprising fifty-eight acres, a water works plant valued at $900,000, eighty-five miles of water mains, well equipped fire department, efficient police department, thirty-two churches, seventeen public school buildings, three sanitariums, a city hospital, two daily and two weekly newspapers, a library, five banks, six theatres, first-class hotels. The State Penitentiary is also located here. The manufacturing industries are many and include acetylene gas generators, advertising sign boards, agricultural tools, aluminum castings, antiseptic cans, automatic machinery, automobiles, automobile accessories, bank and office fixtures, boilers, blank books, carriages and wagons, cement mixers, flour, flour-mill machinery, furnaces, gasoline engines, glass, mirrors, machine tools, pumps, etc. A large and very successful industry is the cultivation of celery, onions and small fruits.

Other towns of the county include Grass Lake, Springport, Brooklyn, Concord, Hanover and Parma. Their shipments consist largely of grain, apples, potatoes and live stock. The transportation facilities of the county are the Grand Trunk, Michigan Central, Lake Shore & Michigan Southern, Cincinnati Northern Railroads, the Detroit United Railways Company and the Michigan United Traction Company.

JACKSON COUNTY

MICHIGAN

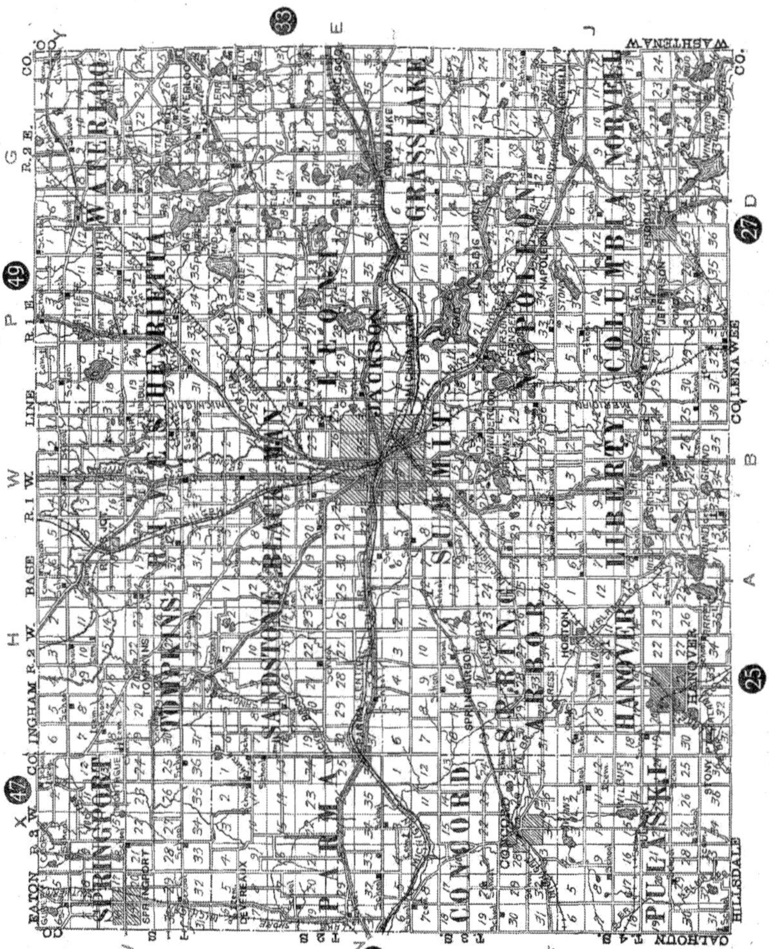

CALHOUN COUNTY.

Calhoun county was laid out in 1829. In 1833 it was organized and named in honor of Vice-President John C. Calhoun. It is located in the southern part of the Lower Peninsula and is bounded on the north by Barry and Eaton counties, on the east by Jackson county, on the south by Branch and Hillsdale counties and on the west by Kalamazoo county. Calhoun has a total land area of 447,452.44 acres, of which 411,801 acres are already devoted to farms. The valuation of taxable property as estimated by the state board of tax commissioners in 1911 is $73,846,732. The county is well supplied with schools, there being a total of 185, supplying positions for 400 teachers with an enrollment of 10,747 students. The total population is 56,638 (1910 census). There are 11 banks, four daily and nine weekly newspapers, telegraph, telephone and rural route service.

Marshall, which is the county seat, has a population of about 5,000 and is located at the confluence of Rice creek with the Kalamazoo river and on the Michigan Central and the Lake Shore & Michigan Southern Railways, and the Michigan United Railway (electric). The city owns an electric lighting plant, the power for which is generated by the water power which was purchased by the city. The city also owns its own system of water works, which cost about $50,000. It has a good school system, ten churches of different denominations, two banks and three daily newspapers, also a court house costing about $80,000. The grounds of the Calhoun Agricultural Society are also located here. Among the most prominent manufactories are flouring mills, cigar factories, furniture factory, carriage factory, a creamery and cold storage food factory, two furnace factories, marble and granite works, also foundry and machine shops.

Other towns of the county include Albion, Athens, Battle Creek, Burlington and Homer. The most important of these are Albion and Battle Creek. The population of Battle Creek is about 30,000. It is located at the confluence of Battle creek and Kalamazoo rivers, on the Michigan Central and Grand Trunk Railroad and on the Michigan United Traction Company. It is 13 miles west of Marshall, the county seat, 45 miles southwest of Lansing and 22 miles east of Kalamazoo.

Battle Creek's manufactories include threshing machines, portable engines, health foods, stoves, oven racks, paper roofing, tables, paper, boilers, electrical goods, wire novelties, steam pumps, printing presses, woodworking machinery, flour, sash, door and blinds, brass goods, furniture, printing ink, railroad cars and engines, etc. One of the largest engine shops of the Grand Trunk system, erected at a cost of about $2,000,000, is located here. This is also the home of the Battle Creek Sanitarium, which is the largest of its kind in the world. There are 4 banks, 14 public and 2 parochial schools, including a new high school building which has just been completed at a cost of about $90,000, and a beautiful public library. The religions of the city are represented by many handsome churches, of which the most prominent are the Baptist, Adventist, Congregational, Episcopal, German Evangelical and Methodist. The city has 8 first-class hotels, 3 daily newspapers and 5 monthly publications, electricity and gas, a municipally-owned water plant, which cost about $800,000, well equipped fire departments and a postoffice building costing $150,000.

The country surrounding Battle Creek is very productive and wheat, oats, corn, hay, fruits and garden products are raised in abundance. Electric street car lines connect with all surrounding points. Transportation facilities of the county are the Grand Trunk, Michigan Central and the Lake Shore & Michigan Southern Railroads, and the Michigan United Railway Company.

CALHOUN COUNTY

MICHIGAN

BATTLE CREEK.
Central National Bank.

MARSHALL.
Commercial Savings Bank.

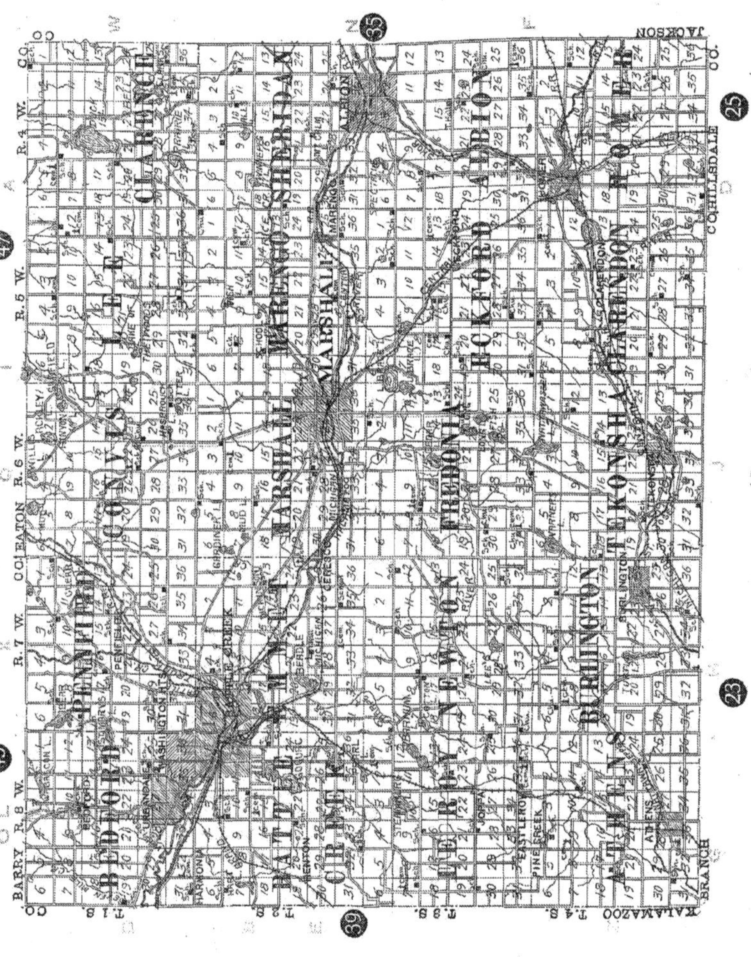

KALAMAZOO COUNTY.

Kalamazoo county was laid out in 1829 and was organized in 1830. It takes its name from the river which was called Ke-Kala-mazoo, which name is said to be of Indian derivation and interpreted by some as meaning "bright, sparkling water." It is located in the southwestern part of the Lower Peninsula and is bounded on the north by Allegan and Barry counties, on the east by Calhoun county, on the south by St. Joseph county and on the west by Van Buren county. The total land area is 359,234.79 acres, of which about 332,000 acres are in beautiful farms. The population is 60,427 (1910 census). In 1911, the state board of tax commissioners placed a valuation of $78,008,142 on all taxable lands. There are 138 schools, which were attended by 10,642 pupils last year, requiring the services of 415 teachers. The county has thirteen banks, two daily and several weekly newspapers. Telephone, telegraph and rural mail service provide for the necessities and add to the comforts of life.

Kalamazoo is the county seat, also the largest city, having about 45,000 inhabitants. It is located on the Michigan Central, Grand Trunk, Lake Shore & Michigan Southern, Grand Rapids & Indiana, Chicago, Kalamazoo & Saginaw and the Kalamazoo, Lake Shore & Chicago Railroads, also the Michigan United Traction Company (electric), 144 miles west of Detroit and 49 south of Grand Rapids. The city has an excellent water system, police and fire departments, municipal electric lighting plant, gas plant, sanitary sewerage system, twenty-two miles of brick and asphalt pavement, hospitals and sanitariums, first-class hotels, beautiful theatres, several parks, including more than eighty-five acres, splendid school system,—the Western State Normal School, a new million-dollar institution, is located here, a beautiful public library, about forty-two churches representing the leading denominations, four banks, two daily and seven weekly newspapers. The principal industries include manufactories of book paper, corsets, wind-mills and tanks, gas lamps and heaters, and regalia for fraternal organizations. There are six paper mills in the city and immediate vicinity, forty-one metal working plants, vehicle works, and numerous plants manufacturing blank books, playing cards, tablets and other paper goods. Kalamazoo is known as the world's center in the growth of celery and peppermint.

Vicksburg is located on the Portage river, at the intersection of the Grand Trunk and the Grand Rapids & Indiana Railways, 13 miles south of Kalamazoo, 23 southwest of Battle Creek and 62 south of Grand Rapids. The population is about 2,000. The city is lighted by electricity, has water works, opera house, good hotels, churches of several denominations, a union school, two banks and two weekly newspapers. The more important industrial interests include a paper-mill, flour-mill, two gasoline engine works, bagging machine factory, cement block works, engine governor works, clothing factory, creamery, etc. Vicksburg is the receiving and shipping point for large quantities of grain, farm produce, wool and flour.

Other towns of importance are Galesburg, where considerable blooded stock is raised; Augusta, Climax and Schoolcraft, all in good agricultural section. Transportation facilities of the county include the Lake Shore & Michigan Southern, Grand Rapids & Indiana, Grand Trunk, Michigan Central and the Chicago, Kalamazoo & Saginaw Railroads, and the Michigan United Traction Company (electric).

KALAMAZOO COUNTY

MICHIGAN

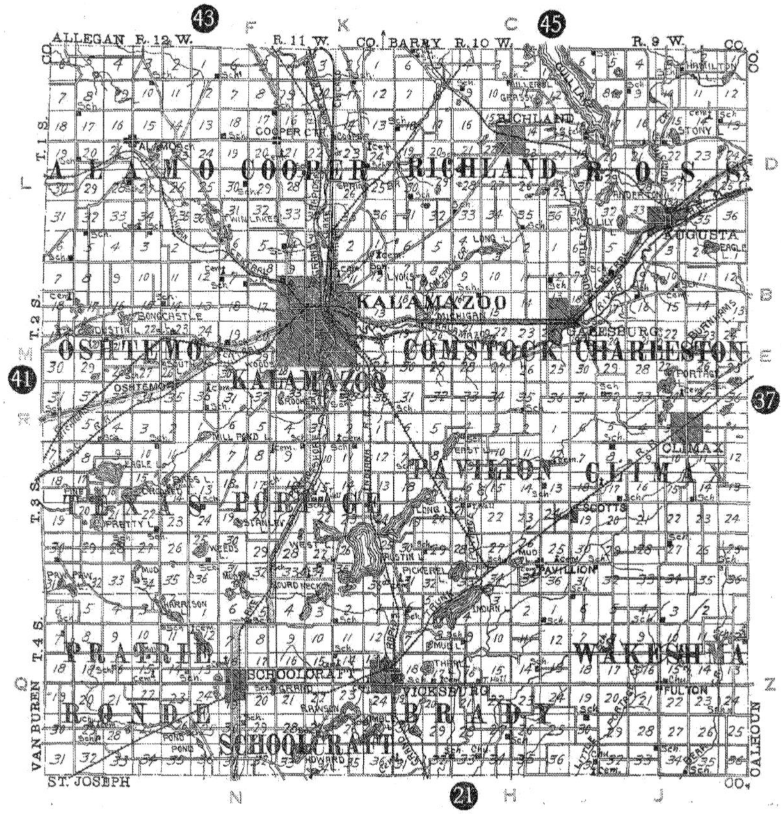

VAN BUREN COUNTY.

Van Buren county was laid out in 1829, was organized in 1837 and named in honor of Secretary of State Martin Van Buren. It is located in the southwest part of the Lower Peninsula and is bounded on the north by Allegan county, on the east by Kalamazoo county, on the south by Cass county, and on the west by Lake Michigan and Berrien county. The total land area is 391,442.62 acres, of which about 362,000 acres are in wonderfully productive farms. The population is 33,185 (1910 census). The valuation of taxable property as estimated by the state board of tax commissioners in 1911, is $35,104,410. There are 155 schools, a total enrollment of 6,824 students, employing 341 teachers. The county has fourteen banks, two daily and nine weekly newspapers. Good telegraph, telephone and rural mail service is found in every locality.

Paw Paw is the judicial seat of the county and has about 1,800 inhabitants. It is situated on the Kalamazoo, Lake Shore & Chicago Railway, and on the Paw Paw river, eighteen miles southwest of Kalamazoo, four from Lawton, where connection is made with the main line of the Michigan Central Railroad, fifteen miles from Hartford, where connection is made with the main line of the Pere Marquette Railroad, and thirty-three from South Haven, where connection is made with the the Michigan Central Railroad and a line of steamers plying to Chicago. Paw Paw is lighted by electricity, has water works, sewers, fire department, churches of many denominations, excellent schools, an opera house, two banks and two weekly newspapers. Wheat, pork, live stock, beans, peaches, apples, grapes and small fruits are shipped.

South Haven is the largest town in the county and has a population of about 4,000. This city occupies a commanding position on the shore of Lake Michigan at the mouth of the Black river, which forms a safe and commodious harbor. It is a station on the Michigan Central Railroad and on the Kalamazoo, Lake Shore & Chicago Railroad, thirty miles northwest of Paw Paw, forty from Kalamazoo, and seventy-five by water from Chicago. It has well-laid-out and shaded streets, is lighted by electricity, has a good system of water works, a fire department, sewerage system, opera house, churches of several denominations, a splendid public school system, a $15,000 public library, a gas plant, two banks, four newspapers, etc. The more prominent industries embrace piano manufacturing, fruit packages and lumber manufactories, canning factory, wood carving works, foundry, planing mills, syrup, pickle, vinegar and basket factories, etc.

Other enterprising towns of the county are Hartford, Lawton, Bangor, Bloomingdale, Decatur, Gobleville, and Lawrence. The surrounding country is well adapted for agriculture and fruit growing and wheat, live stock, peaches and apples are exported. Fruit growing is, however, the principal industry and large quantities of fruit are shipped. The principal transportation facilities of the county are the Michigan Central Railroad, Pere Marquette Railroad, the Kalamazoo, Lake Shore & Chicago Railroad and the Chicago & South Haven Steamship Line.

VAN BUREN COUNTY

MICHIGAN

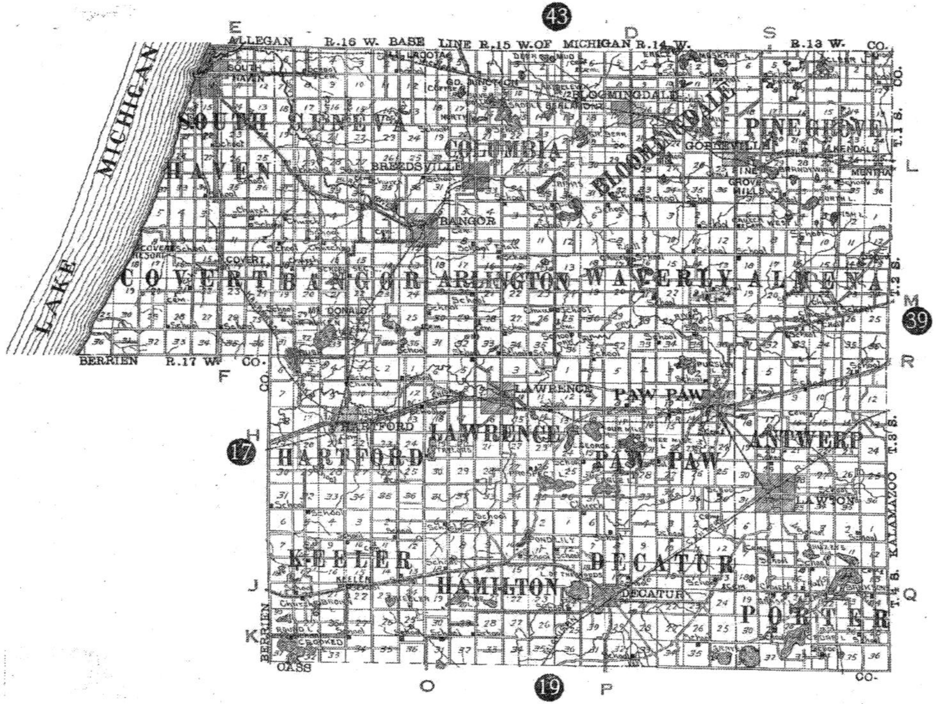

ALLEGAN COUNTY.

Allegan county was laid out in 1831, and was named for an ancient Indian tribe in the Alleghanies. It was organized as a county in 1835. It is located in the western tier of counties near the southern part of the state and is bounded on the entire west side by Lake Michigan. The total land area of the county is 529,873.41 acres, about 475,000 acres of this land being in farms. Taxable property in the county was placed at a valuation of $38,915,767 by the state board of tax commissioners in 1911.

There are 196 schools in the county, which were attended by 8,540 children last year and required a total of 301 teachers. The county has efficient telephone, telegraph and rural mail service, fourteen banks, eight newspapers, etc.

Allegan is the county seat and has a population of about 3,500. It is located on the Kalamazoo river and on the Lake Shore & Michigan Southern Railway, the Michigan Central and the Pere Marquette Railways, twenty miles east of Lake Michigan, thirty-three miles south of Grand Rapids. It is the receiving and distributing point for a rich and thickly settled agricultural section and ships large quantities of grain and general farm produce. It is lighted by electricity, has a municipally-owned water plant, well-paved streets, an efficient fire department, eight churches, a splendid high school and four ward schools, a public library, hospital, three banks, opera house, good hotels, a $100,000 court house, a $10,000 city hall and two weekly newspapers. The most important industries comprise the following: Saw and planing-mills, glass factory, foundry and machine shops, manufactories of candy, cigars, kitchen cabinets, furniture, carriages, wagons, folding boxes, flour, cement blocks, caskets, chemicals, vinegar, patent medicines, etc.

The other principal towns in the county are Douglas, Fennville, Otsego, Plainwell, Saugatuck and Wayland. The main transportation facilities through the county are the Pere Marquette Railway, Grand Rapids & Indiana Railway, Michigan United Railway, Michigan Southern Railway, and Grand Rapids, Holland & Chicago Railway.

ALLEGAN COUNTY

MICHIGAN

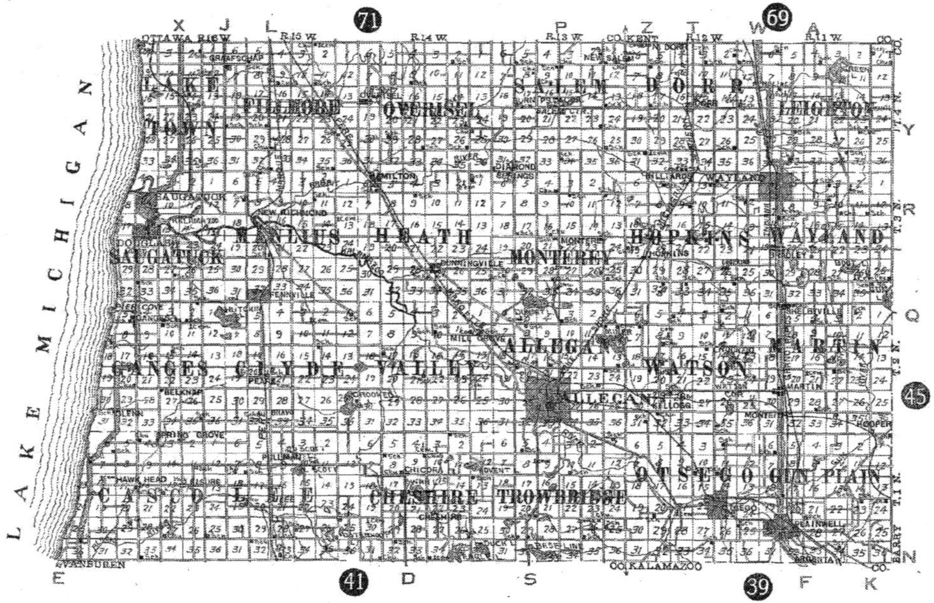

BARRY COUNTY.

Barry county was laid out and organized in 1829 and was named in honor of Postmaster-General William T. Barry. The county is located near the southwestern part of the Lower Peninsular and is bounded by Kent and Ionia counties on the north, Eaton county on the east, Kalamazoo and Calhoun counties on the south and Allegan county on the west. The entire acreage of the county is given as 354,029.41 acres, of which almost 340,000 acres are devoted to excellent farms. In 1911, the state board of tax commissioners placed a value of $21,175,834 upon all taxable land in the county. The county has a good school system throughout, there being a total of 145 schools, requiring 210 teachers, with an enrollment of 4,575 children. Excellent telephone, telegraph and rural mail service is found in every locality. There are also eight banks and eight newspapers.

Hastings, with a population of about 5,000, is the county seat, and was named in honor of E. P. Hastings, formerly a well-known citizen of Detroit. It is located on the Michigan Central and the Chicago, Kalamazoo & Saginaw Railroads, and on the Thornapple river, 32 miles southeast of Grand Rapids. The city is modern, having electricity, gas, water works, fire department, churches of the Adventist, Baptist, Catholic, Christian Science, Episcopal, Methodist, Presbyterian and United Brethren denominations, excellent public schools, first-class hotels, an opera house, a good court house, two banks and two weekly newspapers. There are numerous manufacturing interests, among them being a large felt-boot factory, large table factory, book-case factory, chair factory, international lock and seal factory, press and tool factory, kitchen cabinet factory, planing and flour-mills, cigar factory, gas works and an electric light and power plant.

Other towns in the county are Nashville, Freeport and Middleville. Transportation facilities include the Michigan Central, Pere Marquette, Chicago, Kalamazoo & Saginaw Railroads, and Michigan United Traction Company.

BARRY COUNTY

MICHIGAN

HASTINGS.
Skinner Garage Co.

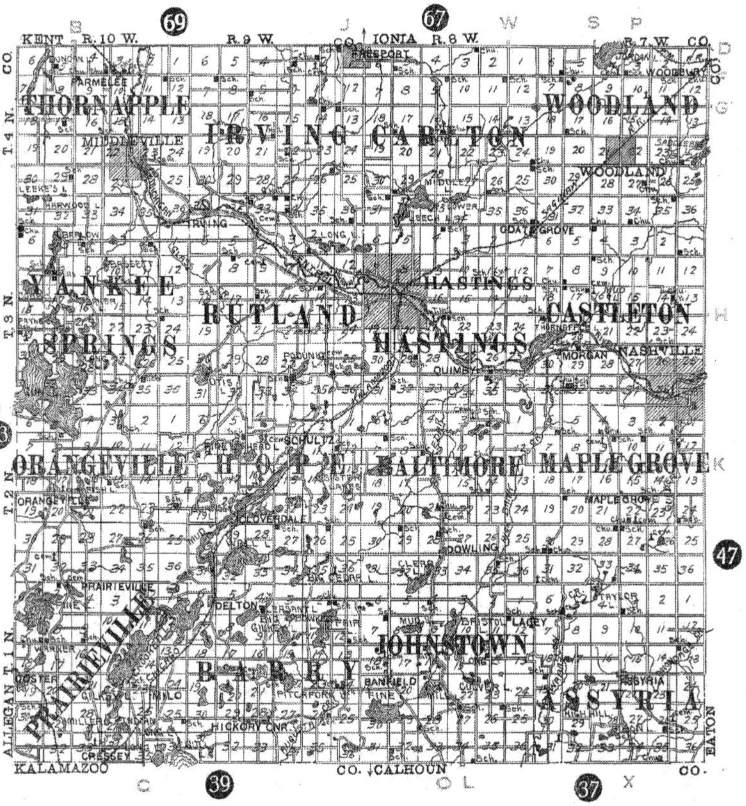

EATON COUNTY.

Eaton county was laid out in 1829 and was organized in 1837, and was named in honor of secretary of war John H. Eaton. This county is located in the south central part of the Lower Peninsula. It is bounded on the north by Ionia and Clinton counties, on the east by Ingham county, on the south by Calhoun and Jackson counties and on the west by Barry county. The total land area is 366,688.45 acres, of which about 345,000 acres are devoted to splendid farms. The 1910 census gives Eaton county a population of 30,499. There are 149 schools, a total enrollment of 5,967 children, requiring the services of 249 teachers. The county has 14 banks, 14 weekly newspapers, good telephone, telegraph and rural mail service. The valuation of taxable property, as estimated by the state board of tax commissioners in 1911, is $33,785,181.

Charlotte is the largest city and the judicial seat of the county. It has a population of about 5,000, is located on the Michigan Central and Grand Trunk Railways, 18 miles southwest of Lansing and 59 miles southwest of Grand Rapids. The city is lighted by electricity and gas, has wide, paved streets, fire department, water works, a number of beautiful parks, churches representing the leading denominations, excellent public schools, a library, three newspapers and two banks. The principal manufacturing industries consist of brass lubricator works, foundry, library and dining table factory, auto accessory works, hay fork pulley factory, flour and grist mills, brick and tile works, scythe factory, iron culvert works, manufactory of wooden specialties, etc.

Other enterprising towns of the county include Grand Ledge, Eaton Rapids, Bellevue, Olivet and Dimondale. Grand Ledge, with a population of about 3,000, is located on the Pere Marquette Railway, sixteen miles northeast of Charlotte and about twelve miles from Lansing. Soft coal is mined to the west of the city, also fire clay for two large sewer pipe works; the city is lighted by electricity, has water works, fire department, telephone service, opera house, two banks, gas works, two union schools, four churches and two weekly newspapers. The manufacturing industries include two chair factories, a foundry, two power companies, sewer pipe and tiling works, flour mill, wire works, paint works, cement block works, planing mill, carriage and wagon works, two grain elevators, etc.

Eaton Rapids, another thriving and prosperous city of the county, with a population of about 2,200, is located on the Grand river, upon the Lansing branch of the Lake Shore & Michigan Southern Railway, and also upon the Michigan Central Railway. It is lighted by electricity, the city owning its own plant; has water works, fire department, churches of several denominations, an excellent system of public schools, public library, two banks and an opera house. The city has several thriving manufacturing industries. The entire county is particularly well adapted to farming and from most every town in the county, quantities of grain, live stock, flour, fruit, butter and eggs are shipped.

Transportation facilities of the county are the Grand Trunk, Michigan Central, Lake Shore & Michigan Southern and the Pere Marquette Railroads.

CHARLOTTE.
J. A. Fritz, Garage.
A. B. Collins & Co., Druggists.
First National Bank.

EATON COUNTY

MICHIGAN

EATON RAPIDS.
R. G. Ferguson, Garage.
F. A. Graham, Prescription Druggist. Both Phones.

GRAND LEDGE.
Wolverine Garage, D. C. Shuart & Son, Dealers in Automobiles and Accessories, 315, 317, 319 South Bridge St.

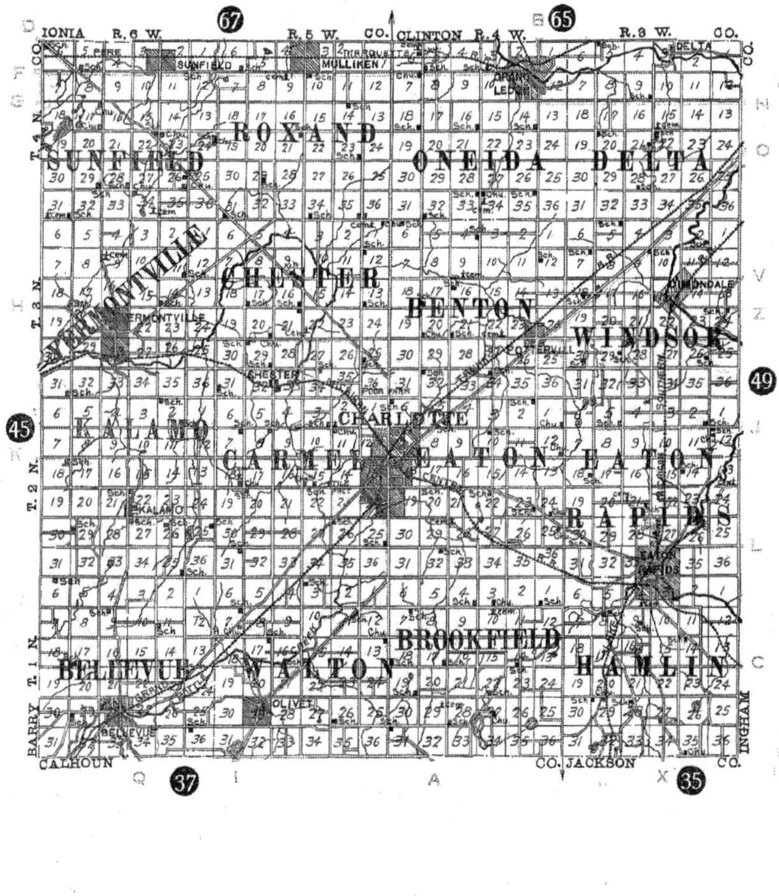

INGHAM COUNTY.

Ingham county was laid out in 1829 and was organized in 1838. The county was named in honor of Secretary of Treasury Samuel D. Ingham. This county is located in the south central part of tthe Lower Peninsula and is bounded on the north by Clinton and Shiawassee counties, on the east by Livingston county, on the south by Jackson county and on the west by Eaton county. The total land area is 355,272.91 acres, of which about 334,000 acres are devoted to splendid farms. The population is about 53,310 (1910 census). The valuation of taxable property, as estimated by the state board of tax commissioners in 1911, is $56,110,681. There are 154 schools, requiring 339 teachers, and an enrollment of 8,843 students. The county has thirteen banks, two daily and nine weekly newspapers. Excellent telegraph, telephone and rural mail service is found in every community throughout the county.

Mason is the county seat and has a population of about 2,000. It is located on the Michigan Central Railway, and on the Michigan United Traction (electric), 12 miles south of Lansing and 25 north of Jackson. It is lighted by electricity, has water works and sewerage system, fire department, a fine court house, a good public school system, school library, an opera house and two weekly newspapers. The country surrounding is rich and fertile and many wonderfully productive farms are found. Live stock, fruit, grain and farm produce are largely shipped.

Lansing, the capital city of the state, has a population of about 40,000. It is located on the Grand Trunk, Michigan Central, the Lake Shore & Michigan Southern and Pere Marquette Railroads, also the Michigan United Traction (electric), 87 miles north of Jackson and 88 northwest of Detroit. The city has beautiful, wide and well paved streets, splendid water works system, is lighted by electricity, excellent police and fire departments, electric light and gas plants, theatres, first-class hotels, sixteen public and five parochial schools, including the new high school just erected at a cost of over $125,000, a public library costing about $35,000, thirty-one churches of most all denominations, a Young Men's Christian Association, a Young Women's Christian Association, two daily and three weekly newspapers, four banks, etc.

The manufacture of automobiles forms the chief industry of Lansing, there being two large automobile plants located here. Other industries include auto wheel works, auto body works, wheelbarrow factory, several gasoline engine plants, cut glass factories, cigar factories, candy factories, machine shops, foundries, etc.

The State Capitol, a magnificent structure in the classic style of architecture, built of stone, brick and iron, and costing, complete, $1,510,130.59, was begun in 1872 and finished in 1878. It occupies a beautiful, elevated site, consisting of four blocks, in the heart of the city. The Michigan Agricultural College, located three miles east of the city, on a farm of 684 acres, divided by the Cedar river, is a great attraction to all who visit the city. The State Industrial School for Boys is located in the eastern part of the city, on a farm of 260 acres. The Michigan School for the Blind is located in the northwest part of the city, on fine grounds of forty-five acres. A postoffice, costing $150,000, has been erected.

Other towns of the county include, Leslie, population, 1,200; Lyons, population, 800, and Williamston, population, 1,200. The country tributary to these towns is among the richest and most productive sections in the state. The soil is adapted to many kinds of grains, fruits, vegetables, etc., and stock raising is an important industry. The transportation facilities of the county include the Grand Trunk, Michigan Central, Pere Marquette, Lake Shore & Michigan Southern Railroads and the Michigan United Traction Company.

INGHAM COUNTY

MICHIGAN

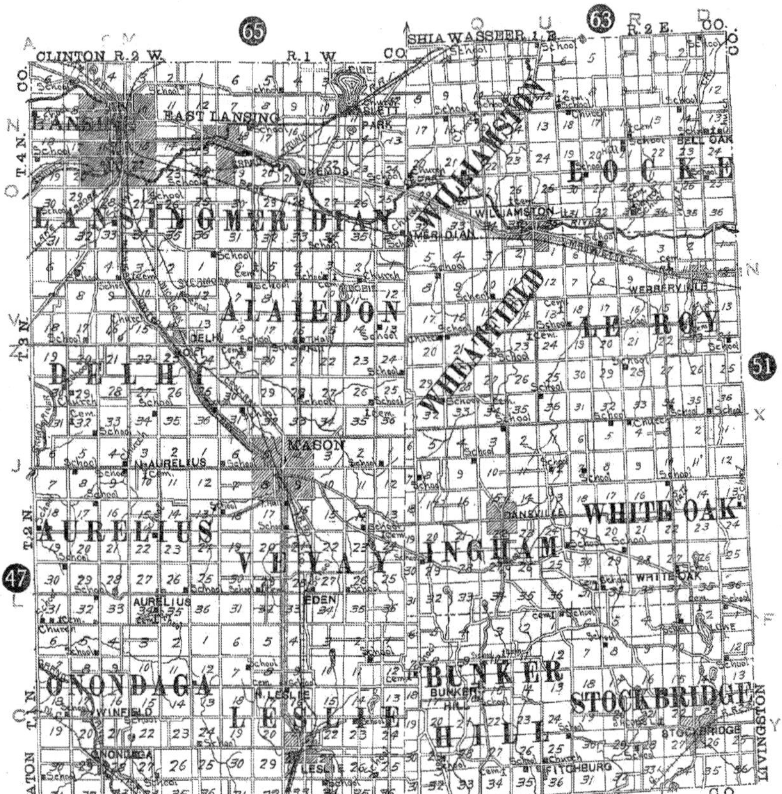

LIVINGSTON COUNTY.

Livingston county was laid out in 1833 and was organized in 1836. It was named in honor of Edward Livingston, then secretary of state and subsequently minister to France. This county is located towards the southeastern part of the Lower Peninsula. It is bounded on the north by Shiawassee and Genesee counties, on the east by Oakland county, on the south by Washtenaw county and on the west by Ingham county. The total land area is 370,871.08 acres, of which about 350,000 acres are in farms which are among the very best in the state. The population is 17,736 (1910 census). In 1911, the state board of tax commissioners placed a valuation of $22,502,238 on all taxable lands in the county. There are 137 schools, 3,413 students in attendance, requiring the services of 199 teachers. The county has eight banks and seven weekly newspapers. Good telegraph, telephone and rural mail service is found in every community.

Howell is the judicial seat, also the largest town in the county, having about 2,500 inhabitants. It is located on the Pere Marquette and Ann Arbor Railroads, 34 miles southeast of Lansing and 54 northwest of Detroit. It is lighted by electricity, has a fine system of water works, a fire department, seven churches, a central high and two ward schools, a $15,000 library, a $25,000 court house, opera house, good hotels, two banks and up-to-date newspapers. A large condensed milk factory, using about 70,000 pounds of milk daily, is located here. Other industries consist of wire specialty works, creamery, flour-mills, planing-mills, cigar factories, grain elevators, etc. This is the location of the State Sanitorium for Tuberculosis and is the second largest Holstein cattle center in America.

Fowlerville has a population of about 1,000. It is located on the Pere Marquette Railroad, 9 miles northwest of Howell and 63 from Detroit. It has Baptist, Lutheran, Methodist Episcopal and Catholic churches, good schools, an opera house, electric lights, a city hall, two banks and two weekly newspapers. The entire county is particularly well adapted for dairying and cattle raising and has some of the largest Holstein dairies in America. The surrounding country is also adapted to agriculture, large quantities of wheat, corn, beans, potatoes and hay being raised.

Other towns of the county are Brighton and Pinckney. The principal transportation facilities of the county are the Pere Marquette, Grand Trunk and Ann Arbor Railroads.

LIVINGSTON COUNTY

MICHIGAN

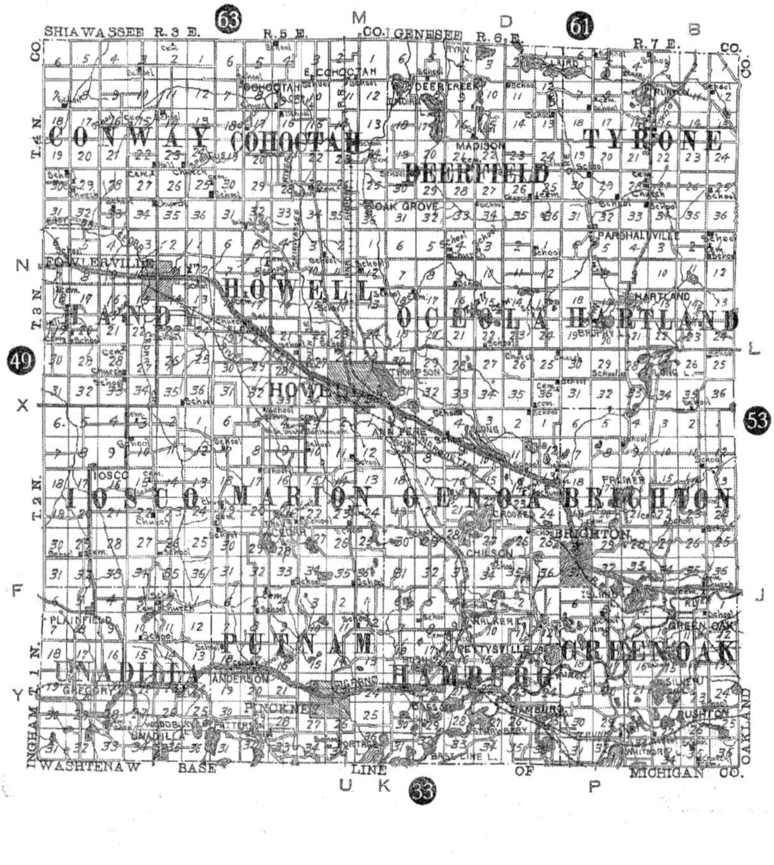

OAKLAND COUNTY.

Oakland county was laid out in 1819 and organized in 1820. The county was so named because of the numerous oak openings. Bela Hubbard, in his "Memorials of a Half Century," speaks of the character of the "openings" as that of "a majestic orchard of oaks and hickories varied by small prairies, grassy loams and clear lakes." It is located in the southeastern part of the Lower Peninsula, and is bounded on the north by Genesee and Lapeer counties, on the east by Macomb county, on the south by Washtenaw and Wayne counties, and on the west by Livingston and Genesee counties. The total land area is 575,400.15 acres, of which about 543,000 acres are in farms which are among the finest in the state. The population is 49,576 (United States census 1910). The valuation of taxable property, as estimated by the state board of tax commissioners in 1911, is $55,543,810. The county has a splendid school system. There are 213 schools, an enrollment of 9,407 students last year, requiring 379 teachers. There are 22 banks, 1 daily and 1 monthly and eleven weekly newspapers. Good telegraph, telephone and rural mail service is found in every locality.

Pontiac, the largest city, also the judicial seat of the county, has about 16,000 inhabitants. It is located on the Clinton river, on the Detroit United Railway (electric), the Grand Trunk, and the Pontiac, Oxford & Northern Railroads, 26 miles northwest of Detroit and 57 miles southwest of Port Huron. The city is beautifully located in the heart of Michigan's inland lake district, has broad and well-shaded streets, is lighted by electricity, has water works, an efficient fire department, sewerage system, churches of the leading denominations, eight graded schools and a $70,000 high school building, a public library, theaters, first class hotels, a public hospital, a court house costing $120,000, a handsome city hall, four banks, a daily and weekly newspaper, and is the location of the Pontiac State Hospital. The larger manufacturing industries included a wire fence factory, spring factory, planing mills, bending works, and manufactories of auto tops, autos, motor trucks, knit goods, paint, leather goods, bean pickers and seeders, woodwork, wheels, oak flooring, vinegar, flour, tools, machinery, etc.

Rochester has a population of about 2,000. It is located at the confluence of the Clinton river and Paint creek, on the Michigan Air Line division of the Grand Trunk Railway, the Bay City division of the Michigan Central Railroad, and on the Flint division of the Detroit United Railway (electric), nine miles northeast of Pontiac and twenty-seven from Detroit. It has Congregational, Methodist, Baptist and Universalist churches, a graded public school, a ladies' library, an opera house, good hotels, two banks and two weekly newspapers. The industries include paper and saw-mills, tile roofing factory, handle factory, woolen mills, foundry, electric light works, etc.

Other enterprising towns of the county include Birmingham, Clarkston, Farmington, Holly, Leonard, Milford, Orion, Ortonville, Oxford, Royal Oak, and South Lyon. The principal transportation facilities of the county are the Michigan Central, Grand Trunk, Pere Marquette, and the Pontiac, Oxford & Northern Railroads, and the Detroit United Railway (electric).

OAKLAND COUNTY

MICHIGAN

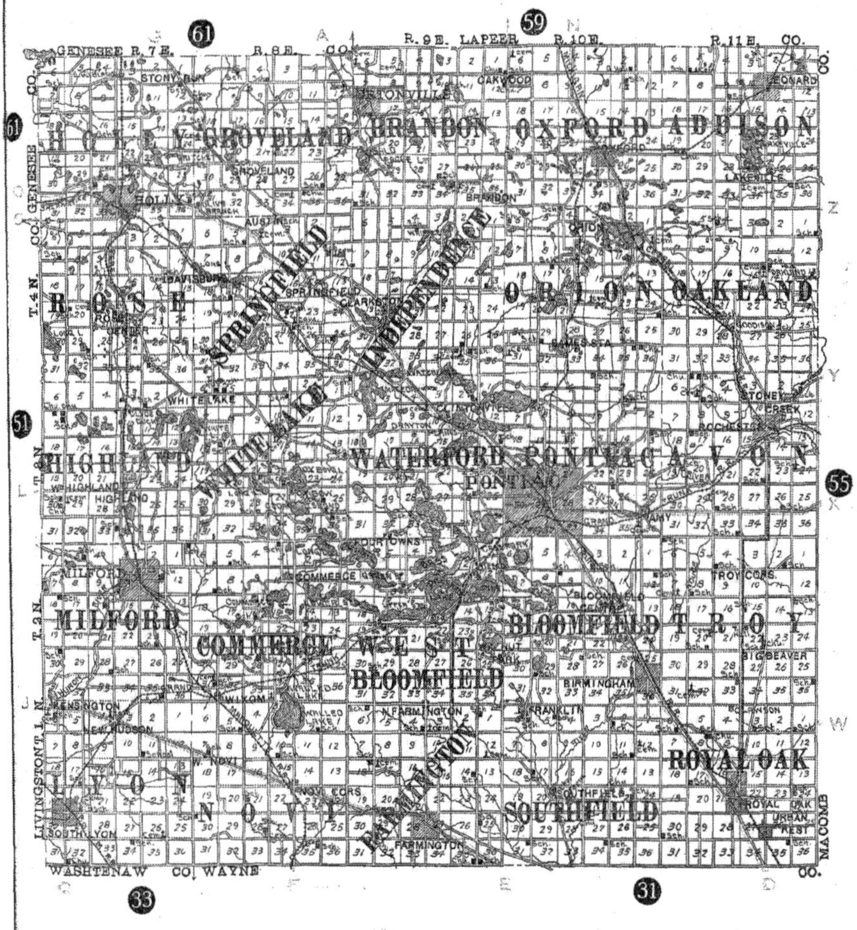

MACOMB COUNTY.

Macomb county was laid out and organized in 1818 and was named in honor of Alex Macomb, a general in the United States army. This county is located in the southeastern part of the Lower Peninsula. It is bounded on the north by Lapeer and St. Clair counties, on the east by St. Clair county, Anchor bay and Lake St. Clair, on the south by Lake St. Clair and Wayne county, and on the west by Oakland county. The total land area is 300,080.20 acres, of which about 287,000 acres are in splendid farms. The population is 32,606 (1910 census). The valuation of taxable property, as estimated by the state board of tax commissioners in 1911, is $41,808,462. The county has 123 schools, attended by 5,808 students last year, requiring 208 teachers. There are seventeen banks, one daily and eleven weekly newspapers. Excellent telegraph, telephone and rural mail serve is found in every community throughout the county.

Mount Clemens is the judicial seat and the largest city in the county. The population is about 9,000. The city is located on the Grand Trunk Railway, 36 miles from Port Huron and 21 from Detroit, and on the Detroit United Railway, two and one-half miles from Lake St. Clair. It has city water works, fire department, electric lights, a fine high school and five ward buildings, a fine public library, churches of the leading denominations, an opera house, three banks, three newspapers, etc. This city is known as the "Carlsbad of America" and is visited every year by thousands of health seekers. The estimated amount now invested in the mineral wells, the hotels, boarding houses and bath houses devoted to the treatment of visitors is about $15,000,000.

Romeo, a town of about 2,000 inhabitants, is located on the Grand Trunk Railroad and on the Detroit United Electric Railway, 20 miles northwest of Mount Clemens and 40 from Detroit. It has a municipally-owned water works and electric light plant, about sixteen miles of sidewalks, churches of the Congregational, Baptist, Christian, Lutheran and Methodist denominations, a central school building valued at $35,000 and two ward schools, a new $10,000 public library, an opera house, two banks and a weekly newspaper. The town is surrounded by one of the best farming districts in the state.

Richmond has a population of about 1,500. It is located on the Grand Trunk and Michigan Central Railways, about 16 miles northeast of Mount Clemens and 38 miles northeast of Detroit. It is supported by a rich agricultural section, and has Congregational, Methodist Episcopal, Baptist, German Evangelical, Lutheran and Catholic churches, two schools, good hotels, an opera house, two banks and two newspapers, and a number of prosperous manufacturing establishments. The shipments comprise grain, butter, eggs, apples and live stock.

Other thriving towns of the county are Armada, Fraser, New Haven, Utica and Warren. The principal transportation facilities of the county include the Grand Trunk, Michigan Central, Pere Marquette Railroads, and the Detroit United Railway (electric).

MACOMB COUNTY

MICHIGAN

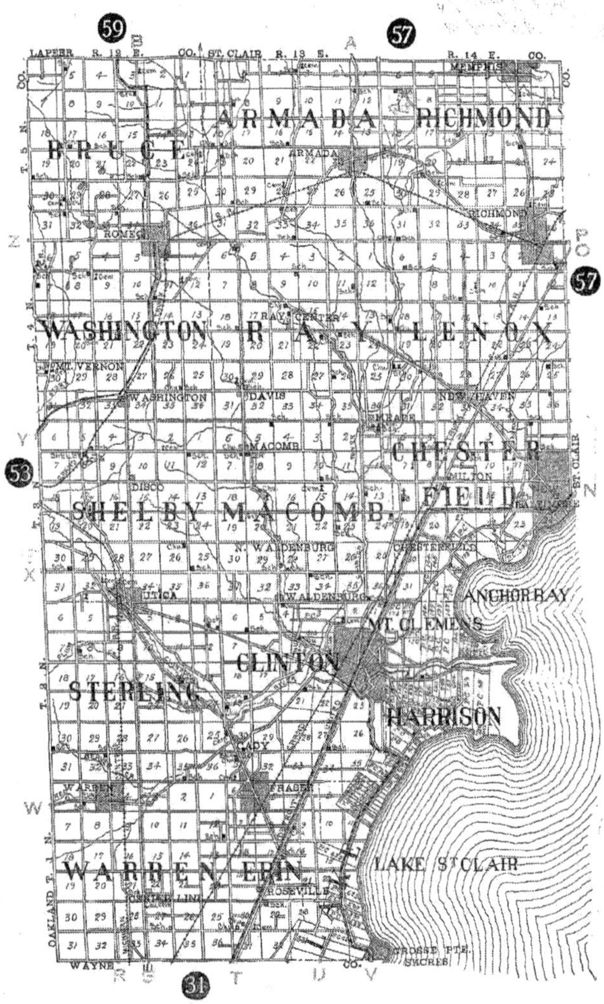

ST. CLAIR COUNTY.

St. Clair county was laid out and organized in 1821 and is thought to have been named in honor of Gen. Arthur St. Clair, first governor of the Northwest Territory. This county is located in about the southeastern part of the Lower Peninsula. It is bounded on the north by Sanilac county, on the east by Lake Huron and the St. Clair river, on the south by Anchor Bay, Lake St. Clair and Macomb county, and on the west by Lapeer county. The total land area of the county is 448,381.12 acres, of which about 415,000 acres are already in wonderfully productive farms. The population is 52,341 (1910 census). The valuation of taxable property, as estimated by the state board of tax commissioners in 1911, is $48,470,323. There are 174 schools, an enrollment of 9,802 students, giving positions to 336 teachers. The county has fifteen banks, one daily and ten weekly newspapers, also good telegraph, telephone and rural mail service.

Port Huron is the judicial seat and largest city in the county and has a population of about 23,000. The city is advantageously located at the foot of Lake Huron at the head of St. Clair river, sixty-five miles by water, and fifty-seven by rail from Detroit, and one hundred and thirteen from Lansing. It has seven miles of water front, three miles of which are given over to ideal homes and bathing beaches. It is a station on the Pere Marquette and the Grand Trunk Railways, with the Detroit United Railway interurban line to Detroit. Two ferry lines connect the city with Sarnia and Port Edward, on the Canadian side of the river. The railway tunnel under the St. Clair river, built by the Grand Trunk Railway, is one of the greatest engineering achievements on the continent. It is over a mile in length from the American to the Canadian side and cost about $3,000,000 to build. This is an important port of entry and a large customs business is transacted. There are two dry docks and three ship yards. The city is lighted by electricity, has broad cement walks, twenty-five miles of good pavement, modern system of water works, thoroughly equipped fire department, police department, about seventy-five acres of public parks, a handsome court house, and city hall, auditorium, opera houses, a customs house and post office building, a $30,000 Y. M. C. A. building, a hospital costing about $40,000, and a detention hospital, churches representing the leading denominations, sixteen public schools including the County Normal, a beautiful library, four banks, one daily and one weekly newspaper, etc. The larger industrial institutions include an engine and thresher works, a sulphite fibre works, a salt factory which is one of the largest in the world, automobile factory, knitting factory, an auto body factory, planing mills, wagon works, broom factories, boiler works, etc.

Other thriving communities of the county are Marine City, St. Clair, Algonac, Capac, Emmet and Yale, all surrounded by good farms. The principal transportation facilities of the county are the Pere Marquette, Grand Trunk, Michigan Central, Port Huron & Southern Railways, Detroit United Railway (electric), Star Cole Line, Detroit & Cleveland Navigation Company, Erie & Michigan Railway and Navigation Company, Northern Steamship Company, Erie & Western Transportation Company (Anchor Line) and the Northern Transportation Company.

ST. CLAIR COUNTY

MICHIGAN

LAPEER COUNTY.

Lapeer county was laid out in 1822 and was organized in 1835. The name was taken from the French word "La Pierre," which means flint stones. It is located in about the east central part of the Lower Peninsula, and is bounded on the north by Tuscola and Sanilac counties, on the east by Sanilac and Saint Clair counties, on the south by Oakland and Macomb counties and on the west by Genesee county. Total land area is 423,535.06 acres, of which about 400,000 acres are in fine farms. The population of the county is 26,033 (1910 census). The valuation of taxable property, as estimated by the state board of tax commissioners in 1911, is $21,060,841. The school system in this county is equal in every respect to that of the other counties. There are 135 schools, attended by 5,491 students, supplying positions for 205 teachers. There are sixteen banks and seven weekly newspapers. Good telephone, telegraph and rural mail service are found throughout the county.

Lapeer is the judicial seat and the largest city in the county, with a population of about 4,000. It is located on the Flint river at the crossing of the Grand Trunk and Michigan Central Railroads, in the heart of one of the richest and most productive agricultural sections in the state, 48 miles west of Port Huron and 60 north of Detroit. There are churches of the Episcopal, Baptist, Methodist Protestant, Presbyterian and Catholic denominations, and public schools which rank among the best in the state. The Michigan Home for the Feeble-Minded and Epileptic is located here on 360 acres of land. The city is lighted by electricity, has a fine water works system, good fire department, complete sewerage system, wide and well-paved streets, a library, first-class hotels, three banks, two live weekly newspapers, etc. The manufacturing industries consist of flour-mills, stove factory, foundry and machine shops, carriage and wagon works, creamery, etc. Other thriving towns of the county are Almont, Clifford, Columbiaville, Dryden, Imlay City, Metamora, North Branch and Otter Lake.

Imlay City is located on the Belle river and on the Grand Trunk Railway, 12 miles east of Lapeer and 59 north of Detroit. It is lighted by electricity, has water works, fire department, churches of the Congregational, Methodist, Episcopal, Baptist, German Lutheran and Catholic denominations, a $20,000 school, a city hall, opera house, two banks and two weekly newspapers. The principal exports of the surrounding country are grain, live stock, lumber and farm products. The principal transportation facilities of the county are the Grand Trunk, Michigan Central and the Pontiac, Oxford & Northern Railroads.

LAPEER COUNTY

MICHIGAN

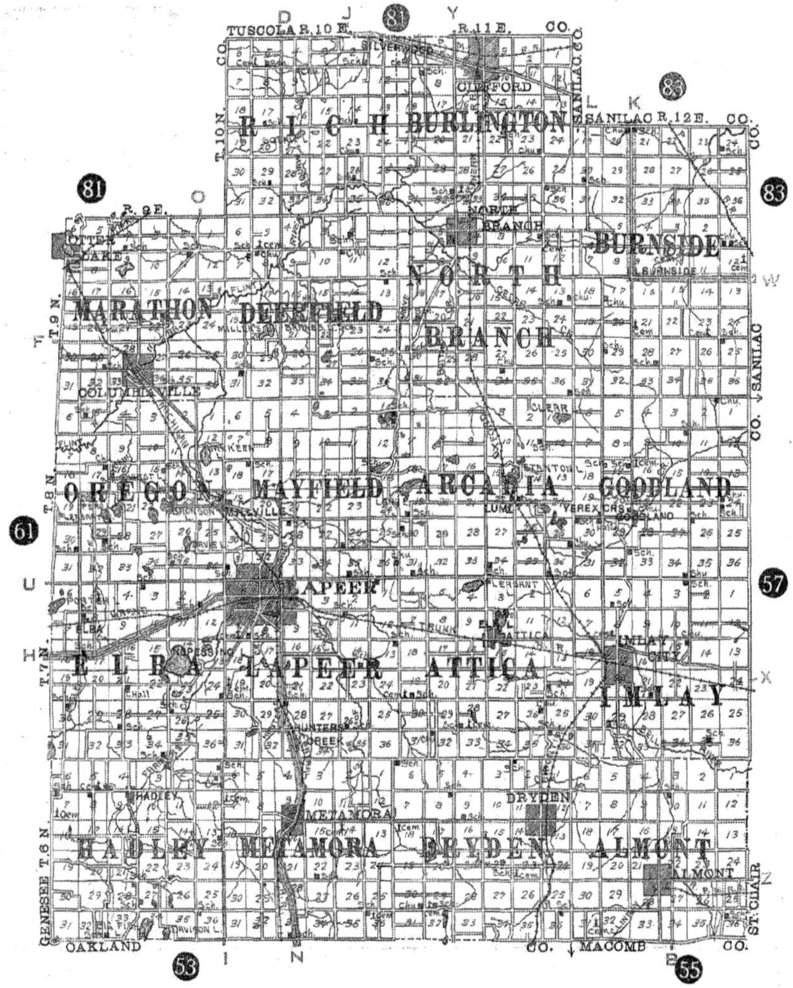

GENESEE COUNTY.

Genesee county was laid out in 1835, organized in 1836, and was named from that part of New York from whence many of its settlers had come. The name originated with the Chennssio tribe of Indians and means "beautiful valley." The county is located in the east central part of the Lower Peninsula. Its boundaries are, Saginaw and Tuscola counties on the north, Lapeer county on the east, Livingston and Oakland counties on the south, and Shiawassee and Saginaw counties on the west. The total land area comprises 408,979.92 acres. Of this number, about 390,000 acres are devoted to farms, which are wonderfully productive. The federal census of 1910 gives the county a population of about 64,555. In 1911, the state board of tax commissioners placed a valuation of $65,385,450 on all taxable lands. There are 177 schools, requiring 380 teachers, and a total of 11,436 students in attendance. The county has nineteen banks, two daily and nine weekly newspapers, exeellent telephone, telegraph and rural mail service.

Flint is the judicial seat of the county, also the largest city. Population 38,550 (census 1910). This city has had a wonderful growth, showing an increase in population during the last decade of about 25,000. It has an area of twelve square miles and is located on both banks of the Flint river, 34 miles from Saginaw, 49 from Lansing and 68 from Detroit. It has excellent facilities for the shipment of the products of its factories. It is on the Grand Trunk and Pere Marquette Railways, also *the Detroit United Electric and the Saginaw & Flint Electric* Railways.

The city is laid out with fine, wide and beautifully shaded streets, is lighted by electricity and gas, has a water works plant valued at $775,000, has 70 miles of water mains, a thoroughly equipped fire department, 15 acres of parks, a police department, 16 public schools employing 150 teachers, 25 churches, 3 hospitals, 12 hotels, efficient sewer system, electric street car system, a public library, a new $125,000 Y. M. C. A. building, a $150,000 Masonic temple, a new city hall, a $100,000 court house, a $75,000 postoffice, 5 banks, a $110,000 high school, theaters, a daily newspaper and two weeklies.

Flint is the home of the Michigan school for the deaf, which is surrounded by 200 acres of beautifully laid out grounds. It is also the location of one of the largest automobile plants in the world, three other growing automobile plants, and an immense quantity of vehicles of almost every description are manufactured. Other industries include an electric stove plant, a steel spring plant, an automobile parts plant, automobile carburetor plant, saw and planing-mills, flour-mills, gasoline engine works, and plants for the manufacture of axles, wheels, carriage hardware, auto bodies, varnish, paint, electric and gas fixtures, pumps, cigars, brooms, cigar boxes, rugs, paper, brick, boilers, mattresses, ladders, woolen goods, potash, show cases, furniture, heaters, etc.

Fenton, located on the Grand Trunk Railway, sixteen miles south of Flint and with a poulation of about 2,500, is the next largest town of the county. It has churches of several denominations, fine high school building, opera house, good hotels, two banks, city hall and fire station and municipally owned water works and electric light plant. Its principal industries include a screen door factory, water works, machinery factory, cement works, flour-mill, creamery, carriage and wagon works, foundry and machine shop, cheese factory and two grain elevators. It is situated in a rich agricultural section and in the vicinity of several attractive lakes, including Long lake, which is surrounded by summer cottages and with which Fenton is connected by an electric railway.

The other principal towns of the county are Flushing, Clio, Davidson, Mount Morris, Montrose, Linden, and Gaines, all of which are located in a highly productive agricultural section and from which grain, hay, fruit, potatoes and other farm products are largely shipped. The principal transportation facilities of the county are the Pere Marquette, Grand Trunk and the Michigan Central Railways, Detroit United Traction Company, and the Saginaw and Flint Railway (electric).

GENESEE COUNTY

MICHIGAN

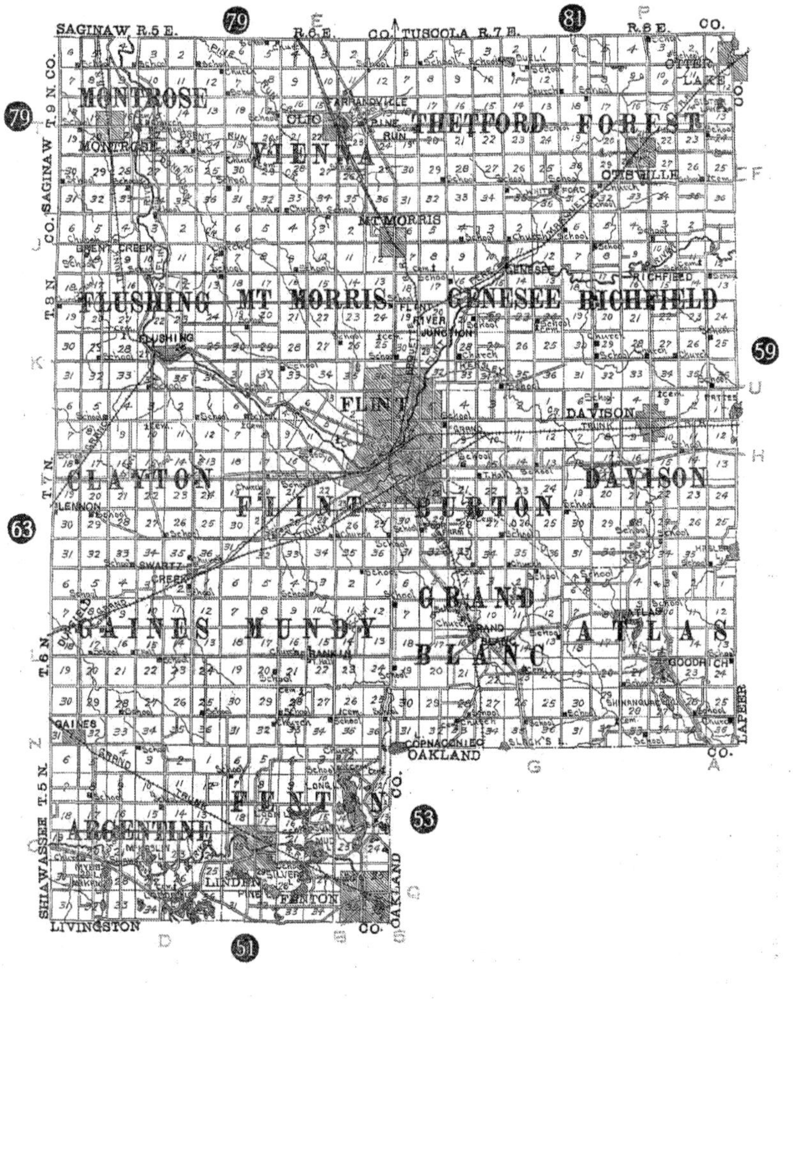

SHIAWASSEE COUNTY.

Shiawassee county was laid out in 1822 and was organized in 1837. The name is taken from the river extending through the county which derives the name from the words meaning "straight ahead." It is located in about the south central part of the Lower Peninsula and is bounded on the north by Saginaw county, on the east by Genesee county, on the south by Ingham and Livingston counties, and on the west by Clinton county. The total land area is 345,200.32 acres. Of this number, about 328,000 acres are in splendid farms. The population is 33,246 (1910 census). The valuation of taxable property, as estimated by the state board of tax commissioners in 1911, is $30,723,205. There are 128 schools, furnishing positions for 251 teachers, and a total enrollment of 6,515 students. The county has twelve banks, two daily and nine weekly newspapers. Telegraph, telephone and rural mail service is found throughout the county.

Corunna, the judicial seat of the county, has a population of about 1,384. It is located on the Grand Trunk Railway and the Ann Arbor Railroad, the Owosso & Corunna Electric Railway, and on both sides of the Shiawassee river, three miles from Owosso, thirty-nine south of Saginaw, thirty northeast of Lansing, twenty-two west of Flint and seventy-five northwest of Detroit. It has Episcopal, Presbyterian, Methodist, Free Methodist and Baptist churches, a fine school house, a library, a beautiful park, a court house costing about $142,000, a bank, two weekly newspapers. Furniture, lumber, flour, robes and cigars are manufactured, and coal is mined and shipped.

Owosso is the largest city in the county and has about 11,000 inhabitants. It is situated on the Shiawassee river and on the Ann Arbor, the Grand Trunk and Michigan Central roads, three miles northwest of Corunna, twenty-eight from Lansing and seventy-eight from Detroit. The city is lighted by electricity, has a municipal water works system, six miles of street paving, sewerage system, fire department, opera house, a $65,000 post office, four school buildings, churches of many denominations, three banks, two daily newspapers, etc. The car shops of the Ann Arbor Railroad are located here, giving employment to a large number of men. The city's manufacturing interests include the second largest casket company in the world, one of the biggest motor truck factories in the United States, a table plant, stove works, iron and engine works, screen door and sash works, one of the largest butter concerns in the State, packing house, artificial ice plant, bundle works, carriage and sleigh works, knitting works, planing mills, flour mill, sugar plant, etc.

Other important towns of the county all located in good agricultural sections are Bancroft, Byron, Durand, Laingsburg, Morrice, Perry, and Vernon. Durand, with a population of about 2,500, is located at the junction of the Grand Trunk, Grand Trunk Western and Ann Arbor Railroads, eight miles southeast of Corunna, seventeen from Flint and sixty-seven from Detroit. The Grand Trunk Railroad has spent something like $300,000 on property in and around Durand, including a round house, one of the largest on its system, a $100,000 depot, coal chutes, carpenter shop and foundry, etc. The city has a municipally-owned electric light and water plant, Congregational, Episcopal, Methodist, Baptist, Christian and Catholic churches, two school buildings, a combination fire hall, council chamber, public library and city office building, a fire department, seven miles of sewers, a creamery, machine and stamping works, a hoop works, flour mill, two grain elevators, a $10,000 Y. M. C. A. building, two banks, a weekly newspaper, etc.

Transportation facilities of the county are the Grand Trunk, Michigan Central, Ann Arbor Railroads, and the Michigan United Traction Company (electric).

SHIAWASSEE COUNTY

MICHIGAN

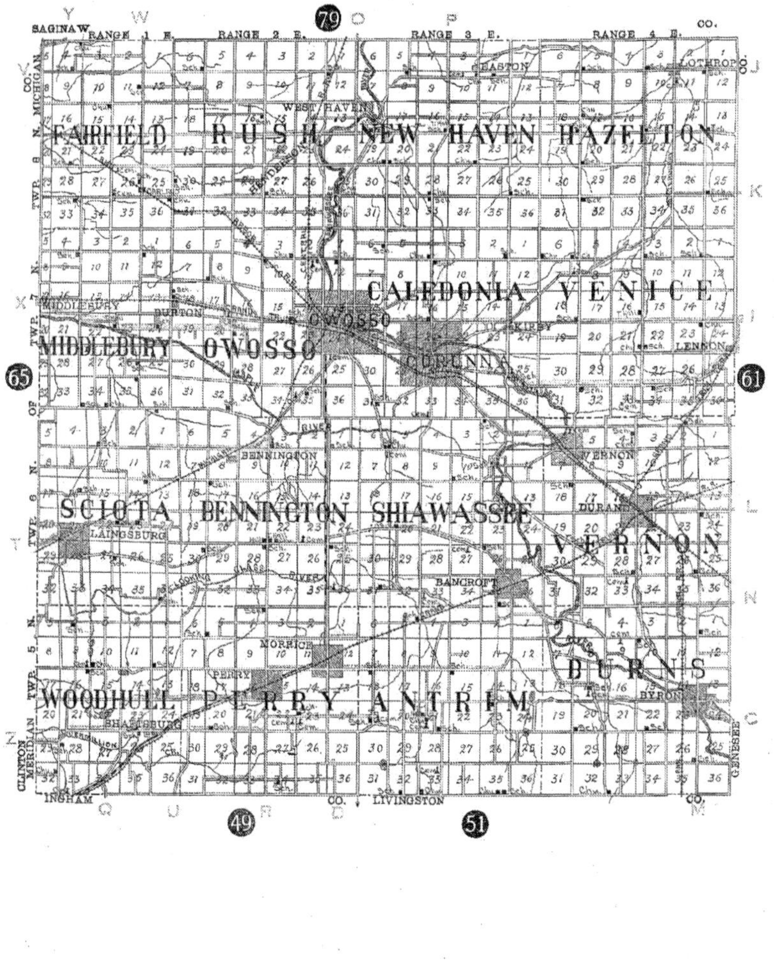

CLINTON COUNTY.

Clinton county was laid out in 1831 and was organized in 1839. The county was named in honor of Dewitt Clinton, through whose efforts the Erie canal had been built, which had a great effect upon the fortunes of Michigan. This county is located in the south central part of the Lower Peninsula. It is bounded on the north by Gratiot county, on the east by Shiawassee and Ingham counties, on the south by Eaton and Ingham counties and on the west by Ionia county. The total land area is 364,972.96 acres, about 352,000 acres of which are already devoted to wonderfully productive farms. The valuation of all taxable property as estimated by the state board of tax commissioners in 1911, is $30,428,680. The federal census of 1910 gives Clinton county a population of 23,129. The school system is equal to that of any of the larger counties, there being 131 schools, attended by 4,385 children and requiring 200 teachers. There are ten banks and five weekly newspapers. Also the best of telegraph, telephone and rural mail service.

St. Johns is the county seat, also the largest town. It has a population of about 3,500, and is located on the Grand Trunk railway and the Michigan United Traction Company (electric) 18 miles north of Lansing, 26 east of Ionia and 98 northwest of Detroit. The city is well laid out and possesses many attractive features, among which are its churches, of which there are Congregational, Episcopal, Baptist, Methodist, Free Methodist, Catholic and German Lutheran denominations. It has municipally-owned electric light and water works plant, a ladies library, three school buildings, opera house, three banks, good hotels and two weekly newspapers. Among the prominent industries are saw- and grist-mills, grain elevators, a foundry, gasoline engine works, heating boiler works, a quilt factory, agricultural implement supply works, drilling and prospecting tool works, canning factory, creamery, two portable building factories, wagon factory and a cider-mill. The town is connected with Lansing by electric railway.

Other thriving towns of the county include Elsie, population 600; Fowler, population 476; Maple Rapids, population 529; Ovid, population 1,100, and Westphalia, population 375. Ovid is located on the Grand Trunk railway and on the Maple river, about 10 miles east of St. Johns, 10 west of Owosso and 24 northeast of Lansing. It has electric light and water works plant, churches of the Congregational, Baptist, Free Methodist and Methodist denominations, a graded public school, opera house, two public halls, a bank and a weekly newspaper. The transportation facilities of the county include the Grand Trunk, Pere Marquette, Ann Arbor and Michigan Central Railroads, and the Michigan United Traction Company (electric).

ELSIE.

C. M. Sheldon & Son, Automobile Garage. General Blacksmithing and Repairing. Agency for Ford Motor Cars.

FOWLER.

Louis Webber, Agent for Ford and Buick. Repairs and Accessories. Storage, 50 Cents Per Day.

CLINTON COUNTY

MICHIGAN

OVID.

G. F. Smith & Son, Distributers of Ford Motor Cars.

ST. JOHNS.

A. T. Smith, Distributor of Ford Motor Cars, Auto Livery, Garage and Supplies. Storage, 50 Cents.
St. Johns National Bank.
Wm. J. Moss Auto Co.

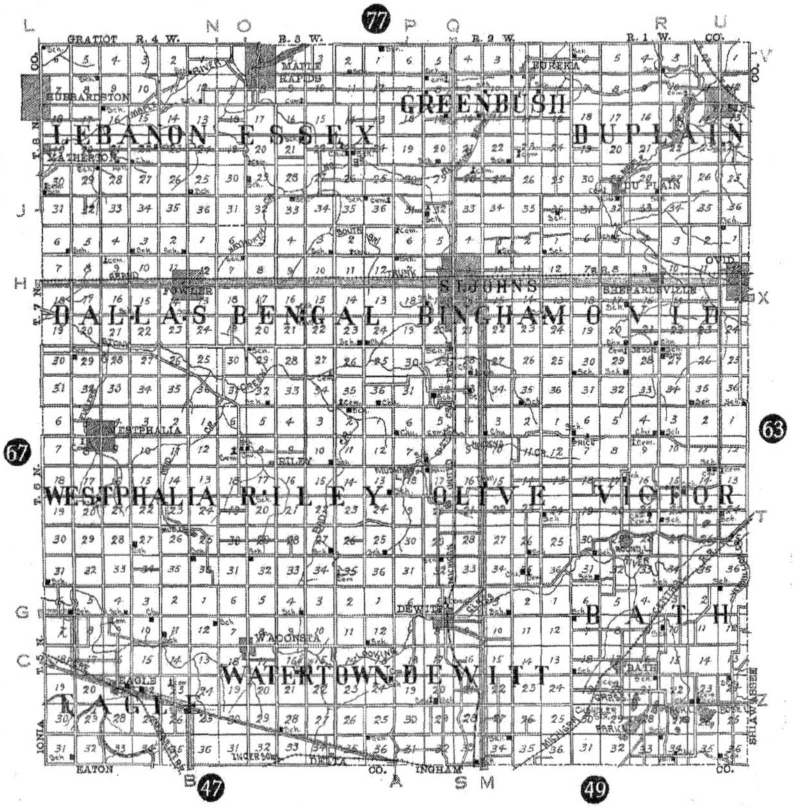

IONIA COUNTY.

Ionia county was laid out in 1831, organized in 1837, and was so named for the ancient Greek district on the west shore of Asia Minor, which for several centuries was famous for its commerce, wealth, high civilization and social development. The county is located in the west central part of the Lower Peninsula. It is bounded on the north by Montcalm county, on the east by Clinton county, on the south by Barry and Eaton counties and on the west by Kent county. The total land area is 366,291.10 acres. Of this number, about 351,500 acres are devoted to splendid farms. The valuation of taxable property, as estimated by the state board of tax commissioners in 1911, is $33,657,700. The population is 32,550 (1910 census). The county has 150 schools, furnishing positions for 259 teachers, and an enrollment of 5,722 students. There are sixteen banks, two daily and ten weekly newspapers. Good telegraph, telephone and rural mail service is found throughout the county.

Ionia is the judicial seat and the largest city of the county, having a population of about 5,500. It is located among the hills along the Grand river, 34 miles east of Grand Rapids and 38 northwest of Lansing. It is a station on the Pere Marquette and Grand Trunk Railways. The city's location on the hills, following the general line of the river and extending far back, makes it one of the most picturesque and attractively arranged places in the state. There are eight churches, three public school buildings, a $50,000 parochial school building, two banks, a $30,000 armory, public library, a fire hall, a $15,000 city hall, opera house, municipally owned water works, handsome court house, electric lighting and water power plant, gas plant, a $65,000 postoffice, two daily and two weekly newspapers.

Among the prosperous industrial establishments are found clothing and skirt factories, auto body factory, gasoline engine and implement works, flour-mills, planing-mills, pottery, Pere Marquette shops, glove factory, furniture factory, washing machine factory, brick and tile works, automobile plant, cigar factories, machine shop, grain elevator, creamery, two monument works, etc. Four miles to the southwest is the Ionia county house, to the west of the city is the Michigan Reformatory, and to the south, the State Hospital. Ionia is the receiving and distributing point for a rich agricultural section and is one of the largest bean shipping points in the United States.

Belding has a population of about 5,000. It is located on the Pere Marquette Railroad and on the Flat river, 15 miles northwest of Ionia. It has churches of several denominations, excellent schools, electric light plant, opera house, three banks, first-class hotels and two live newspapers. Manufacturing industries consist of four silk mills, one basket factory, a canvas coal bag factory, shoe factory, a paper box factory, sash, door and blind factory, a saw-mill, feed-mill, refrigerator factory, etc.

Other important towns of the county are Portland, Hubbardston, Lake Odessa, Muir, Pewamo and Saranac. The surrounding country produces beans, grain, and fruit in abundance. The principal transportation facilities of the county are the Pere Marquette, and the Grand Trunk Railroads.

IONIA COUNTY

MICHIGAN

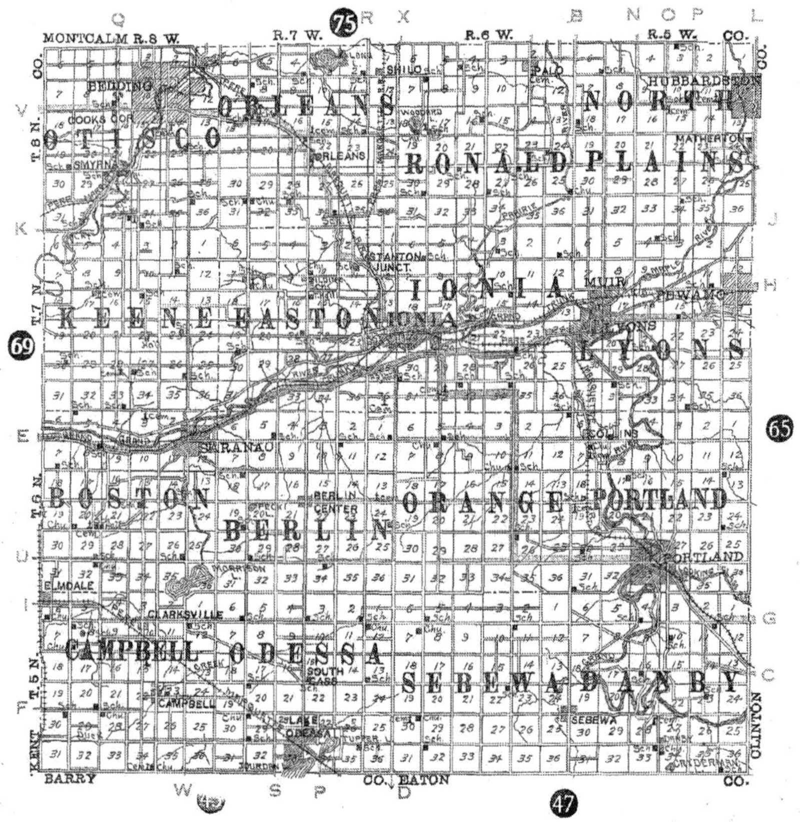

KENT COUNTY.

Kent county was laid out in 1831, organized in 1836, and was named in honor of James Kent, a well-known expounder of the principles of American law. The county is located in the west central part of the Lower Peninsula and is bounded on the north by Newaygo and Montcalm counties, on the east by Montcalm and Ionia counties, on the south by Allegan and Barry counties, and on the west by Muskegon and Ottawa counties. Total land area is 545,815.80 acres, of which about 487,000 acres are in splendid farms. The population is 159,145 (1910 census). In 1911, the state board of tax commissioners placed a valuation of $187,586,358 on all taxable lands. The county has 240 schools, an enrollment of 25,958 students, requiring 881 teachers. There are twenty-two banks, three daily and twenty-two weekly newspapers. There is good telegraph, telephone and rural mail service throughout the county.

Grand Rapids is the judicial seat and the largest city in the county. It is also the second largest city in the state. Population is shown by 1910 census to be 112,571, now estimated at more than 130,000. It is located at the head of navigation on Grand river, in a rich agricultural section, 30 miles from Lake Michigan, and on the Pere Marquette, Grand Rapids & Indiana, Grand Trunk, Michigan Central and Lake Shore & Michigan Southern Railroads, also several electric lines. The city has an area of 17.5 squares miles, 46 miles of paving, 101 miles of public sewers, 135 miles of gas mains, 106 miles of water mains. There are many beautiful parks, covering over 400 acres, 18 theaters and vaudeville houses, 31 public homes and hospitals, and about 100 churches representing nearly every denomination. There are 37 public schools, in addition to which are many private and denominational schools, a beautiful public library, beautiful new postoffice building, an immense water works, police and fire departments, 10 banks, many of which have several branches.

Grand Rapids is one of the largest furniture manufacturing cities in the world and is known the world over as the "Furniture City." A few of the many successful manufacturing industries are, all kinds of furniture, show cases, sticky fly-paper, flour- and grist-mills, gypsum, planing- and interior finish-mills, printeries, foundry and machine shops, carpet sweepers, vehicles, boots and shoes, hosiery and knit goods, railway construction and repair shops, refrigerators, wood turning and carving, mirrors, and ornamental glass, cigars, copper and sheet metal works, etc. It is estimated that in the manufacture of furniture, the annual output is in excess of $10,000,000.

Grand Rapids is the center of one of the finest producing districts in the entire country. The city affords an excellent home market for the products of many nearby farms and orchards, but solid carload lots of potatoes, beans, peaches, apples, small fruits and greenhouse products are also shipped by the commision men.

Other towns of importance are Caledonia, Cedar Springs, Grandville, Lowell, Sparta, Ada, Rockford and Sand Lake, all in good agricultural sections. The principal transportation facilities of the county are the Grand Rapids & Indiana, Pere Marquette, Grand Trunk, Michigan Central, Lake Shore & Michigan Southern, Grand Rapids, Holland & Chicago and the Grand Rapids, Grand Haven & Muskegon Railways and the Michigan United Traction Company.

KENT COUNTY

MICHIGAN

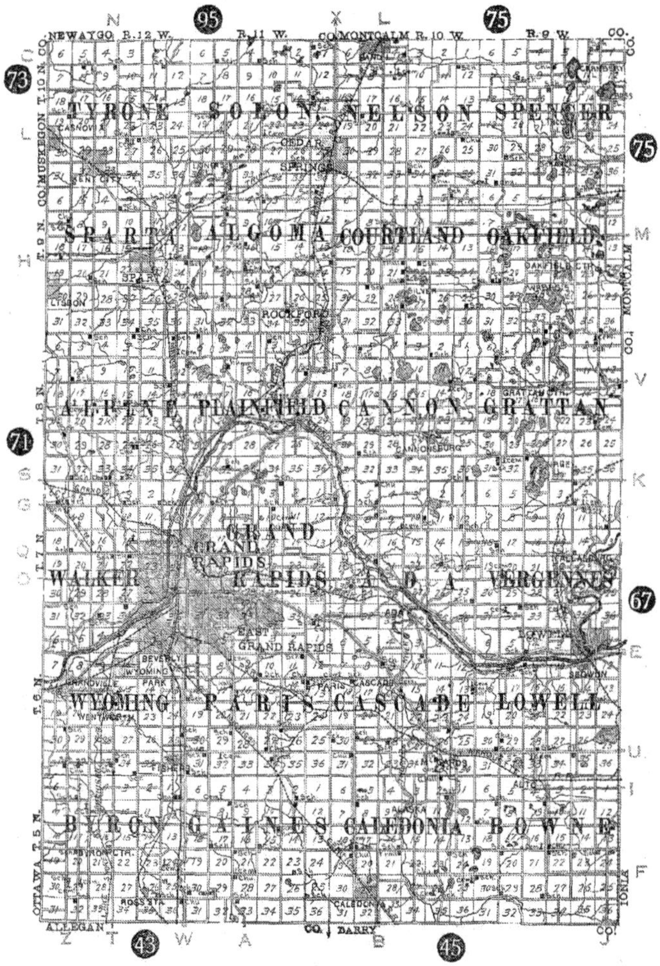

OTTAWA COUNTY.

Ottawa county was laid out in 1831, and was organized in 1837. The name is that of a once powerful tribe of Indians that inhabited the northwestern portion of the Lower Peninsula. This county is located in the western part of the Lower Peninsula and is bounded on the north by Muskegon county, on the east by Kent county, on the south by Allegan county, and on the west by Lake Michigan. The total land area is 357,839.46 acres, of which about 325,000 acres are in splendid farms. The population is 45,301 (1910 census). The valuation of taxable property, as estimated by the state board of tax commissioners in 1911, is $44,347,162. The school system is equal to that of any of the larger counties, there being 136 schools, 10,277 students in attendance, requiring the services of 297 teachers. The county has thirteen banks, two daily and twelve weekly newspapers, also good telegraph, telephone and rural mail service.

Grand Haven, the capital city of the county, has a population of about 5,856. It is the western terminus of the (D. & M. div.) Grand Trunk Railway, 31 miles west of Grand Rapids. It is also a station on the Pere Marquette Railroad, and the Grand Rapids, Grand Haven & Muskegon Railway (electric). The town is picturesquely located at the mouth of the Grand river, on the shore of Lake Michigan, and is one of the most important ports on the shore of the lake. The city has churches representing the leading denominations, a $60,000 high school, one union and five ward school buildings, an institute, a library, an opera house, first class hotels, two banks, a daily and a weekly newspaper. It is lighted by electricity and gas, has an excellent system of water works, good fire department, etc. Grand Haven is in the center of Michigan's great fruit belt and large quantities of grapes and berries are shipped annually. Fishing is also an important interest.

Holland, the largest city in the county, has a population of about 12,000. It is located on the Pere Marquette Railway, and on the Grand Rapids, Holland & Chicago Railway (electric), twenty miles south of Grand Haven and twenty-five southwest of Grand Rapids. It has a good natural harbor at the head of Black Lake and has a permanent channel of eighteen feet. The city is lighted by electricity and gas, has water works, fire department, excellent sewerage system, churches of the leading denominations, a high school and five ward schools and Hope College, said to be the seat of learning of the Reformed church in America. The Western Theological Seminary of the Reformed church in America is also located here. One daily and five weekly newspapers are published here.

Holland is an important fruit market and general farm produce is largely shipped. The leading manufactories are woodenware and leather. There are also planing mills, iron foundries, glass, machinery, tool, chemical engine, screen, basket, piano and furnace factories, a beet sugar factory, the second largest pickle works in the United States, roller flouring mills, canning factories, furniture factories, a railway printing plant, saw mills, shoe factory, etc. Adjacent to the city are located three large summer resorts.

Other thriving towns of the county are Zeeland, Coopersville and Spring Lake. The principal transportation facilities of the county are the Grand Trunk, Grand Rapids & Indiana, Pere Marquette Railroads, Grand Rapids, Grand Haven & Muskegon (electric), Grand Rapids, Holland & Chicago (electric) and the Graham & Morton Transportation Company, Goodrich Steamship Line, Crosby Transportation Company, and the Grand Trunk Car Ferry.

OTTAWA COUNTY

MICHIGAN

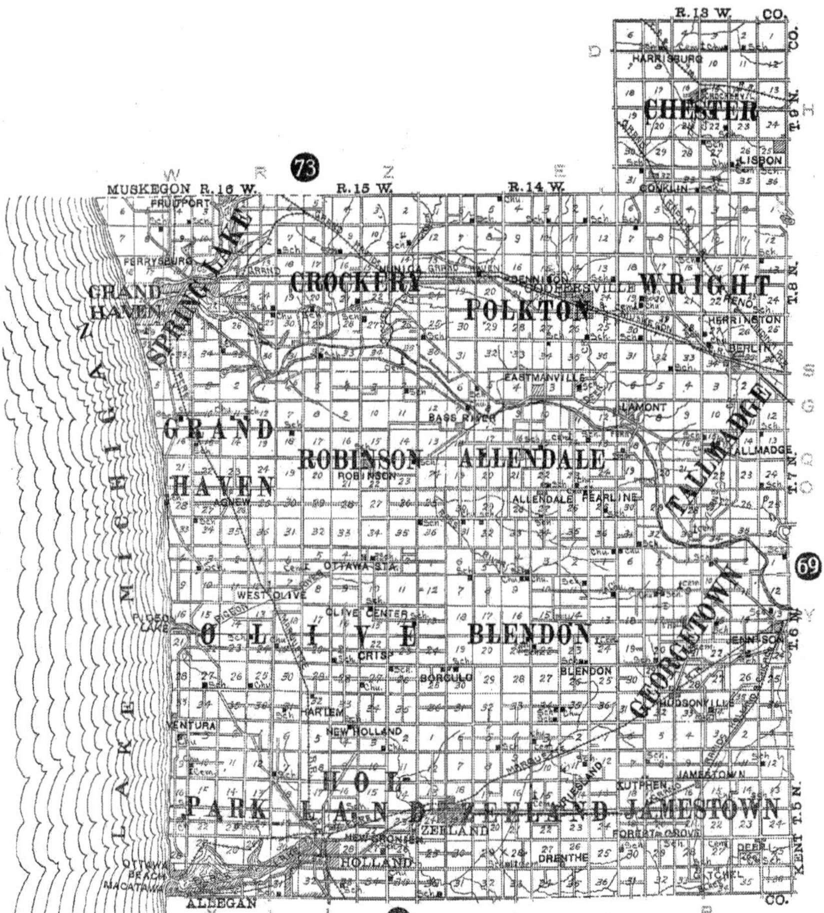

MUSKEGON COUNTY.

Muskegon county was laid out and organized in 1859. It took its name from the river running through it and emptying into Lake Michigan. The word is taken from the Pottawatomie language and is thought to mean "Marshy River." It is located in the extreme west central part of the Lower Peninsula, and is bounded on the north by Oceana and Newaygo counties, on the east by Newaygo and Kent counties, on the south by Ottawa county and on the west by Lake Michigan. The total land area is 322,484.68 acres, of which about 185,000 acres are in fine farms. The population is 40,577 (1910 census). The valuation of taxable land, as estimated by the state board of tax commissioners in 1911, is $29,183,320. There are 118 schools, attended by 8,437 students, requiring the services of 311 teachers. The county has ten banks, two daily and four weekly newspapers, also telegraph, telephone and rural mail service.

Muskegon is the judicial seat, also the largest city in the county, having over 30,000 inhabitants. It is located on the east shore of Lake Michigan, and on the Pere Marquette, Grand Rapids & Indiana and the Grand Trunk Railroads, and the Grand Rapids, Grand Haven & Muskegon Railway (electric). It is one of the best harbors on the east shore of Lake Michigan and is located directly across the lake from Milwaukee, being 84 miles distant from that city and 118 from Chicago, to which cities boat service is maintained all the year round. At this point the Muskegon river broadens out into a beautiful lake six miles long and from one to three miles wide, which empties into Lake Michigan through a channel three hundred feet wide and of sufficient depth to admit into the harbor the largest and heaviest vessels that ply the lakes.

The city has an area of 6 square miles, 35 miles of pavement, 40 miles of public sewers, five public parks, covering 85 acres, a thoroughly equipped fire department, municipally-owned water works, twenty-one public school buildings, one of the best equipped free manual training schools in the United States, many churches of different denominations, first-class hotels, theatres, a beautiful public library costing $230,000, two hospitals, four banks, two daily and one weekly newspapers, etc.

The city is in the great Michigan fruit belt and in the vicinity are some of the finest and most productive sections devoted to raising the small fruits, grapes, peaches, plums and apples. The rich lands of the Muskegon river bottom are especially adapted to the cultivation of celery, which promises to become a most important industry. Among the more prominent industries are iron foundries and machine shops, a refrigerator works, billiard and pool table factory and a curtain roller factory which are among the largest in the world, automobile works, marine motor works, paper-mill, furniture factories, brewery, electric cranes, etc. The city of Muskegon Heights which adjoins the city limits has a population of about 3,000.

Whitehall has a population of about 1,800. It is located at the head of White lake and on the Pere Marquette Railroad, 16 miles north of Muskegon and 5 inland from Lake Michigan. Montague, with about 1,200 inhabitants, located at the head of White lake, opposite Whitehall, on the Pere Marquette Railroad, 10 miles from Muskegan and about 6 from Lake Michigan, is another thriving town of Muskegon county.

The principal transportation facilities of the county are the Pere Marquette, Grand Trunk, Grand Rapids & Indiana and the Grand Rapids, Grand Haven & Muskegon Railroads, and the Goodrich-Crosby Transportation Company's boat lines.

MUSKEGON COUNTY

MICHIGAN

MUSKEGON.
The Union National Bank.
W. W. Barcus, Inc., Real Estate and General Insurance.

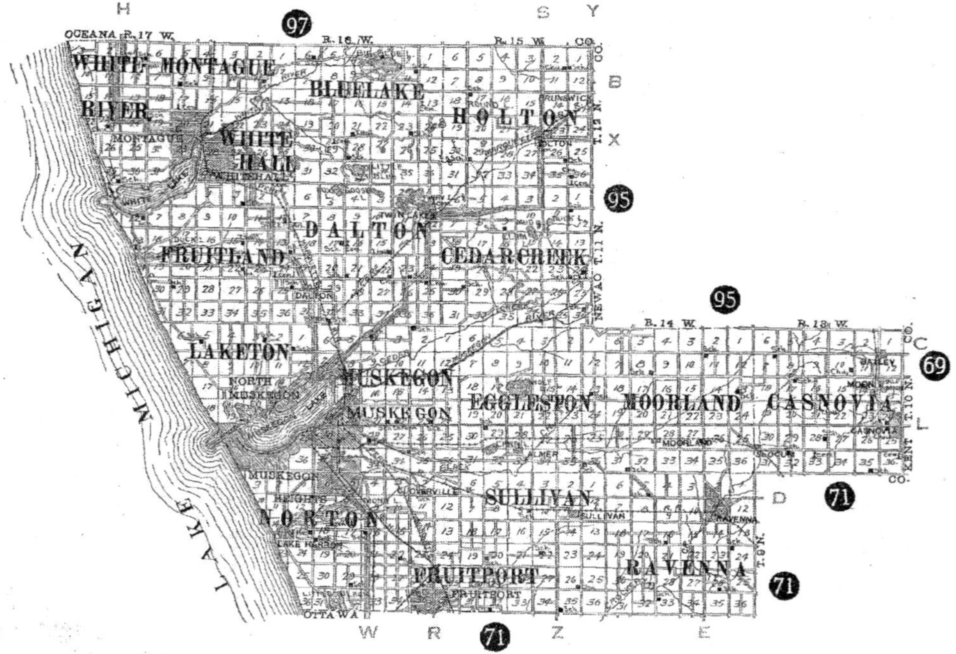

MONTCALM COUNTY.

Montcalm county was laid out in 1831, organized in 1850, and was named in honor of Marquis De Montcalm. It is located in about the west central part of the Lower Peninsula and is bounded on the north by Mecosta and Isabella counties, on the east by Gratiot county, on the south by Ionia and Kent counties, and on the west by Newaygo and Kent counties. The total land area is 454,460.74 acres, about 393,000 acres of which are in splendid farms. The population is 32,069 (1910 census). The valuation of taxable property, as estimated by the state board of tax commissioners in 1911, is $20,829,816. There are 143 schools, with an enrollment of 6,879 students, requiring the services of 289 teachers. The county has eighteen banks, one daily and eleven weekly newspapers, also telegraph, telephone and rural mail service.

Stanton, the county seat, has a population of about 1,200. It is located on the Pere Marquette Railroad, 24 miles north of Ionia and 61 northwest of Lansing. It is lighted by electricity, has water works, churches of the Congregational, Methodist, Free Methodist, Baptist and Catholic denominations, a union school building, two opera houses, a new court house costing about $80,000, a bank and two weekly newspapers. The soil in the vicinity is especially adapted for farming.

Greenville with its 4,200 inhabitants is the largest city in the county. It is located on the Flat river and on the Grand Trunk and Pere Marquette Railroads, 15 miles southeast of Stanton and 41 northeast of Grand Rapids. It is lighted by electricity and gas, has water works, fire department, Episcopal, Congregational, Adventist, Baptist, Catholic, Danish Lutheran and Methodist churches, excellent schools, a ladies' library, two public halls, good hotels, three banks, a daily and weekly newspaper.

The manufacturing interests include three flour-mills, two of the largest refrigerator factories in America, sideboard factory, agricultural implement factories, blast furnace, grain and potato planter factories, planing- and saw-mills, cider-mill, sash and door factories, two electric light and power plants, a potato starch factory, etc. Greenville is known as one of the most important potato markets in the state.

Other important towns include, Howard City, population 1,100; Carson City, population 1,000; Edmore, population 800; Lakeview, population 1,000; McBrides and Sheridan, all surrounded by good farming country. The transportation facilities of the county are the Grand Rapids & Indiana, Pere Marquette and Grand Trunk Railroads.

MONTCALM COUNTY

MICHIGAN

CARSON CITY.
F. Ralph, Garage.

STANTON.
Main Street Garage, Union Tel. 125.

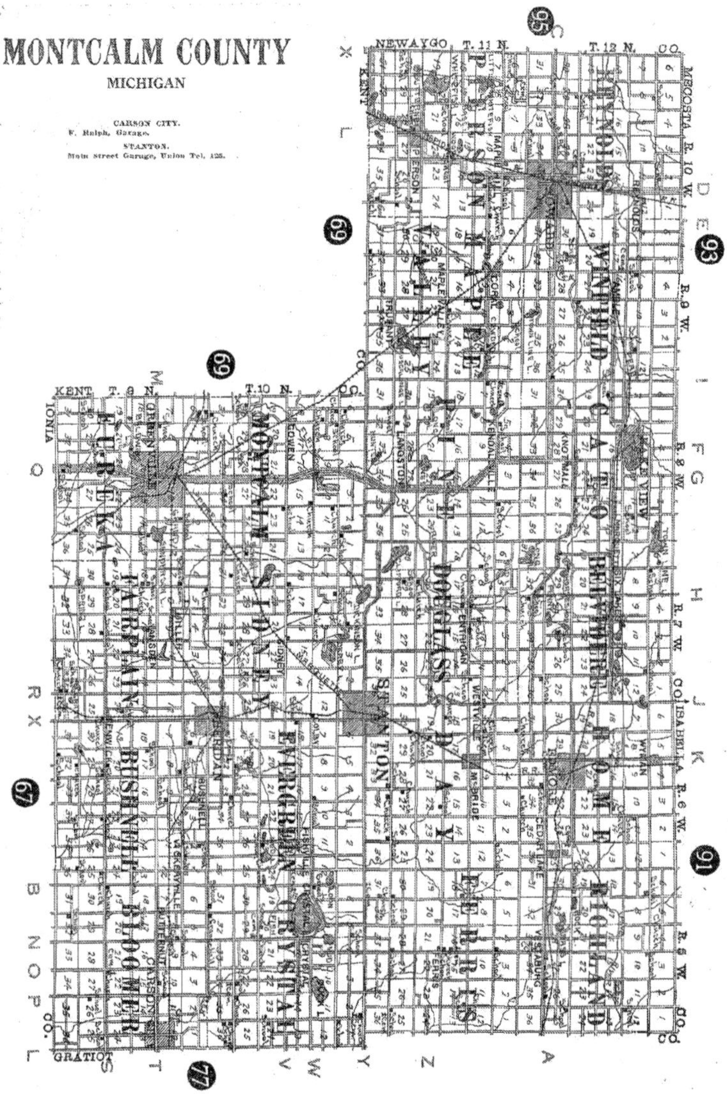

GRATIOT COUNTY.

Gratiot county was laid out in 1831 and was organized in 1855. It was named in honor of Charles Gratiot, who, as captain and engineer, built Fort Gratiot, at the head of the St. Clair river. This county is located in the central part of the Lower Peninsula, and is bounded on the north by Isabelle and Midland counties, on the east by Saginaw county, on the south by Clinton county, and on the west by Montcalm county. The total land area is 364,628.63 acres, of which about 335,000 are in splendid farms. The population is 28,820 (1910 census). The valuation of taxable property, as estimated by the state board of tax commissioners in 1911, is $26,038,121. There are 135 schools, which were attended by 6,544 pupils last year, requiring the services of 320 teachers. The county has seventeen banks and eleven weekly newspapers. Good telegraph, telephone, and rural mail service is found throughout the county.

Ithaca is the capital city of the county and has a population of about 2,000. It is located on the Ann Arbor Railroad, 42 miles north of Lansing. It does a big grain and produce business and is the central supply station for a large and fertile agricultural area. There are churches of the Adventist, Baptist, Methodist, Free Methodist and Presbyterian denominations, also a splendid school system, four banks, good hotels, a $100,000 court house, a sewerage system costing about $60,000, a $45,000 electric light and pumping plant. Has roller flouring-mills, 3 grain elevators, a large creamery, foundry and machine shop, beet lifter factory, brick and tile works. There are two live weekly newspapers published here.

Other towns of importance include Alma, population 8,000; St. Louis, population 2,000; Ashley and Breckenridge. Alma is located on the Pine river and on the Pere Marquette and Ann Arbor Railroads, eight miles south of Ithaca and thirty-seven miles west of Saginaw. The city has paved streets and the boulevard system of street lighting. It has an electric light and water plant, modern sewerage system, good fire department, two banks, first-class hotels, an opera house and newspapers. There are churches of several denominations, and a splendid public school system. Alma College is located here. Prominent industries of the city include a large sugar factory, automatic gasoline engine works, foundry and machine shop, one of the largest creameries in the state, and manufactories of hay presses, overalls and jackets, skirts, heaters, bee smokers, wall board and roofing, chemicals, cement blocks, etc. The principal transportation facilities of the county are the Pere Marquette, Grand Trunk and the Anna Arbor Railroads.

GRATIOT COUNTY

MICHIGAN

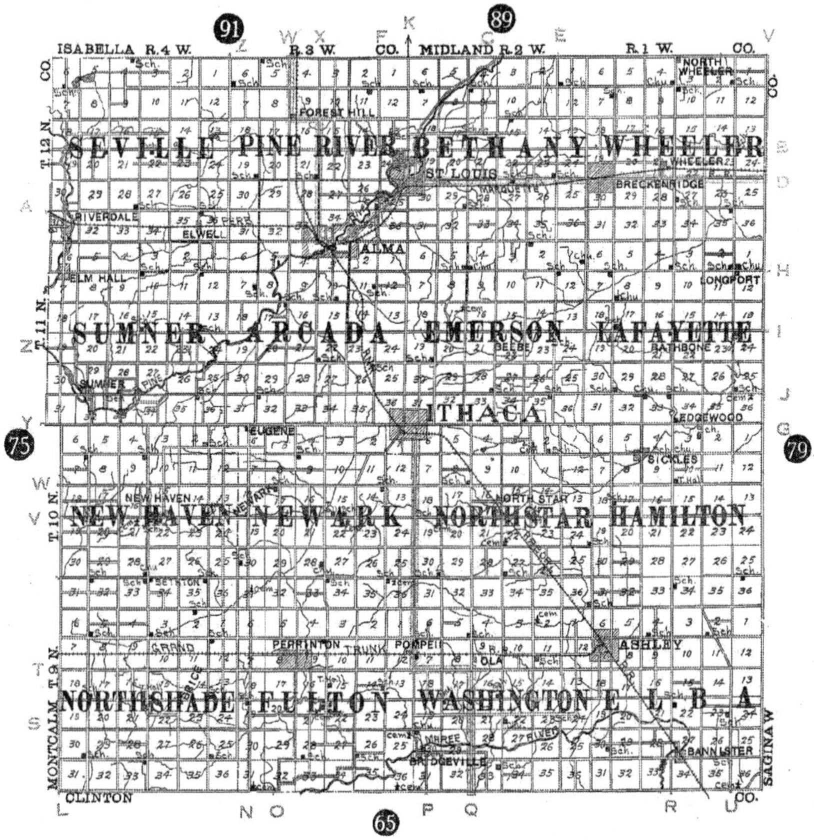

SAGINAW COUNTY.

This county was first laid out in 1822 by Lewis Cass, then governor of Michigan. It was again laid out by the Legislature in 1831 and was finally organized in 1835. The county takes its name from the river and bay of that name. Saginaw county is located in the east central part of the Lower Peninsula. It is bounded on the north by Midland and Bay counties, on the east by Tuscola county, on the south by Shiawassee and Genesee counties, and on the west by Gratiot and Midland counties. The total land area of the county is 520,291.45 acres. Of this number, about 431,000 acres are devoted to farms which are wonderfully productive. The population is 89,290 (1910 census). The valuation of taxable property as estimated by the state board of tax commissioners in 1911, is $82,859,580. There are 193 schools, an enrollment of 15,837 pupils, requiring the services of 482 teachers. The county has seventeen banks, two daily and eleven weekly newspapers. Splendid telegraph, telephone and rural mail service is found in every community.

Saginaw, the largest city and judicial seat of the county, has a population of about 50,510 (U. S. census 1910). It is located on the Grand Trunk Railway system, the Michigan Central Railroad, Pere Marquette, the Saginaw & Bay City (electric) and the Saginaw & Flint Railway (electric), ninety-three miles northwest of Port Huron and ninety-eight northwest of Detroit, at the point where the Bad Cass, Shiawassee and Tittabawassee rivers and Swan creek unite to form the Saginaw river. Down these rivers were floated 16,000,000,000 feet of logs and in the early days Saginaw was dependent on activity as a lumber center. It is said more logs have gone down the Saginaw river than have been floated on any other stream in the world and the Saginaw manufacturing district has manufactured more pine timber than any other district in the world. Coal and salt have taken the place of lumber in an industrial way; above ground the fertile fields of the Saginaw valley have shown what resources can be developed in the way of sugar beets and the foundation has been laid for the long list of staple industries. There are numerous coal mines in the neighborhood of the city.

Saginaw has an area of about twelve square miles, 220 miles of streets, 62 miles of paving, 113 miles of public sewers, 30 miles of electric street railway, several parks covering in all about 240 acres, a first class water works plant, 101 miles of water mains, a thoroughly equipped fire department, police department, 26 public schools, one of the finest manual training schools in the country, costing about $250,000, a number of parochial schools, churches of the leading denominations, several hospitals, beautiful first class hotels, theatres, magnificent federal building and free library, etc. The city has a great diversity of industries, some of which are automobiles and auto parts, agricultural implements, maple flooring, wood alcohol, barrels, beer and malt, lumbering tools, boilers, brass castings, brick, carriages, corsets, coal cars, elevators, furniture, gas engines, glass, matches, motors, underwear, portable houses, patent medicine, pianos, railroad machinery, sash, doors, and blinds, saws, seed cleaning machinery, wagons, wheelbarrows, windmills, woolen goods, etc.

Other important towns of the county are Chesaning, Frankenmuth, Merrill, and St. Charles. A very fine quality of bituminous coal has been found at a depth of from 218 to 300 feet where a test has been made in this county. The principal transportation facilities of the county are the Michigan Central, Pere Marquette, Grand Trunk railways, Saginaw & Flint Railway (electric) and the Saginaw & Bay City (electric).

BIRCH RUN.

Claude Reid, Garage.

SAGINAW.

Saginaw Cadillac Company.
Electric Vehicle Service Co., Storage Batteries, Mazda Auto Lamps, Electrical Auto Accessories.
Valley Home Telephone Company.
The Second National Bank of Saginaw, Mich.
B. G. Appleby Co., Real Estate.

SAGINAW COUNTY

MICHIGAN

SAGINAW.

Eastman & Range Garage, Cole and Stearns Cars. Day and Night Service.
Birss Bros., Automobile Accessories and Hardware.
Culver-Deisler Co., Prescription Druggists.

ST. CHARLES.

St. Charles Auto Co., Agency Chevrolet Cars.

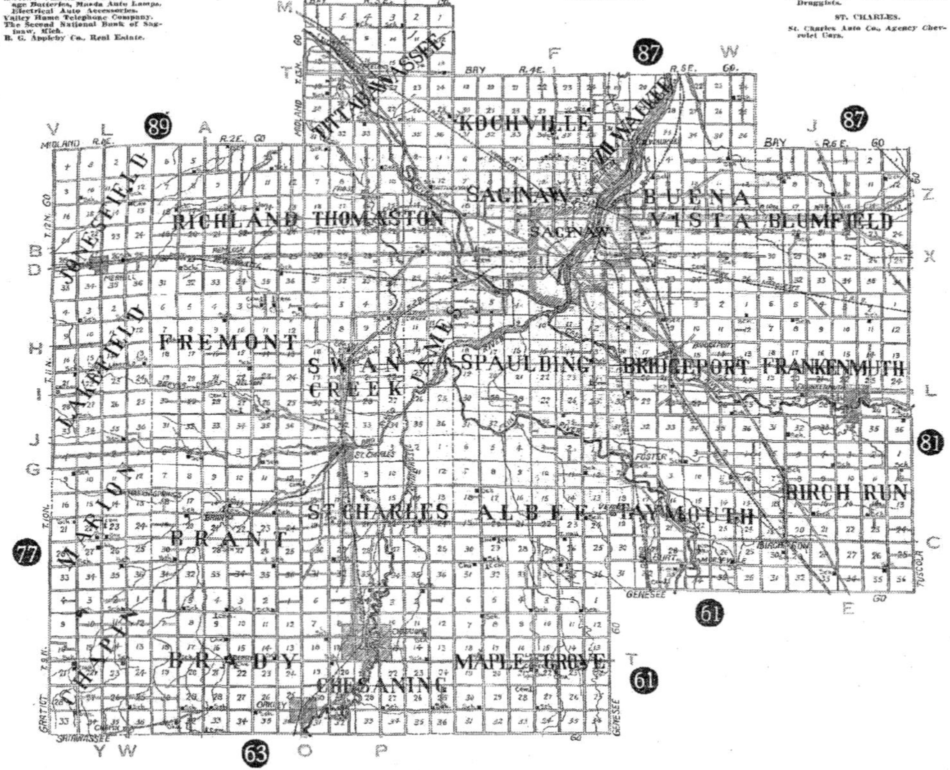

TUSCOLA COUNTY.

This county was laid out in 1840 and was organized in 1850. The name is thought to mean "level lands." It is located in about the east central part of the Lower Peninsula and is bounded on the north by Saginaw bay and Huron county, on the east by Sanilac county, on the south by Lapeer and Genesee counties, and on the west by Saginaw and Bay counties. The total land area is 454,440.14 acres. Of this number about 451,000 acres are devoted to fine farms. The population is 34,913 (1910 census). In 1911 the state board of tax commissioners placed a valuation of $26,092,395 on all taxable lands. There are 157 schools, an enrollment of 7,693 students, requiring the services of 248 teachers. The county has twenty-three banks and ten weekly newspapers, also good telegraph, telephone and rural mail service in every community.

Caro is the county seat and the largest town. The population is 2,500. This town is located on the Caro branch, Bay City division, Michigan Central Railroad and the Detroit, Bay City & Western Railway, thirty-two miles southeast of Bay City, thirty-nine miles north of Lapeer and one hundred miles northwest of Detroit. It is lighted by electricity, has an excellent system of water works, a voluntary fire department, good hotels, churches of the leading religious denominations, good schools, two banks, two newspapers and one of the largest beet sugar factories in the state.

Vassar, another town in the county, is advantageously located on the Cass river and on the Michigan Central and Pere Marquette Railroads, thirteen and one-half miles southwest of Caro and eighty-six from Detroit. It is surrounded and supported by a rich agricultural section, is lighted by electricity, has broad, well shaded and well paved streets, a fine system of water works, a fire department, natural drainage aided by a sanitary sewerage system, a public library, opera house, good hotels, several churches, a splendid public school system, four banks and two newspapers. The manufacturing interests include flour and feed mills, shipping crate factory, machine shop, milk condensing factory, dye factory, cement block works, grain elevators, etc. Other towns in the county are Cass City, Fairgrove, Gagetown, Kingston, Mayville, Millington, and Reese, all in a good agricultural section. The transportation facilities of the county are the Michigan Central Railroad, Pere Marquette Railroad, Pontiac, Oxford & Northern Railroad, Detroit & Huron Railroad, Detroit, Bay City & Western Railroad.

TUSCOLA COUNTY

MICHIGAN

CARO.
H. S. Myers & Co., Garage. Buick Cars.

CASS CITY.
Treadgold's Drug Store.

VASSAR.
William Grant, Garage.

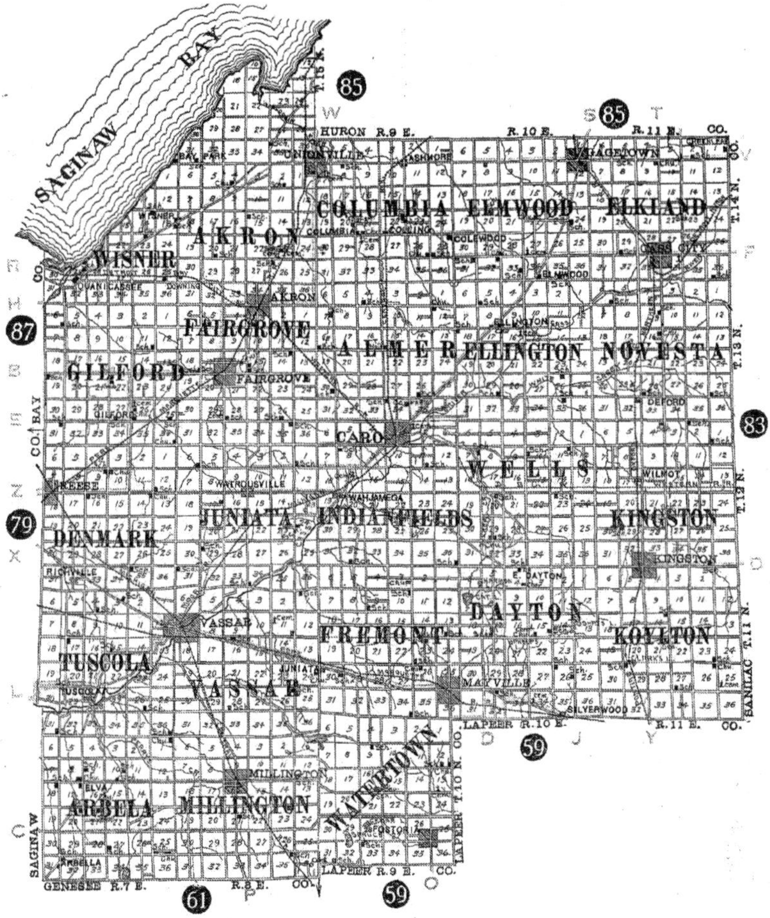

SANILAC COUNTY.

Sanilac county was laid out in 1822 and was organized in 1848. The county takes its name from a famous Indian chief who took part in the early wars between the Iroquois and Wyandottes. It is located in the extreme eastern part of the Southern Peninsula. Its boundaries are Huron county on the north, Lake Huron on the east, Lapeer and St. Clair counties on the south, and Lapeer and Tuscola counties on the west. The total land area is 616,213.60 acres. Of this number about 552,000 acres are devoted to splendid farms. The population is 33,930 (1910 census). The valuation of taxable property as estimated by the state board of tax commissioners in 1911, is $25,979,830. There are 159 schools, furnishing positions for 79 teachers and an enrollment of 8,659 students. The county has 20 banks and 12 weekly newspapers. Good telegraph, telephone and rural mail service is found in nearly every locality.

Sandusky is the judicial seat of the county and has a population of about 1,000. It is located on the Pere Marquette Railway, eight miles west of Carsonville and forty-six northwest of Port Huron; has Episcopal, Methodist, and Presbyterian churches, electric light and power plant, opera house, water works, sewerage, good hotels, two banks and two weekly newspapers.

Croswell, the largest town in the county, has about 1,500 inhabitants. It is located on the Black river and on the Pere Marquette Railway, twenty miles southeast of Sandusky, twenty-six above Port Huron and ninety above Detroit. It has a large area of fine agricultural territory tributary for which it is the receiving and distributing point. It is lighted by electricity, has good sewerage system, water works, churches of many denominations, excellent public schools, opera house, sugar factory, brick and tile works, flour mill, creamery, bridge and culvert works, two banks, two newspapers, etc.

Other towns of the county include Marlette, Applegate, Brown City, Deckerville, Forestville, and Lexington, all in a good agricultural section. The principal transportation facilities of the county are the Pere Marquette, Detroit, Bay City & Western, and the Detroit & Huron Railroads.

SANILAC COUNTY
MICHIGAN

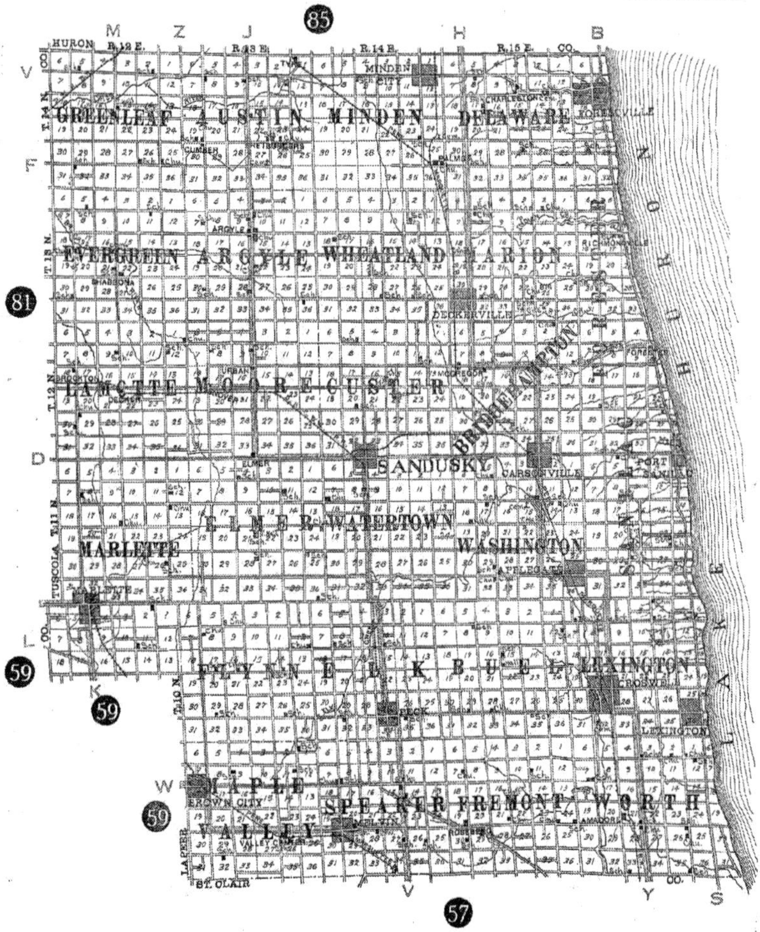

HURON COUNTY.

Huron county was laid out in 1840 and was organized in 1859. The county was named for the lake bordering on the north, east and west, and the lake, in turn, was so called from a tribe of Indians called the Hurons, who lived there. The county is located in the eastern part of the Lower Peninsula in what is known as the "Thumb" district. It is bounded on the north by Lake Huron, on the east by Lake Huron, on the south by Tuscola and Sanilac counties, and on the west by that part of Lake Huron known as Saginaw bay and by Tuscola county. The total land area is 536,982.68 acres. Of this number, about 472,000 acres are devoted to farms, some of which are of the best in the eastern part of the state. The total population of the county is 34,758 (1910 census). In 1911, the state board of tax commissioners placed a valuation of $24,866,457 on all taxable land. There are 126 schools, which were attended by 8,475 pupils last year, requiring 222 teachers. The county has 17 banks and 11 weekly newspapers. Also good telegraph, telephone and rural mail service throughout.

Bad Axe is the judicial seat of the county and has a population of about 2,000. It is located on the Pere Marquette and Grand Trunk Railroads, 63 miles northwest of Port Huron. It has Baptist, Episcopal, German Evangelical, Mennonite, Methodist, Presbyterian and Catholic churches, a $40,000 high school, water works, opera house, good hotels, a $40,000 court house, two banks and two newspapers. This is the trading center for a productive agriculture section and large quantities of grain, hay, seed, produce and live stock are shipped.

Harbor Beach has a population of about 2,000, and is located on the shore of Lake Huron and the Pere Marquette Railroad, 18 miles east of Bad Axe and 60 miles above Port Huron. It is a great grain market for the whole of the Huron Peninsula. There are Baptist, Free Methodist, Lutheran, Methodist Episcopal, Presbyterian and Catholic churches, good schools, a library, an opera house, three public halls, two banks, water works, fire department, electric lighting plant, and two live newspapers. Manufactories consist of flour, corn starch, wheat starch, macaroni, food pastes, cement tile, building blocks, and butter. As a summer resort, the surroundings are splendid.

Other towns of the county are Caseville, Elkton, Kinde, Owendale, Pigeon, Port Austin, and Port Hope, whose shipments consist largely of wheat, cattle, hay, sugar beets and flax. The principal transportation facilities of the county are the Grand Trunk, Pere Marquette, Pontiac, Oxford & Northern, Michigan Central and the Detroit & Huron Railroads, also the Detroit & Cleveland Navigation Company.

HURON COUNTY

MICHIGAN

BAD AXE.

Bad Axe Auto Company, Automobiles. Repairing and General Machine Work, Plumbing, Heating, Electrical Work.

Dunlap Garage Company, Buick Distributors for Huron County.

The Misses Skinner, Books, Stationery, Music, Eastman Kodaks and Supplies.

PIGEON.

Diebel Auto Company, Automobiles, Storage, Repairs and Supplies.

Harder Garage and Salesroom, Automobiles, Accessories and Repairs.

PORT AUSTIN.

Point of Pines Hotel. Steam Heat, Sample Room, Bus to All Trains.

Dan Allan, Garage and Sales Room, Automobile Accessories and Repairs, Stationery and Marine Engines, Repairing.

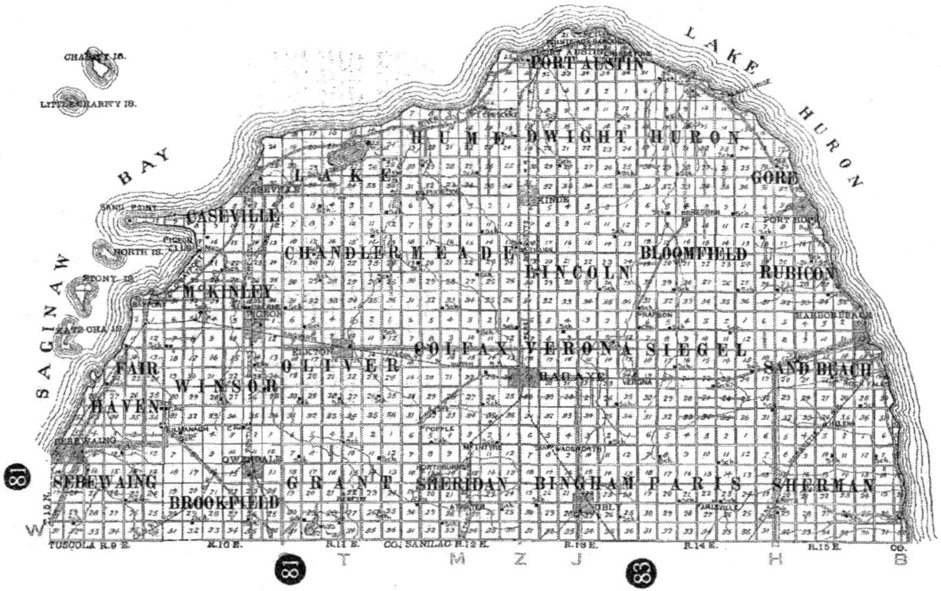

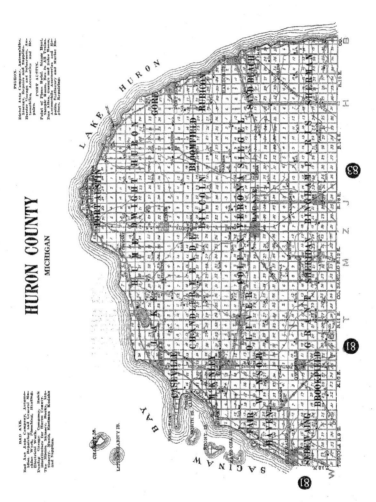

BAY COUNTY.

Bay county was laid out in 1831 and was at that time called Arenac. In 1857 it was organized and took the name of Bay, because of its location on the bay of Saginaw. The total land area of the county is 284,626.09 acres, of which about 215,000 acres are in good farms. Bay county is located in the eastern part of the Lower Peninsula and is bounded entirely on the east by Saginaw bay. It has a population of 68,238 (1910 census). In 1911, the state board of tax commissioners placed the value of taxable land throughout the county at $89,331,544. There are a total of 93 schools, with an enrollment of 12,085 children, requiring 322 teachers. The county has 17 banks, 8 newspapers, telegraph, telephone and rural route service.

Bay City is the county seat and has a population of 45,166 (U. S. census 1910). It is a natural railroad, deep water and manufacturing center, and occupies an ideal location at a point where the Saginaw river flows into Saginaw bay, and is surrounded by a rich and productive farming section. It is a little more than 100 miles north of Detroit, the chief city of the state. It has nearly 200 miles of streets; 85 miles of paving, over 100 miles of sewers, 25 miles of electric street railway, 50 miles of gas mains, 10 public parks covering 35 acres and valued at $800,000, a water works plant valued at $1,000,000, 100 miles of water mains, a $147,000 municipal electric lighting plant, a fire department comprising ten station houses, a police department, 18 public school buildings, 19 parochial schools, public library, theaters, 3 hospitals, first-class hotels, 8 banks, a $300,000 city hall, State armory, an $80,000 Y. M. C. A. building, a $200,000 postoffice and beautiful churches of nearly every denomination. There are two daily and three weekly newspapers published in Bay City.

In 1860, the inexhaustible salt basin that underlies this section was tapped, the success of which resulted in the manufacture of salt, which has since developed into immense proportions. The first beet sugar plant to be erected in the state was built in Bay City in 1898. Since then other large and modern beet sugar plants have been put into operation. The beet sugar industry has proved to be a large factor in the success of this locality as a manufacturing community. Close to the limits of the city are coal mines, with a large annual output, which are now supplying some of the railroads and many manufacturing plants. The fishing on Saginaw bay gives employment to a large number of people. Pickerel, bass, white-fish, perch, catfish, sturgeon and other fish are caught. The city's industries include saw-mills, sash and door factories, largest plant in the United States for making wooden pipe, large woodenware factory, veneer works, hardwood flooring mill, large Portland cement plant, railroad locomotive wrecking crane works, denatured alcohol plant, chemical company, etc.

Other important cities of the county are Pinconning and Essexville. Pinconning, with a population of about 800, is located on the Michigan Central and Detroit & Mackinac Railroads, and on the Pinconning river, one and one-half miles from Saginaw bay and 19 miles above Bay City. It is lighted by electricity, has Catholic, German Lutheran, Methodist and Presbyterian churches, public school, library, two banks, a weekly newspaper, water works, etc.

Essexville is a town of about 1,600 and is located on the east bank of the Saginaw river near its mouth, and about three miles below Bay City, of which it is, in fact, a suburb. Has Baptist, Congregational and Catholic churches, sugar factory, chemical works, shingle-mill, etc. A street railway affords communication with Bay City.

The transportation facilities of the county include the Michigan Central, Pere Marquette, Grand Trunk, Detroit & Mackinac Railroads, the Erie & Michigan Railway and Navigation Company, and the Saginaw & Bay City Electric.

BAY COUNTY

MICHIGAN

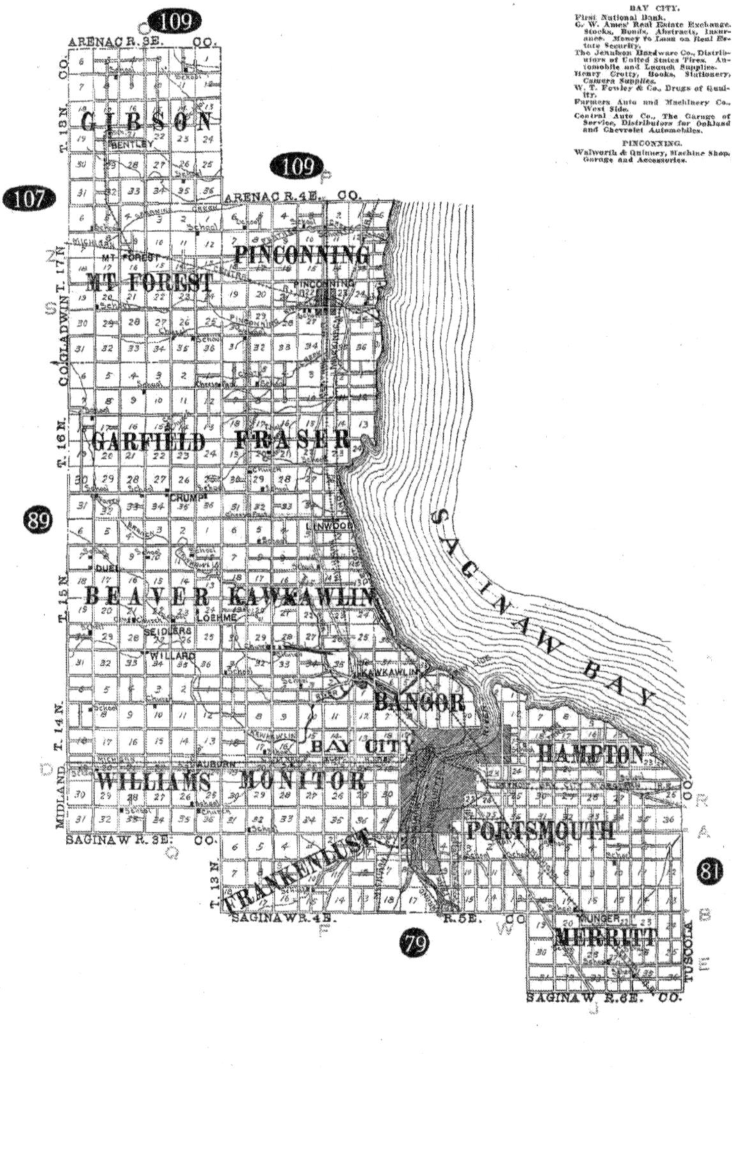

BAY CITY.

First National Bank.

G. W. Ames' Real Estate Exchange. Stocks, Bonds, Abstracts, Insurance. Money to Loan on Real Estate Security.

The Jennison Hardware Co., Distributors of United States Tires. Automobile and Launch Supplies.

Henry Gretty, Books, Stationery, Camera Supplies.

W. T. Fowler & Co., Drugs of Quality.

Farmers Auto and Machinery Co., West Side.

Central Auto Co., The Garage of Service, Distributors for Oakland and Chevrolet Automobiles.

PINCONNING.

Walworth & Quinney, Machine Shop, Garage and Accessories.

MIDLAND COUNTY.

Midland county was laid out in 1831 and was organized in 1850. The name is descriptive of the geographical location of this county as it is very nearly in the center of the Lower Peninsula. It is bounded on the north by Gladwin county, on the east by Bay and Saginaw counties, on the south by Gratiot and Saginaw counties, and on the west by Isabella county. The total land area is 330,470.23 acres, of which about 177,000 acres are in farms which are very productive. The population is 14,005 (1910 census). The valuation of all taxable lands, as estimated by the state board of tax commissioners in 1911, is $9,239,473. There are 87 schools, supplying positions for 125 teachers, and 3,812 children in attendance. The county has four banks and three weekly newspapers. Telegraph, telephone and rural mail service is found in nearly every locality.

Midland, the county seat and largest town of the county, has about 3,000 inhabitants. It is located at the confluence of the Tittabawassee and Chippewa rivers, and on the Pere Marquette and Michigan Central Railroads, about 20 miles northwest of Saginaw and 18 west of Bay City. It is well laid out, with broad and well-shaded streets, has churches of the Episcopal, Presbyterian, Methodist, Baptist, German Lutheran and Catholic denominations, six good schools, a free library, an opera house, has good sewerage and water works, good hotels, two banks and two weekly newspapers. The manufacturing industries consist of flour, lumber, shingle, lath, cider and heading-mills, pickle depots, brick and tile works, cigar factories, electric lighting plant, chemical works, a bleaching powder factory, foundry, machine shops, etc. The surrounding country produces excellent crops of wheat, oats, hay, beans, sugar beets, etc.

Coleman has a population of about 1,100. It is located on the Pere Marquette Railway, 20 miles northwest of Midland and 40 from Saginaw. Has Episcopal, Presbyterian, Methodist, Latter Day Saint and Catholic churches, good educational advantages, an electric lighting plant, a bank and a weekly newspaper. The county's transportation facilities include the Michigan Central and Pere Marquette Railroads.

MIDLAND COUNTY

MICHIGAN

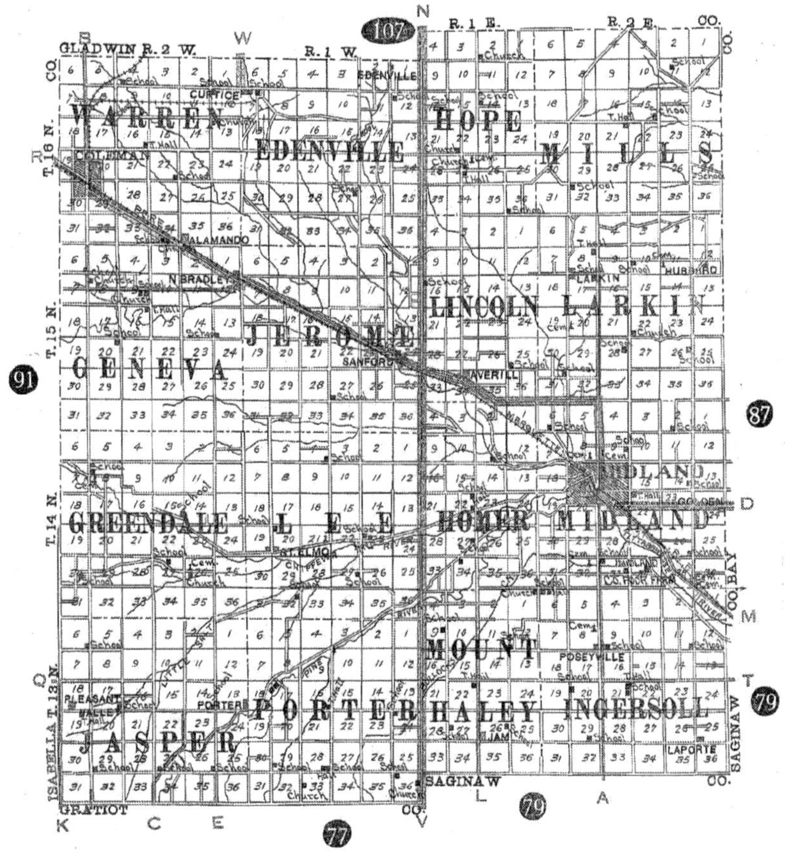

ISABELLA COUNTY.

Isabella county was laid out in 1831 and was organized in 1859, being named in honor of Queen Isabella of Spain. It is located in the central part of the Lower Peninsula and is bounded on the north by Clare county, on the east by Midland county, on the south by Montcalm and Gratiot counties and on the west by Mecosta county. The total land area is 368,746 acres, of which about 300,000 acres are devoted to farms which are very productive. The federal census of 1910 gives the county a population of 23,029. The valuation of taxable property, as estimated by the state board of tax commissioners in 1911, is $16,028,215. The school system is equal to that of any of the larger counties, there being 118 schools, requiring the services of 152 teachers, and an attendance of 4,806 students. The county has eight banks and four weekly newspapers. Good telephone, telegraph and rural mail service is to be had in every community.

Mount Pleasant, the capital city of the county, contains about 4,500 people. It is located on the Chippewa river, and on the Ann Arbor and Pere Marquette Railroads, 53 miles northwest of Saginaw and 149 from Detroit. The city has an excellent system of public improvements, is lighted by gas and electricity, a good sewerage and drainage system, a good water works, fire department, paved streets, a forty-acre park, opera house, two banks, first-class hotels, a fine court house, public library, two weekly newspapers, churches of the Adventist, Baptist, Disciples, Episcopal, German Lutheran, Methodist, Presbyterian, Unitarian and Catholic denominations, splendid school system, etc. The city's industrial interests include, among others, a milk condensing plant, veneer works, chicory factory, calcium works, cigar factories, flour-mill, planing-mill, grain elevators, light and fuel plant, hub and lath-mill, foundry, etc. The surrounding country is rich and productive and produces a wide diversity of crops.

Shepherd has a population of about 1,000. It is located on the Ann Arbor Railroad and on Salt river, 7 miles southeast of Mount Pleasant. It has Baptist, Christian, Methodist, United Brethren and Catholic churches, a graded public school, an opera house, two banks and a weekly newspaper. The principal transportation facilities of the county are the Ann Arbor and Pere Marquette Railroads.

ISABELLA COUNTY

MICHIGAN

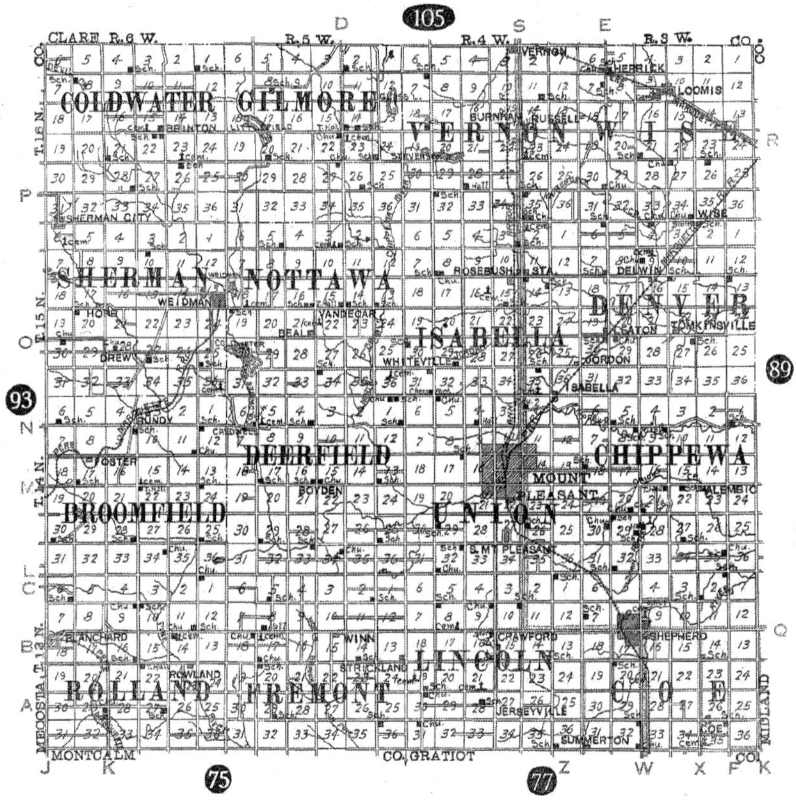

MECOSTA COUNTY.

Mecosta county was laid out in 1840 and was organized in 1859. The name is that of a once famous Pottawatomie chief and is thought to mean "bear cub." This county is located in about the west central part of the Lower Peninsula and is bounded on the north by Osceola county, on the east by Isabella county, on the south by Montcalm county, and on the west by Newaygo county. The total land area comprises 362,778.58 acres. Of this number, about 286,000 acres are devoted to good farms. The population is 19,466 (1910 census). In 1911, the state board of tax commissioners placed a valuation of $10,936,441 on all taxable lands. There are 113 schools, which were attended by 4,383 pupils last year, requiring the services of 162 teachers. The county has six banks, two daily and five weekly newspapers. Telephone, telegraph and rural mail service is found throughout the county.

Big Rapids, the judicial seat and largest city of the county, has a population of about 5,000. It is located on the Grand Rapids & Indiana and the Pere Marquette Railroads, 56 miles north of Grand Rapids. The city is named after the big rapids of the Muskegon river, which flows through it and furnishes unexcelled water power. It is lighted by electricity, has a good water works system, fire and police departments, excellent sewerage system, a public library, an opera house, a court house costing about $30,000, good hotels, paved streets, two banks and three newspapers. The religious and educational advantages include Congregational, Episcopal, Methodist, Baptist, Presbyterian, Catholic, Norwegian Lutheran, German Lutheran and Swedish Lutheran churches, a central high and three ward schools, and the Ferris institute, which is known throughout the country. Among the city's prominent industries are planing and saw-mills, maple floor factories gas light and fuel plant, electric light and power plant, machine shop and manufactories of furniture, cigars, brooms, flour, spring seats, hot blast grates, saw-filing machinery, carriages, veneer, brick, etc.

Other thriving communities of the county are Barryton, Mecosta, Morley and Stanwood. The principal transportation facilities of the county are the Grand Rapids & Indiana and the Pere Marquette Railroads.

MECOSTA COUNTY

MICHIGAN

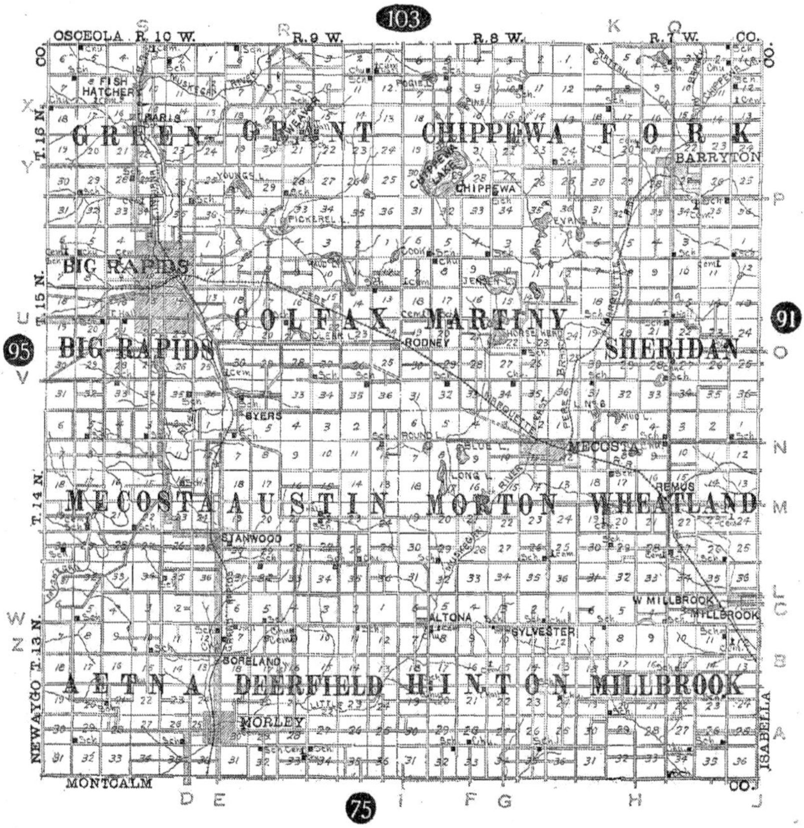

NEWAYGO COUNTY.

Newaygo county was laid out in 1840 and organized in 1851, the name being that of a famous Chippewa chief. It is located in the west central part of the Lower Peninsula, and is bounded on the north by Lake county, on the east by Mecosta and Montcalm counties, on the south by Muskegon and Kent counties, and on the west by Oceana and Muskegon counties. The total land area is 542,741.08 acres. Of this number, about 326,000 acres are devoted to farms which are very productive. The population is 19,220 (1910 census). The valuation of taxable land, as estimated by the state board of tax commissioners in 1911, is $13,884,005. There are 127 schools, furnishing positions for 185 teachers, and an enrollment of 4,706 students. The county has seven banks, five weekly newspapers, also telephone, telegraph and rural mail service.

White Cloud, which is the county seat, has a population of about 700. It is located on the White river, and on the Pere Marquette Railroad, 55 miles northeast of Muskegon and 45 north of Grand Rapids. It owns and operates its own electric light and water works plant, has a fire department, public hall, excellent schools, churches of the Congregational, Methodist, Swedish Evangelical and Catholic denominations, two banks and two weekly newspapers.

Fremont, the largest town of the county, has about 2,000 inhabitants. It is located on the Pere Marquette Railroad, 12 miles northeast of Newaygo, 24 northeast of Muskegon, and 58 north of Grand Rapids. Has Congregational, Methodist, United Brethren, Holland, Disciples, and Catholic churches, public hall, water works, good schools, flour mills, saw mill, tannery, canning factory, pickle factory, electric lighting plant, two banks, a weekly newspaper, etc.

Other towns of the county include Grant (population 500) and Newaygo (population 1,300). Principal transportation facility of the county is the Pere Marquette Railroad.

NEWAYGO COUNTY

MICHIGAN

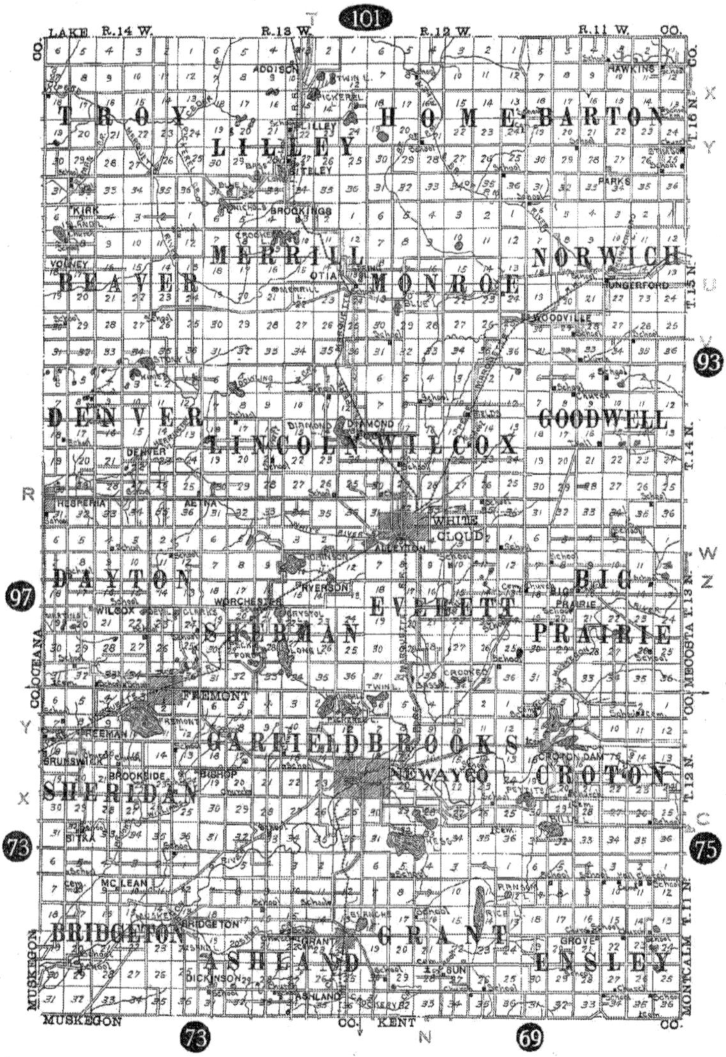

OCEANA COUNTY.

Oceana county was laid out in 1831, and was organized in 1855. It is so named because of its bordering upon the large fresh water sea or ocean. It is located in the extreme west central part of the Lower Peninsula. The boundaries are Mason county on the north, Newaygo county on the east, Muskegon county on the south, and Lake Michigan on the west. The total land area is 345,410.25 acres. Of this number, about 244,000 acres are devoted to fine farms. The population is 18,379 (1910 census). In 1911, the state board of tax commissioners placed a valuation of $11,-858,671 on all taxable land. There are 95 schools, furnishing positions for 156 teachers, and a total of 4,314 pupils in attendance. The county has eight banks, seven weekly newspapers, also splendid telegraph, telephone and rural mail service.

Hart, the judicial seat and largest town in the county, has a population of about 1,800. It is located on the Pere Marquette Railroad, and on the south branch of the Pentwater river, eight miles south of Pentwater, and forty-two north of Muskegon. It is lighted by electricity, has water works, fire department, a high school building erected at a cost of about $50,000, churches of several denominations, two banks and three weekly newspapers. The industries include saw, flour, planing and shingle-mills, canning factories, etc. The shipments comprise peaches, plums, small fruits, potatoes, lumber, flour, wheat, canned goods and wool.

Pentwater has a population of about 1,400. This town is located on the shore of Lake Michigan at the outlet of Pentwater lake, and on the Pere Marquette Railroad, eight miles northwest of Hart and forty-four north of Muskegon. It is lighted by electricity, has Baptist, Episcopal, Methodist, Church of Christ and Catholic churches, excellent educational advantages, a public library, an opera house, a fire department, water works, a fruit canning factory, two banks and a weekly newspaper. The shipments consist of lumber, lath, shingles, tanbark, fish and large quantities of apples, peaches, potatoes and produce.

Other towns of the county are Hesperia, Shelby and Walkerville. The principal transportation facilities of the county are the Pere Marquette Railroad, The Northern Michigan Transportation Company and the Hill Boat Line.

OCEANA COUNTY

MICHIGAN

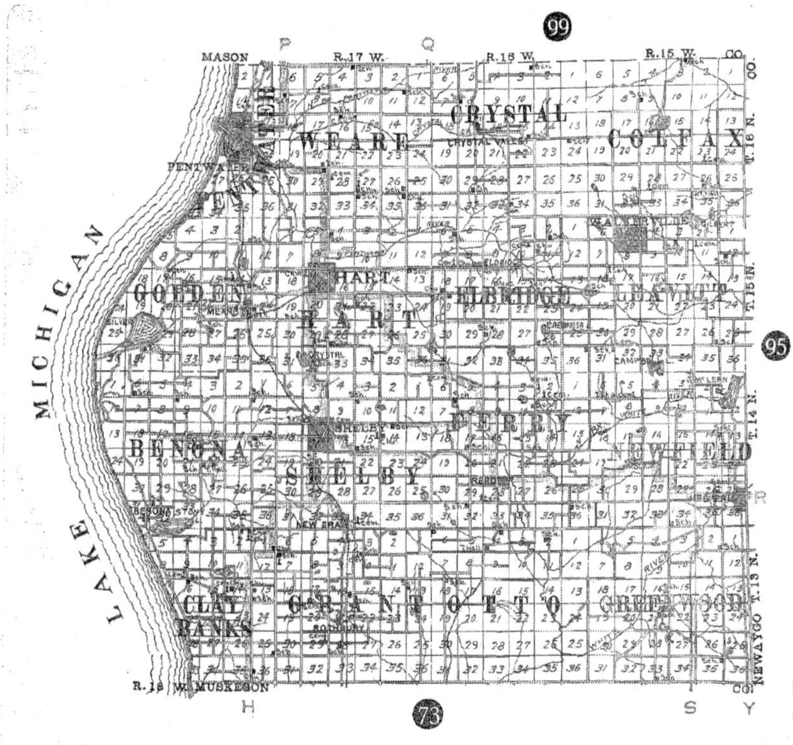

MASON COUNTY.

This county was originally laid out in 1840 and was named Notipekago, the Indian name of Pere Marquette river. Later, in 1843, the name was changed and the present name given in honor of Stevens T. Mason, the first governor of the state. The county was organized in 1855. It is located in the extreme west central part of the Lower Peninsula, is bounded on the north by Manistee county, on the east by Lake county, on the south by Oceana county, and on the west by Lake Michigan. The total land area is 315,526.87 acres, of which about 172,000 acres are in fine farms. The population is 21,832 (1910 census). The valuation of taxable land, as estimated by the state board of tax commissioners in 1911, is $13,791,430. The county has a school system equal to those of the larger counties, there being 78 schools, attended by 4,834 students, requiring the services of 153 teachers. There are eight banks, one daily and five weekly newspapers. Good telegraph, telephone and rural mail service is found in nearly all localities.

Ludington is the judicial seat, also the largest city in the county, having about 9,132 inhabitants. It is situated about half way up the east shore of Lake Michigan at the mouth of the Pere Marquette river, 98 miles from Milwaukee and 156 from Chicago. It is the western terminus of the Pere Marquette Railroad, and is in the heart of the Michigan fruit belt. The city has paved streets, good sewerage system, excellent schools, a fine public library, an efficient fire department, electric light and power plant, an opera house, first-class hotels, domestic gas for fuel and light, a municipally-owned water works system, churches of the Congregational, Episcopal, Danish Episcopal, German Lutheran, Methodist, Baptist, Norwegian Baptist, Presbyterian, Swedish Lutheran and Catholic denominations, two banks, three newspapers, etc. Among the more prominent industrial establishments are saw- and shingle-mills, several big salt factories, including one of the largest salt producing plants in the world, one of the largest manufactories of game boards in the world, watch case factory, foundry, machine shops, boiler works, planing- and feed-mill, a cannery, boat and engine works, cigar factories, manufactories of wood type and printers' specialties, vehicle specialties, woodenware, enameled wood goods, baskets, sash, doors and blinds, snuff, wooden bowls, a grain elevator, etc. Ludington is famous for its summer resort facilities.

Other towns of the county are Scottville (population, 1,400) and Custer (population, 325). Scottville is located on the Pere Marquette Railroad and on the Pere Marquette river, 9 miles east of Ludington and 40 west of Reed City. It is supported by a rich farming district, and has churches of several denominations, a graded public school, water works, an opera house, flour-mill, grain elevator, butter factory, two banks and a weekly newspaper. Quantities of grain, butter, fruit, flour, potatoes and produce are shipped.

The transportation facilities of the county include the Manistee & Grand Rapids, Ludington & Northern and the Pere Marquette Railroads, the Pere Marquette Steamship Line, the Northern Michigan Transportation Company.

MASON COUNTY

MICHIGAN

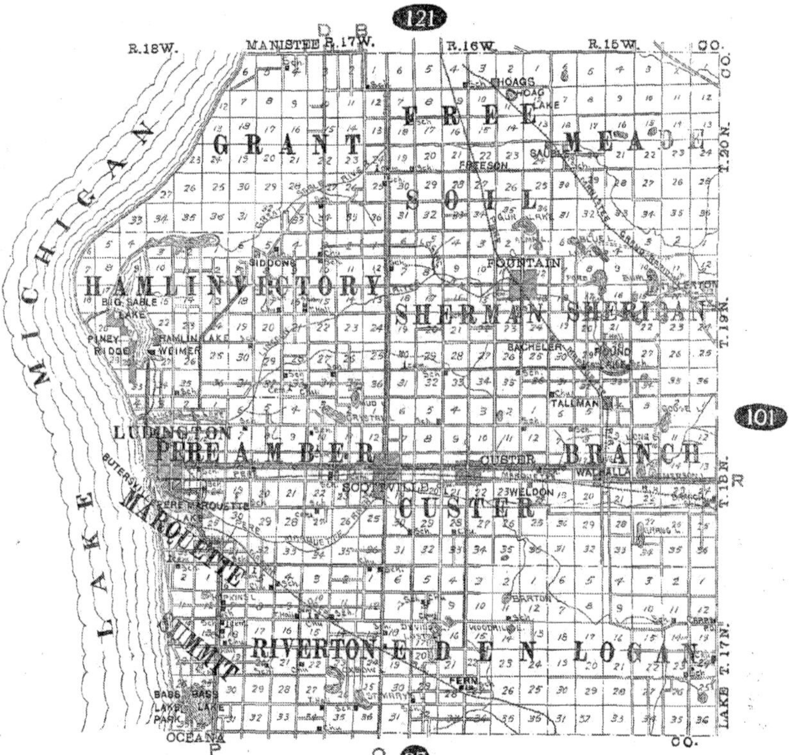

LAKE COUNTY.

Lake county was laid out in 1840 and was first named Aishcum, the name of a Pottawatomie chief. In 1843 the name was changed. The county was finally organized in 1871. The name Lake is peculiarly inappropriate to this county, as it is an inland county and contains but few lakes of any size. It is located in about the west central part of the Lower Peninsula. Its boundaries are: Manistee and Wexford counties on the north, Osceola county on the east, Newaygo county on the south, and Mason county on the west. The total land area of the county is 365,393.85 acres. Of this number, about 88,000 acres are now in farms. The population is 4,934. In 1911, the state board of tax commissioners placed a valuation of $4,267,298 on all taxable lands. There are 48 schools, requiring the services of 67 teachers, and an enrollment of 1,237 students last year. The county has two banks, two weekly newspapers and good telegraph, telephone and rural mail service.

Baldwin is the county seat, and has a population of about 550. It is located on the Pere Marquette river and on the Pere Marquette Railroad, 74 miles north of Grand Rapids. It has Congregational and Episcopal churches, a graded public school, good hotels, a $10,000 court house and a weekly newspaper. In the immediate vicinity are to be found some of the finest trout streams in northern Michigan. Live stock, potatoes and huckleberries are shipped.

Luther is the largest town in the county. Population, 900. It is located on the Little Manistee river and on the Manistee & Grand Rapids Railroad, 18 miles northeast of Baldwin. It has churches of Baptist, Christian, Episcopal, Methodist and Catholic denominations, a graded public school, a bank and a weekly newspaper. Transportation facilities of the county are the Manistee & Grand Rapids and the Pere Marquette Railroads.

LAKE COUNTY

MICHIGAN

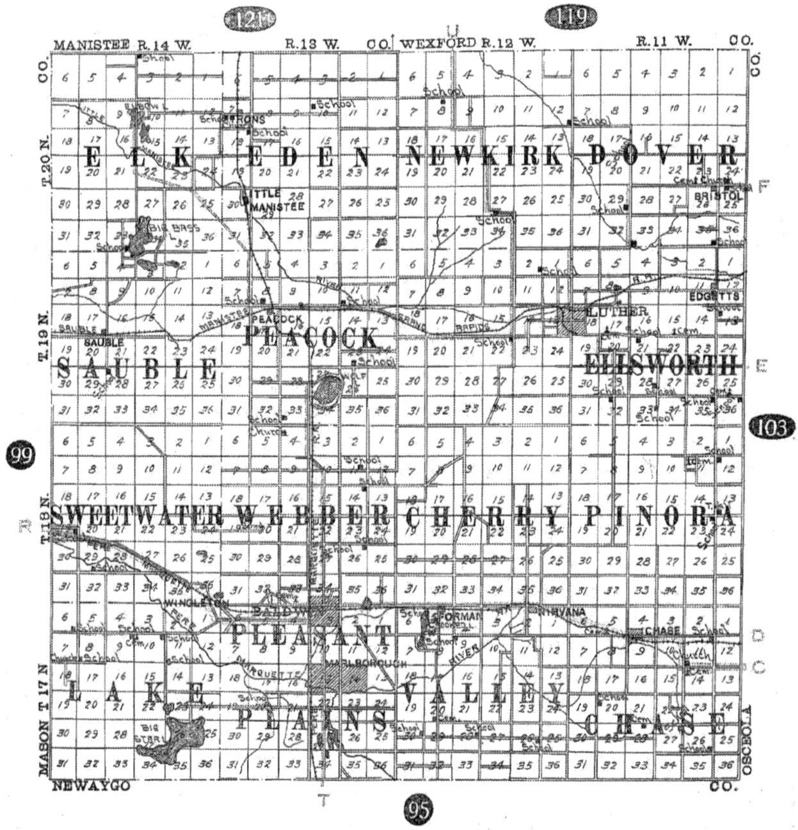

OSCEOLA COUNTY.

Osceola county was laid out in 1840 and was originally called "Unwattin," the name o fa famous Ottawa chief. Later, in 1843, the name was changed to Osceola, which is said to mean "black drink." The county was finally organized in 1869. This county is located in about the northwestern part of the Lower Peninsula. It is bounded on the north by Wexford and Missaukee counties, on the east by Clare county, on the south by Mecosta county, and on the west by Lake county. The total land area is 367,237.05 acres, and about 240,000 acres are already in good productive farms. The population is 17,889 (1910 census). The valuation of all taxable property, as estimated by the state board of tax commissioners in 1911, is $10,307,176. The school system in this county is good. There are 98 schools, furnishing positions for 150 teachers, and a total enrollment of 4,127 students. The county has nine banks and seven weekly newspapers. Also telegraph, telephone and rural mail service.

Hersey is the judicial seat of the county. The village has about 350 inhabitants, and is located at the confluence of the Hersey and Muskegon rivers, on the Pere Marquette, and Grand Rapids & Indiana Railroads. It has churches of the Congregational, German Evangelical and Methodist Episcopal denominations, an electric light and power plant, a bank and a weekly newspaper.

Reed City, the largest town of the county, has a population of about 2,000. This town is located on the Hersey river at the intersection of the Pere Marquette and Grand Rapids & Indiana Railroad, four miles west of Hersey, forty-eight east of Ludington, and sixty-eight north of Grand Rapids. It is also in a good agricultural section. It is lighted by electricity, has a good water works system, good hotels, an opera house, grain elevator, excellent educational advantages, a library, churches of the Congregational, Baptist, Lutheran, German Lutheran, Mennonite, Swedish, German Methodist, Methodist and Catholic denominations, two banks and two weekly newspapers. There are manufactories of shingles, maple flooring, saw, planing, heading, flour and woolen mills, foundry, etc.

Other towns of the county include Evart (population about 1,400), Le Roy, Marion and Tustin. Evart is situated on the Pere Marquette railroad, between Saginaw and Ludington. It has good hotels, an opera house, good school system, Baptist, Catholic, Methodist and Presbyterian churches, two libraries, electric light and water works plant, fire department, two banks and a weekly newspaper. The shipments include lumberman's tools, lumber, farm produce and grain.

The transportation facilities of the county include the Grand Rapids & Indiana, Pere Marquette, Manistee & Grand Rapids and the Ann Arbor Railroads.

OSCEOLA COUNTY

MICHIGAN

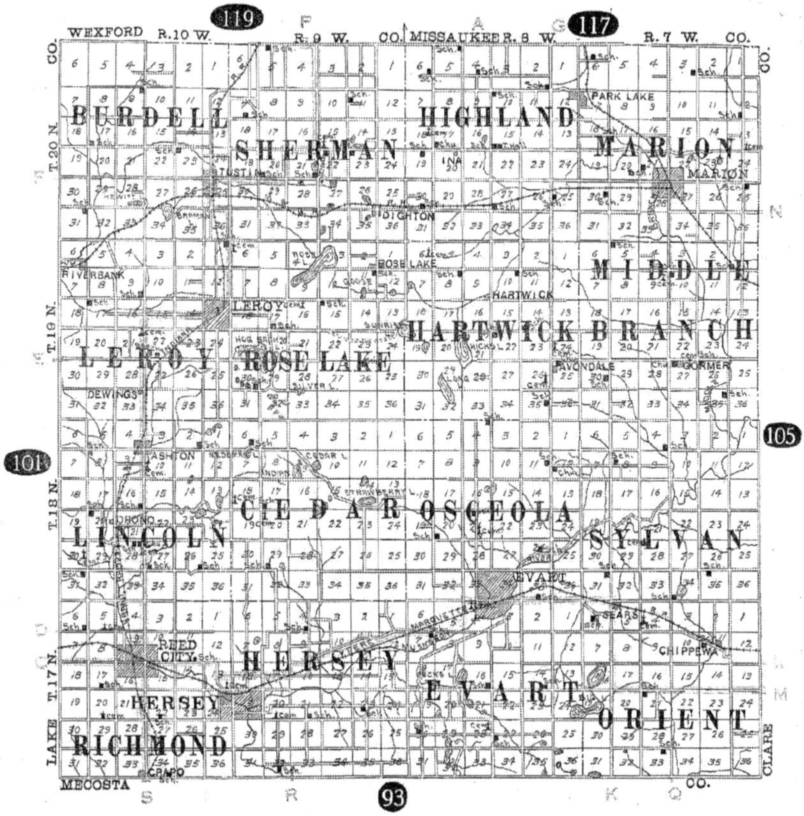

CLARE COUNTY.

Clare county was laid out in 1840 and was at that time called Kaykakee, which in the Chippewa language means "pigeon hawk." Later, in 1843, the name was changed to Clare, taken from the name of a county in Ireland. The county was organized in 1871. This county is located in the north central part of the Lower Peninsula. It is bounded on the north by Missaukee and Roscommon counties, east by Gladwin county, south by Isabella county, and west by Osceola county. The total land area is 364,756.51 acres, about 185,000 acres of which are already devoted to farms. The valuation of all taxable property, as estimated by the state board of tax commissioners in 1911, is $4,071,360. In 1910 the county had a population of 9,240. The total number of schools in the county is 71, furnishing positions for 102 teachers and about 2,376 scholars in attendance. The county has 6 banks and 4 weekly newspapers, also good telephone, telegraph and rural mail service. The county is rich in agriculture and stock raising.

Harrison is the county seat and has a population of about 800. It is located on the shore of Budd lake, one of the most beautiful inland bodies of water in northern Michigan. It is a station on the Pere Marquette Railway, 72 miles from Saginaw. It has Catholic, Congregational, Methodist and United Brethren churches, good schools, electric light, water works, opera house, two banks and a weekly newspaper.

Other towns of the county include Clare, which is the largest town in the county and has a population of about 1,400 and Farwell, with a population of about 585. Clare is located on the Pere Marquette and Ann Arbor railways, 15 miles south of Harrison, 50 miles from Saginaw and 94 miles from Lansing and is surrounded by excellent farms. It is lighted by electricity, has water works, churches of the Baptist, Catholic, Congregational, Free Methodist, German Lutheran and Methodist denominations, a $25,000 school building, public hall, opera house, good hotels, two banks and two weekly newspapers. Manufacturing industries include saw, shingle and planing mills, flour-mill, stave and heading factories, electric lighting plant, foundry, machine shops, creamery, pickle salting station, etc. The chief shipments include lumber, shingles, hoops, handles, staves, heading, bark, telegraph poles, wheat, hay, produce and cattle. The principal transportation facilities of the county are the Pere Marquette and Ann Arbor railroads.

CLARE.
Clare County Savings Bank.
J. T. Brown & Sons, Garage.
Mrs. A. E. Mussell, Druggist.

CLARE COUNTY

MICHIGAN

FARWELL.
William Ruston, Pharmacist.

ROSEBUSH.
F. C. Matteson, General Merchandise.

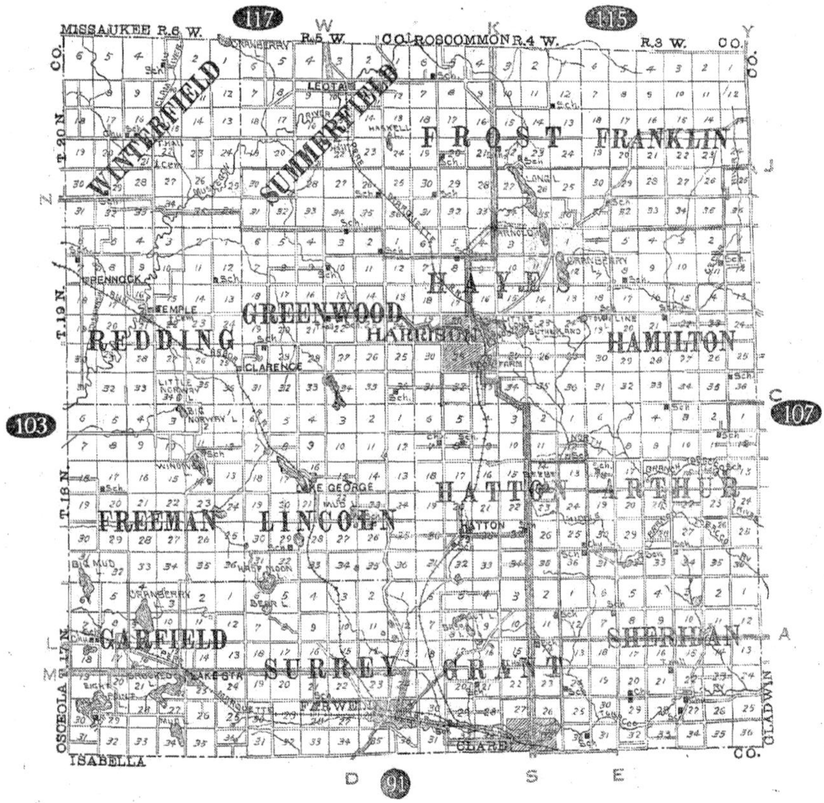

GLADWIN COUNTY.

Gladwin county was laid out in 1831 and was organized in 1855. It was named in honor of Major Henry Gladwin, who was in command of Fort Detroit during the Indian war. It is located in the northeast central part of the Lower Peninsula. Is bounded on the north by Roscommon and Ogemaw counties, on the east by Arenac and Bay counties, on the south by Midland county and on the west by Clare county. The total land area is 330,761.78 acres. Of this number, about 130,000 acres are in farms. The population is about 8,418 (federal census 1910). In 1911, the state board of tax commissioners placed a valuation of $4,393,873 on all taxable land in the county. There are 61 schools, an enrollment of 2,477 children, furnishing positions for 86 teachers. The county has three banks, two weekly newspapers, also telephone, telegraph and rural mail service.

Gladwin is the county seat, also the largest city. Has a population of about 1,200. It is located on the Michigan Central Railroad and on the Cedar river, 47 miles northwest of Bay City. It is lighted by electricity, has water works, excellent sewerage, churches of the Episcopal, Free Methodist, Catholic, Methodist and Presbyterian denominations, a $20,000 public school, an opera house, two banks, saw, planing and shingle-mills, flour-mills, basket factory, electric lighting plant and a weekly newspaper.

Beaverton, a thriving community in Gladwin county, has a population of about 500. It is located on the Pere Marquette Railroad at the confluence of the middle, north and south branches of the Tobacco and Cedar rivers, 9 miles south of Gladwin and 52 northwest of Saginaw. It is lighted by electricity, has a good water works system, churches of several denominations, a graded public school, opera house, a bank and a weekly newspaper. Transportation facilities of the county are the Michigan Central and Pere Marquette Railroads.

GLADWIN COUNTY

MICHIGAN

BEAVERTON.

W. C. Wickham, Ford Service Station.

GLADWIN.

Ford Service Station, M. Robert Morris.

Smith & Behnke, Garage and Repairing.

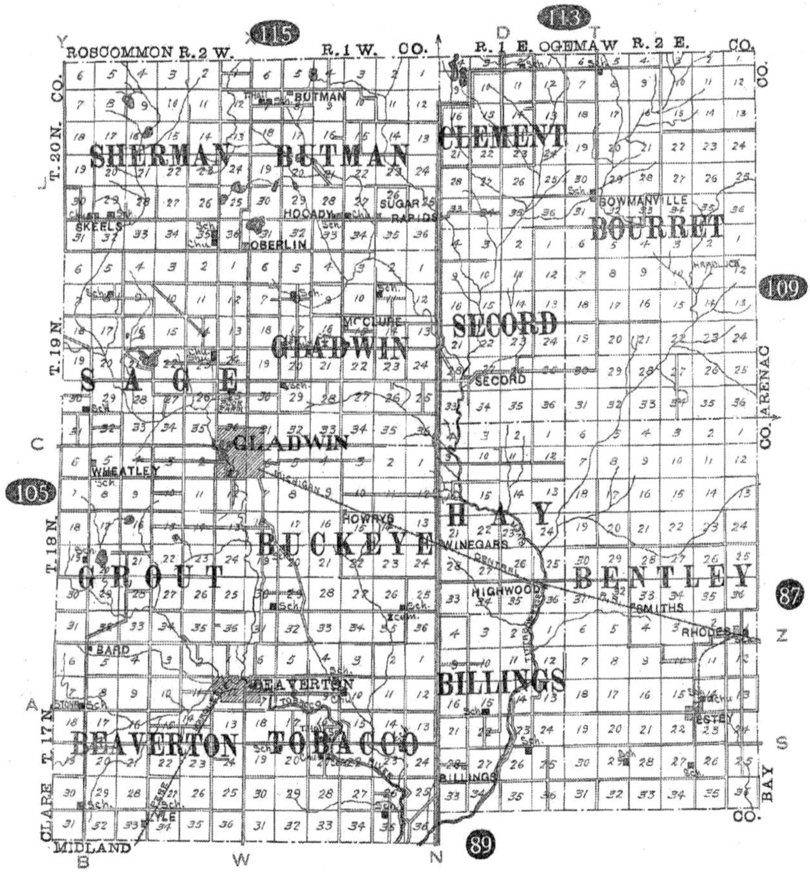

ARENAC COUNTY.

Arenac county was laid out in 1831, and in 1857 it was incorporated into the newly formed Bay county. In 1883 it was re-established with its present limits. It is located in the northeastern part of the Lower Peninsula and is bounded entirely on the east by Saginaw bay. The total land area of the county is 235,097.58 acres, of which about 115,000 acres are good productive farms. The last census taken in 1910, gives Arenac a population of 9,640 inhabitants. There are forty-five schools in the county, with an enrollment of 2,665 children, requiring the services of 75 teachers. Also seven banks and three newspapers.

Standish is the county seat and has a population of about 1,000. It is located on the middle branch of the Pine river and on the Michigan Central Railroad. The town is well located, being but five miles west of the shore of Saginaw bay and 28 miles north of Bay City. It is the trade center of a productive contributory section. It is modern in many respects, having broad, shaded and well laid out streets, a good electric lighting plant, an abundance of pure water, good sewerage system, fire department, churches of the Baptist, Catholic, Christian, Congregational and Methodist denominations, good public school system, court house, opera house, good hotels, two banks and a weekly newspaper.

Other important towns of the county are Au Gres and Omer. The main transportation facilities of the county are the Detroit & Mackinac and the Michigan Central Railroads.

ARENAC COUNTY

MICHIGAN

STANDISH.
Ireland's Garage.

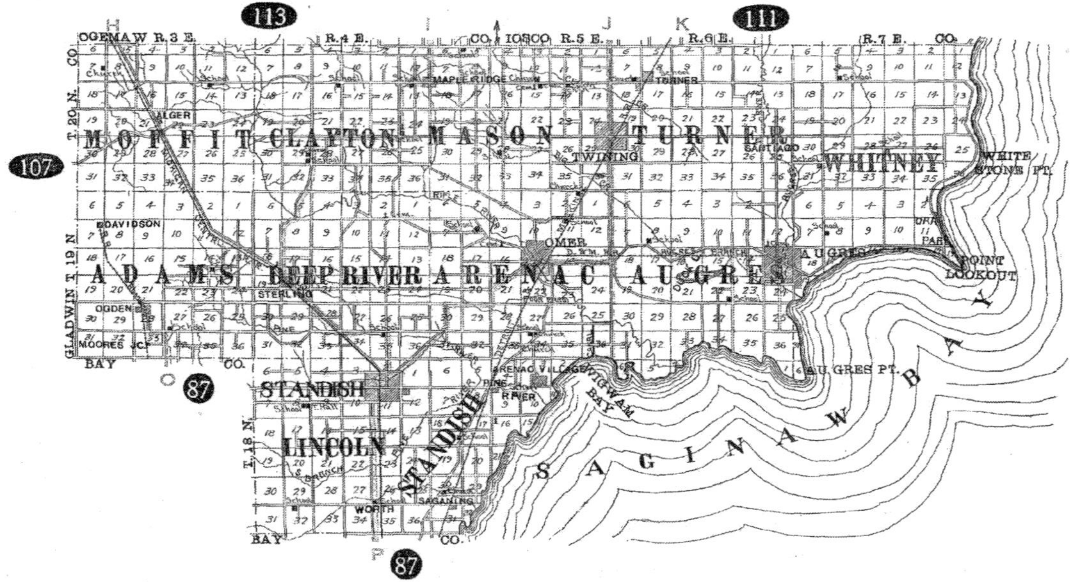

IOSCO COUNTY.

This county was laid out in 1840, and was then called Kanotin, the name of a famous Ottawa chief. During the same year the name was changed to that which it now bears, and means "water of light." The county was finally organized in 1857. It is located in the northeastern part of the Lower Peninsula, is bounded on the north by Alcona county, on the east by Lake Huron, on the south by Arenac county, and on the west by Ogemaw county. The total land area of the county is 354,821.51 acres, of which about 115,000 acres are devoted to good farms. The population of the county is about 9,753 (1910 census). The valuation of taxable property, as estimated by the state board of tax commissioners in 1911, is $3,575,893. Educational advantages offered in Iosco county are equal in many respects to those of the larger counties. There are schools, requiring 69 teachers, and 2,178 students in attendance. The county has six banks and three weekly newspapers. Good telegraph, telephone and rural mail service is to be found in the county.

Tawas City is the judicial seat of the county and is located on the Detroit & Mackinac Railway, at the mouth of the Tawas river, on the indentation of Saginaw bay, known as Tawas bay, one of the best natural harbors on Lake Huron, 60 miles by rail from Bay City. Has Baptist, two German Lutheran, Methodist and Presbyterian churches, excellent public schools, two Lutheran schools, a county normal school, a public library, a bank, a court house, two grain elevators and a weekly newspaper. The shops of the Detroit & Mackinac Railroad are also located here. The population of the town is about 1,300.

East Tawas is the largest town in the county and has a population of about 1,500. It is located on the Detroit & Mackinac Railway, and on the north shore of Tawas bay, one and one-half miles above Tawas City and 61 by rail from Bay City. It is lighted by electricity, has water works, fire department, churches of the Baptist, Episcopal, Methodist, Presbyterian and Catholic denominations, good schools, an opera house, two banks and a weekly newspaper.

Other thriving towns of the county include Au Sable, Oscoda and Whittemore. The leading transportation facilities of the county are the Detroit & Mackinac and the Au Sable & Northwestern Railroads, the Detroit & Cleveland Navigation Company and the Erie & Michigan Railway and Navigation Company.

IOSCO COUNTY

MICHIGAN

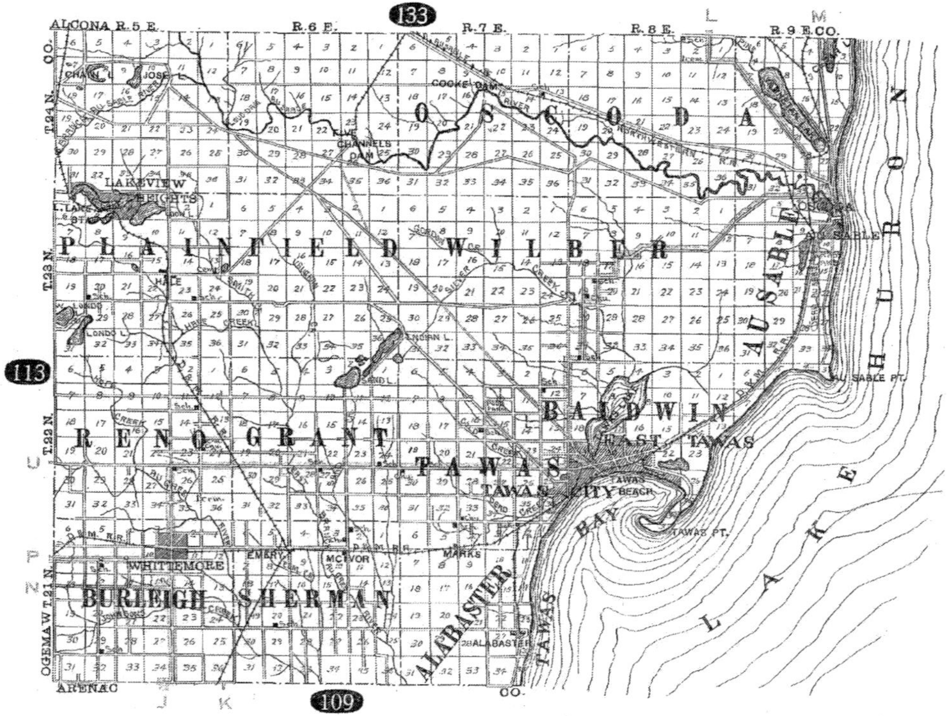

OGEMAW COUNTY.

Ogemaw county was laid out and organized in 1840. The name is taken from the Chippewas, and the meaning of which is "chief." This county is located in about the northeastern part of the Lower Peninsula. It is bounded on the north by Oscoda county, on the east by Iosco county, on the south by Gladwin and Arenac counties, and on the west by Roscommon county. The total land area is 366,811.14 acres, about 145,000 acres of which are already in good farms. The population is 8,907 (census 1910). The valuation of taxable land as estimated by the state board of tax commissioners in 1911, is $4,817,885. The school system is equal to that of most of the larger counties. There are 59 schools, 2,842 students in attendance, requiring the services of 82 teachers. The county has five banks and four weekly newspapers. Also good telegraph, telephone and rural mail service.

West Branch is the judicial seat and largest town of the county. The population is about 1,800. It is located on the Mackinaw division of the Michigan Central Railroad, 53 miles northwest of Bay City and 162 northwest of Detroit. It is lighted by electricity, has well-shaded and paved streets, a handsome court house, good water and drainage system, opera house, fire department, a public library, Episcopal, Methodist and Catholic churches, two banks and two live newspapers. The industrial enterprises include saw and planing mills, machine shop, flour mill, electric lighting plant, creamery, etc. Large quantities of live stock, clover seed and huckleberries are shipped.

Rose City has about 550 inhabitants, and is located on a branch of Rifle river, and on the Detroit and Mackinac Railroad, fifteen miles northeast of West Branch. It has Free Methodist, Lutheran and Methodist Episcopal churches, a bank and a weekly newspaper. The transportation facilities of the county are the Michigan Central, and Detroit & Mackinac Railroads.

OGEMAW COUNTY

MICHIGAN

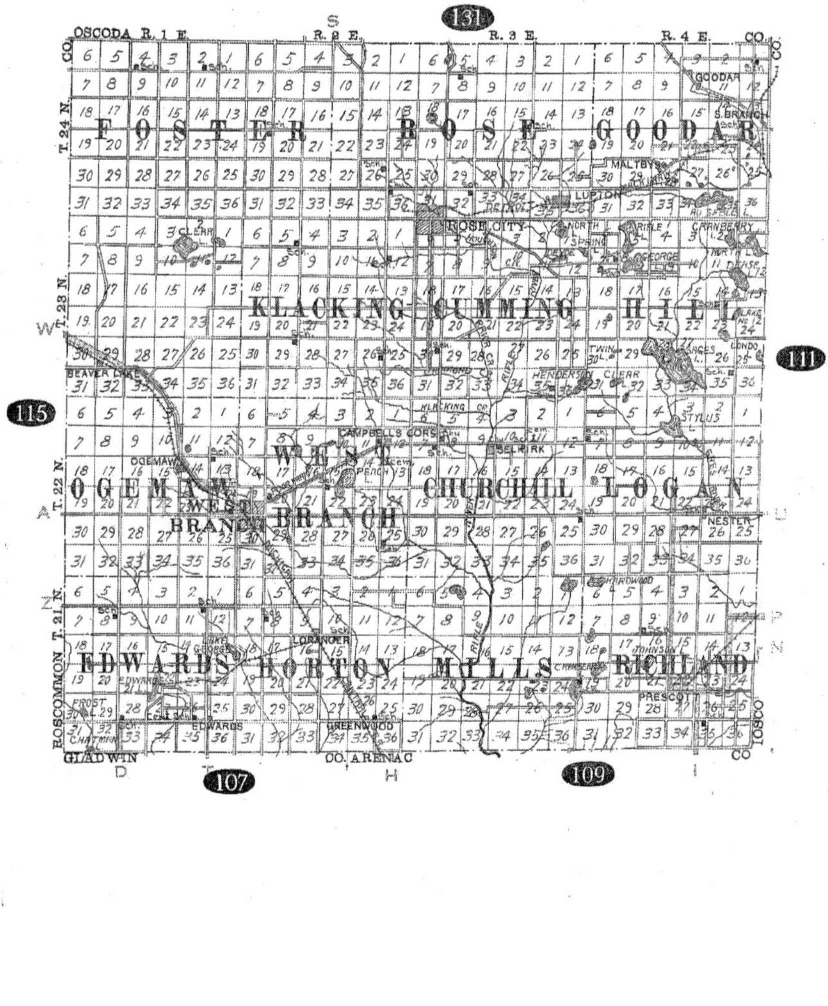

ROSCOMMON COUNTY.

Roscommon county was laid out in 1840 and was at that time called Mikenauk, the name of a famous Ottawa chief. Later, in 1843 the name was changed and in 1875 the county was finally organized. The name Roscommon was taken from a county in the central part of Ireland. This county is located in about the north central part of the Lower Peninsula. Is bounded on the north by Crawford county, on the east by Ogemaw county, on the south by Clare and Gladwin counties, and on the west by Missaukee county. The total land area is 338,315.33 acres, with about 84,000 acres now converted into farms. The population is 2,274 (1910 census). The valuation of taxable property, as estimated by the state board of tax commissioners in 1911, is $2,028,967. The county has a good school system, there being 27 schools, an enrollment of 551 students, and supplying positions for 38 teachers. There is one bank and one weekly newspaper, also telegraph and telephone service in the county.

Roscommon is the county seat and has a population of about 550. It is a station on the Michigan Central Railroad, forty-three miles south of Gaylord, seventy-seven northwest of Bay City, and one hundred and five south of Mackinaw City. It has Congregational, Methodist and Catholic churches, a graded public school, electric light and water works plant, a bank and a weekly newspaper. The transportation facilities of the county are the Michigan Central and Grand Rapids & Indiana Railroads.

ROSCOMMON COUNTY

MICHIGAN

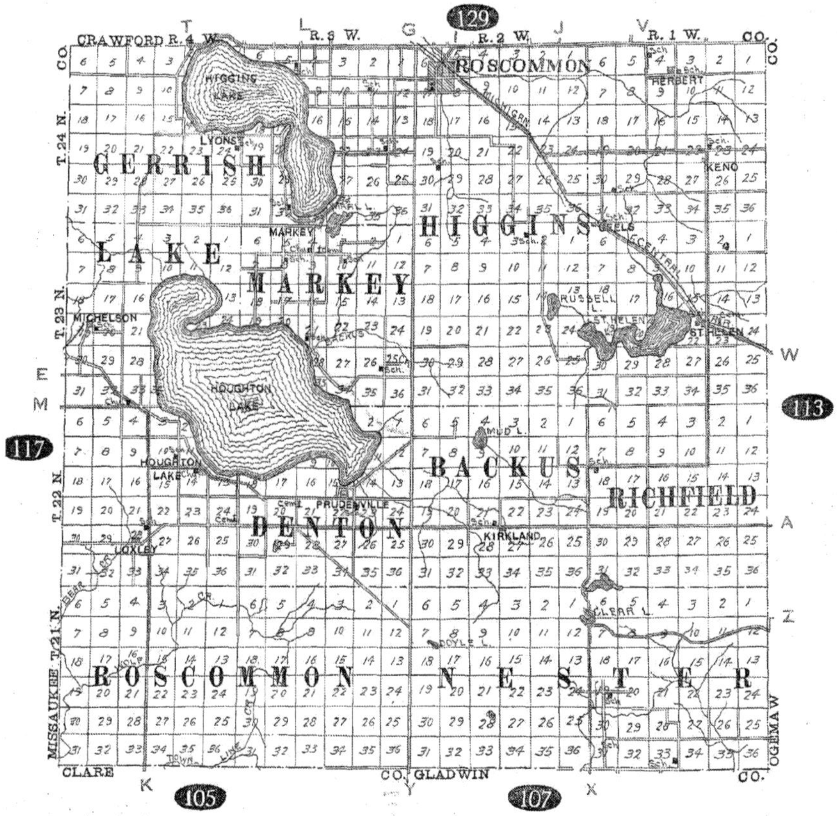

MISSAUKEE COUNTY.

Missaukee county was laid out in 1840 and was organized in 1871. It was named for a famous Ottawa chief and the name is thought to mean "at large mouth of river." The county is located in about the north central part of the Lower Peninsula. Is bounded on the north by Kalkaska county, on the east by Roscommon county, on the south by Osceola and Clare counties and on the west by Wexford county. The total land area is 363,280.57 acres, of which about 148,000 acres are now devoted to farms. The population is 10,606 (1910 census). The valuation of taxable property, as estimated by the state board of tax commissioners in 1911, is $5,575,611. There are 68 schools, which were attended by 2,707 students last year, requiring 102 teachers. The county has four banks and three weekly newspapers. Also telegraph, telephone and rural mail service.

Lake City is the largest town, also the county seat, and has a population of about 800. It is situated on the Grand Rapids & Indiana Railway, 16 miles from Cadillac and 113 from Grand Rapids. It is the receiving and distributing point for a tributary section having good agricultural possibilities. Has electric light and water works plant, churches of the Methodist, Episcopal, Free Methodist, Presbyterian and Catholic denominations, a good school system, an opera house, flour- and saw-mills, two banks and two weekly newspapers.

McBain has a population of about 780. It is located on the Ann Arbor Railway, 10 miles south of Lake City. It has Methodist and Presbyterian churches, a bank and a weekly newspaper. The principal transportation facilities of the county are the Ann Arbor, Grand Rapids & Indiana and the Pere Marquette Railroads.

MISSAUKEE COUNTY

MICHIGAN

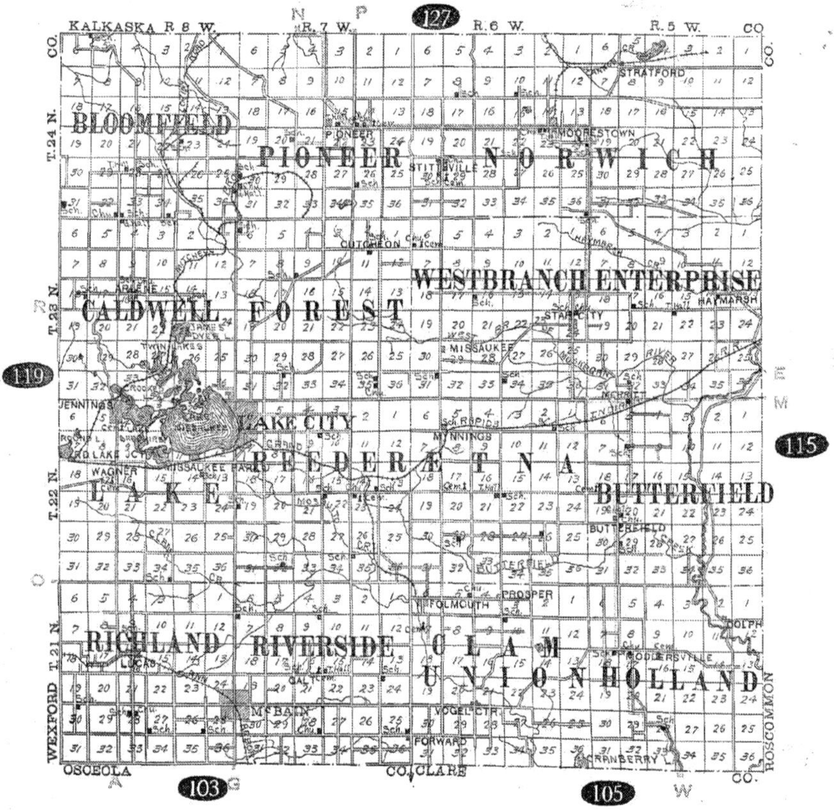

WEXFORD COUNTY.

This county was laid out in 1843 and was organized in 1869. It was originally named "Kautawabet" and is the last of the changes to Irish names. It is located in about the northwestern part of the Lower Peninsula and is bounded on the north by Grand Traverse county, on the east by Missaukee county, on the south by Lake and Osceola counties, and on the west by Manistee county. The total land area is 366,675.60 acres, of which about 148,000 acres are devoted to farms. The population is 20,769 (1910 census). In 1911, the state board of tax commissioners placed a valuation of $15,544,273 on all taxable lands. There are 88 schools, a total enrollment of 5,175 students, furnishing positions for 201 teachers. The county has eight banks, three daily and five weekly newspapers, also telegraph, telephone and rural mail service.

Cadillac is the judicial seat, also the largest city in the county and has a population of about 10,000. It is attractively located on the shore of Lake Cadillac and on the Grand Rapids & Indiana and Ann Arbor Railways, ninety-eight miles north of Grand Rapids. It dates its settlement from 1871, previous to which time it was the heart of an unbroken wilderness, surrounded by forests of both pine and hard wood timber. The city has electric and gas lights, a water works system, an excellent system of sewerage, a beautiful new court house, a fine city hall, public library, graded schools, a first class high school, two banks, two daily and two weekly newspapers, churches of the leading denominations, etc. The principal shipments consist of large quantities of potatoes, other farm products, lumber, veneer, fruit packages, store furniture, broom handles, last blocks, billiard cues, lath, maple flooring, charcoal, wood alcohol, pig iron, saw mill machinery, chemicals, carriage stock and shingles. Other industries include boiler shops, stave and heading works, basket and brick works, a woodenware factory, table factory, smelting works, flouring mills, etc.

Other towns of the county include Buckley, Harrietta, Manton, Mesick, and Sherman. Manton, which is located in a good agricultural section, is a station on the Grand Rapids & Indiana Railroad, twelve miles north of Cadillac and one hundred and ten from Grand Rapids. It owns and operates its own electric light and water works plant, has a sanitary sewerage system, wide and well laid out streets, an opera house, good hotel, a public school building costing about $16,000, churches of the leading denominations, a school and township library, a bank and a live weekly newspaper. The industries include two saw mills, stave mill, flour mill, pickle factory, lumber mill, grist mill, etc. The transportation facilities of the county are the Ann Arbor Railroad, Grand Rapids & Indiana Railroad, Manistee & Northeastern Railroad and the Manistee & Luther Railroad.

WEXFORD COUNTY

MICHIGAN

CADILLAC.
George Van Liew, Michigan Clover, Grain, Farm Bargains.

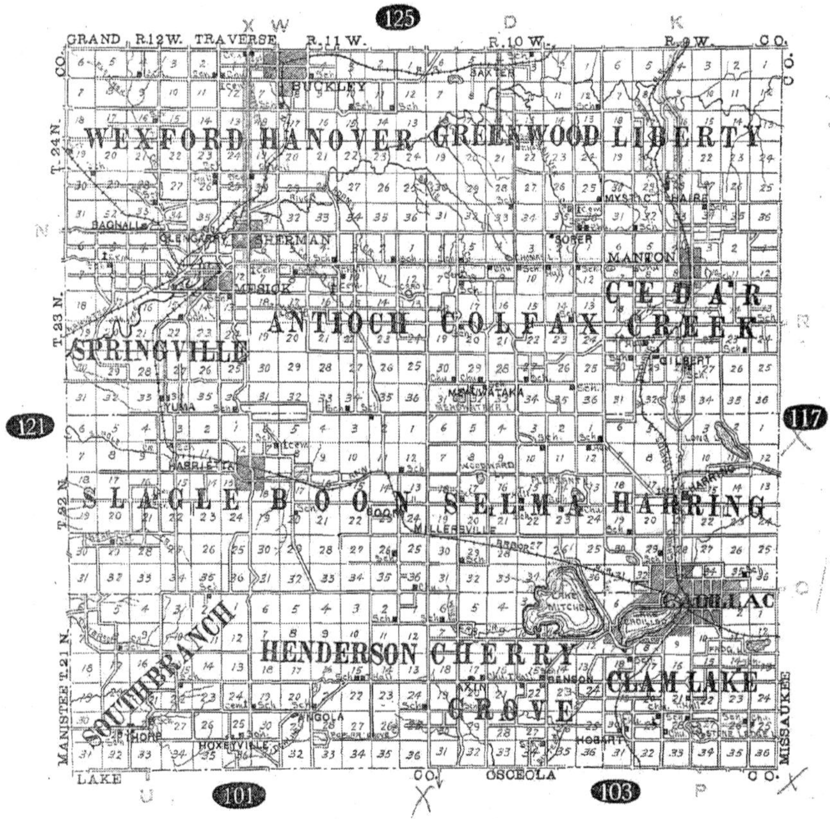

MANISTEE COUNTY.

Manistee county was laid out in 1840 and was organized in 1855. The name is taken from the river which flows through it and empties into Lake Michigan within its borders. The word is of Indian origin and is supposed to mean "river with islands." It is located in the western part of the Lower Peninsula, and is bounded on the north by Benzie county, on the east by Wexford county, on the south by Mason and Lake counties, and on the west by Lake Michigan. The total land area of the county is 350,101.39 acres. Of this number about 145,000 acres are in farms. The population is 26,688 (1910 census). The valuation of taxable land, as estimated by the state board of tax commissioners in 1911, is $18,195,005. The county has 776 schools, an enrollment of 5,283 students, requiring the services of 181 teachers. There are seven banks, two daily and seven weekly newspapers. Good telegraph, telephone and rural mail service is found in nearly every locality.

Manistee is the county seat and the largest city, having about 12,381 inhabitants (1910 census). It is beautifully located on the shore of Lake Michigan, at the mouth of the Manistee river, 175 miles by water from Chicago. It is a station on the Pere Marquette, Manistee & Northeastern and the Manistee & Grand Rapids Railroads. The city is situated in the famous northern Michigan fruit belt and has a tributary territory of great productiveness. It has well-paved and shaded streets, a modern electric lighting plant, a municipally-owned water works, a modernly-equipped fire department, two hospitals, a public library, an opera house, beautiful parks, first-class hotels, three banks, two daily and two weekly newspapers, also a good school system. There are churches of the Congregational, Baptist, Episcopal, German Lutheran, Methodist, Unitarian and Catholic denominations. This city is well known as a summer resort. The more important industrial interests include saw,- shingle- and planing-mills, salt blocks, a modernly equipped dry dock and shipyard, iron works, brewery, tower clock factory, cooperage machinery works, emery wheel works, furniture factories, saw and tool works, shoe factory, lumber and mill carts, carriages, wagons and sleighs, flour-mills, brick and tile works, novelty works, broom factory, boiler and engine works, cigar factories, glove, candy and shirt factories, etc.

Other towns of the county are Bear Lake, Copemish and Onekama. Transportation facilities of the county are the Manistee & Northeastern, Arcadia & Betsey River, Pere Marquette, Ann Arbor, Manistee & Luther, and the Manistee & Grand Rapids Railroads, the Northern Michigan Transportation Company, and the Pere Marquette line of steamers.

MANISTEE COUNTY

MICHIGAN

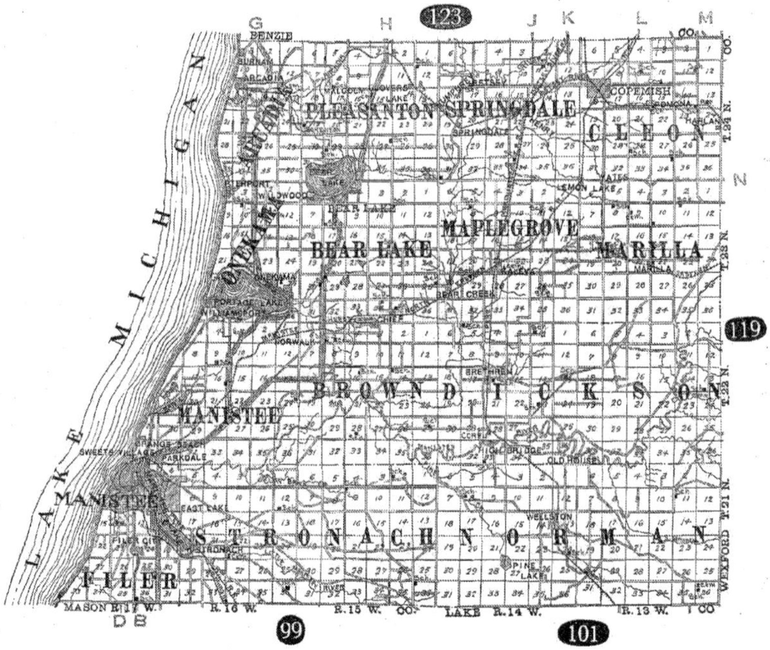

BENZIE COUNTY.

In 1863 the county of Benzie was laid out and organized, being taken from the lower part of Leelanau county. The derivation is uncertain, one explanation being that it is a corruption of "Betsey," the name of a river running through the county, which in turn is a corruption of the French name of the river, Riviere Aux Bec Scies, and is translation of the Indian name of the river Una-zig-o-ze-bee. Another explanation is that it was taken from the word "Benzonia," a place located in that county and which was the county seat. Benzie county is located in the northwestern part of the Lower Peninsula and is bounded on the north by Leelanau county, on the east by Grand Traverse county, on the south by Manistee county and on the west by Lake Michigan. The total land area is 204,192.43 acres, 98,588 acres of which are devoted to farms. The federal census of 1910 gives the county a population of about 10,638. In 1911, the state board of tax commissioners placed a valuation of $6,313,143 on all taxable land. A school system is by no means lacking in Benzie county, there being a total of 57 schools, furnishing positions for 100 teachers and has an enrollment of 2,792 children. Good telephone, telegraph and rural mail service is to be found. The county has 4 banks and 6 newspapers.

The judicial seat of the county is Honor, a little town of about 550 inhabitants. It is located on the Platte river and on the Manistee & Northeastern and Pere Marquette Railroads. It has a Congregational church, a newspaper, a bank, hotels, saw and veneer-mills, etc.

Other towns of the county include Frankfort, Benzonia, Lake Ann, Alberta and Thompsonville. Frankfort, with a population of over 1,600, is the largest town in Benzie county. It is a port of entry on Lake Michigan, located on the Ann Arbor Railroad, 16 miles southwest of Honor, the county seat, 28 miles from Manistee, and 40 miles from Traverse City. It is picturesquely situated and has a magnificent harbor, with eighteen feet of water in the channel. It has a lighthouse and life saving station, is supplied with electric light and water works, churches of several denominations, a $25,000 school building, library, hotels and a daily newspaper. During the season, numerous lines of steamers connect Frankfort with Manistee, Milwaukee and Chicago, Mackinac, Charlevoix, Manistique and other points north, also Ann Arbor car ferries, which run the year round. Like many other sections of Benzie county, Frankfort is a great fruit center, there being many acres of land in that county adapted to the raising of fruits.

Benzonia has a population about the same as that of Honor, the two towns being within six miles of each other. Has a Congregational church, the Benzonia Academy (a Congregational institution), a bank and a weekly newspaper.

The main transportation facilities of the county are the Pere Marquette, Manistee & Northeastern and the Ann Arbor Railroads. Also the Northern Michigan Transportation Company.

BENZIE COUNTY

MICHIGAN

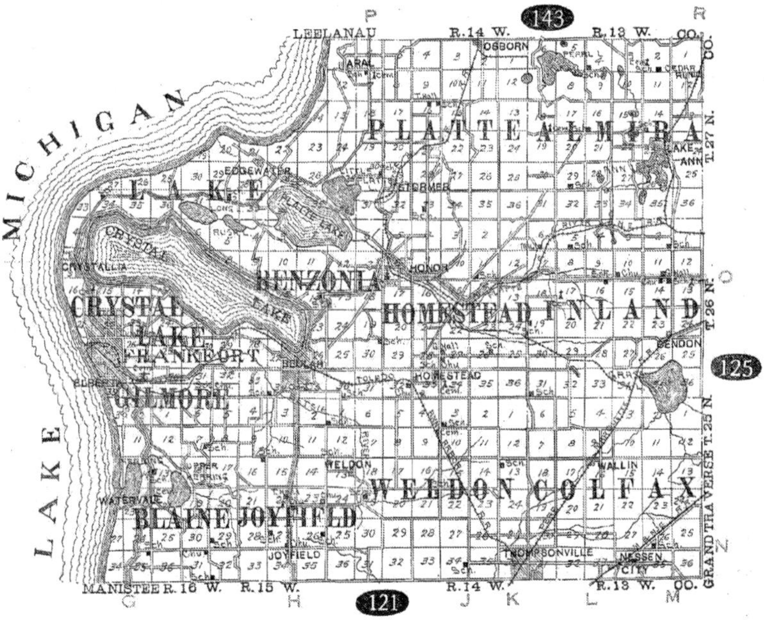

GRAND TRAVERSE COUNTY.

Grand Traverse county was laid out in 1840 and was then called Omeena, taken from the Indian language and meaning "the point beyond." Later, in 1851, the county was organized and the name changed to that which it now bears. The county takes its name from the bay upon which it borders. It is located in the northwestern part of the Lower Peninsula, and is bounded on the north by Leelanau county, Grand Traverse bay and Antrim county, on the east by Kalkaska county, on the south by Wexford county and on the west by Benzie county. The total land area of the county is 299,277.98 acres. Of this number, about 178,000 acres are devoted to farms, which are wonderfully productive. The population is 23,784 (federal census 1910). In 1911, the state board of tax commissioners placed a valuation of $15,056,946 on all taxable lands. The county has a good school system. There are 73 schools, employing 159 teachers and an enrollment of 5,128 students. There are six banks, one daily and two weekly newspapers, also good telephone, telegraph and rural mail service.

Traverse City is the largest city and the judicial seat of the county. It has a population of about 12,500, is located on the Pere Marquette, Grand Rapids & Indiana and the Manistee & Northeastern Railroads, at the head of the west arm of Grand Traverse bay, where the Boardman river, its chief tributary, enters the bay. This city has long been famous as a summer resort. It is also the gateway to the Grand Traverse region, a region of one of the most beautiful and healthful summer places of recreation in the Northwest. The country surrounding Traverse City has long been settled and is rich in farming and fruit lands. The Northern Michigan Asylum is located there.

Prominent manufacturing interests consist of one of the largest oval wood dish factories in the world, as well as one of the largest basket factories in the state, potato implement factory, canning factory, candy factory, iron works, flour and feed mills, tanneries, brick and tile works, foundry and machine shops. Sash doors, electrical appliances, gasoline engines, boats, chairs, cigar boxes, refrigerators, lumber, motor boats, flooring, caskets, shoes, brick machines, carriages, wagons, vinegar, etc., are also manufactured. The religious and educational interests are represented by twenty-three church organizations, a high school and four ward schools. There are three banks, a city library, a hospital, theaters and two newspapers. The city is lighted by electricity and gas, has a good water works plant, good police and fire departments, and well paved streets. In the immediate vicinity one finds good brook trout and bass fishing.

Other thriving communities of the county are Fife Lake and Kingsley. Kingsley is located on the Grand Rapids & Indiana Railroad, 18 miles southeast of Traverse City. Has Baptist, German Lutheran and Methodist churches, a bank, flour and planing-mills, electric light and water works.

Fife Lake is located on the body of water from which it takes its name, 26 miles southeast of Traverse City and 87 southwest of Petoskey. It is a station on the Grand Rapids & Indiana Railroad and is a shipping point for a large lumbering and potato growing region. Has churches of several denominations, good public school system, two hotels, a bank and a weekly newspaper. The principal transportation facilities of the county are the Pere Marquette, Grand Rapids & Indiana and the Manistee & Northeastern Railroads, also the Northern Michigan Transportation Company.

GRAND TRAVERSE COUNTY

MICHIGAN

TRAVERSE CITY.
West Michigan Garage, Purvis & Wynkoop.

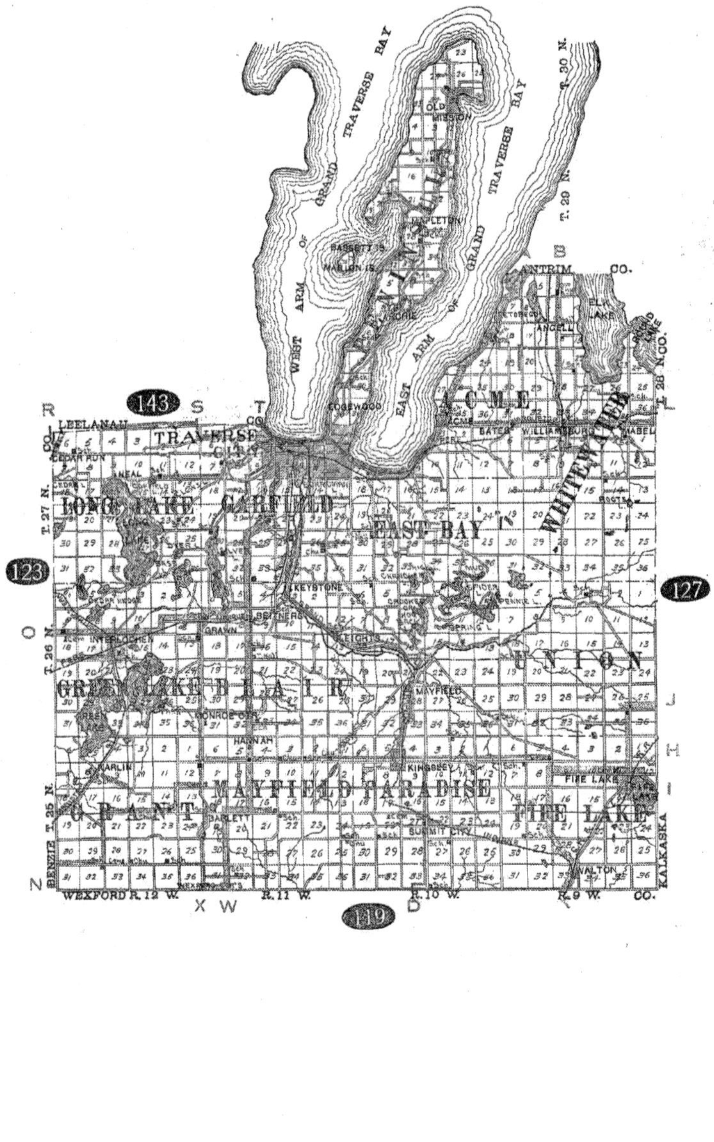

KALKASKA COUNTY.

Kalkaska county was laid out in 1840, and was at that time called Wabassee, the name of a Pottawatomie chief. In 1843 the name was changed to Kalkaska, and later in 1871 the county was finally organized. This county is located in the northern part of the Lower Peninsula. It is bounded on the north by Antrim county, on the east by Crawford county, on the south by Missaukee county and on the west by Grand Traverse county. The total land area of the county is 359,069.30 acres. Of this number, about 81,000 acres are already devoted to good farms. The population is 8,097 (1910 census). The valuation of taxable property, as estimated by the state board of tax commissioners in 1911, is $8,082,745. The county has 55 schools, supplying positions for 77 teachers, and last year's report showed a total of 1,072 children in attendance. There are two banks and one weekly newspaper, and good telegraph, telephone and rural mail service is to be found.

Kalkaska is the largest town, also the judicial seat of the county. It is located on the Pere Marquette and the Grand Rapids & Indiana Railroads, 137 miles north of Grand Rapids. It has electric lights, good water works system, an up-to-date school system, churches of the Congregational, Methodist, Baptist, Christian Science and Disciples denominations, a $17,000 court house, a light and power plant, two banks and two weekly newspapers. The industries include a saw-mill, cant-hook works, grist- and planing-mill, cycle works, etc. Lumber, ginseng, live stock, farm and dairy products are shipped. Principal transportation facilities of the county are the Pere Marquette, Grand Rapids & Indiana and the Manistee & North-eastern Railroads.

KALKASKA COUNTY

MICHIGAN

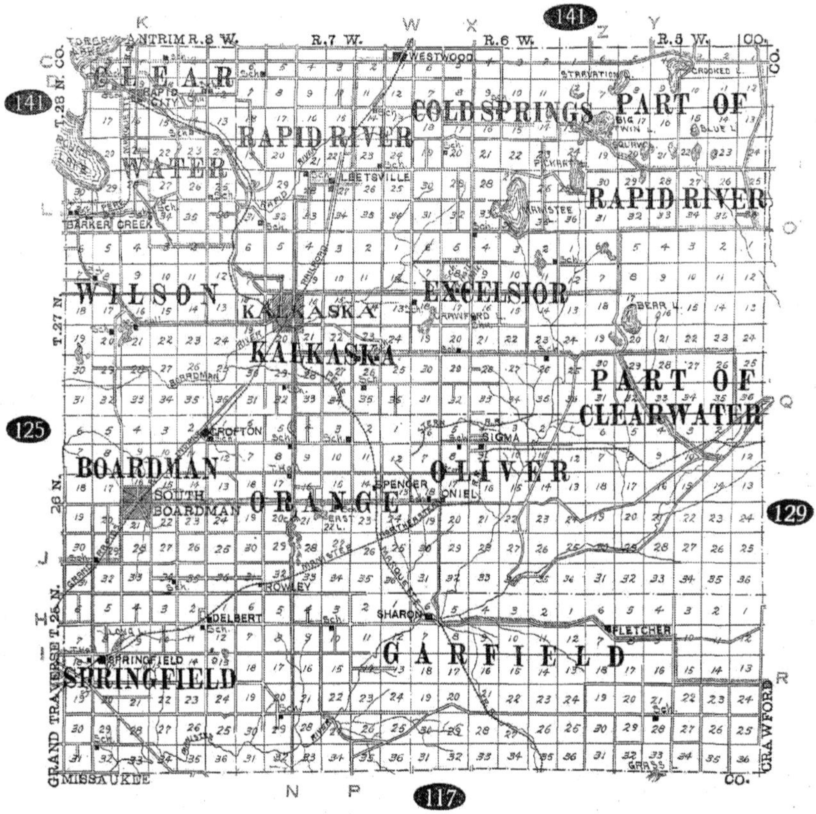

CRAWFORD COUNTY.

Crawford county was originally called Shawono, the name of a famous Chippewa chief. The word means "southern." Later, in 1848, the name was changed to Crawford, being named in honor of Col. William Crawford who was captured by Indians and burned at the stake. It is located in the north central part of the Lower Peninsula. Is bounded on the north by Otsego county, on the east by Oscoda county, on the south by Roscommon county and on the west by Kalkaska county. The county has a total land area of 350,845.89 acres. Of this number, about 40,000 acres are in farms. The population is 3,934 (1910 census). The valuation of taxable property, as estimated by the state board of tax commissioners in 1911, is $4,471,377. There are 24 schools, requiring the services of 48 teachers, and last year's report showed a total of 1,003 scholars in attendance. The county has two banks and 1 weekly newspaper. Also good telegraph and telephone service.

Grayling is the largest town and also the judicial seat of the county. Has a population of about 2,000, is 92 miles northwest of Bay City and 90 from Mackinaw. It is the division point of the Michigan Central Railroad between Bay City and Mackinaw. The Manistee & Northeastern Railroad was extended to Grayling via Walton Junction about two years ago and opened up direct communication to Chicago by way of Lake Michigan through Manistee and also a new route south and east by way of the Grand Rapids & Indiana and the Pennsylvania roads. The town is lighted by electricity, has water works, fire department, opera house, fine court house, a bank, a weekly newspaper and the Grayling Mercy Hospital, costing about $25,000. Has churches of the Catholic, Lutheran, Methodist Episcopal, Presbyterian and Protestant Methodist denominations, and good schools.

Principal transportation facilities of the county are the Michigan Central, Detroit & Charlevoix and the Manistee & Northeastern Railroads.

CRAWFORD COUNTY

MICHIGAN

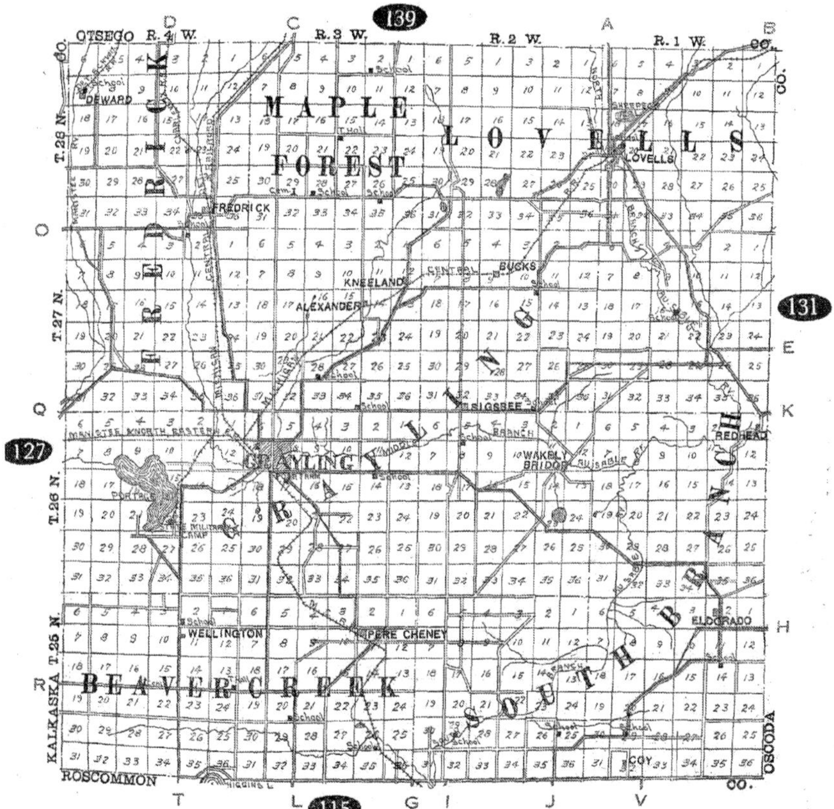

OSCODA COUNTY.

Oscoda county was laid out and organized in 1840. The name is of Indian origin and is said to mean "pebbly prairie." It is located in the northeastern part of the Lower Peninsula and is bounded on the north by Montmorency county, on the east by Alcona county, on the south by Ogemaw county, and on the west by Crawford county. The total land area is 364,769.48 acres. Of this number about 60,000 acres are now devoted to farms. The population is 2,027. The valuation of taxable property, as estimated by the state board of tax commissioners in 1911, is $2,264,747. There are 20 schools, 521 students in attendance, requiring the services of 33 teachers. The county has two banks, one weekly newspaper, telegraph, telephone and rural mail service.

Mio, the county seat, has a population of about 300. It is situated on the Au Sable river, 15 miles from Comins, its shipping point. It has a Methodist church, a bank and a weekly newspaper. The transportation facility of the county is the Au Sable & Northwestern Railroad.

OSCODA COUNTY

MICHIGAN

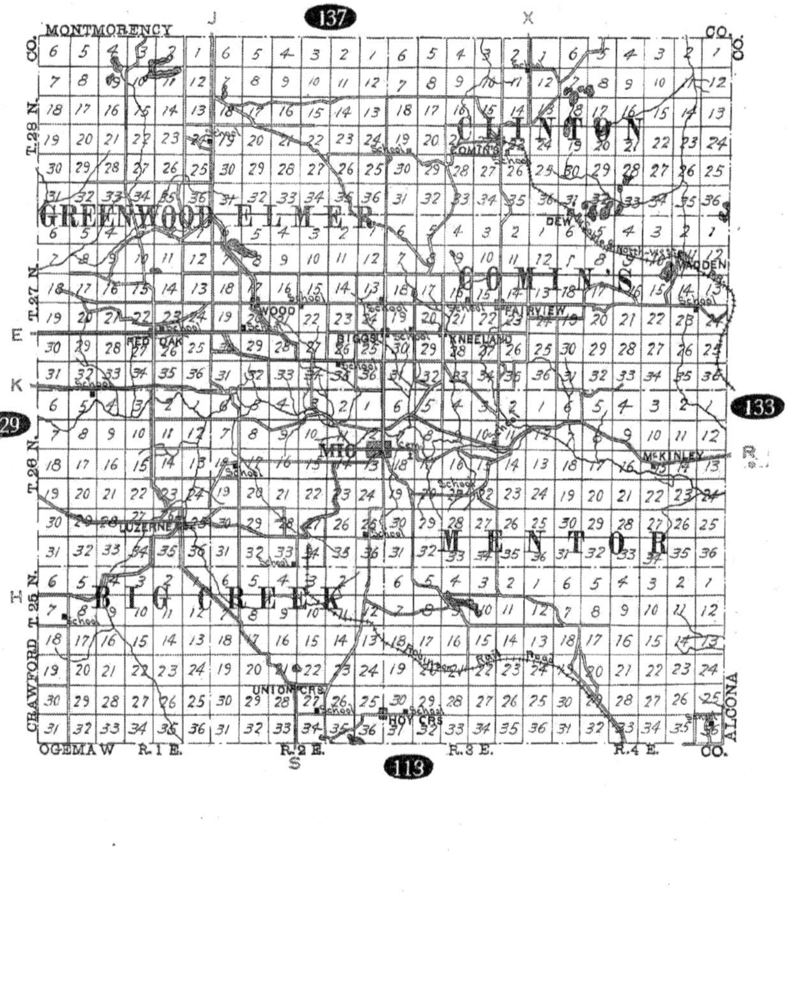

ALCONA COUNTY.

Alcona county was first laid out in 1840 and was first called Negwegon, after a well known Chippewa chief. It was afterwards named Alcona, meaning, "A fine or excellent plain," and was organized as a county in 1869. It is one of the eastern tier of counties and is located towards the northern part of the Lower Peninsula. The total land area is 435,247.34 acres, of which 105,000 acres are in farms, producing good crops. The population is 5,703 (1910 census). The valuation of taxable property as estimated by the state board of tax commissioners in 1911, is $2,921,885. The county has a large lake frontage, being bounded entirely on the east by Lake Huron.

There are 43 schools which were attended by 1,357 pupils last year, requiring the services of 48 teachers. The county has telephone, telegraph and rural mail service, 3 banks and 2 newspapers. One paper is published at Harrisville and the other at Lincoln.

Harrisville, which is the county seat, has a population of about 500 and is located on the main line of the Detroit & Mackinac Railroad, on the west shore of Lake Huron in Harrisville township, about 200 miles above Detroit, 100 above Bay City and 34 miles south of Alpena. There are Baptist, Catholic, Presbyterian and Methodist churches, new six-room high school, court house, agricultural hall, good hotel, roller flouring-mills, creamery, contract seed house, electric lighting plant, a bank and one newspaper.

The other principal towns are Lincoln and Mikado, both located on the Detroit & Mackinac Railroad to the southwest of Harrisville—each having a bank and churches of different denominations, hotel, flour-mills, etc.

The principal transportation facilities of the county are the Detroit & Mackinac Railroad and the Au Sable & Northwestern Railroad.

ALCONA COUNTY

MICHIGAN

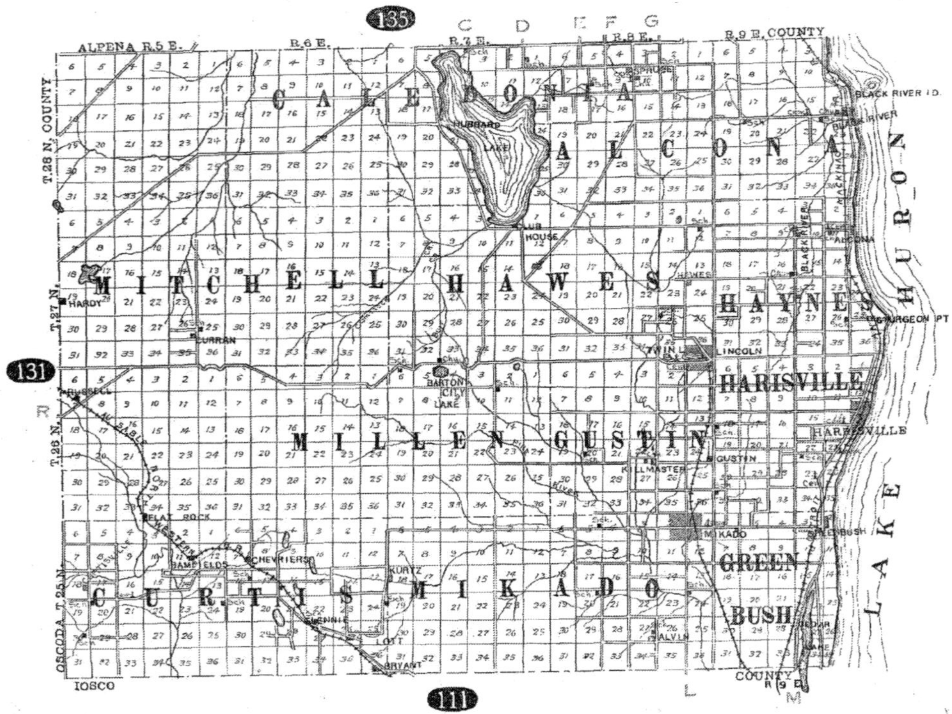

ALPENA COUNTY.

Alpena county was laid out in 1840 and was first called Animickee, after a well known Chippewa chief. Later the name was changed to Alpena, meaning the "Partridge Country." Alpena county was organized in 1857. It is located in the northeastern part of the Lower Peninsula and is bounded on the entire east by Lake Huron. The land area of the county is 371,153.39 acres, of which 150,000 acres are already devoted to farms. The entire population is given at 19,965 (1910 census). In 1911, the state board of tax commissioners placed the value of taxable property in the county at $12,949,233.

There are a total of 76 schools, requiring the services of 131 teachers, while last year's report shows a total of 3,493 children in attendance. The county has good telephone, telegraph and rural mail service.

Alpena is the judicial seat of Alpena county, and has a population of 12,706 (U. S. census 1910). It is beautifully located on Thunder bay, at the mouth of Thunder Bay river, and is a station on the Detroit & Mackinac Railroad. The city owns and operates an excellent water works system and electric lighting plant, costing in the neighborhood of $250,000, has a good sewerage system, paved streets, a police department, fire department, two opera houses, first class hotels, a $20,000 court house, $100,000 postoffice building, public library, a $75,000 depot, a $50,000 city hall and a $30,000 public hospital are now being constructed. The county has three banks, two of them being located in Alpena.

The religious and educational advantages of Alpena are very good, there being churches of the following denominations: Adventist, two Baptist, three Catholic, Congregational, Episcopal, Free Methodist, Hebrew, Latter Day Saints, Two German Evangelical Lutheran, Norwegian Lutheran, Methodist Episcopal and Presbyterian churches. There are nine public and six parochial schools, also a well-equipped business college. The city has three newspapers, two published daily and one weekly. One finds Alpena supplied with numerous industrial establishments, some of which are as follows: Lumber, shingle and planing-mills, factories manufacturing all kinds of lumber products, an automobile factory, pulp works, flour and grist mills, two tanneries, two veneer works, paper-mill, mattress works, breweries, electric light plant, power plant, cement works, foundry, rug and cigar factories, quarries, etc.

A government fish hatchery is located at Alpena. The bay forms an excellent harbor and during the season of navigation, steamers bring in many visitors, making Alpena quite popular as a summer resort. A large portion of the surrounding country is rich, fertile soil, capable of producing all cereals and roots adapted to the climate in abundance as well as some very fine fruit. Transportation facilities throughout the county include the following: Detroit & Mackinac Railroad, Boyne City, Gaylord & Alpena Railroad, and the Detroit & Cleveland Navigation Company.

ALPENA COUNTY

MICHIGAN

ALPENA.

Alpena County Savings Bank, Capital $100,000, Surplus $125,000.

Alpena Garage (C. A. Reynolds). Cadillac, Hupmobile and Studebaker Machines. Fireproof Storage. Auto Repairing.

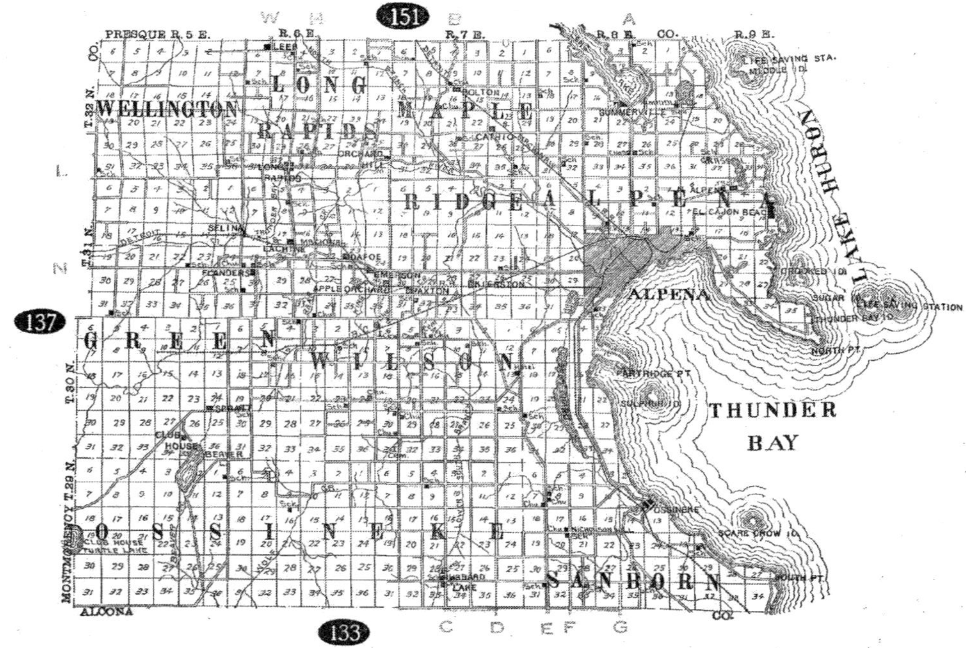

MONTMORENCY COUNTY.

In 1840, this county was laid out and was then named Cheonoquet, for a Chippewa chief. The name is supposed to mean "Big Cloud." In 1848 the county was organized and the present name given it. It is uncertain what the name Montmorency commemorates. This county is located in the northern part of the Lower Peninsula. Is bounded on the north by Cheboygan and Presque Isle counties, on the east by Alpena county, on the south by Oscoda county, and on the west by Otsego county. The total land area is 355,528.77 acres, and about 56,000 acres are already devoted to farms. The population is 3,755 (1910 census). In 1911, the state board of tax commissioners placed a valuation of $2,022,828 on all taxable land. The county has 32 schools, furnishing positions for 37 teachers, and an enrollment of 743 students. There are three banks and three weekly newspapers. Telephone, telegraph and rural mail service is also to be found.

Atlanta is the county seat and has about 200 inhabitants. It is located 14 miles from Lewiston, which is on the Michigan Central Railroad, and is the shipping point, and 30 west of Alpena. Has a Congregational church, a bank and a weekly newspaper.

Hillman has a population of about 500, and is located on Thunder Bay river, and on the Detroit & Mackinac Railroad, 16 miles northeast of Atlanta and 24 from Alpena. Has Episcopal, Presbyterian, Methodist Episcopal and Catholic churches, a bank and a weekly newspaper.

The principal transportation facilities of the county are the Michigan Central, Detroit & Mackinac and the Boyne City, Gaylord & Alpena Railroads.

MONTMORENCY COUNTY

MICHIGAN

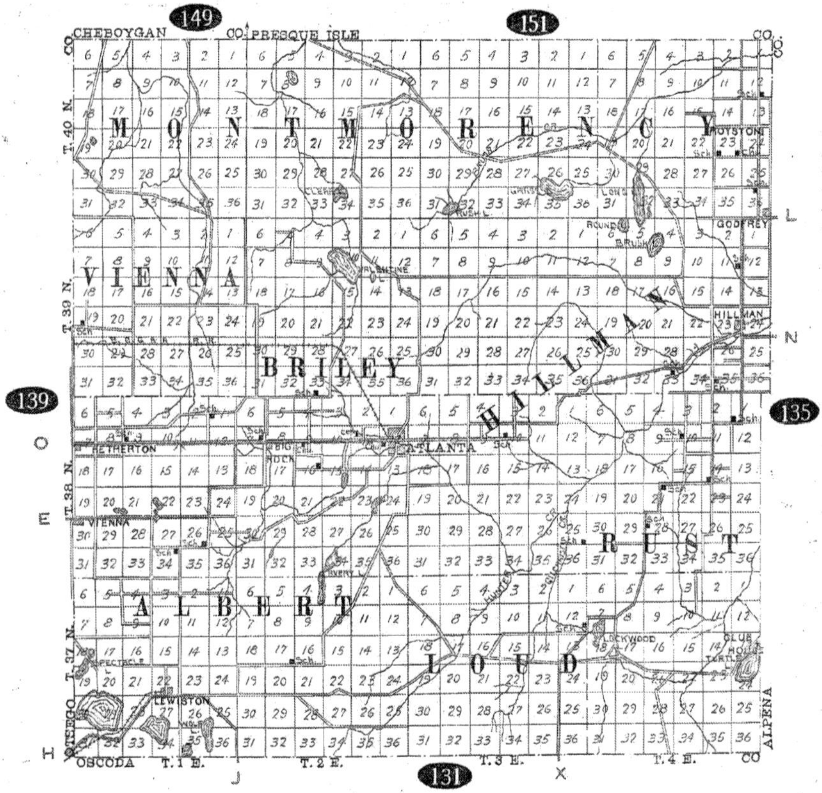

OTSEGO COUNTY.

This county was first laid out in 1840, and was at that time called "Okkuddo." In 1843 the name was changed to Otsego, which is said to mean "clear water." The county was organized in 1875. It is located in the northern part of the Lower Peninsula. The boundaries are Cheboygan county on the north, Montmorency county on the east, Crawford county on the south and Antrim and Charlevoix counties on the west. The total land area is 334,272.96 acres. Of this number, about 60,000 acres are already in good farms. The population is 6,552 (1910 census). The valuation of taxable property, as estimated by the state board of tax commissioners in 1911, is $6,914,039. A good school system is to be found throughout the county. There are 40 schools, an enrollment of 1,042 students, furnishing positions for 72 teachers. The county has five banks and two weekly newspapers, while good telegraph, telephone and rural mail service is also to be found.

Gaylord, the judicial seat of the county, has about 1,800 inhabitants. It is located on the Michigan Central, and the Boyne City, Gaylord & Alpena Railroads, 63 miles south of Mackinaw City. It is the trading point for a prosperous agricultural section, has Congregational, Methodist, Baptist and Catholic churches, a high school building erected at a cost of about $27,000, municipally-owned water works and electric light plant, opera house, two banks and a weekly newspaper. A woodenware factory, a grist-mill and a motor car plant comprise the chief industries.

Vanderbilt, with about 550 inhabitants, is located on the Michigan Central Railroad, eight and one-half miles north of Gaylord; has Congregational and Methodist churches, a shingle mill and a bank. Transportation facilities of the county are the Michigan Central, Boyne City, Gaylord & Alpena and the Detroit & Charlevoix Railroads.

OTSEGO COUNTY

MICHIGAN

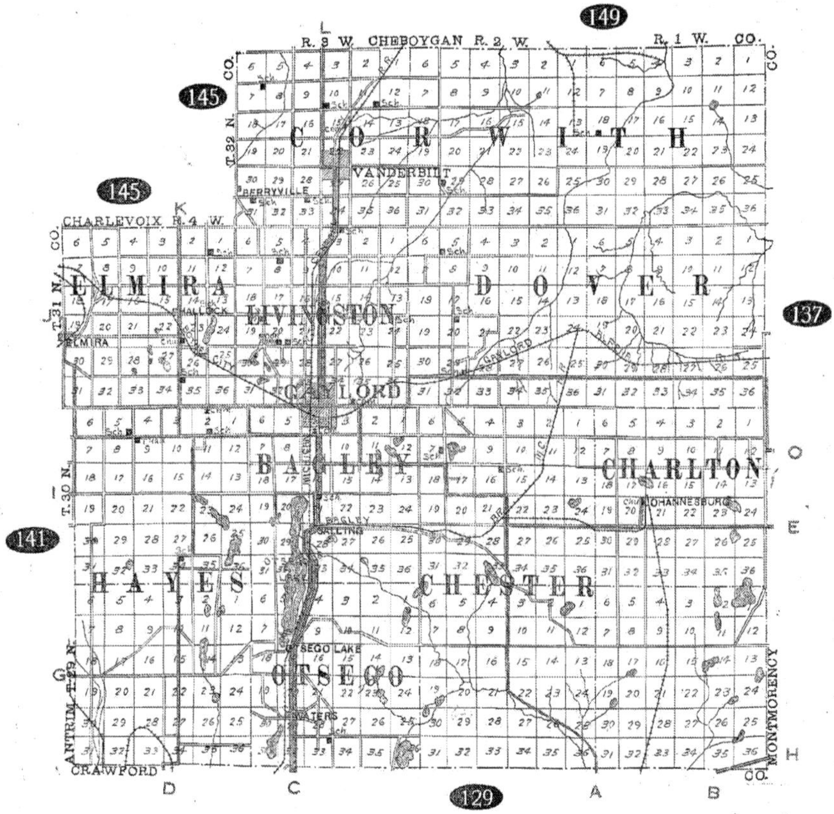

ANTRIM COUNTY.

Antrim county was laid out in 1840 and was first called Meegisee, meaning "Eagle," and was named after a famous Chippewa chief, and later, in 1843, it was changed to the name it now bears. The name "Antrim" is that of a county in the northeastern part of Ireland. The county was finally organized in 1863. It is located in the northwestern part of the Lower Peninsula and is bounded on the entire west by Grand Traverse bay and Torch lake, forming a peninsula of part of the coast line. The total land area of this county is 305,558.44 acres, with nearly 120,000 acres already in splendid farms. The valuation of taxable property, as gien out by the state board of tax commissioners in 1911, is $10,805,174. The population is 15,692 (1910 census).

Antrim county has a total of 78 schools, employing 136 teachers and an attendance of 3,405 children last year. There is good telephone, telegraph and rural route service in the county.

Bellaire is the capital of the county and has a population of about 1,400. It is located on the Pere Marquette Railroad and East Jordan & Southern Railroad, 37 miles south of Charlevoix. There are Congregational, Methodist and Catholic churches, good schools, electric lighting plant, a bank and a weekly newspaper. A few of the industries include: Feed and grist-mills, saw-mills, etc.

Other important towns of the county include: Elk Rapids, Mancelona and Central Lake. Elk Rapids is a town of about 1,800 inhabitants and is picturesquely located on Grand Traverse bay, at the mouth of the Elk river, and is a station on the Pere Marquette Railway, 34 miles southwest of Bellaire. The town is lighted by electricity, has a fine water system, churches of the Episcopal, Methodist, Catholic, German Reformed, Presbyterian and Norwegian Lutheran denominations, a $24,000 school building, good public library, a bank and two weekly newspapers. There is a good market for apples, potatoes, peas and other farm products which are raised in the vicinity. Manufacturing industries include iron and chemical company, saw and flour-mills and a cigar factory.

Mancelona, located 12 miles southeast of Bellaire on the Grand Rapids & Indiana Railroad, has a population the same as that of Elk Rapids. It is surrounded by a fertile tributary section with agricultural resources and possibilities, making it rich in opportunities and for which it is the trade center. There are churches of the Congregational, Episcopal, Methodist, German Reform and Catholic denominations, a good school system, a township library, opera house, good hotels, a bank and two weekly newspapers. There are a number of prosperous industries, including saw-mills, planing-mills, flour-mill, creamery, and manufactories of veneer, screens, brooms, hoops, cheese box material, gasoline engines, etc.

Central Lake has a population of about 1,000 and is located eight miles north of Bellaire on the Pere Marquette Railroad. It is well known as a summer resort. Has Congregational, Free Methodist and Methodist Episcopal churches, good schools, electric lighting, two banks and a weekly newspaper.

Principal transportation facilities of the county are the Grand Rapids & Indiana, Pere Marquette, Boyne City, Gaylord & Alpena, Detroit & Charlevoix and the East Jordan & Southern Railroads, and the Northern Michigan Transportation Company.

ANTRIM COUNTY

MICHIGAN

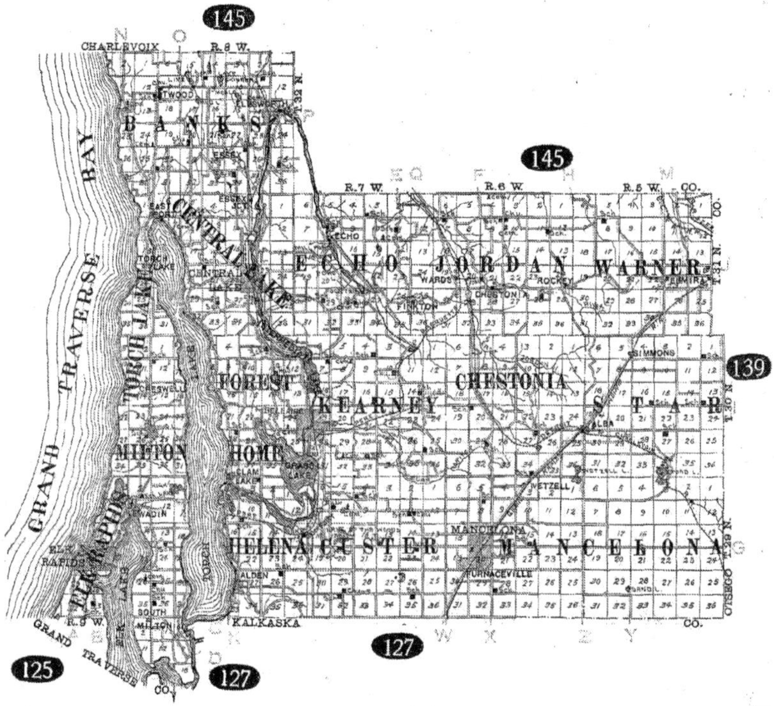

LEELANAU COUNTY.

Leelanau county was laid out in 1840 and was organized in 1863. The name—according to an Indian legend—means "Delight of Life." This county is located in the northern part of the Lower Peninsula. Its boundaries are Lake Michigan on the west and north, Grand Traverse Bay on the east, and Benzie and Grand Traverse counties on the south. The total land area of the county is 220,233.58 acres, of which about 180,000 acres are in good farms. The population is 10,608 (1910 census). The valuation of taxable property, as estimated by the state board of tax commissioners in 1911, is $6,388,512. There are 61 schools, supplying positions for 84 teachers, and an enrollment of 2,885 students. The county has five banks and three weekly newspapers, also telegraph, telephone and rural mail service.

Leland is the county seat and has a population of about 400. It is located at the mouth of Leelanau river, the outlet of Lake Leelanau, on the west shore of the peninsula forming Leelanau county, 25 miles northwest of Traverse City and four and one-half north of Provemont, its nearest railroad point. There are Lutheran and Methodist churches and a weekly newspaper is published. Leland has become popular as an ideal summer resort.

Empire, the largest town in the county, has about 650 inhabitants. It is located on the shore of Lake Michigan and on the Manistee & Northeastern Railroad, 28 miles southwest of Leland and about the same distance from Traverse City. It has Catholic and Methodist churches, a bank and a weekly newspaper. Other towns of the county are Northport, population, 600, and Suttons Bay, population, 600. The transportation facilities of the county are the Empire & Southeastern, Manistee & Northeastern, Traverse City, Leelanau & Manistique Railroads and the Northern Michigan Transportation Company.

LEELANAU COUNTY

MICHIGAN

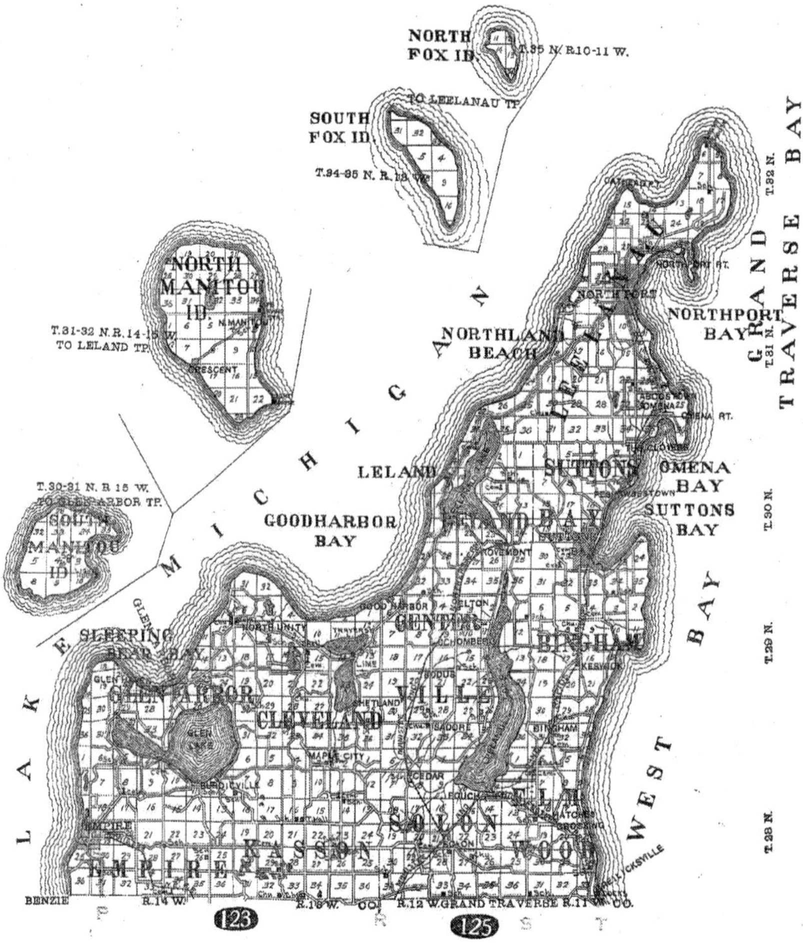

CHARLEVOIX COUNTY.

Charlevoix county was laid out in 1840 and was at that time called Keshkauko, the name of a leading chief of the Chippewas. In 1843 the name was changed to Charlevoix, in honor of Pierre Francois Xavier de Charlevoix, the French Jesuit missionary, traveler and historian. The country was organized during the year 1869. It is located in the northwestern part of the Lower Peninsula; is bounded on the north by Emmet county, on the east by Cheboygan and Otsego counties, on the south by Otsego and Antrim counties and on the west by Lake Michigan. The total land area is 266,224.98 acres, 127,625 acres of which are devoted to farms. The population is 19,157 (1910 census). There are 77 schools in Charlevoix county, with an enrollment of about 4,536 students, requiring the services of 168 teachers. There are 7 banks, one daily and six weekly newspapers in the county, also telegraph, telephone and rural mail service.

Charlevoix is the capital city of the county and has a population of about 2,500. It is beautifully located on the shore of Lake Michigan at the entrance to Pine Lake and its ideal attractions and many charms have made it famous as a summer resort. It is located on the Pere Marquette Railroad, 210 miles north of Grand Rapids. The city owns and controls its own electric light and water plants, has churches of the Baptist, Congregational, Episcopal, Methodist and Catholic denominations, an up-to-date public school system, public library, good hotels, two banks an opera house and two weekly newspapers. There are saw and shingle-mills, and manufactories of flour, beet sugar, cement, boilers, boats and launches, rustic furniture and bridges. A large shipping trade is done in wood, bark, ties, cedar posts, lumber and fish.

Other cities of importance are Boyne City, Boyne Falls and East Jordan. Boyne City, with a population of 5,218 (1910 census), is located on the Boyne City, Gaylord & Alpena Railway, and Pine lake, 16 miles southeast of Charlevoix. The city is lighted by electricity, has perfect natural drainage supplemented by a splendid sewerage system, fire department, paved streets and good water for domestic and industrial purposes. In the hills surrounding the city to the north and south is a never-failing supply of flowing wells and spring water which is furnished to users through 16 miles of mains. There are churches of the Baptist, Evangelical, German Evangelical, Methodist, Presbyterian and Roman Catholic denominations, a first class public school system, two banks, first-class hotels, a hospital and two newspapers.

In the list of manufacturing industries of Boyne City, that of the manufacture of lumber constitutes one of the most important industries. The city is destined to become one of the largest manufacturing centers in the state for lumber, lath, shingles, flooring, veneer, sash, doors, and other timber products, as well as for furniture and carriages. The industrial interests include some of the largest hard wood lumber mills in the world, large veneer plant, planing-mills, largest shingle plant in the state, manufactories of boxes and baskets, charcoal, brick and tile, chemicals, etc. Principal transportation facilities of the county are the Pere Marquette, Boyne City, Gaylord & Alpena, Detroit & Charlevoix, Grand Rapids & Indiana Railways, and the Northern Michigan Transit Company.

CHARLEVOIX COUNTY

MICHIGAN

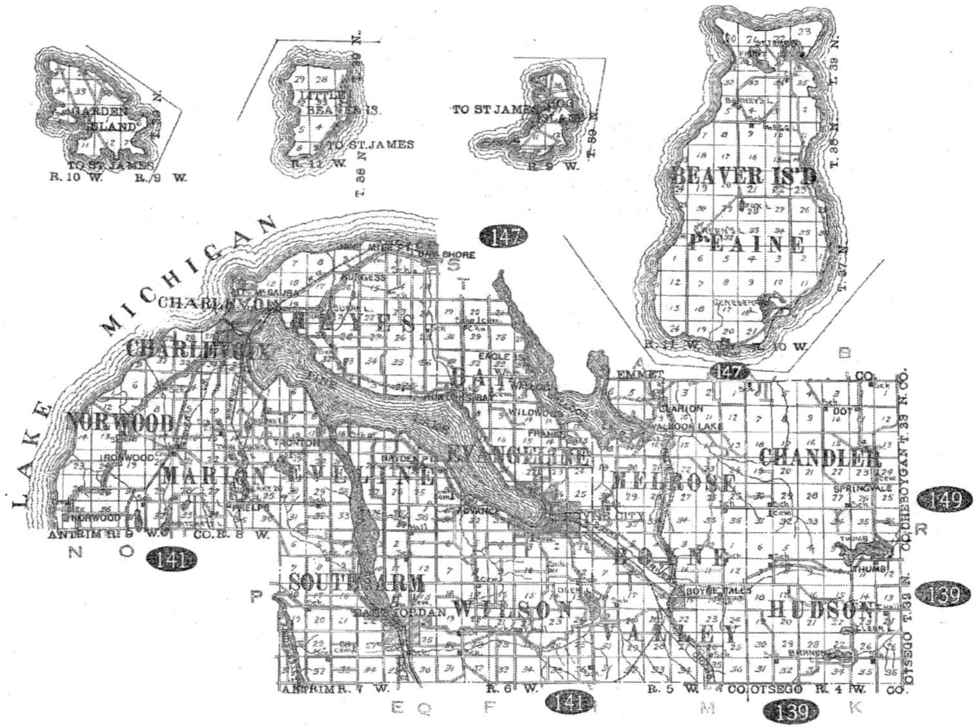

EMMET COUNTY.

Emmet county was laid out in 1840 and was first called Tonedagana. In 1843 the name was changed to Emmet, in honor of the Irish patriot, Robert Emmet. The county was finally organized in 1853. It is located in the extreme northern part of the Lower Peninsula, is bounded on the north by Lake Michigan and the straits of Mackinac, on the east by Cheboygan county, on the south by Charlevoix county and on the west by Lake Michigan. The total land area of the county is 300,855.39 acres. About 125,000 acres are now being farmed with great success. The population is 18,561 (1910 census). The valuation of taxable property, as estimated by the state board of tax commissioners in 1911, is $16,048,690. The school system is equal to that of most any of the larger counties, there being 78 schools, attended by 3,765 children and requiring 150 teachers. There are five banks, one daily and four weekly newspapers. Good telegraph, telephone and rural mail service is found. The county in general is well adapted for farming.

Petoskey, with a population of over 5,000, is the judicial seat and also the largest city in the county. The county seat was originally located at Harbor Springs, but was removed to Petoskey by a vote of the people of the county in 1910. It is located on the Grand Rapids & Indiana and the Pere Marquette Railways, at the mouth of Bear river, on Little traverse bay, which is six miles wide and nine miles long. The city is lighted by electricity, has water works, fire department, gas plant, an opera house, two banks, a beautiful court house erected at a cost of about $30,000, two weekly newspapers, churches of the Adventist, Baptist, Catholic, Christian Science, Episcopal, German Evangelical, German Lutheran, German Methodist, Methodist, Mennonite and Presbyterian denominations, excellent public schools, a public library, first class hotels and numerous substantial manufacturing and business houses. Paper, leather, sectional blocks and lumber are the leading manufactured articles.

Other towns of importance are Alanson, population 500; Harbor Springs, population 2,000, and Pellston, population 1,200. The largest of these is Harbor Springs, which is located on the Grand Rapids & Indiana Railroad, eight miles north of Petoskey, on the north side of a fine land-locked harbor formed by the projection of Harbor Point across the northern part of Little Traverse bay. It is one of the best natural harbors upon the entire chain of Great Lakes. Climate, location and natural beauty have made Harbor Springs famous as a summer resort. There are churches of Baptist, Catholic, Episcopal, Methodist and Presbyterian denominations, excellent schools, water works, good hotels, a boat factory, a bank and a newspaper. Large quantities of grain, produce, lumber, wood, maple sugar and fish are shipped.

The principal transportation facilities of the county are the Grand Rapids & Indiana and the Pere Marquette Railroads, the Northern Steamship Company, Northern Transportation Company and the Goodrich Transportation Company.

EMMET COUNTY

MICHIGAN

CHEYBOYGAN COUNTY.

Cheyboygan county was laid out and named in 1840, and was organized in 1853. It was named from a river of the same name and has many meanings ascribed to it. The county is located in the extreme northern part of the Lower Peninsula. It is bounded on the north by Lake Huron, on the east by Presque Isle county, on the south by Otsego and Montmorency counties and on the west by Charlevoix and Emmet counties. The total land area comprises 462,489.73 acres. Of this number, 120,418 acres are devoted to farms. It has a total population of 17,872 (1910 census). The valuation of taxable property as estimated by the state board of tax commissioners in 1911, is $12,006,821. The county has splendid educational advantages. There are in all, 84 schools, requiring 139 teachers, with a total enrollment of 4,138 students. There are 6 banks, 1 daily and 8 weekly newspapers in the county, also telegraph, telephone and rural mail service.

Cheboygan is the judicial seat of the county and has a population of about 8,000. It is a thriving manufacturing and shipping point and the lake port of one of the best farming sections in Michigan, located in the straits of Mackinac at the mouth of the Cheboygan and Black rivers and on the Michigan Central and the Detroit & Mackinac Railroads. In addition to its rail facilities, it has many boat lines connecting with nearly every large port on the lakes. The city is thoroughly modern, has well paved streets, fine sewerage system, water works, a well equipped fire department, 10 miles of water mains, police department, 9 public schools, a county normal school, 3 parochial schools, public library, opera house, first class hotels, 3 banks, churches of different denominations, electric light, gas and power plant and 3 newspapers.

This section grows large quantities of such fruits as cherries, plums, and apples. Potatoes, hay, oats, barley, corn and rye are raised in abundance. The principal industries of the city are saw-mills, one of the largest tanneries west of New York, large paper-mill, foundries, snow plow works, automobile factory, fire kindle factory, cannery, flour mill, sash, door and blind factory, wood turning works, boiler works, machine shops, cigar factories, packing industries, planing mills, etc. The other principal towns are Tower and Wolverine. The transportation facilities of the county are the Michigan Central and the Detroit & Mackinac Railroads, the Detroit & Cleveland Navigation Company, Northern Michigan Navigation Company and the Arnold Transportation Company.

CHEBOYGAN COUNTY

MICHIGAN

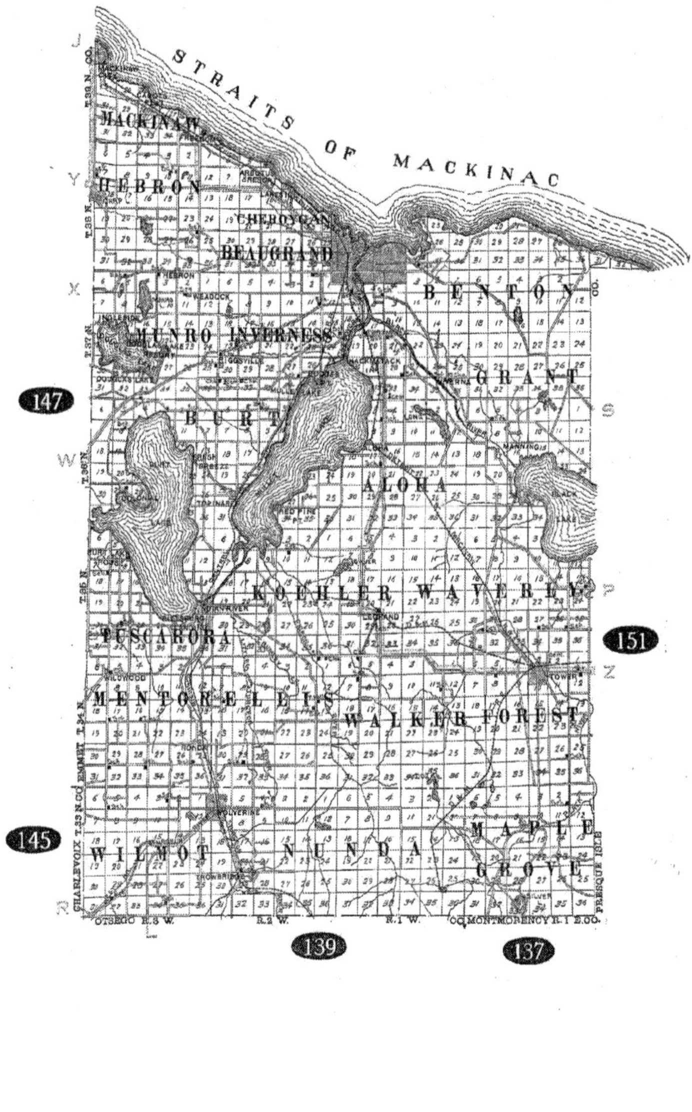

PRESQUE ISLE COUNTY.

This county was laid out in 1840, and was organized in 1871. The county was so named from the narrow peninsula—presque isle—jutting out into Lake Huron toward the southern end of the county. It is located in the extreme northeastern part of the Lower Peninsula and is bounded on the north by Cheboygan county and Lake Huron, on the east by Lake Huron, on the south by Montmorency and Alpena counties, and on the west by Cheboygan county. The total land area is 428,874.97 acres. About 182,000 acres are already in good farms. The population of the county is 11,249 (1910 census). In 1911, the state board of tax commissioners placed a valuation of $5,457,792 on all taxable land. There are a total of fifty schools, 2,360 scholars in attendance, requiring 74 teachers. The county has four banks and four weekly newspapers, also telephone, telegraph and rural mail service.

Rogers, the judicial seat of the county, has a population of about 700. It is located on the shore of Lake Huron, thirty-five miles northwest of Alpena, forty-five southeast of Cheboygan, and eleven and three-quarter miles from Metz Depot on the Detroit & Mackinac Railroad. It has Methodist, Lutheran and Catholic churches, a bank and a weekly newspaper.

The largest town in the county is Onaway, which has about 2,700 inhabitants. It is located on the Detroit & Mackinac Railway, twenty-seven miles southwest of Rogers, twenty-six miles southeast of Cheboygan, and forty-six miles northwest of Alpena, in the midst of timbered lands, agricultural lands and trout streams. It has Episcopal, Methodist, Baptist and Catholic churches, good schools, municipally-owned electric light and water plant, opera house, two public halls, good hotels, two banks and two weekly newspapers. The industries include manufactories of bicycle and automobile steering wheel rims, cooperage, saw mills, a foundry and machine shop, shingle mills, handle factory, stave and heading mills, planing mill, hoop mill, etc. Onaway is located near two of the best trout streams in northern Michigan—the Black and Rainy rivers.

Millersburg, with its 550 inhabitants, is located on the Detroit & Mackinac Railway, and on the Ocqueoc river, eighteen miles southwest of Rogers, and midway between Alpena and Cheboygan. It has Methodist, Presbyterian and Catholic churches, a graded public school, a bank and a weekly newspaper. The principal transportation facility of the county is the Detroit & Mackinac Railroad.

PRESQUE ISLE COUNTY

MICHIGAN

ONAWAY.
Onaway State Savings Bank. Capital $20,000, Surplus and Profits $30,000.

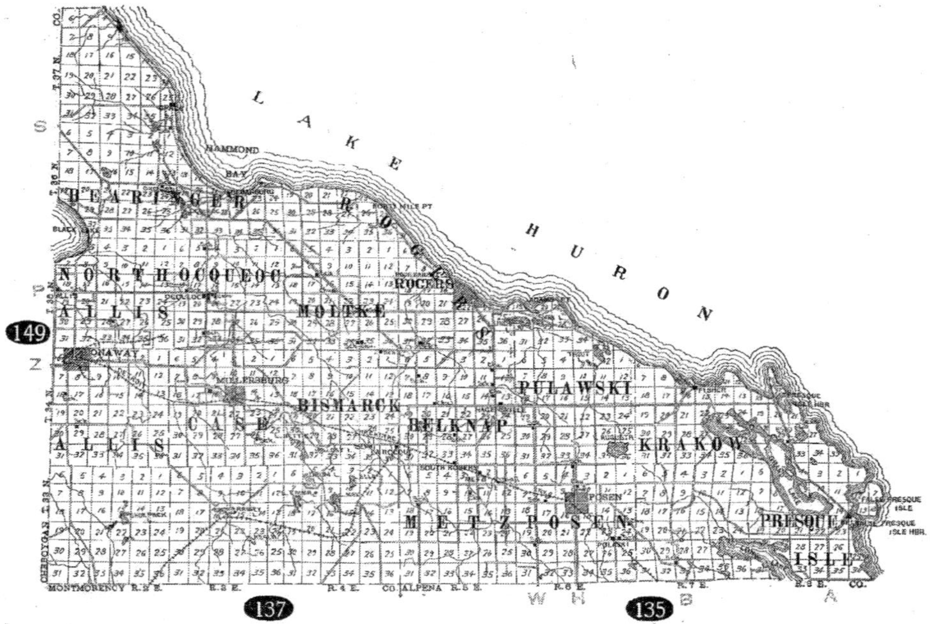

MACKINAC COUNTY

Mackinac county was laid out and organized in 1818. The county was first called Michilimackinac, in memory of an ancient Indian tribe which at one time occupied this territory. Later, the name was changed to that which it now bears. This county is located in about the southeastern part of the Upper Peninsula. It is bounded on the north by Luce and Chippewa counties, on the east by Chippewa county, on the south by Lake Michigan, Straits of Mackinac and Lake Huron, and on the west by Schoolcraft county. The total land area is 650,2255.42 acres, of which about 59,000 acres have been converted into good farms. The population of the county is 9,249 (1910 census). The valuation of taxable land, as estimated by the state board of tax commissioners in 1911, is $8,001,963. There are 60 schools, which were attended by 1,980 pupils last year, requiring the services of 77 teachers. The county has two banks and two weekly newspapers, also good telegraph, telephone and rural mail service.

St. Ignace has about 2,500 inhabitants and is the largest town and also the judicial seat of the county. It is located on the Duluth, South Shore & Atlantic Railroad, and the car ferries which run from St. Ignace to Mackinac City connect with the Michigan Central and the Grand Rapids & Indiana Railroads. It has fine, broad streets, good cement walks, electric lights, the purest of water, a bank and two newspapers.

St. Ignace has won the reputation of being one of the finest and most healthful summer resorts in the Upper Peninsula, and the thousands of people who visit here annually enjoy her natural beauty. In the woodland lakes and trout streams, hidden in the nearby forests, are perch, black bass, pike, pickerel, Mackinac trout and brook trout. A large amount of shipping passes through her waters on the way to and from Chicago, Buffalo, Detroit and Duluth.

Mackinac island is picturesquely located on the south shore of Mackinac county, in the straits of Mackinac, 18 miles northwest of Cheboygan, 5½ from St. Ignace, the nearest rail approach, and 9 from Mackinaw. The island is famous as a summer resort and is a paradise for the lover of outdoor sports, boating and fishing. Among its historic landmarks is Mackinac Island Park, ceded by the United States to the state of Michigan for the purpose of a state park. The park comprises old Fort Mackinac, with 35 buildings, the military reservation of 104 acres and the old National Park of 911 acres. Fort Mackinac is the second oldest fortification now standing in the United States. The religions are represented by churches of the Episcopal, Catholic and Union Mission denominations. There is also a public school.

Transportation facilities of the county include the Minneapolis, St. Paul & Sault Ste. Marie; Duluth, South Shore & Atlantic and Manistique Railroads, and the Arnold Steamship Line, Northern Michigan Transportation Company, Goodrich Transportation Company, Erie and Michigan Railway and Navigation Company, Canadian, Atlantic Transportation Company, Mutual Transportation Company and the Detroit & Cleveland Navigation Company.

MACKINAC COUNTY

MICHIGAN

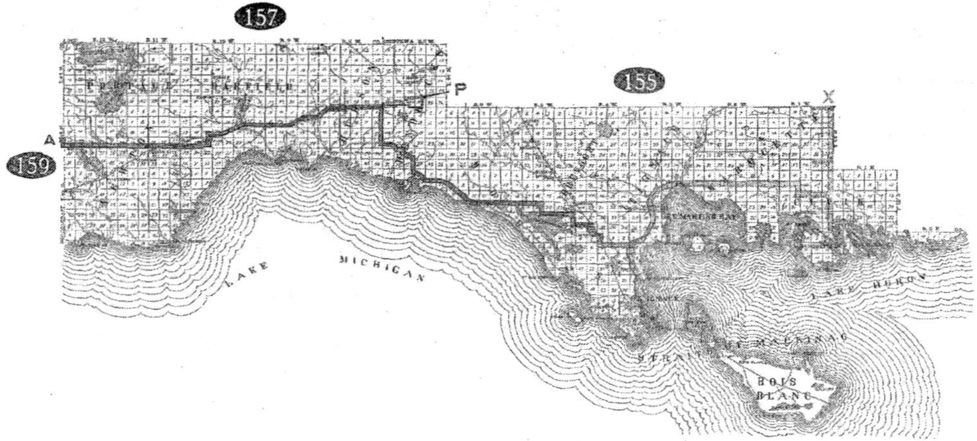

CHIPPEWA COUNTY.

Chippewa county was laid out and organized in 1826, and was at one time part of Michilimackinac county. The name was taken from the Chippewa Ojibway Indians, the largest of the Algonquin tribes. The county is located in the extreme eastern part of the Upper Peninsula and is bounded on the north by Lake Superior and White Fish bay, on the east by Lake George, St. Mary's river, Mud lake, and a portion of the North channel, on the south by Mackinac county and Lake Huron, and on the west by Luce county. The county has a total land area of 999,960.22 acres, with about 176,000 acres devoted to farms. A considerable acreage of the agricultural land in Chippewa county is being very successfully devoted to dairying and stock raising. The federal census of 1910 gives Chippewa county a population of 24,472. In 1911, the state board of tax commissioners placed a valuation of $19,784,939 on all taxable lands in the county. There is a good school system throughout the county, there being 90 schools, requiring 166 teachers, and last year's records show a total of 5,516 children in attendance. In the county may be found good telegraph, telephone, and rural mail service. There are 5 banks, 1 daily and 2 weekly newspapers.

Sault Ste. Marie is the judicial seat of the county, as well as being the largest city, and has a population of 12,615 (1910 census). It is located on the St. Mary's river, near the outlet of Lake Superior, opposite the famous Sault rapids, 170 miles east of Marquette. Here is the location of one of the greatest ship canals in the world through which commerce of the Great lakes passes on its way to and from Lake Superior and Lake Huron. The city's position on the St. Mary's river on a series of rapids which made necessary the ship canal is responsible for a second great attraction at this point—the power canal with all its attendant possibilities. In this enterprise is realized the utilization of the natural forces inherent in the waters of Lake Superior as they flow over a sandstone rock ledge about half a mile long and half a mile wide, with a fall of twenty feet. Water power developments have been planned, attempted and carried out and locks by which boats have been enabled to pass these falls have been constructed and operated during the past one hundred years, but it has been left to this day and generation to witness the practical consummation of the greatest possibilities in both directions, since of this formerly dormant power more than half has now been brought under control, while locks are now in operation and being improved, capable of passing, up and down, the largest fleet of merchant carrying vessels on the face of the globe.

Lake Superior covers an area of some 30,000 square miles, fed from a water shed of hundreds of thousands of square miles, the Sault rapids being its only outlet. The quantity discharged fluctuates with the varying conditions of precipitation and evaporation, from about 3,000,000 to 7,000,000 cubic feet per minute, which, rushing over the Sault rapids, represents an equivalent of 130,000 to 260,000 horsepower. The freight movement to and from Lake Superior consists largely of such commodities as hard and soft coal, ore, wheat and lumber. The total tonnage of these commodities that passed through the canal during the season of 1912 was 72,472,676 net tons, an increase of 18,955,400 tons over the shipments of the year previous. The work of widening the Soo ship canal is now under way.

Sault Ste. Marie is lighted by electricity, has a complete sewerage system, efficient fire department, and the purest water is supplied by a $200,000 system of water works. There are churches of the Baptist, Catholic, Disciples, Episcopal, Finnish and Swedish Evangelical Lutheran, Free Methodist, Methodist Episcopal and Presbyterian denominations, a high school and six ward schools, a public library, a handsome court house which was erected at a cost of about $75,000, a city hall, a beautiful new federal building, well laid out streets, three banks, first class hotels, a daily and two weekly newspapers. Situated as it is, among ideal surroundings, "The Soo" has gained the reputation of being one of the finest summer resorts in the country.

The shipping facilities of the county are exceptionally good and include the Minneapolis, St. Paul & Sault Ste. Marie and the Duluth, South Shore & Atlantic Railroads, the Erie & Michigan Railway and Navigation Company, Northern Michigan Navigation Company, Erie & Western Transportation Company, Northern Steamship Line, Canadian Pacific Steamship Company, the Mutual Anchor Line and the C. D. & G. B. Transportation Company.

CHIPPEWA COUNTY

MICHIGAN

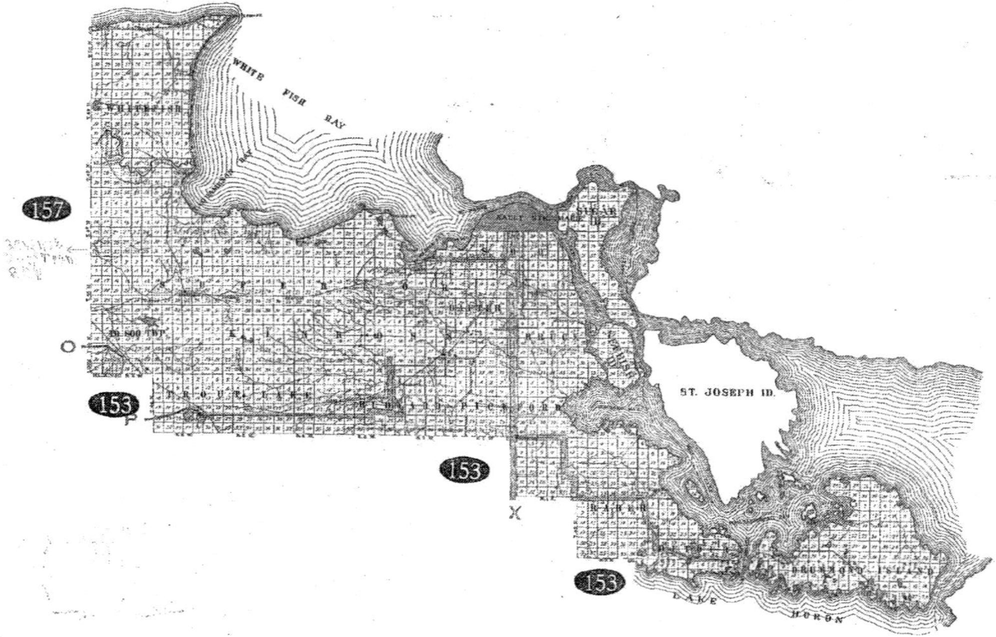

LUCE COUNTY.

Luce county was laid out and organized in 1887, after being separated from Chippewa and Mackinac counties, of which it was a part. It was named in honor of Cyrus G. Luce, then governor of the state. The total land area of the county is 582,654.15 acres. Of this number, about 21,000 acres have already been converted into farms. This county is located in the northeastern part of the Upper Peninsula. Is bounded on the north by Lake Superior, on the east by Chippewa county, on the south by Mackinac county, and on the west by Alger and Schoolcraft counties. The population is 4,004 (1910 census). The valuation of taxable property, as estimated by the state board of tax commissioners in 1911, is $6,256,418. The county has 17 schools, an enrollment of 902 students, requiring the services of 38 teachers. There is one bank and one weekly newspaper, while telegraph, telephone and rural mail service add to the conveniences.

Newberry is the county seat, also the largest town, population, 1,800. It is located on the Duluth, South Shore & Atlantic Railroad, 55 miles northwest of St. Ignace, 56 southwest of Sault Ste. Marie and 96 southeast of Marquette. It has good system of water works, electric lights, churches of the Episcopal, Presbyterian, Methodist, Lutheran and Catholic denominations, a graded public school, an opera house, a bank and a weekly newspaper. Newberry is surrounded by good agricultural lands and is rapidly developing, being settled by a prosperous farming community. The Upper Peninsula Hospital for the insane is located here. The principal transportation facility of the county is the Duluth, South Shore & Atlantic Railroad.

LUCE COUNTY

MICHIGAN

NEWBERRY.
Newberry Garage. Special Attention to Tourists.
Newberry Hotel. Rates, $2 and $2.50 with Bath. Special Attention to Tourists.

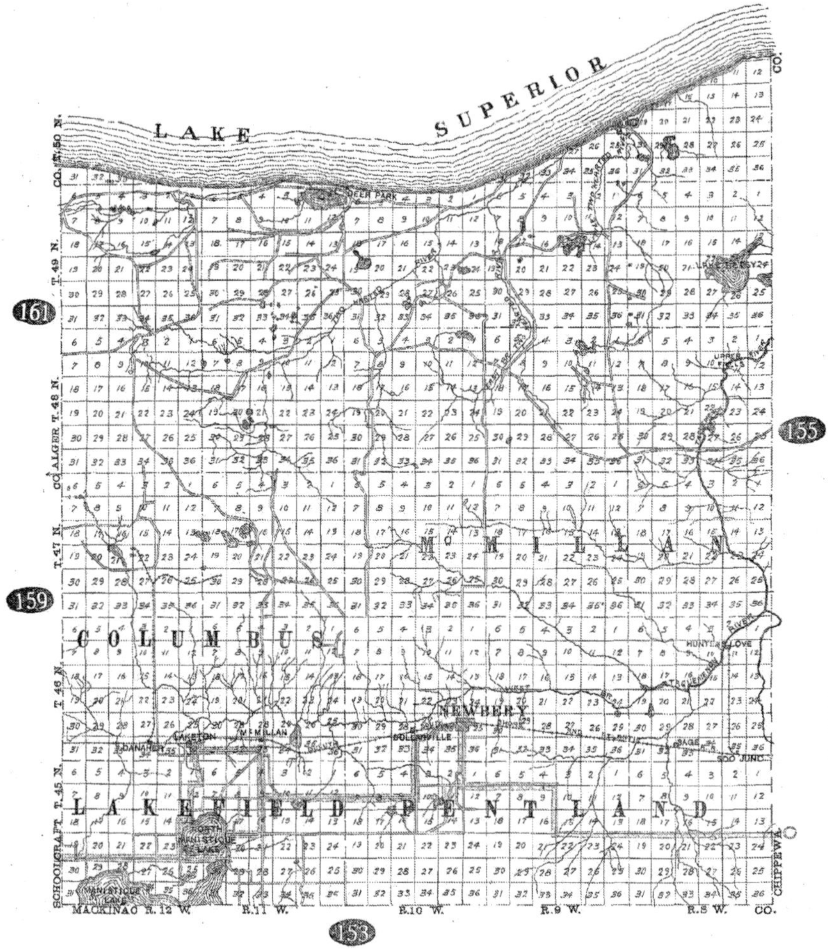

SCHOOLCRAFT COUNTY.

This county was laid out and organized in 1843 and was named in honor of Henry Rowe Schoolcraft, whose name is associated with his researches in all matters connected with the Indians. This county is located in about the central part of the Upper Peninsula. It is bounded on the north by Alger county, on the east by Luce and Mackinac counties, on the south by Lake Michigan and on the west by Alger and Delta counties. The total land area is 758,095.70 acres, of which about 46,000 acres are now in good farms. Population, 8,681 (1910 census). The valuation of taxable property, as estimated by the state board of tax commissioners in 1911, is $8,390,564. The school system is equal to that of many of the larger counties, there being 34 schools, an enrollment of 1,848 students requiring the services of 79 teachers. The county has two banks and two weekly newspapers, telegraph, telephone and rural mail service.

Manistique, the largest city and judicial seat of the county, has a population of about 5,000. It occupies a beautiful location on the shore of Lake Michigan, at the mouth of the Manistique river, 90 miles by water from St. Ignace, 107 from Sault Ste. Marie and 269 from Chicago. It is a station on the Milwaukee, St. Paul & Sault Ste. Marie Railway, and on the Manistee & Northeastern railroads. The city is electrically and gas lighted, has a good sewer system, a fine system of water works, well equipped fire department, beautiful churches of the leading denominations, an opera house, hospital, a splendid school system, two banks and two progressive newspapers. The principal industries include lumber mills, chemical works, lime factory, box factory, tannery, planing mills, etc. The magnificent areas of scenery, good hunting and fishing has made Manistique well known as a summer resort.

Transportation facilities of the county include the Duluth, South Shore & Atlantic Railway, Manistique Railway, Ann Arbor Car Ferry, Manistee & Lake Superior Railway, and the Minneapolis, St. Paul & Sault Ste. Marie Railway.

SCHOOLCRAFT COUNTY

MICHIGAN

MANISTIQUE.
Haggins Garage and Repair Shop.

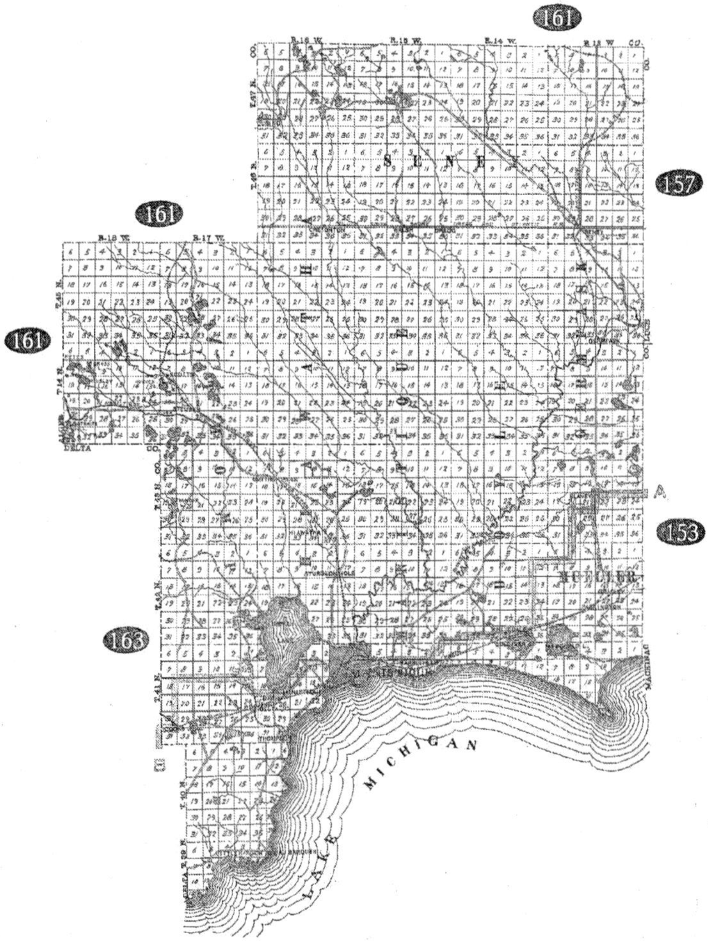

ALGER COUNTY.

Alger county was laid out and organized in 1885 and was named in honor of Russell A. Alger, then governor of Michigan, and afterwards secretary of war and United States senator. This county is located in the northern part of the Upper Peninsula and is bounded on the north and part of the west by Lake Superior. The total land area of the county is 589,948.58 acres, having about 30,000 already converted into farms. The valuation of taxable property as estimated by the state board of tax commissioners in 1911, is $9,436,997. The population is 7,675 (1910 census).

There are a total of 29 schools, which were attended by 1,545 children last year, requiring the services of 61 teachers. The county has telephone and telegraph service, two banks and one newspaper, which is published at Munising.

Munising is the county seat and has a population of about 3,000. It is located on the Munising, Marquette & Southeastern Railway; Duluth, South Shore & Atlantic Railway, and the Minneapolis, St. Paul & Sault Ste. Marie Railroad. There are churches of different denominations, a high school building, costing about $60,000, water works, electric lighting plant, opera house, a live weekly newspaper, two banks, and a court house, costing about $40,000. The industries include lumber mills, woodenware plant, a tannery and a paper factory which is one of the most modern in the United States. The plant is in operation night and day and is run by electricity. The streams throughout the county are planted each year with brook trout and the nearby lakes teem with bass and perch, making Munising one of the best fishing spots in Michigan.

Grand Marais, on the shore of Lake Superior has a population of about 1,000. The village is lighted by elecricity, has a fire department and a municipal pumping station. Water pipes are laid in all streets and water is furnished to every resident free, absolutely no charge being made and no restrictions as to how much is used or for what purpose. There are churches of the Catholic, Methodist and Episcopal denominations, excellent schools, opera house, hotels, telephone exchange, etc. Lumbering is the principal industry and fishing is extensively carried on.

The principal transportation facilities of the county are the Munising, Marquette & Southeastern Railway, Duluth, South Shore & Atlantic Railway, and the Minneapolis, St. Paul & Sault Ste. Marie Railway.

ALGER COUNTY

MICHIGAN

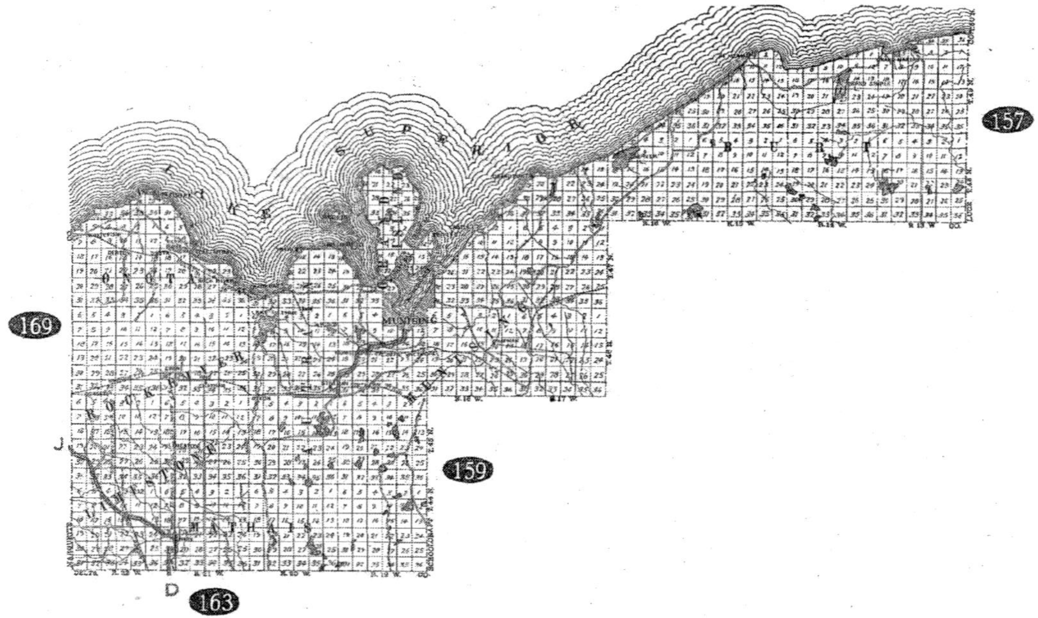

DELTA COUNTY.

Delta county was laid out in 1843 and was organized in 1861. The county as originally laid out included not only the present territory, but also Menominee and part of Dickinson, Marquette and Iron counties, giving it the shape of the Greek letter "Delta" from which the county takes its name. It is located in the south central part of the Upper Peninsula. Is bounded on the north by Alger county, on the east by Schoolcraft county and Lake Michigan; on the south by that part of Lake Michigan known as Green bay, and on the west by Menominee and Marquette counties. The total land area of the county is 748,215.44 acres. Of this number, about 113,000 acres are in profitable farms. The federal census of 1910 gives Delta county a population of about 30,108. In 1911, the state board of tax commissioners placed a valuation of $18,848,782 on all taxable lands. The county has a good school system. There are 82 schools, supplying positions for 199 teachers and an enrollment of 6,776 children. There are six banks, two daily and five weekly newspapers, also good telephone, telegraph and rural mail service in the county.

Escanaba is the largest city, as well as being the capital city of the county. It has a population of about 14,000, is located on the Chicago & Northwestern and the Escanaba & Lake Superior railroads. Its situation is as beautiful as it is advantageous for commerce. It is located on a point of land dividing Green bay from Little Bay de Noc, the latter forming one of the best harbors on the entire chain of lakes. It is easy of approach, having an entrance three miles in width and depth sufficient to float the largest vessels. The city is one of the two great shipping points for iron ore. The statistics of the port and its capabilities are almost incredible to any one who has not already something like a just appreciation of the magnitude of the iron interests of this great region. Its six enormous iron docks have a capacity of 95,000 tons, at which 30 vessels can be loaded simultaneously and from 20,000 to 30,000 tons can be shipped in twenty-four hours. The docks are lighted by electric lights and are kept in full operation day and night. There are also large merchandise and commercial docks, handling 150,000 tons of coal annually. The fish trade is an important industry, daily shipments being large.

The city is lighted by electricity, has broad and well paved streets, water works, fire and police departments, electric street railway, 2 Baptist, 3 Catholic, Episcopal, 4 Lutheran, 2 Methodist, Presbyterian and Swedish Mission churches, a high school building costing about $40,000, a public library, hospital, first class hotels, a handsome court house costing about $27,000, 2 daily and 4 weekly newspapers, 3 banks, 3 theaters, etc. Good farming and hardwood timber land lies within a few miles of the city and the Escanaba river which rises in the iron region and here flows into the lake, furnishes splendid water power.

Other towns of importance are Gladstone, population 4,211; Garden, Ford River and other small but thriving towns. Gladstone is located on the west shore of Little Bay de Noc, seven miles north of Escanaba with which it is connected by electric railway. It is a station on the main line of the Milwaukee, St. Paul & Sault Ste. Marie railroad. Has a municipal electric lighting plant, a water works plant built at a cost exceeding $35,000, fire department, opera house, two banks and two weekly newspapers. Has churches of the Congregational, Baptist, Catholic, Evangelical Lutheran, Methodist, Presbyterian, Swedish, Finnish Baptist and Swedish Mission denominations. Excellent boating, bathing and fishing make this city an ideal summer resort. The Soo Line has made this point its water terminus and has erected a grain elevator, flour, iron and coal docks, which are among the largest individual docks on the lakes.

The transportation facilities of the county are the Minneapolis, St. Paul & Sault Ste. Marie, Chicago & Northwestern, Escanaba Traction Company, and the Escanaba & Lake Superior railroads, the Arnold Steamship Line, and the Goodrich Steamship Company.

DELTA COUNTY

MICHIGAN

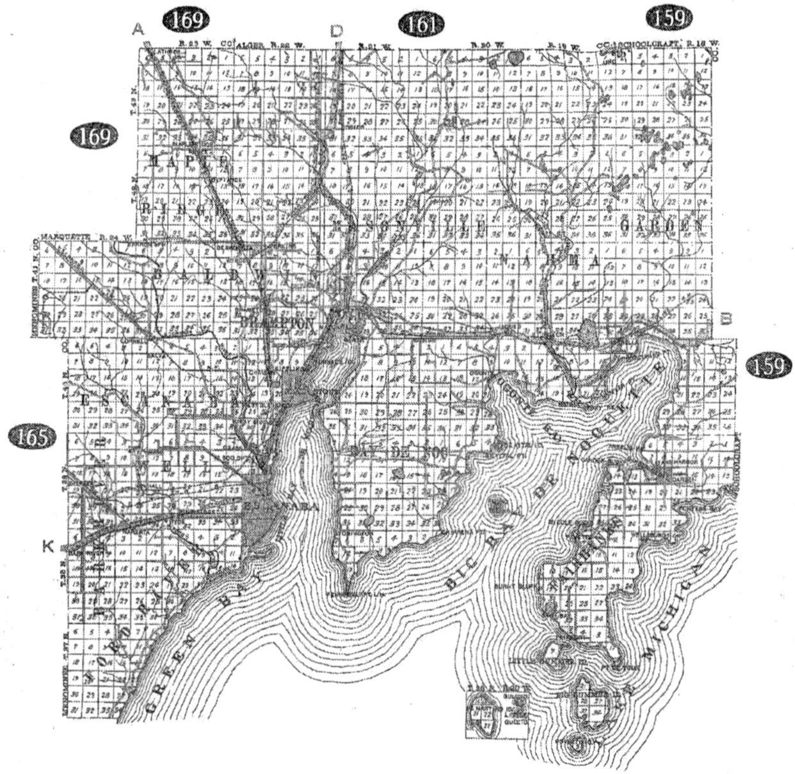

MENOMINEE COUNTY.

Menominee county was laid out by the Legislature in 1861 as Bleeker county, but the following session, in 1863, it was organized and the name changed to that which it now bears. The word Menominee is derived from the Chippewas and means "good grain." It is located in the extreme south central part of the Upper Peninsula. Is bounded on the north by Dickinson, Marquette and Delta counties, on the east by Delta county and Green bay, on the south by Green bay and Wisconsin, and on the west by Wisconsin and Dickinson counties. The total land area is 670,297.43 acres. Of this number, about 168,000 acres are devoted to fine productive farms. The population is 25,648 (1910 census). The valuation of taxable property, as estimated by the state board of tax commissioners in 1911, is $19,678,938. There are 101 schools, attended by 6,445 students, requiring 195 teachers. The county has six banks, one daily and two weekly newspapers, also good telegraph, telephone and rural mail service.

Menominee, the county seat and largest city, has about 12,000 inhabitants. It is prettily located at the mouth of Menominee river, on the shore of Green bay, on the Chicago & Northwestern, Chicago, Milwaukee & St. Paul and the Wisconsin & Michigan Railroads, 264 miles from Chicago and 187 from Marquette. The city is lighted by electricity and gas, has good water works system, paved streets, splendid sewerage system, a well-equipped fire department, a public library, first-class hotels, a postoffice completed at a cost of about $50,000, an opera house, three banks, one newspaper, etc. The manufacturing industries include an immense beet sugar plant, one of the largest manufactories of children's vehicles in the United States, the second largest saw-mill-machinery manufactory and steel casting plant in the country, an electric manufacturing plant, one of the largest and best-equipped canning plants in the world, also several smaller industries. There are churches of the Episcopal, Methodist, Presbyterian, Baptist, German Methodist, Lutheran, Norwegian Lutheran, Catholic, Seventh Day Adventist, Swedish Lutheran and Swedish Methodist denominations. There are nine public schools, a high school building costing $65,000. The Menominee County School of Agriculture and Domestic Science is located here. The surrounding country is a productive agricultural section.

Other towns of the county are Daggett and Stephenson. The principal transportation facilities of the county are the Chicago & Northwestern, Wisconsin & Michigan, Minneapolis, St. Paul & Sault Ste. Marie and the Chicago, Milwaukee & St. Paul Railroads.

MENOMINEE COUNTY

MICHIGAN

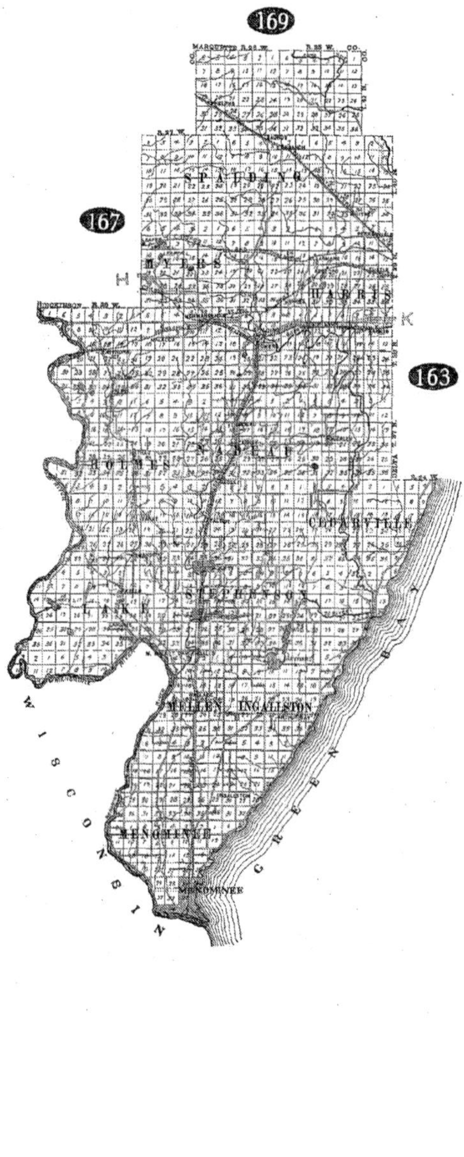

DICKINSON COUNTY.

Dickinson county, which was at one time part of Menominee, Iron and Marquette counties, was organized in 1891, and was named in honor of Postmaster General Don M. Dickinson. The county is located in the south central part of the Upper Peninsula and is bounded on the north by Marquette county, on the east by Marquette and Menominee counties, on the south by Menominee county and Wisconsin and on the west by Iron county and Wisconsin. The total land area of the county is 491,925.00 acres. Of this number, about 24,000 acres are devoted to farms. The 1910 census gives the county a population of 20,524. In 1911, the state board of tax commissioners placed a valuation of $23,132,495 on all taxable land in the county. There are a total of 44 schools, requiring the services of 164 teachers and an enrollment of 5,560 children. The county has three banks, one daily and three weekly newspapers.

Iron Mountain is the judicial seat and the largest city in the county. It has a population of about 10,000, and is located on the Chicago & Northwestern and the Chicago, Milwaukee and St. Paul Railroads, 72 miles northwest of Menominee. It is lighted by electricity and gas, has water works, fire department and excellent sewerage. There are churches of the Baptist, Catholic, Episcopal, German Lutheran, Methodist Episcopal, Presbyterian; Swedish Mission, Swedish Methodist, Swedish Baptist and Swedish Lutheran denominations, nine handsome school buildings, a library costing $20,000, a fine opera house, an $85,000 county building, two banks, a daily newspaper, etc. The Actual Business College, located here, occupies a prominent place among the commercial educational institutions of the state.

This is the location of the famous Chapin iron mine, one of the largest and best in the Upper Peninsula, producing a very rich hematite ore, from which is made the best Bessemer iron and steel. The mine is worked at a depth of about 1,500 feet. The plant is of the most modern description, and immense hydraulic machinery, costing about $500,000, has been constructed to convey compressed air into the mine and is used for operating all machinery connected with the mine. There are other iron mines surrounding the city and, with carriage and wagon works, cement works, etc., are the principal industries of the place.

Norway, another town in Dickinson county, has a population of about 5,000, is located on the Chicago & Northwestern and the Michigan & Wisconsin railroads, eight miles east of Iron Mountain. Mining, farming and lumbering are the principal industries. There are churches of the Baptist, Catholic, Lutheran, Methodist Episcopal, Norwegian and Swedish Mission denominations, good schools, a convent, a bank and one weekly newspaper.

Vulcan, also in Dickinson county, with a population estimated at nearly 3,000, is located on the Chicago & Northwestern railway, ten miles southwest of Iron Mountain, the county seat, and two miles from Norway. Among the principal industries are the manufacture of brick and the mining and handling of iron ore in large quantities. There are churches of several denominations. The transportation facilities of Dickinson county are the Escanaba & Lake Superior, Chicago & Northwestern, Chicago, Milwaukee & St. Paul, and the Wisconsin & Michigan railroads.

DICKINSON COUNTY

MICHIGAN

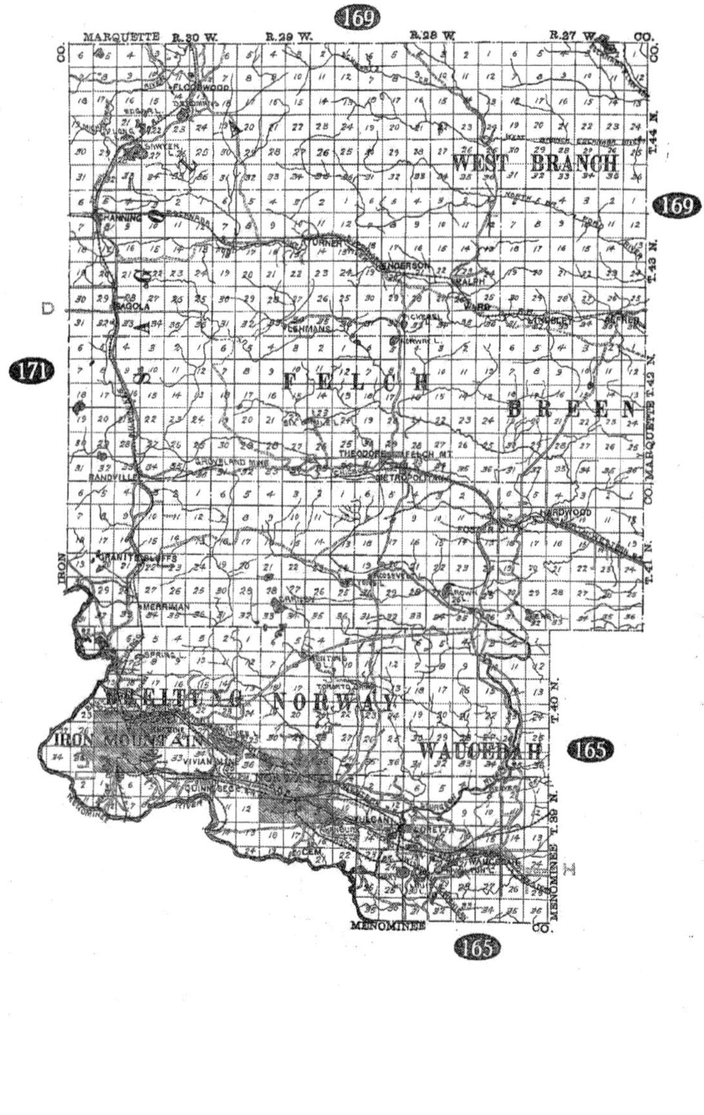

MARQUETTE COUNTY.

Marquette county was laid out in 1843 and was organized in 1851 and was named in honor of Father Jaques Marquette, who established several missions among the Indians. It is located in the northern part of the Upper Peninsula, is bounded on the north by Lake Superior, east by Alger and Delta counties, south by Dickinson, Menominee and Delta counties, and west by Iron and Baraga counties. The total land area is 1,182,851.15 acres. Of this number, about 68,000 acres are in farms. The total population is 46,739 (1910 census). In 1911, the state board of tax commissioners placed a valuation of $74,089,264 on all taxable lands. The county has 92 schools, furnishing positions for 342 teachers, and a total enrollment of 10,253 students. There are ten banks, two daily and six weekly newspapers. There is also good telegraph, telephone and rural mail service.

Marquette is the county seat and has about 12,000 inhabitants. It is picturesquely located on the south shore of Lake Superior on an inlet known as Marquette Bay, 170 miles west of Sault Ste. Marie. It is the metropolis of the mining interests of the Lake Superior iron region. The first iron dock was built in 1845.

This city is the general headquarters of the Duluth, South Shore & Atlantic Railroad, also the home office of the Lake Superior and Ishpeming Railway. It has wide and well-laid-out streets, a complete sewerage system, thoroughly equipped fire department, good water works, police department, municipal light and power plant, a public library, a normal school library, an opera house, a $250,000 court house, first-class hotels, three hospitals, a $60,000 city hall. This is also the location of the Upper Peninsula State Prison and House of Correction. The school property includes ten buildings, the high school, which includes the manual training school, costing about $100,000. There are churches of the leading denominations, also three banks, one weekly and two daily newspapers.

The manufacturing interests comprise iron works, foundry and machine shops, saw- and planing-mills, brewery, powder plant, charcoal works, carriage and wagon works, boiler and sheet iron works, gas light plant, etc. There is also a large stone quarry within the city limits.

Ishpeming, the largest city in the county, has a population of about 12,448 (1910 census). It is located on the Duluth, South Shore & Atlantic, Chicago & Northwestern and the Lake Superior & Ishpeming Railroads, 15 miles southwest of Marquette and three west of Negaunee. It is the largest city and one of the most important mining centers in the Lake Superior iron district, having located within its corporate limits eight iron mines; there is also a smelting furnace, a boiler shop, carriage and wagon factories, etc. There are churches of the leading denominations, good public and parochial schools, an opera house, a public library. The city is lighted by gas and electricity, has a good water works system, efficient fire department, two banks, four weekly newspapers, etc.

Negaunee has a population of about 8,460 (1910 census). It is located on the Duluth, South Shore & Atlantic, Chicago & Northwestern and the Lake Superior & Ishpeming Railways, in the heart of the iron district, twelve miles southwest of Marquette and three from Ishpeming. The city is lighted by electricity, has water works, a well-equipped fire department, Episcopal, Methodist, Presbyterian, Catholic, Swedish and Finnish Lutheran churches, six school buildings, an opera house, a library, three banks and a weekly newspaper.

The principal transportation facilities of the county are the Chicago, Milwaukee & St. Paul, Escanaba & Lake Superior, Chicago & Northwestern, Munising, Marquette & Southeastern, Lake Superior & Ishpeming, and the Duluth, South Shore & Atlantic Railroads, the Erie & Western Transportation Company and the Northern Steamship Company.

MARQUETTE COUNTY

MICHIGAN

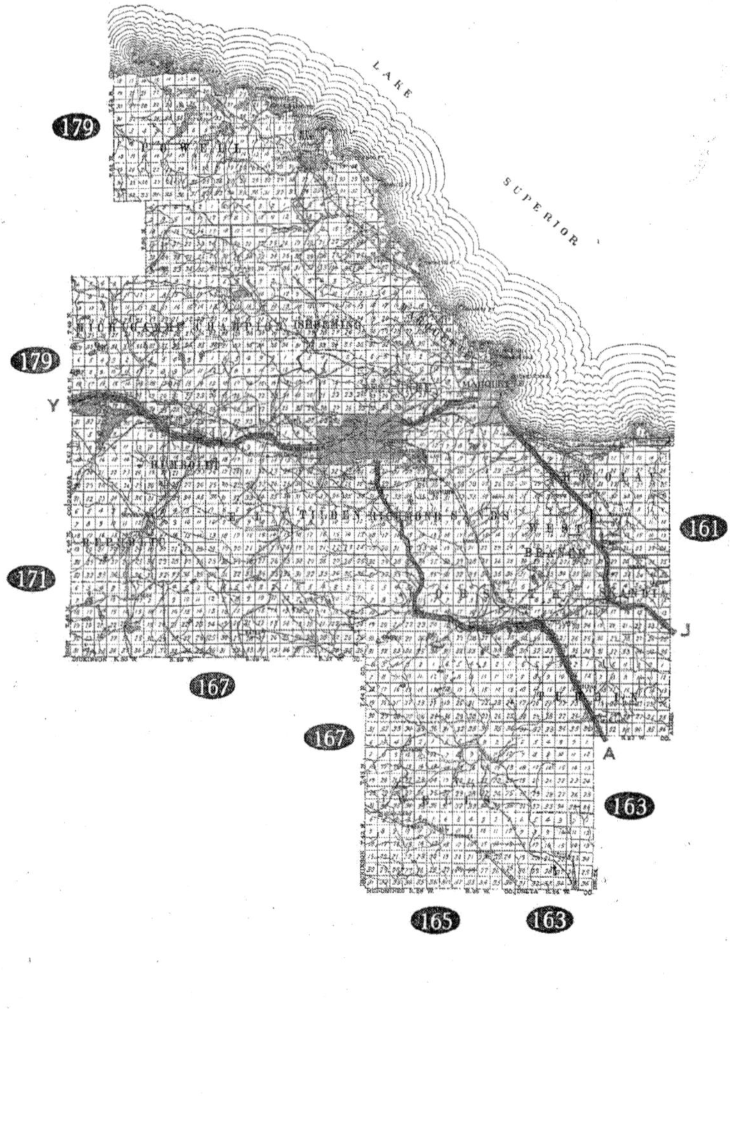

IRON COUNTY.

Iron county was laid out and organized in 1885. It was so named because of the heavy iron deposits which are found throughout. It is located in the southwestern part of the Upper Peninsula, is bounded on the north by Houghton and Baraga counties, on the east by Marquette and Dickinson counties, on the south by Wisconsin and on the west by Gogebic and Ontonagon counties. The total land area of the county is 760,148.11 acres. Of this number, about 80,000 acres are now devoted to farms. The population is 15,164 (1910 census). In 1911, the state board of tax commissioners placed a valuation of $30,314,143 on all taxable land. The county has 41 schools, furnishing positions for 141 teachers, and last year's records showed a total of 3,807 students in attendance. There are three banks and two weekly newspapers, also telegraph and telephone service in the county.

Crystal Falls is the largest city, also the county seat. It has a population of about 3,500. The city is located on the Paint river and on the Chicago & Northwestern and the Chicago, Milwaukee & St. Paul Railroads, 18 miles east of Iron river and 17 from Florence, Wisconsin. In the vicinity are twenty-nine iron mines. The city owns and operates its own water works and electric light plant, has a good fire department, sanitary sewerage, a good public school system, including a high school erected at a cost of about $65,000, churches of the Episcopal, Methodist, Presbyterian, Baptist, Catholic, Swedish and Finnish Lutheran and Swedish Methodist denominations, a $60,000 court house, an opera house, a bank and a weekly newspaper.

Iron River has a population of about 3,000. It is located on the Chicago & Northwestern Railroad, 17 miles west of Crystal Falls. It has churches of the following denominations: Episcopal, Methodist, Presbyterian, Swedish Baptist, Swedish Lutheran and Catholic, a good school system, including a high school erected at a cost of about $35,000, water works, fire department, a bank and a weekly newspaper. The principal transportation facilities of the county are the Chicago, Milwaukee & St. Paul and the Chicago & Northwestern Railroads.

IRON COUNTY

MICHIGAN

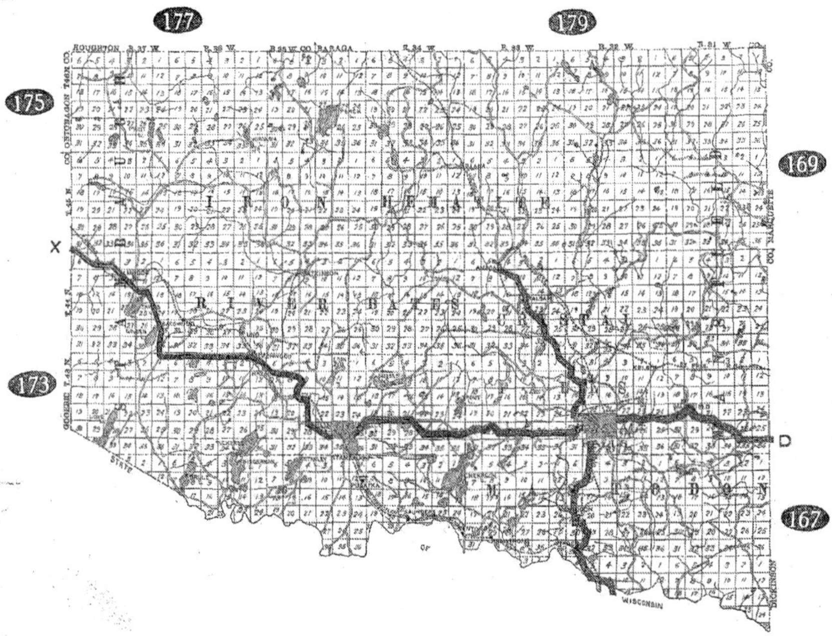

GOGEBIC COUNTY.

Gogebic county was laid out and organized in 1887 and was named for the Gogebic iron district. It is also probable that the name was taken from Lake Agogebic, which is partly in this county and partly in Ontonagon county. It is located in the extreme western part of the Upper Peninsula. It is bounded on the north by Lake Superior and Ontonagon county, on the east by Ontonagon and Iron counties, on the south by Wisconsin, and on the west by Wisconsin. The total land area of the county is 712,032.76 acres. Of this number, about 15,000 acres are in farms. The valuation of all taxable property, as is estimated by the state board of tax commissioners in 1911, is $56,467,012. The total population of the county is about 23,333 (1910 census). This county has a good school system, there being 48 schools, attended by 5,420 children, and requiring 190 teachers. There are four banks and three weekly newspapers. Good telephone and telegraph service is found in the county.

Bessemer is the capital city of the county and has a population of about 4,500. It is located on the Duluth, South Shore & Atlantic, the Minneapolis, St. Paul & Sault Ste. Marie and the Michigan & Northwestern Railways, 47 miles east of Ashland, Wisconsin. It is the center of the famous Gogebic iron range, with many large producing mines in the immediate vicinity. The city has electric light, water works, churches of the German Evangelical, Catholic, Methodist, Presbyterian, and Swedish Evangelical denominations, fine school facilities, including a new high school building, costing about $45,000, a $50,000 court house, a public library, an opera house, city hall, a bank, and a weekly newspaper.

Other cities of importance include Ironwood and Wakefield. Ironwood is the largest city in the county and has a population of about 13,000. It is located on the Chicago & Northwestern and the Minneapolis, St. Paul & Sault Ste. Marie Railroads, and on the Montreal river, a small stream which forms the boundary line between the states of Michigan and Wisconsin. Iron mining is the chief industry, there being within the city's limits several large iron mines, producing the highest grade Bessemer ore found in this country. The city is lighted by electricity, has water works, fire department, opera house, two hospitals, a bank, good hotels, churches of the Swedish Lutheran, Methodist Episcopal, Presbyterian, Sewdish Baptist, Swedish Mission, Swedish Methodist, Finnish, and Catholic denominations, ten school buildings, a manual training school, erected at a cost of about $80,000, a public library and two weekly newspapers.

Wakefield is located on the Chicago & Northwestern Railroad, six miles east of Bessemer. Has Lutheran, Methodist, and Catholic churches and a bank. Iron mining is the chief industry throughout the county.

The shipping facilities of the county are the Chicago & Northwestern, Duluth, South Shore & Atlantic, Minneapolis, St. Paul & Sault Ste. Marie Railways, and the Ironwood & Bessemer Railway and Light Co.

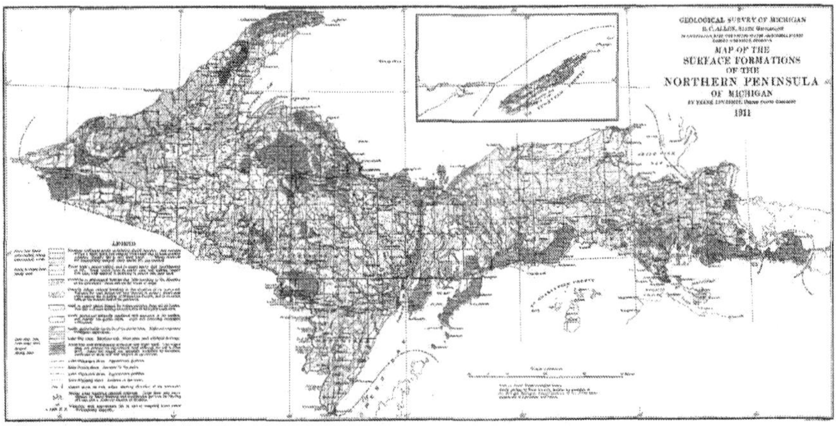
GEOLOGICAL SURVEY OF MICHIGAN
MAP OF THE
SURFACE FORMATIONS
OF THE
NORTHERN PENINSULA
OF MICHIGAN
1911
LEGEND

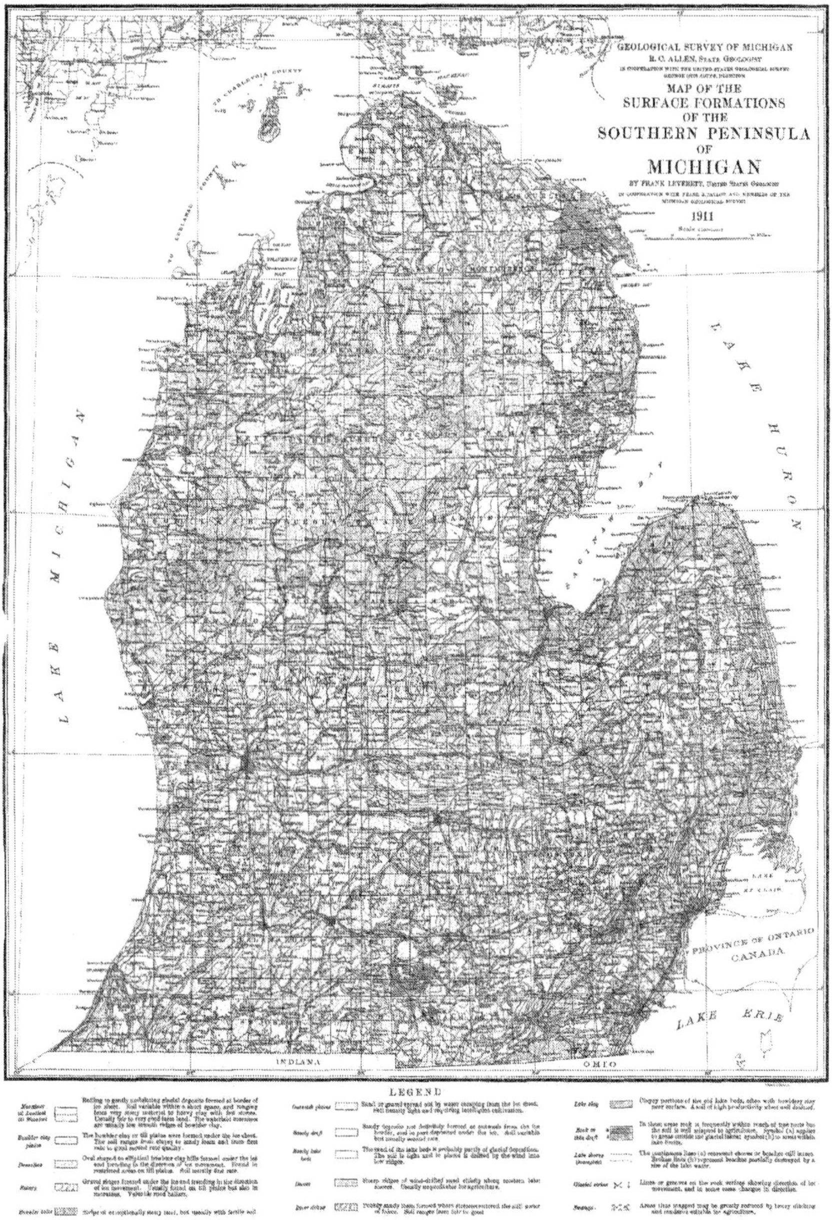
GEOLOGICAL SURVEY OF MICHIGAN
R. C. ALLEN, STATE GEOLOGIST
MAP OF THE
SURFACE FORMATIONS
OF THE
SOUTHERN PENINSULA
OF
MICHIGAN
BY FRANK LEVERETT, UNITED STATES GEOLOGIST
1911
LAKE MICHIGAN
LAKE HURON
SAGINAW BAY
LAKE ST. CLAIR
PROVINCE OF ONTARIO
CANADA
LAKE ERIE
INDIANA
OHIO
LEGEND

GOGEBIC COUNTY

MICHIGAN

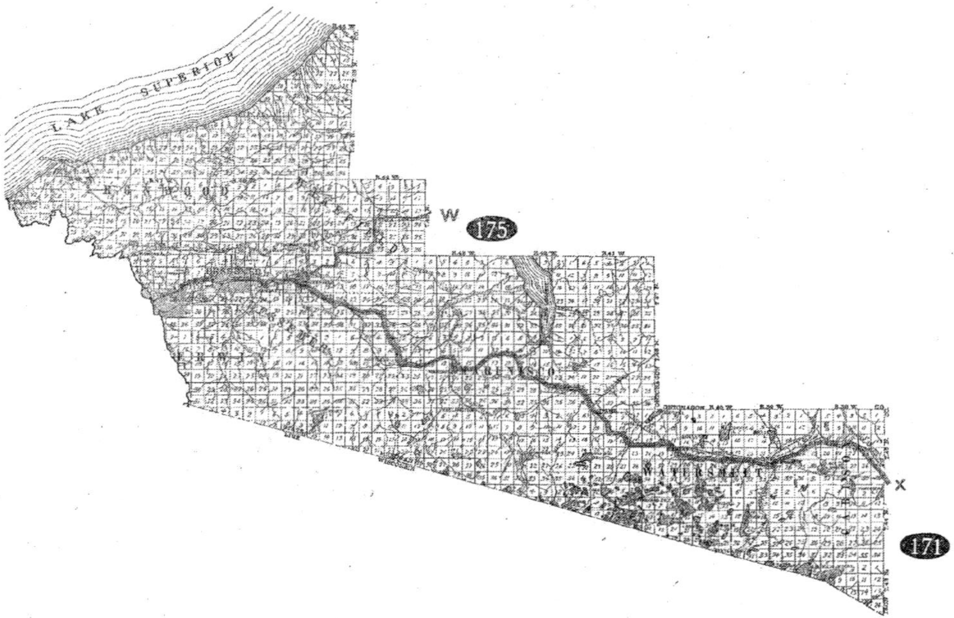

ONTONAGON COUNTY.

Ontonagon county was laid out in 1848, was organized in 1848. The county was originally much larger and included that territory known as Isle Royal. It took its name from the river of the same name, emptying into Lake Superior. The word "Ontonagon" is thought to mean "fishing place." It is located in the extreme northwestern part of the Upper Peninsula. Is bounded on the north by Lake Superior, on the east by Houghton and Iron counties, on the south by Gogebic county, and on the west by Gogebic county and Lake Superior. The total land area is 844,758.71 acres. About 39,000 acres are already in good farms. The population is 8,650 (1910 census). The valuation of taxable property, as estimated by the state board of tax commissioners in 1911, is $15,597,875. The county has a good school system. There are 55 schools, an enrollment of 2,484 students, requiring 99 teachers. There are six banks and two weekly newspapers. There is also good telephone and telegraph service.

Ontonagon is the county seat and has about 2,000 inhabitants. It is situated on the south shore of Lake Superior at the mouth of the Ontonagon river, and is a station on the Chicago, Milwaukee & St. Paul Railway. It owns and operates its own water and electric light plants, has Episcopal, Presbyterian, Methodist Episcopal, Swedish Lutheran and Roman Catholic churches, fine schools, two banks, a weekly newspaper, etc. This locality is fast becoming known as a healthful summer resort.

In the vicinity of Ontonagon are several billion feet of hemlock, pine, ash, basswood, birch, maple, elm, cedar, and other timber of the finest quality, making it a fine location for saw mills, furniture factories, stave and heading mills, tanneries, pulp and paper mills, woodenware plants, chemical plants, etc. Clays and shales for the manufacture of paving brick and fine face brick are found in abundance. The agricultural possibilities of this locality are good and fine farms are numerous. The soil is adapted to the growing of many kinds of grains, vegetables and fruits.

The principal transportation facilities of the county are the Duluth, South Shore & Atlantic, Chicago & Northwestern, Chicago, Milwaukee & St. Paul, and the Copper Range Railroad, also the United States & Dominion Transportation Company.

ONTONAGON COUNTY

MICHIGAN

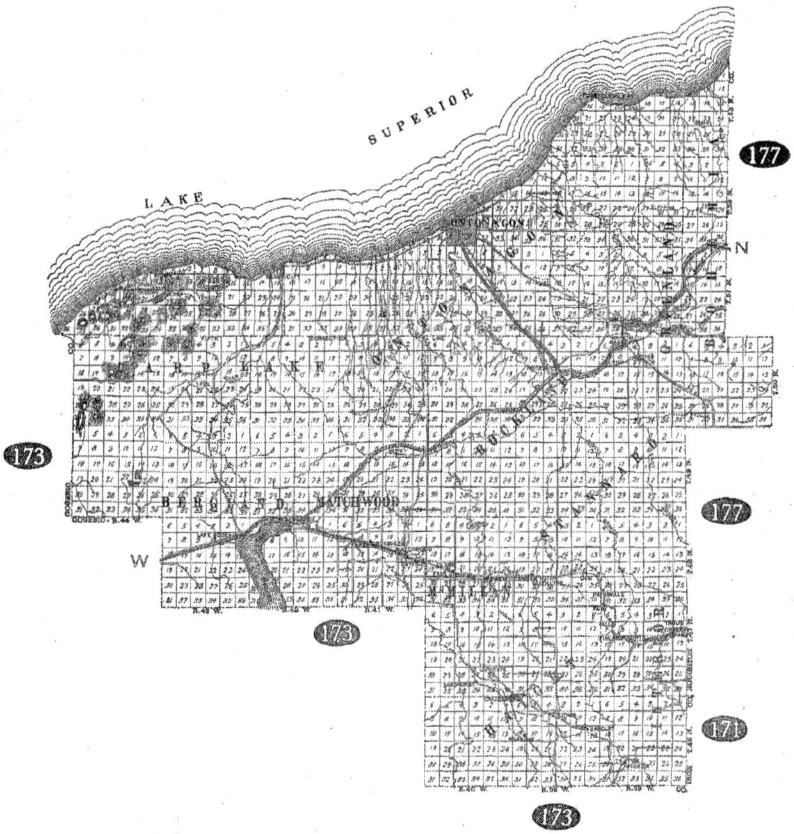

HOUGHTON COUNTY.

Houghton county was laid out and organized in 1845, and was named in honor of Douglas Houghton, first state geologist of Michigan. It is bounded on the north by Keweenaw county and Lake Superior, on the east by Keweenaw bay and Baraga county, on the south by Iron county and on the west by Ontonagon county and Lake Superior. The total land area of the county is 647,466.14 acres, of which about 95,000 acres are devoted to farms. The population is 88,098 (1910 census). The valuation of taxable property, as estimated by the state board of tax commissioners in 1911, is $117,626,097. The educational advantages offered are equal to those of any other county throughout the state. There are 135 schools, 19,169 students in attendance, requiring the services of 668 teachers. There are 13 banks, 5 daily and 8 weekly newspapers. The county also has telephone, telegraph and rural mail service.

Houghton is the county seat and has a population of about 5,500. It is located on the Duluth, South Shore & Atlantic, the Copper Range and the Mineral Range Railroads, and on the south shore of Portage lake, 14 miles from the mouth of Portage river, 10 from Lake Superior on the west and 94 northwest of Marquette. It is in the midst of the Lake Superior copper region, a strip of country four to six miles in width, extending from southwest to northwest, through the entire length of Keweenaw peninsula and beyond. This range is very rich in native copper, and some of the most productive mines in the world are located in the vicinity of the town. Houghton contains one of the finest court houses in the Upper Peninsula, a city hall, Catholic, Episcopal, Methodist Episcopal and Presbyterian churches, two banks, daily and weekly newspapers, and a public school building costing $60,000. The Michigan College of Mines is also located here.

Calumet is the largest city in the county and has a population of about 30,000. It is located on the Mineral Range, the Copper Range, the Keweenaw Central and the Hancock & Calumet Railroads, 14 miles north of Houghton and four from Lake Linden, its shipping point by water. The city is well lighted by electricity, has good police and fire departments, excellent drainage and sewer system, two systems of water works, opera house, handsome parks, two hospitals, first class hotels, splendid school system, handsome churches, three banks, two daily and three weekly newspapers. Calumet is the site of the famous Calumet and Hecla copper mine, one of the richest in the world. The machinery used for elevating the copper rock to the surface and for pumping and condensing air for the drills is all on an immense scale and of the most perfect design. The stamp mills and furnaces at Lake Linden are said to be the largest in the world.

Other important cities of the county include Laurium, population, 9,000; Hancock, population, 9,000; Hubbell, population, about 1,200, and Lake Linden, population about 2,500. The transportation facilities of the county are the Duluth, South Shore & Atlantic, Copper Range, Mineral Range, Keweenaw Central, Chicago, Milwaukee & St. Paul Railroads, Houghton Traction Company (electric), United States and Dominion Transportation Company, Erie and Western Transportation Company, Northern Steamship Company and the Mutual Transit Company.

HOUGHTON COUNTY

MICHIGAN

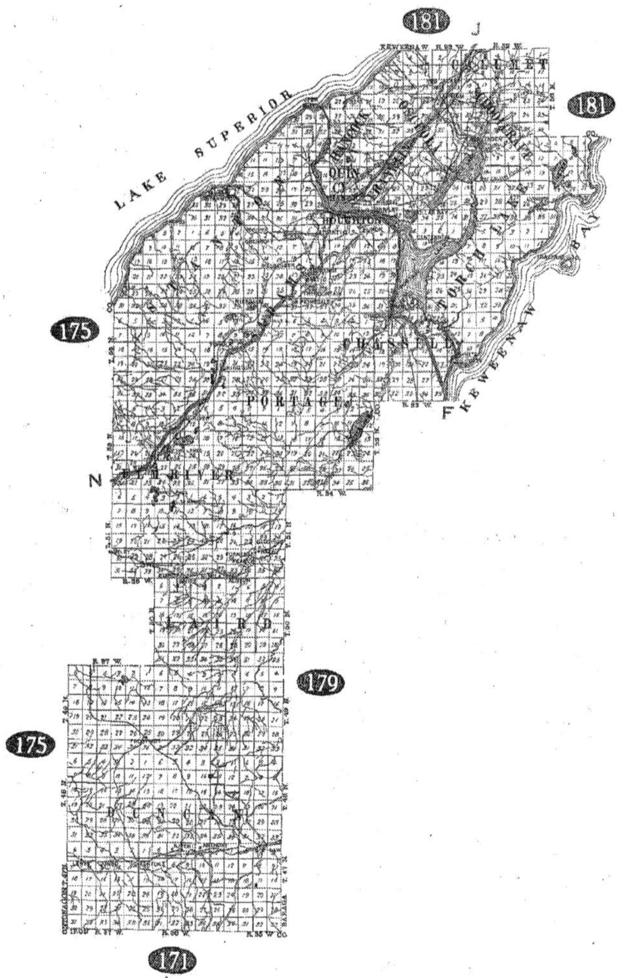

BARAGA COUNTY.

Baraga county was laid out and organized in 1875. It was named in honor of Bishop Frederick Baraga, the great Indian apostle of the Northwest, who labored among the Indians from 1831 until his death in 1868. This county is located in the northwest part of the Upper Peninsula and is bounded almost entirely on the north by that part of Lake Superior known as Keweenaw bay. It has a land area of 582,805.56 acres, of which about 35,000 acres are already in farms. The 1910 census gives Baraga a population of about 6,127. In 1911 the state board of tax commissioners placed a value of $7,613,042 on all taxable property. The county has a good school system. There are 31 schools, requiring 49 teachers, and last year's report shows a total of 1,611 children in attendance. The county has telegraph, telephone and rural mail service. There are two banks and two weekly newspapers, one published in Baraga and the other at L'Anse.

L'Anse is the judicial seat of the county and has a population of about 1,000. The town is located at the head of l'Anse bay, on the Duluth, South Shore & Atlantic Railway, 32 miles south of Houghton and 68 miles northwest of Marquette. It is almost ideal as a summer resort, with a climate delightfully cool and refreshing, and within a short distance are streams well supplied with brook trout, while deer and other game are plentiful. L'Anse has electric street lights, water works, fire department, court house, good schools, good hotel, town hall and a progressive newspaper. There are also a number of slate, graphite and brownstone quarries in the immediate vicinity.

Baraga is a station on the Duluth, South Shore & Atlantic Railway and is located on Keweenaw bay, five miles by rail or two miles across the bay from L'Anse and twenty-six miles south of Houghton. The beauty of location, the coolness of the climate and surrounded as it is by excellent trout streams, make it an ideal summer resort.

Transportation facilities are the Duluth, South Shore & Atlantic, Chicago, Milwaukee & St. Paul and the Mineral Range Railroads.

BARAGA COUNTY

MICHIGAN

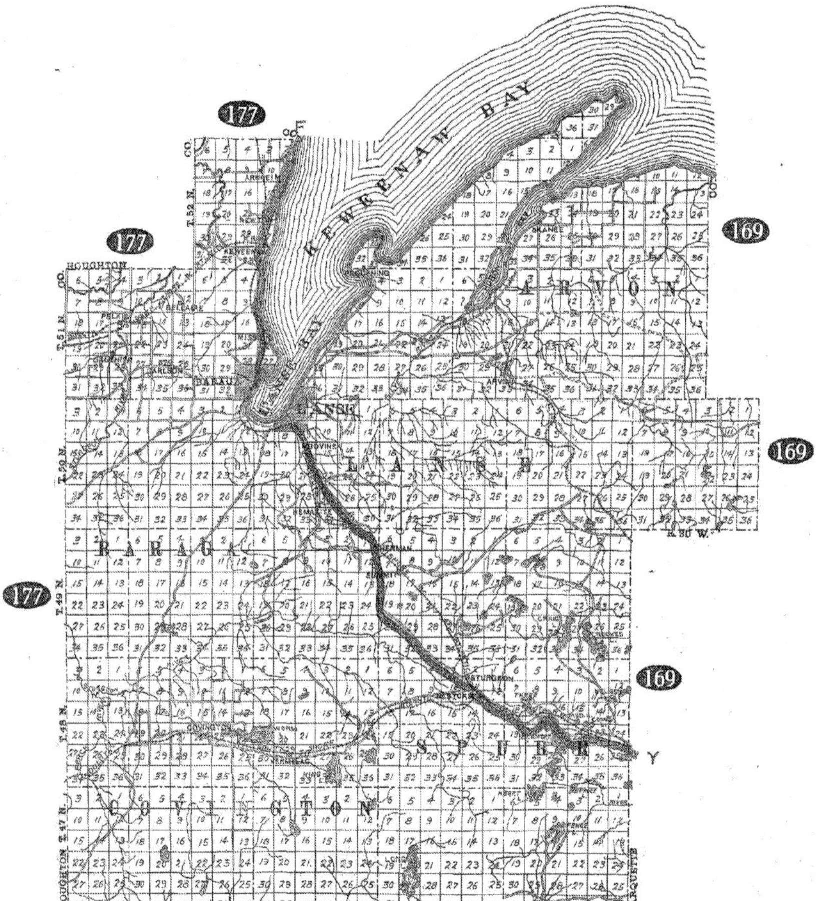

KEWEENAW COUNTY.

Keweenaw county was laid out and organized in 1861, and included Manitou and Isle Royal. The name is taken from the Indian word "Ki-wi-wai-ni-ning," meaning a portage or a place where a portage is made. This county is of peninsular formation and is located in the extreme northern part of the Upper Peninsula. It is bounded on the north, east and west by Lake Superior, and on the south by Lake Superior and Houghton county. The total land area is 318,468.31 acres. Of this number about 3,000 acres are devoted to farms, although the county is particularly noted for its copper mines. The population is 7,156 (1910 census). The valuation of taxable property, as estimated by the state board of tax commissioners in 1911, is $16,784,418. The school system of the county is good and consists of 15 schools, an enrollment of 1,713 students, requiring the services of 50 teachers. There is one bank and one weekly newspaper. The county has good telegraph and telephone service.

Eagle River has a population of about 200, and is the judicial seat of the county. It is located on the north shore of the Keweenaw peninsula on Lake Superior, at the mouth of the stream from which it derives its name. It is two miles from Phoenix, the nearest railroad approach. It has a Methodist church. The banking facilities are at Calumet, 16 miles distant.

Ahmeek has a population of about 1,200 and is the largest town in the county. It is eleven miles from Eagle river and two and one-half miles from Mohawk. The principal transportation facilities of the county are the Mineral Range, Keweenaw Central Railroads, and the Houghton Traction Company.

KEWEENAW COUNTY

MICHIGAN

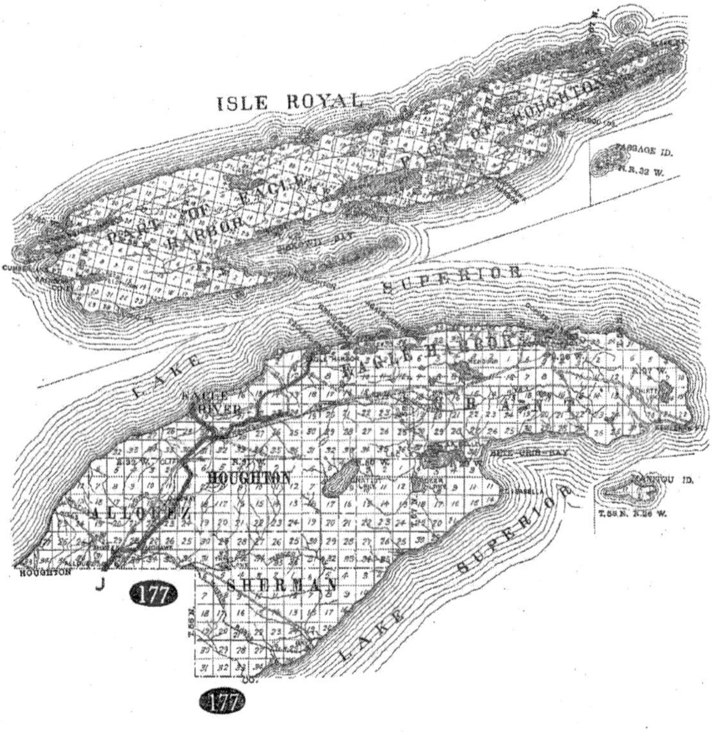

POPULATION OF TOWNSHIPS, CITIES AND VILLAGES

Alcona County, 5,703

Alcona twp.	336
Caledonia twp.	616
Curtis twp.	589
Greenbush twp.	394
Gustin twp.	555
Lincoln village	182
Harrisville city	441
Harrisville twp.	761
Hawes twp.	804
Haynes twp.	651
Mikado twp.	652
Mikado village	190
Millen twp.	282
Mitchell twp.	282

Alger County, 7,675

Au Train twp.	400
Burt twp.	1,375
Grand Island twp.	32
Limestone twp.	418
Mathias twp.	526
Munising twp.	3,847
Munising village	3,052
Onota twp.	147
Rock River twp.	1,206

Allegan County, 39,819

Allegan city	2,418
Allegan twp.	1,141
Casco twp.	1,796
Cheshire twp.	1,248
Clyde twp.	1,194
Fennville village	835
Dorr twp.	1,658
Fillmore twp.	1,882
Ganges twp.	1,092
Gunplain twp.	2,474
Plainwell village	1,493
Heath twp.	1,610
Hopkins twp.	1,845
Laketown twp.	1,056
Lee twp.	959
Leighton twp.	1,153
Manlius twp.	1,150
Martin twp.	1,185
Monterey twp.	1,253
Otsego twp.	2,828
Otsego village	2,012
Overisel twp.	1,461
Salem twp.	1,577
Saugatuck twp.	2,048
Douglas village	485
Saugatuck village	621
Trowbridge twp.	1,253
Valley twp.	468
Watson twp.	1,042
Wayland twp.	1,846
Wayland village	726

Alpena County, 19,965

Alpena city	12,706
Alpena twp.	988
Green twp.	758
Long Rapids twp.	1,212
Maple Ridge twp.	781
Ossineke twp.	1,006
Sanborn twp.	847
Wilson twp.	1,634

Antrim County, 15,692

Banks twp.	1,663
Central Lake twp.	1,187
Central Lake village	418
Chestonia twp.	312
Custer twp.	591
Echo twp.	724
Elk Rapids twp.	1,775
Elk Rapids village	1,871
Forest Home twp.	942
Bellaire village	1,056
Helena twp.	762
Jordan twp.	426
Kearney twp.	1,071
Mancelona twp.	3,384
Mancelona village	1,306
Milton twp.	737
Star twp.	551
Torch Lake twp.	829
Warner twp.	438

Arenac County, 9,640

Adams twp.	608
Arenac twp.	664
Au Gres city	402
Au Gres twp.	413
Clayton twp.	851
Deep River twp.	867
Lincoln twp.	781
Mason twp.	853
Twining village	267
Moffat twp.	861
Omer city	707
Standish city	828
Standish twp.	1,280
Turner twp.	585
Whitney twp.	684

Baraga County, 6,127

Arvon twp.	395
Baraga twp.	2,549
Baraga village	1,071
Covington twp.	849
L'Anse twp.	2,088
L'Anse village	788
Spurr twp.	165

Barry County, 22,633

Assyria twp.	978
Baltimore twp.	1,035
Barry twp.	1,323
Carlton twp.	1,160
Freeport village	407
Castleton twp.	2,343
Nashville village	1,346
Hastings city	4,383
Hastings twp.	954
Hope twp.	999
Irving twp.	1,081
Johnstown township	927
Maple Grove twp.	1,085
Orangeville twp.	777
Prairieville twp.	802
Rutland twp.	927
Thornapple twp.	1,740
Middleville village	905
Woodland twp.	1,380
Woodland village	304
Yankee Springs twp.	611

Bay County, 68,238

Bangor twp.	1,218
Bay City	45,166
Beaver twp.	1,787
Frankenlust twp.	1,245
Fraser twp.	1,802
Garfield twp.	901
Gibson twp.	919
Hampton twp.	3,023
Essexville village	1,477
Kawkawlin twp.	1,493
Merritt twp.	1,326
Monitor twp.	2,196
Mount Forest twp.	781
Pinconning twp.	2,162
Pinconning village	877
Portsmouth twp.	1,031
Williams twp.	2,409

Benzie County, 10,638

Almira twp.	896
Lake Ann village	211
Benzonia twp.	1,355
Benzonia village	363
Blaine twp.	649
Colfax twp.	761
Thompsonville village	612
Crystal Lake twp.	3,024
Frankfort village	1,236
Gilmore twp.	906
South Frankfort village	681
Homestead twp.	1,113
Inland twp.	605
Joyfield twp.	412
Lake twp.	790
Platte twp.	148
Weldon twp.	1,164

Berrien County, 53,622

Bainbridge twp.	1,798
Benton twp.	3,021
Benton Harbor city	9,185
Berrien twp.	1,583
Eau Claire village	392
Bertrand twp.	825
Buchanan twp.	2,092
Buchanan village	1,882
Chikaming twp.	1,094
Galien twp.	1,265
Galien village	485
Hagar twp.	1,072
Lake twp.	2,768
Baroda village	248
Lincoln twp.	1,728
Stevensville village	243
New Buffalo twp.	1,110
New Buffalo village	328
Niles city	5,156
Niles twp.	1,062
Oronoko twp.	2,137
Berrien Springs village	880
Pipestone twp.	1,397
Royalton twp.	1,168
St. Joseph city	5,936
St. Joseph twp.	606
Shoreham village	225
Sodus twp.	1,260
Three Oaks twp.	1,158
Three Oaks village	1,175
Watervliet twp.	2,092
Coloma village	761
Watervliet village	796
Weesaw twp.	1,407

Branch County, 25,605

Algansee twp.	1,261
Batavia twp.	1,015
Bethel twp.	1,248
Bronson twp.	1,948
Bronson village	1,080
Butler twp.	1,114
California twp.	878
Coldwater city	5,945
Coldwater twp.	1,322
Gilead twp.	720
Girard twp.	1,122
Kinderhook twp.	691
Matteson twp.	882
Noble twp.	502
Ovid twp.	891
Quincy twp.	2,407
Quincy village	1,247
Sherwood twp.	1,216
Sherwood village	346
Union twp.	1,492
Union City village	1,240

Calhoun County, 56,638

Albion city	5,833
Albion twp.	724
Athens twp.	1,491
Athens village	631
Battle Creek city	25,267
Battle Creek twp.	1,381
Bedford twp.	1,008
Burlington twp.	1,150
Burlington village	281
Clarence twp.	801
Clarendon twp.	814
Convis twp.	749
Eckford twp.	910
Emmett twp.	1,928
Fredonia twp.	720
Homer twp.	1,883
Homer village	1,008
Lee twp.	840
Le Roy twp.	1,025
Marengo twp.	1,029
Marshall city	4,236
Marshall twp.	681
Newton twp.	556
Pennfield twp.	1,191
Sheridan twp.	936
Tekonsha twp.	1,407
Tekonsha village	543

Cass County, 20,624

Calvin twp.	1,461
Dowagiac city	5,088
Howard twp.	881
Jefferson twp.	805
La Grange twp.	2,904
Cassopolis village	1,358
Marcellus twp.	1,808
Marcellus village	1,041
Mason twp.	587
Milton twp.	593
Newberg twp.	1,161
Ontwa twp.	839
Penn twp.	1,105
Vandalia village	371
Pokagon twp.	971
Porter twp.	1,741
Silver Creek twp.	873
Volinia twp.	945
Wayne twp.	804

Charlevoix County, 19,157

Bay twp.	405
Boyne City	5,218
Boyne Valley twp.	952
Boyne Falls village	305
Chandler twp.	397
Charlevoix city	2,420
Charlevoix twp.	297
Evangeline twp.	325
Eveline twp.	768
Hayes twp.	804
Hudson twp.	673
Marion twp.	636
Melrose twp.	675
Norwood twp.	300
Peaine twp.	373
St. James twp.	608
South Arm twp.	3,126
East Jordan village	2,516
Wilson twp.	408

Cheboygan County, 17,872

Aloha twp.	323
Beaugrand twp.	443
Benton twp.	1,091
Burt twp.	537
Cheboygan city	6,859
Ellis twp.	311
Forest twp.	1,004
Tower village	345
Grant twp.	152
Hebron twp.	304
Inverness twp.	1,047
Koehler twp.	182
Mackinaw twp.	790
Mackinaw City village	435
Mentor twp.	455
Munro twp.	543
Nunda twp.	1,238
Wolverine village	724
Tuscarora twp.	650
Walker twp.	153
Waverly twp.	391
Wilmot twp.	206

Chippewa County, 24,472

Bay Mills twp.	223
Bruce twp.	1,324
Dafter twp.	815
Detour twp.	825
Detour village	771
Drummond twp.	694
Kinross twp.	344
Pickford twp.	1,476
Raber twp.	882
Rudyard twp.	1,363
Sault Ste. Marie city	12,615
Soo twp.	683
Sugar Island twp.	623
Superior twp.	1,321
Trout Lake twp.	312
Whitefish twp.	399

Clare County, 9,240

Arthur twp.	724
Clare city	1,350
Franklin twp.	121
Freeman twp.	129
Frost twp.	278
Garfield twp.	425
Grant twp.	818
Greenwood twp.	463
Hamilton twp.	361
Harrison city	543
Hatton twp.	781
Hayes twp.	362
Lincoln twp.	146
Redding twp.	650
Sheridan twp.	604
Summerfield twp.	219
Surrey twp.	932
Farwell village	532
Winterfield twp.	433

Clinton County, 23,129

Bath twp.	1,621
Bengal twp.	960
Bingham twp.	951
Dallas twp.	1,593
Fowler village	476
De Witt twp.	1,305
Duplain twp.	1,731
Elsie village	592
Eagle twp.	1,007
Eagle village	125
Essex twp.	1,335
Maple Rapids village	580
Greenbush twp.	1,180
Lebanon twp.	1,014
Hubbardston village	430
Olive twp.	903
Ovid twp.	2,169
Ovid village	1,078
Riley twp.	1,101
St. Johns city	3,154
Victor twp.	853
Watertown twp.	1,211
Westphalia twp.	2,499
Westphalia village	360

Crawford County, 3,934

Beaver Creek twp.	341
Frederic twp.	776
Grayling twp.	2,087
Grayling village	1,775
Maple Forest twp.	471
South Branch twp.	259

Delta County, 30,108

Baldwin twp.	753
Bark River twp.	1,290
Bay de Noc twp.	530
Brampton twp.	516
Cornell twp.	454
Escanaba city	13,194
Escanaba twp.	946
Fairbanks twp.	481
Ford River twp.	1,148
Garden twp.	1,205
Garden village	497
Gladstone city	4,211
Maple Ridge twp.	733
Masonville twp.	2,109
Nahma twp.	1,858
Wells twp.	1,466

Dickinson County, 20,524

Breen twp.	965
Breitung twp.	929
Felch twp.	772
Iron Mountain city	9,216
Norway city	4,074
Norway township	1,764
Sagola twp.	825
Waucedah twp.	675
West Branch twp.	582

Eaton County, 30,499

Bellevue twp.	1,881
Bellevue village	925
Benton twp.	1,365
Potterville village	488
Brookfield twp.	1,115
Carmel twp.	975
Charlotte city	4,886
Chester twp.	1,088
Delta twp.	1,225
Eaton twp.	918
Eaton Rapids city	2,094
Eaton Rapids twp.	1,068
Grand Ledge city	2,893
Hamlin twp.	844
Kalamo twp.	1,223
Oneida twp.	1,120
Roxand twp.	1,280
Mulliken village	411
Sunfield twp.	1,331
Sunfield village	385
Vermontville twp.	1,063
Vermontville village	650
Walton twp.	1,370
Olivet village	627
Windsor twp.	1,347
Dimondale village	361

Emmet County, 15,361

Bear Creek twp.	1,600
Bliss twp.	654
Carp Lake twp.	847
Center twp.	441
Cross Village twp.	406
Friendship twp.	487
Littlefield twp.	1,084
Alanson village	473
Little Traverse twp.	2,268
Harbor Springs village	1,805
McKinley twp.	2,150
Pellston village	1,089
Maple River twp.	750
Petoskey city	4,778
Pleasant View twp.	428
Readmond twp.	660
Resort twp.	786
Springvale twp.	727
West Traverse twp.	830

Genesee County, 64,555

Argentine twp.	821
Atlas twp.	1,120
Burton twp.	987
Clayton twp.	1,069
Davison twp.	1,047
Davison village	672
Fenton twp.	3,067
Fenton village	2,331
Linden village	380
Flint city	38,550
Flint twp.	1,081
Flushing twp.	4,075
Flushing village	989
Forest twp.	1,271
Otisville village	312
Gaines twp.	1,199
Gaines village	238
Genesee twp.	1,476
Mount Morris village	518
Grand Blanc twp.	1,844
Montrose twp.	1,612
Montrose village	443
Mount Morris twp.	1,121
Mundy twp.	1,199
Richfield twp.	1,101
Thetford twp.	1,084
Vienna twp.	1,882
Clio village	810

Gladwin County, 8,413

Beaverton city	418
Beaverton twp.	581
Bentley twp.	449
Billings twp.	270
Bourret twp.	217
Buckeye twp.	398
Butman twp.	120
Clement twp.	175
Gladwin city	988
Gladwin twp.	1,185
Grout twp.	872
Hay twp.	179
Sage twp.	808
Sherman twp.	543
Tobacco twp.	860

Gogebic County, 23,333

Bessemer city	4,583
Bessemer twp.	1,106
Carson twp.	150
Erwin twp.	689
Ironwood city	12,821
Ironwood twp.	635
Marenisco twp.	495
Wakefield twp.	3,474
Wakefield village	714
Watersmeet twp.	536

Grand Traverse County, 23,784

Acme twp.	731
Blair twp.	891
East Bay twp.	605
Fife Lake twp.	887
Fife Lake village	346
Garfield twp.	932
Grant twp.	885
Green Lake twp.	780
Long Lake twp.	742
Mayfield twp.	877
Paradise twp.	1,747
Kingsley village	487
Peninsula twp.	1,583
Traverse City	12,115
Union twp.	219
Whitewater twp.	900

Gratiot County, 28,820

Alma city	3,734
Arcada twp.	1,087
Bethany twp.	1,457
Elba twp.	1,793
Ashley village	613
Emerson twp.	1,238
Fulton twp.	1,796
Perrinton village	288
Hamilton twp.	850
Ithaca twp.	2,012
Ithaca village	1,878
Lafayette twp.	1,357
New Haven twp.	1,266
Newark twp.	1,213
North Shade twp.	1,340
North Star twp.	1,234
Pine River twp.	1,148
St. Louis city	1,940
Seville twp.	1,389
Sumner twp.	1,241
Washington twp.	1,338
Wheeler twp.	2,050
Breckenridge village	505

Hillsdale County, 29,673

Adams twp.	1,408
North Adams village	440
Allen twp.	1,252
Amboy twp.	1,817
Cambria twp.	1,873
Camden twp.	1,865
Camden village	392
Montgomery village	383
Fayette twp.	1,947
Jonesville village	1,306
Hillsdale city	5,001
Hillsdale twp.	447
Jefferson twp.	1,857
Litchfield village	690
Pittsford twp.	1,305
Moscow twp.	588
Litchfield twp.	1,641
Ransom twp.	1,431
Reading twp.	2,104
Reading village	1,103
Scipio twp.	895
Somerset twp.	1,181
Wheatland twp.	1,397
Woodbridge twp.	1,107
Wright twp.	2,163
Waldron village	525

Houghton County, 88,098

Adams twp.	5,519
South Range village	1,007
Calumet twp.	32,845
Laurium village	8,537
Red Jacket village	4,211
Chassell twp.	1,328
Duncan twp.	565
Elm River twp.	1,018
Franklin twp.	5,679
Hancock city	8,981
Hancock twp.	551
Laird twp.	850
Osceola twp.	7,745
Portage twp.	8,308
Houghton village	5,113
Quincy twp.	1,097
Schoolcraft twp.	4,183
Lake Linden village	2,325
Stanton twp.	3,307
Torch Lake twp.	8,218
Hubbell village	1,059

POPULATION OF TOWNSHIPS, CITIES AND VILLAGES—Continued

Huron County, 34,758

Bad Axe city 1,886
Bingham twp 1,409
Ubly village 442
Bloomfield twp 855
Brookfield twp 1,154
Owendale village 280
Caseville twp 578
Caseville village 412
Chandler twp 1,289
Colfax twp 1,091
Dwight twp 1,389
Kinde village 304
Fairhaven twp 1,021
Gore twp 167
Grant twp 941
Harbor Beach city 1,886
Hume township 706
Huron twp 918
Lake twp 399
Lincoln twp 1,025
McKinley twp 741
Meade twp 1,159
Oliver twp 1,725
Elkton village 538
Paris twp 1,090
Pointe Aux Barques twp 37
Port Austin twp 1,241
Port Austin village 532
Rubicon twp 404
Port Hope village 344
Sand Beach twp 1,132
Sebewaing twp 2,752
Sebewaing village 1,347
Sheridan twp 906
Sherman twp 1,417
Sigel twp 1,315
Verona twp 441
Winsor twp 2,108
Pigeon village 697

Ingham County, 83,310

Alaiedon twp 856
Aurelius twp 1,136
Bunker Hill twp 981
Delhi twp 1,415
East Lansing city 902
Ingham twp 1,402
Dansville village 249
Lansing city 31,324
Lansing twp 1,760
Leroy twp 1,297
Webberville village 345
Leslie twp 2,014
Leslie village 1,052
Locke twp 1,045
Mason city 1,743
Meridian twp 1,322
Onondaga twp 1,031
Stockbridge twp 1,204
Stockbridge village 608
Vevay twp 817
Wheatfield twp 784
White Oak twp 841
Williamston twp 1,068
Williamston village 1,042

Ionia County 33,550

Belding city 4,129
Berlin twp 1,248
Boston twp 1,784
Saranac village 845
Campbell twp 1,436
Danby twp 1,030
Easton twp 3,073
Ionia city 5,430
Ionia twp 1,476
Lyons village 611
Keene twp 947
Lyons twp 2,232
Muir village 465
Pewamo village 290
North Plains twp 1,292
Odessa twp 2,379
Lake Odessa village 1,328
Orange twp 1,048
Orleans twp 1,134
Otisco twp 1,085
Portland twp 2,743
Portland village 1,832
Ronald twp 1,120
Sebewa twp 1,104

Iosco County 9,753

Alabaster twp 332
Au Sable city 448
Au Sable twp 506
Baldwin twp 213
Burleigh twp 433
East Tawas city 1,432
Grant twp 225
Oscoda twp 1,250
Oscoda village 894
Plainfield twp 821
Reno twp 338
Sherman twp 428
Tawas city 1,641
Tawas twp 980
Whittemore city 214
Wilber twp 288

Iron County 13,164

Bates twp 273
Crystal Falls city 3,775
Crystal Falls twp 1,684
Hematite twp 1,315
Iron River twp 3,085
Iron River village 2,450
Mansfield twp 343
Mastodon twp 385
Stambaugh twp 4,350
Stambaugh village 1,822

Isabella County 25,039

Broomfield twp 787
Chippewa twp 1,018
Coe twp 2,176
Shepherd village 885
Coldwater twp 1,010
Deerfield twp 1,032
Denver twp 981
Fremont twp 1,190
Gilmore twp 740
Isabella twp 1,043
Lincoln twp 1,184
Mount Pleasant city 3,972
Nottawa twp 1,293
Rolland twp 1,217
Sherman twp 908
Union twp 1,409
Vernon twp 1,289
Wise twp 1,121

Jackson County 53,426

Blackman twp 1,248
Columbia twp 1,377
Brooklyn village 602
Concord twp 1,307
Concord village 548
Grass Lake twp 1,219
Grass Lake village 700
Hanover twp 1,248
Hanover village 364
Henrietta twp 872
Jackson city 31,433
Leoni twp 1,406
Liberty twp 880
Napoleon twp 807
Norvell twp 635
Parma twp 1,119
Parma village 500
Pulaski twp 843
Rives twp 1,143
Sandstone twp 1,258
Spring Arbor twp 823
Springport twp 1,244
Springport village 584
Summit twp 1,175
Tompkins twp 876
Waterloo twp 682

Kalamazoo County 55,422

Alamo twp 1,089
Brady twp 1,290
Vicksburg village 1,034
Charleston twp 833
Augusta village 494
Galesburg village 656
Climax twp 1,432
Climax village 485
Comstock twp 1,918
Cooper twp 975
Kalamazoo city 48,487
Kalamazoo twp 8,080
Oshtemo twp 1,111
Pavilion twp 1,002
Portage twp 816
Prairie Ronde twp 758
Richland twp 864
Richland village 375
Ross twp 1,253
Schoolcraft twp 2,377
Schoolcraft village 814
Texas twp 786
Wakeshma twp 1,148

Kalkaska County 5,897

Boardman twp 1,240
Boardman village 328
Clearwater twp 875
Cold Springs twp 545
Excelsior twp 755
Garfield twp 278
Kalkaska twp 1,830
Kalkaska village 1,515
Oliver twp 323
Orange twp 391
Rapid River twp 610
Springfield twp 336
Wilson twp 219
Township 25, range 5 96
Township 25, range 6 93
Township 26, range 5 71
Township 28, range 5 125

Kent County 159,145

Ada twp 1,281
Alpine twp 1,308
Rockford village 848
Algoma twp 1,426
Bowne twp 1,274
Byron twp 2,343
Caledonia twp 1,509
Caledonia village 422
Cannon twp 887
Cascade twp 1,219
Courtland twp 1,104
Gaines twp 1,311
Grand Rapids city 112,571
Grand Rapids twp 4,598
East Grand Rapids village 800
Grattan twp 1,030
Lowell twp 2,172
Lowell village 1,761
Nelson twp 1,874
Cedar Springs village 847
Sand Lake village 370
Oakfield twp 878
Paris twp 2,572
Plainfield twp 1,633
Solon twp 1,350
Sparta twp 3,049
Lisbon village 98
Sparta village 1,253
Spencer township 1,016
Tyrone twp 1,780
Casnovia village 278
Kent City village 467
Vergennes twp 840
Walker twp 2,558
Wyoming twp 5,364
Grandville village 982

Keweenaw County 7,156

Allouez twp 3,872
Ahmeek village 760
Eagle Harbor twp 196
Houghton twp 448
Grant twp 258
Sherman twp 585

Lake County 4,836

Chase twp 339
Cherry Valley twp 239
Dover twp 371
Eden twp 148
Elk township 223
Ellsworth twp 780
Luther village 620
Lake township 261
Newkirk twp 674
Pinora twp 328
Pleasant Plains twp 680
Baldwin village 502
Marlborough village 37
Sweet Water twp 149
Webber twp 255

Lapeer County 26,013

Almont twp 1,676
Almont village 675
Arcadia twp 1,128
Attica twp 1,158
Burlington twp 1,134
Clifford village 208
Burnside twp 1,584
Deerfield twp 1,918
Dryden twp 1,239
Dryden village 371
Elba twp 830
Goodland twp 682
Hadley twp 1,371
Imlay twp 3,225
Imlay City village 1,175
Lapeer city 3,949
Lapeer twp 587
Marathon twp 1,054
Columbiaville village 349
Otter Lake village 270
Mayfield twp 1,018
Metamora twp 1,043
Metamora village 370
North Branch twp 1,794
North Branch village 717
Oregon twp 897
Rich twp 1,110

Leelanau County 10,908

Bingham twp 741
Centerville twp 1,081
Cleveland twp 586
Elmwood twp 744
Empire twp 1,212
Empire village 378
Glen Arbor twp 506
Kasson twp 888
Leelanau twp 1,668
Northport village 524
Leland twp 1,248
Solon twp 706
Suttons Bay twp 1,301
Suttons Bay village 409

Lenawee County 47,907

Adrian city 10,763
Adrian twp 1,045
Blissfield twp 2,405
Blissfield village 1,674
Cambridge twp 1,281
Onsted village 358
Clinton twp 1,475
Clinton village 1,011
Deerfield twp 1,308
Deerfield village 443
Dover twp 1,279
Clayton village 373
Fairfield twp 1,009
Franklin twp 1,184
Hudson city 2,178
Hudson twp 1,344
Macon twp 1,015
Madison twp 1,318
Medina twp 1,459
Ogden twp 1,698
Palmyra twp 1,385
Raisin twp 1,340
Ridgeway twp 1,340
Britton village 370
Riga twp 1,487
Addison village 474
Rollin twp 1,085
Seneca twp 1,892
Morenci village 1,516
Tecumseh twp 2,708
Tecumseh village 2,332
Woodstock twp 1,531

Livingston County 17,784

Brighton twp 1,407
Brighton village 787
Cohoctah twp 1,305
Conway twp 1,164
Deerfield twp 816
Genoa twp 742
Green Oak twp 601
Hamburg twp 767
Handy twp 1,840
Fowlerville village 905
Hartland twp 830
Howell twp 2,086
Howell village 2,835
Iosco twp 752
Marion twp 1,388
Oceola twp 758
Putnam twp 1,118
Pinckney village 477
Tyrone twp 823
Unadilla twp 908

Luce County 4,924

Columbus twp 413
Lakefield twp 634
McMillan twp 3,861
Newberry village 1,732
Pentland twp 1,278

Mackinac County 9,249

Bois Blanc twp 215
Brevort twp 693
Clark twp 870
Garfield twp 1,196
Hendricks twp 441
Hudson twp 585
Mackinac Island city 714
Marquette twp 130
Moran twp 473
Newton twp 818
Portage twp 358
St. Ignace city 2,132
St. Ignace twp 402

Macomb County 32,606

Armada twp 1,758
Armada village 748
Bruce twp 1,987
Romeo village 1,787
Chesterfield twp 1,381
New Baltimore village 858
Clinton twp 1,866
Fraser village 330
Erin twp 2,223
Harrison twp 800
Lenox twp 2,251
New Haven village 478
Richmond village 1,277
Macomb twp 1,538
Mount Clemens city 7,707
Ray twp 1,540
Richmond twp 2,171
Memphis village 587
Shelby twp 2,187
Utica village 499
Sterling twp 1,675
Warren twp 2,843
Warren village 297
Washington twp 1,833

Manistee County 20,988

Arcadia twp 854
Bear Lake twp 1,384
Bear Lake village 301
Brown twp 752
Cleon twp 1,387
Copemish village 480
Dickson twp 425
Filer twp 1,060
Manistee city 12,381
Manistee twp 2,986
Maple Grove twp 802
Marilla twp 550
Onekama twp 780
Onekama village 334
Pleasanton twp 685
Springdale twp 381
Stronach twp 733

Marquette County 45,739

Champion twp 1,096
Chocolay twp 852
Ely twp 415
Forsyth twp 2,402
Humboldt twp 504
Ishpeming city 10,498
Ishpeming twp 587
Marquette city 11,503
Marquette twp 185
Michigamme twp 840
Negaunee city 6,180
Negaunee twp 187
Powell twp 738
Republic twp 2,180
Richmond twp 921
Sands twp 159
Skandia twp 546
Tilden twp 1,158
Turin twp 302
Wells twp 340
West Branch twp 501

Mason County 21,832

Amber twp 661
Branch twp 495
Custer twp 1,287
Custer village 277
Eden twp 813
Freesoil twp 1,391
Grant twp 673
Hamlin twp 345
Logan twp 392
Ludington city 8,133
Meade twp 87
Pere Marquette twp 843
Riverton twp 1,438
Scottville city 801
Sheridan twp 387
Sherman twp 1,362
Summit twp 368
Victory twp 1,070

Mecosta County 19,466

Aetna twp 963
Morley village 385
Austin twp 648
Big Rapids city 4,519
Big Rapids twp 609
Chippewa twp 869
Colfax twp 841
Deerfield twp 1,061
Fork twp 1,310
Barryton village 411
Grant twp 561
Green twp 1,208
Hinton twp 1,033
Martiny twp 720
Mecosta twp 681
Stanwood village 145
Millbrook twp 1,231
Morton twp 385
Mecosta village 342
Sheridan twp 748
Wheatland twp 1,291

Menominee County 25,648

Cedarville twp 1,160
Harris twp 1,961
Holmes twp 967
Ingallston twp 831
Mellen twp 1,862
Menominee city 10,507
Menominee twp 1,493
Meyer twp 1,629
Nadeau twp 1,918
Spalding twp 1,729
Stephenson twp 2,810
Daggett village 256
Stephenson village 587

Midland County 14,005

Coleman city 966
Edenville twp 519
Geneva twp 629
Greendale twp 852
Homer twp 570
Hope twp 781
Ingersoll twp 1,238
Jasper twp 895
Jerome twp 515
Larkin twp 777
Lee twp 414
Lincoln twp 332
Midland city 2,367
Midland twp 1,028
Mills twp 297
Mount Haley twp 655
Porter twp 681
Warren twp 309

Missaukee County 10,686

Aetna twp 631
Bloomfield twp 350
Butterfield twp 333
Caldwell twp 637
Clam Union twp 1,361
Enterprise twp 374
Forest twp 389
Lake twp 1,446
Lake City village 745
McBain city 540
Norwich twp 603
Pioneer twp 138
Reeder twp 1,380
Richland twp 1,187
Riverside twp 641
West Branch twp 425

Monroe County 37,517

Ash twp 1,849
Bedford twp 2,213
Berlin twp 1,067
Dundee twp 2,042
Dundee village 1,079
Erie twp 1,477
Exeter twp 1,339
Maybee village 310
Frenchtown twp 1,779
Ida twp 1,853
La Salle twp 1,268
London twp 1,192
Milan twp 1,812
Milan village 1,253
Monroe city 9,858
Monroe twp 1,141
Raisinville twp 1,699
Summerfield twp 2,008
Petersburg village 596
Whiteford twp 1,626

Montcalm County 32,069

Belvidere twp 1,227
Bloomer twp 2,040
Carson City village 848
Bushnell twp 1,178
Sheridan village 488
Cato twp 1,673
Lakeview village 881
Crystal twp 1,475
Day twp 1,460
McBride village 220
Douglass twp 1,152
Eureka twp 710
Evergreen twp 1,308
Fairplain twp 1,171
Ferris twp 1,158
Greenville city 4,045
Home twp 1,819
Edmore village 752
Maple Valley twp 1,608
Montcalm twp 1,181
Pierson twp 1,129
Pierson village 183
Pine twp 1,115
Reynolds twp 1,541
Howard City village 1,040
Richland twp 1,200
Sidney twp 1,414
Stanton city 1,012
Winfield twp 982

Montmorency County 3,755

Albert twp 882
Avery twp 182
Briley twp 508
Hillman twp 832
Hillman village 411
Montmorency twp 546
Rust twp 470
Vienna twp 324

Muskegon County 40,577

Blue Lake twp 143
Casnovia twp 1,486
Cedar Creek twp 392
Dalton twp 828
Egelston twp 277
Fruitland twp 784
Fruitport twp 858
Fruitport village 339
Holton twp 815
Laketon twp 243
Montague twp 1,318
Montague village 943
Moorland twp 711
Muskegon city 24,462
Muskegon twp 1,344
Muskegon Heights city 1,990
North Muskegon city 352
Norton twp 810
Ravenna twp 1,485
Sullivan twp 413
Whitehall twp 1,362
Whitehall village 1,437
White River twp 461

Newaygo County 19,220

Ashland twp 1,078
Grant village 429
Barton twp 611
Beaver twp 643
Big Prairie twp 449
Bridgeton twp 516
Brooks twp 1,088
Newaygo village 1,397
Croton twp 481
Croton village 65
Dayton twp 2,416
Fremont village 1,900
Denver twp 1,126
Hesperia village 469
Ensley twp 1,184
Everett twp 676
Garfield twp 1,418
Goodwell twp 400
Grant twp 780
Home twp 408
Lincoln twp 454
Merrill twp 327
Norwich twp 403
Sheridan twp 2,368
Sherman twp 789
Troy twp 217
Wilcox twp 1,098
White Cloud village 846

Oakland County 49,676

Addison twp 1,943
Leonard village 343
Avon twp 2,659
Rochester village 1,316
Bloomfield twp 3,438
Birmingham village 1,807
Brandon twp 1,125
Ortonville village 377
Commerce twp 788
Farmington twp 3,788
Farmington village 564
Groveland twp 775
Highland twp 1,040
Holly twp 2,278
Holly village 1,537
Independence twp 1,144
Clarkston village 345
Lyon twp 1,127
South Lyon village 615
Milford twp 1,669
Milford village 975
Novi twp 1,039
Oakland twp 702
Orion twp 1,383
Orion village 717
Oxford twp 1,534
Oxford village 1,101
Pontiac city 14,532
Pontiac twp 863
Rose twp 843
Royal Oak twp 2,803
Royal Oak village 1,671

POPULATION OF TOWNSHIPS, CITIES AND VILLAGES—Continued

Southfield twp.	1,269
Springfield twp.	821
Troy twp.	1,307
Waterford twp.	2,069
West Bloomfield twp.	1,153
White Lake twp.	842

Oceana County 14,378

Benona twp.	1,160
Claybanks twp.	732
Colfax twp.	408
Crystal twp.	789
Elbridge twp.	1,487
Ferry twp.	991
Golden twp.	879
Grant twp.	924
Greenwood twp.	594
Hart twp.	2,862
Hart village	1,253
Leavitt twp.	1,071
Walkerville village	271
Newfield twp.	905
Otto twp.	258
Pentwater twp.	1,237
Pentwater village	1,129
Shelby twp.	2,811
Shelby village	1,206
Weare twp.	1,067

Ogemaw County 8,367

Churchill twp.	573
Cumming twp.	568
Edwards twp.	661
Foster twp.	337
Goodar twp.	427
Hill twp.	486
Horton twp.	338
Klacking twp.	380
Logan twp.	372
Richland twp.	903
Rose City	542
Rose twp.	730
West Branch city	1,376
West Branch twp.	1,216

Ontonagon County 8,650

Bohemia twp.	207
Carp Lake twp.	339
Greenland twp.	1,826
Haight twp.	216
Interior twp.	419
McMillan twp.	458
Matchwood twp.	354
Ontonagon twp.	2,437
Ontonagon village	1,364
Rockland twp.	1,843
Stannard twp.	408

Osceola County 17,889

Burdell twp.	1,183
Tustin village	271
Cedar twp.	248
Evart twp.	1,072
Evart village	1,380
Hartwick twp.	652
Hersey twp.	1,004
Hersey village	315
Highland twp.	1,427
Le Roy twp.	1,335
Le Roy village	331
Lincoln twp.	1,026
Marion twp.	1,508
Marion village	787
Middle Branch twp.	686
Orient twp.	275
Osceola twp.	1,785
Richmond twp.	3,655
Reed City village	1,691
Rose Lake twp.	701
Sherman twp.	1,257
Sylvan twp.	724

Oscoda County 2,327

Big Creek twp.	432
Clinton twp.	307
Comins twp.	748
Elmer twp.	305
Mentor twp.	547

Otsego County 5,554

Bagley twp.	1,420
Gaylord village	1,338
Charlton twp.	181
Chester twp.	225
Corwith twp.	1,086
Vanderbilt village	596
Dover twp.	356
Elmira twp.	404
Hayes twp.	294
Livingston twp.	1,767
Otsego Lake twp.	483

Ottawa County 45,301

Allendale twp.	1,186
Blendon twp.	1,700
Chester twp.	1,189
Crockery twp.	1,547
Georgetown twp.	2,239
Grand Haven city	5,856
Grand Haven twp.	913
Holland city	10,490
Holland twp.	8,538
Jamestown twp.	1,804
Olive twp.	1,089
Polkton twp.	2,141
Coopersville village	814
Robinson twp.	892
Spring Lake twp.	1,929
Spring Lake village	802
Tallmadge twp.	1,312
Wright twp.	1,059
Zeeland city	1,982
Zeeland twp.	1,800

Presque Isle County 11,249

Allis twp.	549
Bearinger twp.	144
Belknap twp.	1,253
Bismarck twp.	385
Case twp.	890
Millersburg village	615
Krakow twp.	485
Metz twp.	789
Moltke twp.	568
North Allis twp.	458
Ocqueoc twp.	397
Onaway city	2,702
Posen twp.	1,296
Posen village	267
Presque Isle twp.	165
Pulawski twp.	489
Rogers twp.	928
Rogers village	708

Roscommon County 2,274

Backus twp.	66
Denton twp.	76
Gerrish twp.	387
Higgins twp.	503
Roscommon village	425
Markey twp.	197
Nester twp.	230
Richfield twp.	401
Roscommon twp.	496

Saginaw County 89,290

Albee twp.	1,694
Birch Run twp.	1,422
Blumfield twp.	1,481
Brady twp.	1,525
Oakley village	237
Brant twp.	1,169
Bridgeport twp.	1,764
Buena Vista twp.	2,737
Carrollton twp.	2,238
Chapin twp.	727
Chesaning twp.	3,819
Chesaning village	1,843
Frankenmuth twp.	2,014
Frankenmuth village	802
Freemont twp.	1,149
James twp.	607
Jonesfield twp.	1,237
Merrill village	585
Kochville twp.	849
Lakefield twp.	788
Maple Grove twp.	2,382
Marion twp.	911
Richland twp.	1,678
Saginaw city	50,510
Saginaw twp.	1,444
St. Charles twp.	2,604
St. Charles village	1,451
Spaulding twp.	832
Swan Creek twp.	578
Taymouth twp.	1,610
Thomas twp.	1,162
Tittabawassee twp.	1,238
Zilwaukee twp.	711

St. Clair County 52,341

Berlin twp.	1,214
Brockway twp.	653
Burtchville twp.	456
Casco twp.	1,413
China twp.	1,180
Clay twp.	2,183
Algonac village	1,294
Clyde twp.	751
Columbus twp.	864
Cottrellville twp.	1,070
East China twp.	327
Emmet twp.	1,049
Emmet village	292
Fort Gratiot twp.	397
Grant twp.	810
Greenwood twp.	687
Ira twp.	1,050
Kenockee twp.	1,171
Kimball twp.	1,151
Lynn twp.	618
Marine city	3,770
Mussey twp.	1,718
Capac village	701
Port Huron city	18,863
Port Huron twp.	1,364
Riley twp.	1,324
St. Clair city	3,023
St. Clair twp.	1,336
Wales twp.	1,318
Yale city	1,328

St. Joseph County 25,499

Burr Oak twp.	1,369
Burr Oak village	707
Colon twp.	1,712
Colon village	862
Constantine twp.	1,910
Constantine village	1,344
Fabius twp.	763
Fawn River twp.	601
Florence twp.	651
Flowerfield twp.	884
Leonidas twp.	1,104
Lockport twp.	686
Mendon twp.	1,606
Mendon village	768
Mottville twp.	494
Nottawa twp.	1,811
Centreville village	618
Park twp.	804
Sherman twp.	601
Sturgis city	5,035
Sturgis twp.	498
Three Rivers city	5,072
White Pigeon twp.	1,850
White Pigeon village	667

Sanilac County 33,930

Argyle twp.	1,203
Austin twp.	968
Bridgehampton twp.	1,307
Carsonville village	401
Brown City	610
Buel twp.	1,110
Croswell city	1,363
Custer twp.	1,052
Delaware twp.	1,516
Forestville village	234
Elk twp.	1,320
Peck village	274
Elmer twp.	833
Evergreen twp.	1,601
Flynn twp.	955
Forester twp.	687
Fremont twp.	1,613
Greenleaf twp.	842
Lamotte twp.	1,012
Lexington twp.	1,431
Lexington village	410
Maple Valley twp.	1,013
Marion twp.	1,740
Deckerville village	628
Marlette twp.	1,498
Marlette village	1,062
Minden twp.	900
Minden City village	338
Moore twp.	1,098
Sandusky city	908
Sanilac twp.	1,385
Port Sanilac village	310
Speaker twp.	1,279
Melvin village	242
Washington twp.	1,604
Applegate village	158
Watertown twp.	884
Wheatland twp.	815
Worth twp.	1,036

Schoolcraft County 8,681

Cusino twp.	383
Doyle twp.	524
Germfask twp.	307
Hiawatha twp.	859
Inwood twp.	874
Manistique city	4,732
Manistique twp.	490
Mueller twp.	318
Seney twp.	120
Thompson twp.	753

Shiawassee County 33,246

Antrim twp.	810
Bennington twp.	1,031
Burns twp.	1,232
Byron village	427
Caledonia twp.	1,494
Corunna city	1,384
Fairfield twp.	835
Hazelton twp.	1,390
Middlebury twp.	734
New Haven twp.	1,411
Owosso city	9,639
Owosso twp.	1,330
Perry twp.	1,077
Morrice village	476
Perry village	739
Rush twp.	1,181
Sciota twp.	1,244
Laingsburg village	782
Shiawassee twp.	1,617
Bancroft village	543
Venice twp.	1,281
Vernon twp.	3,772
Durand village	2,315
Vernon village	485
Woodhull twp.	749

Tuscola County 34,913

Akron twp.	2,274
Almer twp.	1,330
Arbela twp.	1,075
Columbia twp.	1,073
Unionville village	492
Dayton twp.	1,201
Denmark twp.	2,001
Reese village	463
Elkland twp.	2,043
Cass City village	1,158
Ellington twp.	870
Elmwood twp.	1,005
Gagetown village	358
Fairgrove twp.	2,004
Fairgrove village	487
Fremont twp.	1,739
Mayville village	687
Gilford twp.	1,301
Indian Fields twp.	1,997
Caro village	2,372
Juniata twp.	1,049
Kingston twp.	1,235
Kingston village	209
Koylton twp.	932
Millington twp.	1,575
Millington village	423
Novesta township	1,021
Tuscola twp.	1,176
Vassar twp.	2,269
Vassar village	1,830
Watertown twp.	1,171
Wells twp.	851
Wisner twp.	883

Van Buren County 33,185

Almena twp.	808
Antwerp twp.	2,320
Lawton village	1,042
Arlington twp.	1,300
Bangor village	1,158
Bangor twp.	3,124
Bloomingdale twp.	2,251
Bloomingdale village	301
Gobleville village	387
Columbia twp.	1,471
Breedsville village	219
Covert twp.	1,822
Decatur twp.	2,106
Decatur village	1,280
Geneva twp.	1,130
Hamilton twp.	952
Hartford twp.	2,397
Hartford village	1,298
Keeler twp.	1,027
Lawrence twp.	1,761
Lawrence village	602
Paw Paw twp.	2,773
Paw Paw village	1,643
Pine Grove twp.	1,322
Porter twp.	904
South Haven city	3,577
South Haven twp.	1,218
Waverly twp.	1,095

Washtenaw County 44,714

Ann Arbor city	14,817
Ann Arbor twp.	989
Augusta twp.	1,165
Bridgewater twp.	861
Dexter twp.	645
Freedom twp.	921
Lima twp.	839
Chelsea village	1,708
Lodi twp.	1,032
Saline village	810
Lyndon twp.	628
Manchester twp.	1,368
Manchester village	1,041
Northfield twp.	1,106
Pittsfield twp.	979
Salem twp.	1,034
Saline twp.	1,617
Scio twp.	1,832
Dexter village	725
Sharon twp.	867
Superior township	917
Sylvan twp.	2,409
Webster twp.	734
York twp.	2,007
Ypsilanti city	6,230
Ypsilanti twp.	1,088

Wayne County 531,591

Brownstown twp.	2,045
Canton twp.	1,119
Dearborn twp.	2,781
Dearborn village	911
Detroit city	465,766
Ecorse tp.	6,398
Ecorse village	1,065
Ford City village	1,080
Oakwood village	781
River Rouge village	4,162
Gratiot twp.	1,560
St. Clair Heights village	1,252
Greenfield twp.	4,095
Highland Park village	4,120
Grosse Pointe twp.	2,870
Grosse Pointe village	820
Grosse Pointe Farms village	842
Grosse Pointe Park village	296
Hamtramck twp.	7,122
Hamtramck village	3,559
Huron twp.	1,930
Livonia twp.	1,383
Monguagon twp.	2,307
Trenton village	1,224
Nankin twp.	3,066
Wayne village	1,273
Northville twp.	2,274
Northville village	1,002
Plymouth twp.	2,346
Plymouth village	1,671
Redford twp.	2,170
Redford village	318
Romulus twp.	1,630
Springwells twp.	1,870
Sumpter twp.	1,318
Taylor twp.	1,238
Van Buren twp.	1,759
Belleville village	466
Wyandotte city	8,287

Wexford County 20,769

Antioch twp.	640
Sherman village	280
Boon twp.	1,178
Harrietta village	370
Cadillac city	8,375
Cedar Creek twp.	2,159
Manton village	1,069
Cherry Grove twp.	481
Clam Lake twp.	604
Colfax twp.	754
Greenwood twp.	432
Hanover twp.	612
Buckley village	364
Haring twp.	418
Henderson twp.	282
Liberty twp.	370
Selma twp.	923
Slagle twp.	436
South Branch twp.	240
Springville twp.	1,206
Mesick village	310
Wexford twp.	810

Agriculture—United States

Farm Property—Average Value of Each Class of Farm Property per Acre of Land in Farms, With Increases, by Divisions and States: 1910 and 1900.

DIVISION OR STATE.	All farm property 1910	All farm property 1900	Increase Amt.	Increase Per ct.	Land 1910	Land 1900	Increase Amt.	Increase Per ct.	Buildings 1910	Buildings 1900	Per ct. of increase	Implements and machinery 1910	Implements and machinery 1900	Per ct. of increase	Live stock 1910	Live stock 1900	Per ct. of increase
United States	$46.64	$24.37	$22.27	91.4	$32.40	$15.57	$16.83	108.1	$7.00	$4.24	65.8	$1.46	$0.89	64.0	$5.60	$3.67	52.6
GEOGRAPHIC DIVISIONS:																	
New England	43.99	31.12	12.88	41.3	19.38	13.79	5.59	40.5	17.05	11.91	43.2	2.54	1.75	44.9	4.62	3.54	30.5
Middle Atlantic	68.52	51.51	17.01	33.0	33.86	27.19	6.67	24.5	22.70	16.23	39.9	2.68	1.87	43.3	8.08	5.49	47.4
East North Central	85.81	48.86	36.95	75.6	61.52	34.15	27.37	78.6	13.95	8.08	72.4	2.23	1.41	58.4	8.28	5.20	59.2
West North Central	58.18	28.96	29.22	100.9	43.21	19.37	23.84	123.1	6.71	3.77	78.0	1.30	0.80	62.2	6.39	4.64	37.8
South Atlantic	28.44	13.94	14.50	104.0	18.15	8.63	9.52	110.3	5.81	2.94	97.6	0.95	0.51	86.3	3.53	1.86	89.8
East South Central	26.78	14.72	12.06	81.9	16.28	8.72	7.56	86.7	5.03	2.75	81.7	0.92	0.60	53.3	4.23	2.46	72.2
West South Central	22.69	9.18	13.51	147.2	16.06	5.40	10.66	197.4	2.44	1.05	132.4	0.71	0.44	61.4	3.48	2.28	53.1
Mountain	29.52	12.96	16.56	127.8	19.73	6.12	13.61	222.4	2.44	1.18	106.8	0.63	0.31	102.4	6.53	5.26	24.1
Pacific	54.17	23.49	30.68	130.6	41.75	17.79	23.98	140.1	4.32	2.38	80.9	1.29	0.72	79.2	4.60	2.60	76.9
NEW ENGLAND:																	
Maine	29.65	17.43	12.22	71.9	12.73	7.53	5.20	73.4	11.62	7.48	55.3	2.30	1.40	64.3	4.00	2.72	47.1
New Hampshire	31.91	23.78	8.13	34.2	12.79	9.53	3.26	34.2	12.74	9.36	36.1	1.81	1.43	26.6	3.67	2.97	23.7
Vermont	31.15	22.96	8.22	35.8	12.52	9.70	2.82	29.1	11.62	7.89	47.3	2.18	1.60	36.3	3.56	2.76	28.6
Massachusetts	78.75	58.04	20.71	35.7	36.60	27.53	9.07	32.8	30.82	22.30	38.4	4.02	2.81	43.1	7.23	5.02	43.6
Rhode Island	74.43	59.24	15.19	25.6	33.60	29.16	4.48	14.8	29.15	21.39	36.3	4.02	2.79	44.1	7.28	5.60	29.9
Connecticut	72.93	49.01	23.92	48.8	33.03	22.68	10.35	45.6	30.25	19.48	55.4	3.16	2.14	47.7	6.48	4.73	37.0
MIDDLE ATLANTIC:																	
New York	65.89	47.23	18.66	39.5	32.13	24.34	7.79	32.0	21.65	14.88	45.5	3.80	2.47	53.8	8.31	5.54	50.0
New Jersey	99.05	66.71	32.35	48.4	48.23	32.86	15.37	46.8	36.13	21.37	69.1	5.09	3.28	55.2	9.58	6.20	54.6
Pennsylvania	67.43	54.29	13.14	24.2	33.92	29.70	4.22	14.2	22.00	16.67	32.0	3.81	2.63	44.9	7.45	5.29	40.9
EAST NORTH CENTRAL:																	
Ohio	78.95	48.95	30.00	61.3	55.34	35.35	19.99	56.9	13.38	8.90	50.3	2.12	1.48	43.3	8.19	5.14	59.3
Indiana	84.91	45.27	39.64	87.6	62.38	31.83	30.55	96.0	12.49	7.13	75.2	1.92	1.45	32.4	8.11	5.07	60.0
Illinois	120.08	61.12	58.96	96.5	95.02	46.17	48.85	105.8	12.29	7.07	73.8	2.27	1.37	65.7	9.49	5.91	60.6
Michigan	57.49	39.31	18.18	46.2	32.48	24.12	8.36	34.7	15.09	9.05	66.7	2.64	1.64	61.0	7.28	4.50	61.8
Wisconsin	67.10	40.87	26.23	64.2	48.30	29.71	18.59	62.6	13.79	7.83	75.7	2.51	1.47	70.7	7.53	4.85	55.3
WEST NORTH CENTRAL:																	
Minnesota	53.33	30.08	23.25	77.3	36.82	21.31	15.51	72.6	8.79	4.20	109.3	1.89	1.15	64.3	5.84	3.39	72.3
Iowa	110.40	53.06	57.34	108.1	82.58	36.35	46.23	127.2	13.42	6.96	92.8	2.81	1.68	67.3	11.58	8.06	43.7
Missouri	59.35	30.39	28.96	95.3	41.80	20.46	21.34	104.3	7.81	4.37	78.7	1.47	0.84	75.0	8.26	4.72	75.0
North Dakota	34.29	16.42	17.87	108.8	25.60	11.15	14.54	130.4	3.25	1.64	98.2	1.54	0.90	71.1	3.81	2.73	39.6
South Dakota	44.82	15.60	29.22	187.3	34.09	9.92	24.17	243.7	3.94	1.62	143.2	1.30	0.64	103.1	4.82	3.42	41.0
Nebraska	53.85	25.01	28.84	115.3	41.50	16.27	25.57	153.9	5.13	3.04	68.8	1.15	0.83	38.6	5.75	4.86	18.3
Kansas	47.01	20.74	26.27	126.7	35.45	12.77	22.68	177.6	4.60	2.68	71.6	1.11	0.71	56.3	5.58	4.38	27.5
SOUTH ATLANTIC:																	
Delaware	50.79	28.17	22.62	80.3	33.63	22.29	11.34	50.9	17.54	10.00	75.4	3.09	2.02	53.0	6.36	3.92	62.4
Maryland	56.59	39.58	17.01	43.0	32.32	23.28	9.04	38.8	15.48	10.50	46.9	2.35	1.67	40.7	6.44	4.03	59.8
District of Columbia	1,398.06	1,358.86	39.22	2.9	1,186.53	1,142.68	43.85	3.8	171.19	185.39	-7.7	15.25	16.23	-6.0	25.21	14.76	70.8
Virginia	32.08	16.25	15.83	97.3	20.24	10.08	10.16	100.8	7.05	3.56	98.0	0.93	0.50	86.0	3.84	2.11	82.0
West Virginia	31.39	19.14	12.25	64.0	20.65	12.60	8.05	63.9	5.72	3.19	79.3	0.70	0.47	48.9	4.50	2.87	56.8
North Carolina	23.96	10.28	13.68	133.1	15.29	6.24	9.05	145.0	5.06	2.32	118.1	0.82	0.40	105.0	2.79	1.32	111.4
South Carolina	29.02	10.98	18.04	164.3	19.89	7.14	12.75	178.6	4.74	1.93	145.6	1.04	0.47	121.3	3.31	1.43	131.5
Georgia	21.34	8.65	12.69	146.7	13.74	5.25	8.49	161.7	4.04	1.70	137.6	0.78	0.37	110.3	2.98	1.33	124.1
Florida	27.25	12.36	14.89	120.5	17.84	7.06	10.78	152.7	4.65	2.29	103.1	0.85	0.45	88.9	3.92	2.56	53.1
EAST SOUTH CENTRAL:																	
Kentucky	34.87	21.43	13.44	62.7	21.83	13.24	8.59	64.9	6.80	4.14	64.3	0.94	0.70	34.3	5.29	3.35	57.9
Tennessee	30.56	16.77	13.79	82.2	18.53	9.93	8.60	86.6	5.44	3.19	70.5	1.06	0.75	41.3	5.32	2.88	84.6
Alabama	17.83	8.67	9.16	105.6	10.46	4.84	5.62	116.1	3.44	1.67	106.0	0.79	0.42	88.1	3.16	1.75	80.6
Mississippi	22.97	11.20	11.77	105.1	13.69	6.30	7.39	117.3	4.82	2.28	111.8	0.62	0.35	75.9	4.05	2.34	73.1
WEST SOUTH CENTRAL:																	
Arkansas	22.97	10.90	12.07	110.7	14.13	6.62	7.51	113.4	3.68	1.84	100.0	0.97	0.53	83.0	4.23	2.25	88.0
Louisiana	28.85	17.95	10.90	60.7	17.99	9.74	8.25	84.7	4.76	3.02	57.6	1.83	1.46	25.3	4.28	2.61	64.0
Oklahoma	31.82	12.07	19.75	163.6	22.49	6.50	15.99	246.0	3.11	0.93	234.4	0.94	0.46	104.3	5.28	4.19	26.0
Texas	19.73	7.65	12.08	157.9	14.33	4.70	9.63	204.9	1.17	0.50	133.8	0.61	0.24	152.5	2.85	1.96	45.2
MOUNTAIN:																	
Montana	23.65	9.55	14.10	148.1	16.74	4.45	12.29	276.2	1.83	0.79	131.6	0.78	0.31	151.6	6.32	4.40	43.6
Idaho	57.79	20.99	36.80	175.3	41.63	11.07	30.56	276.1	4.73	2.13	123.0	1.26	1.03	22.2	9.42	6.76	39.3
Wyoming	19.37	8.21	11.26	135.5	10.41	2.88	7.53	261.6	1.05	0.48	118.2	0.43	0.17	152.9	7.20	4.52	59.3
Colorado	36.22	17.09	19.22	113.6	27.31	9.54	17.77	186.3	3.38	1.69	100.0	0.95	0.50	90.0	5.18	5.09	1.7
New Mexico	14.15	10.48	3.67	35.0	5.77	2.38	3.39	142.4	1.16	0.60	93.3	0.37	0.22	68.2	3.56	4.91	-27.5
Arizona	60.26	15.50	44.76	288.8	33.97	5.90	28.07	475.8	3.06	1.17	161.5	1.43	0.40	257.5	20.80	8.00	160.0
Utah	41.38	16.26	25.12	154.5	29.28	9.75	19.53	200.3	5.32	2.59	105.4	1.32	0.71	85.9	8.47	5.22	62.3
Nevada	22.25	11.18	11.07	99.0	12.69	5.17	7.52	145.5	1.60	0.91	75.8	0.58	0.35	65.7	7.05	4.74	48.7
PACIFIC:																	
Washington	54.43	16.95	37.48	221.1	44.19	11.89	32.30	271.7	4.66	1.92	142.7	1.43	0.74	93.2	4.17	2.61	59.8
Oregon	45.21	17.15	28.06	163.6	35.23	11.23	24.00	213.7	3.76	1.91	96.9	1.43	0.82	73.3	4.75	3.37	41.0
California	57.81	27.63	30.18	109.2	47.16	21.87	25.29	115.6	4.78	2.69	77.7	1.31	0.74	77.0	4.57	2.33	96.1

[1] A minus sign (—) denotes decrease.

Farm Land and Farm Property—Averages per Farm by Divisions and States: 1910 and 1900.

DIVISION OR STATE.	Average acres per farm: All farm land 1910	All farm land 1900	Improved land 1910	Improved land 1900	Average value per farm: All farm property 1910	All farm property 1900	Land 1910	Land 1900	Buildings 1910	Buildings 1900	Implements and machinery 1910	Implements and machinery 1900	Live stock 1910	Live stock 1900
United States	138.1	146.2	75.2	72.2	$6,444	$3,563	$4,476	$2,276	$994	$620	$199	$131	$774	$536
GEOGRAPHIC DIVISIONS:														
New England	104.4	107.1	38.4	42.4	4,583	3,333	2,066	1,477	1,782	1,276	209	190	526	390
Middle Atlantic	92.2	82.4	62.6	63.4	6,319	4,759	3,122	2,512	2,094	1,601	358	296	745	350
East North Central	103.0	102.4	79.2	76.3	9,007	5,004	6,437	3,496	1,402	827	239	147	929	532
West North Central	209.6	189.5	148.0	127.0	12,196	5,488	9,097	3,870	1,407	715	322	186	1,368	917
South Atlantic	93.3	108.4	42.6	47.9	2,684	1,511	1,694	905	542	319	88	55	360	232
East South Central	78.2	89.9	42.2	44.5	2,094	1,324	1,278	784	394	250	72	54	350	236
West South Central	179.3	233.8	61.8	52.7	4,060	2,140	2,880	1,264	437	245	127	103	616	528
Mountain	324.5	456.9	86.8	82.9	9,351	5,922	6,402	2,608	701	338	209	156	2,119	2,400
Pacific	270.3	331.8	116.1	132.5	14,043	7,864	10,829	5,993	1,721	768	260	241	1,232	871
NEW ENGLAND:														
Maine	104.0	106.2	39.3	40.3	3,220	2,064	1,441	832	1,119	793	241	148	419	289
New Hampshire	120.1	123.1	34.3	36.7	3,833	2,927	1,616	1,211	1,530	1,181	217	176	470	360
Vermont	142.6	142.5	50.0	64.2	4,445	3,270	1,755	1,384	1,697	1,128	311	238	682	519
Massachusetts	77.5	83.4	31.5	36.3	6,135	4,843	2,858	2,295	2,401	1,885	313	224	562	419
Rhode Island	83.8	82.0	33.7	34.1	6,294	4,909	2,636	2,481	2,442	1,765	337	231	819	472
Connecticut	81.5	82.6	36.9	39.5	5,944	4,266	2,608	1,946	2,468	1,600	338	154	528	400
MIDDLE ATLANTIC:														
New York	102.2	99.9	68.8	65.8	6,532	4,715	3,283	2,451	2,212	1,486	186	247	849	531
New Jersey	75.9	82.0	53.9	57.1	7,640	5,479	3,767	2,694	2,777	1,998	361	280	734	506
Pennsylvania	84.8	86.4	57.5	58.9	5,715	4,590	2,873	2,566	1,873	1,440	325	227	643	457
EAST NORTH CENTRAL:														
Ohio	88.6	88.5	70.7	69.5	6,934	4,332	4,727	2,968	1,354	726	188	132	735	466
Indiana	98.6	97.4	78.6	75.2	8,336	4,419	6,164	3,083	1,235	694	196	121	807	494
Illinois	129.1	124.2	111.4	104.9	15,502	7,585	12,270	5,722	1,717	982	292	179	1,226	704
Michigan	91.3	86.4	62.0	58.0	5,251	3,396	2,973	2,081	1,281	752	241	142	656	289
Wisconsin	118.9	117.0	67.2	66.2	7,976	4,581	5,448	3,126	1,620	918	289	179	598	357
WEST NORTH CENTRAL:														
Minnesota	177.3	168.7	125.8	119.2	9,430	5,160	6,527	3,616	1,558	723	351	195	1,055	576
Iowa	156.3	151.2	133.6	130.8	17,259	8,023	12,910	5,497	2,006	1,093	440	253	1,811	1,220
Missouri	124.8	119.3	88.7	80.4	7,405	3,625	5,216	2,441	975	521	183	100	1,031	564
North Dakota	382.3	342.9	275.1	262.5	13,109	5,631	9,812	3,831	1,241	501	596	310	1,456	936
South Dakota	335.1	362.4	203.8	214.6	15,018	5,654	11,625	3,590	1,330	558	435	232	1,629	1,236
Nebraska	297.8	246.1	188.0	151.7	16,026	6,155	12,430	4,004	1,533	749	341	236	1,714	1,196
Kansas	244.0	240.7	168.2	144.7	11,467	4,922	8,648	3,074	1,122	641	273	170	1,426	1,163
SOUTH ATLANTIC:														
Delaware	93.2	110.1	68.5	77.8	5,338	4,394	3,234	2,454	1,681	1,101	296	222	629	434
Maryland	102.4	112.4	69.6	79.4	5,839	4,445	3,341	2,696	1,600	1,191	242	157	666	434
District of Columbia	22.9	31.6	23.7	22.1	30,092	42,882	23,132	36,060	4,751	5,850	426	505	784	466
Virginia	105.9	118.6	53.6	60.1	3,397	1,927	2,146	1,190	747	428	95	59	402	250
West Virginia	103.7	114.7	57.1	63.2	3,253	2,196	2,147	1,446	593	366	73	54	445	329
North Carolina	88.4	101.3	34.7	37.1	2,119	1,041	1,332	652	447	233	53	40	287	134
South Carolina	76.6	90.0	34.6	37.2	2,222	989	1,523	642	363	174	50	43	286	130
Georgia	92.6	117.3	42.3	47.2	1,995	1,016	1,273	616	374	200	72	44	276	157
Florida	105.0	106.9	36.1	37.0	2,863	1,321	1,874	755	498	314	90	48	412	274
EAST SOUTH CENTRAL:														
Kentucky	85.6	93.7	55.4	58.6	2,960	2,007	1,869	1,241	583	387	80	65	454	314
Tennessee	81.6	90.6	44.2	46.6	2,450	1,513	1,510	809	444	282	87	68	430	271
Alabama	78.9	92.7	35.9	38.8	1,408	802	825	449	271	154	62	39	250	162
Mississippi	67.6	82.6	32.8	34.4	1,554	925	926	520	292	168	62	44	274	193
WEST SOUTH CENTRAL:														
Arkansas	81.1	93.1	37.6	38.9	1,554	1,065	1,146	588	294	166	79	49	335	260
Louisiana	88.6	95.4	43.6	40.9	2,409	1,712	1,635	929	413	289	137	246	371	249
Oklahoma	132.7	[1]212.9	92.3	[1]79.4	4,828	[1]2,570	3,413	[1]1,283	477	196	142	[1]87	802	[1]591
Texas	269.1	357.2	65.5	55.6	5,311	2,733	3,999	1,669	503	285	136	53	763	683
MOUNTAIN:														
Montana	516.7	885.9	128.9	199.8	11,228	8,815	8,654	3,960	948	700	402	275	3,268	3,881
Idaho	171.5	181.4	90.2	85.9	9,911	3,880	7,149	2,031	615	391	346	186	1,616	1,260
Wyoming	727.6	1,333.0	114.5	120.6	15,217	12,971	8,002	3,845	859	579	334	224	5,961	6,423
Colorado	263.1	383.6	91.7	92.1	10,643	6,500	7,855	3,638	990	845	257	103	1,530	2,022
New Mexico	313.9	416.5	41.1	30.6	4,498	4,397	2,770	1,407	363	230	116	93	1,249	2,517
Arizona	135.1	332.2	38.0	43.8	8,142	6,163	4,590	1,965	536	280	194	132	2,822	2,978
Utah	156.7	212.4	68.1	53.2	6,997	3,858	4,580	2,070	833	549	206	151	1,328	1,108
Nevada	1,009.0	1,174.7	279.7	262.3	22,402	13,129	13,119	6,079	1,311	1,021	586	407	7,115	5,572
PACIFIC:														
Washington	208.4	256.6	113.4	104.4	11,346	4,338	9,208	2,991	971	491	297	183	870	667
Oregon	230.8	283.0	93.9	92.9	11,609	4,621	9,046	2,157	984	536	289	187	1,307	940
California	316.7	397.4	120.1	131.9	18,308	10,950	14,525	8,091	1,513	1,068	414	294	1,847	928

[1] Includes Indian Territory.

MICHIGAN.

Area, 57,980 sq. m.
Population, 2,810,173.

COUNTIES.

COUNTY.	CO. SEAT.	INDEX.	POP.
Alcona,	Harrisville	L 28	5,791
Alger,	Munising	E 19	7,675
Allegan,	Allegan	T 21	[illegible]
Alpena,	Alpena	J 28	[illegible]
Antrim,	Bellaire	K 22	15,692
Arenac,	Standish	N 27	9,640
Baraga,	L'Anse	D 14	6,127
Barry,	Hastings	T 23	[illegible]
Bay,	Bay City	P 27	[illegible]
Benzie,	Honor	L 20	[illegible]
Berrien,	Saint Joseph	W 19	[illegible]
Branch,	Coldwater	W 23	[illegible]
Calhoun,	Marshall	V 24	[illegible]
Cass,	Cassopolis	W 20	[illegible]
Charlevoix,	Charlevoix	I 22	19,157
Cheboygan,	Cheboygan	H 25	17,872
Chippewa,	Sault Ste. Marie	F 25	24,472
Clare,	Harrison	N 24	[illegible]
Clinton,	St. Johns	S 25	[illegible]
Crawford,	Grayling	L 25	[illegible]
Delta,	Escanaba	G 18	[illegible]
Dickinson,	Iron Mt.	F 16	[illegible]
Eaton,	Charlotte	T 24	[illegible]
Emmet,	Petoskey	H 23	[illegible]
[illegible]			
Saint Joseph,	Centreville	W 22	25,499
Sanilac,	Sandusky	Q 30	33,930
Schoolcraft,	Manistique	F 20	8,681
Shiawassee,	Corunna	R 26	33,324
Tuscola,	Caro	Q 28	34,913
Van Buren,	Paw Paw	V 21	33,185
Washtenaw,	Ann Arbor	U 27	44,714
Wayne,	Detroit	U 29	531,590
Wexford,	Cadillac	N 23	20,769
Total			2,810,173

TOWNS.

Roman type are Post Offices.
Italic type have no Post Office.
Full Face type, County Seat.
r. d., *rural delivery.*
× Population not reported.

TOWN. COUNTY. INDEX. POP.

Abbottsford, Saint Clair ... R 30 ... 25
Abbotts, Gogebic ... E 8 ... ×
Abronia (r. d. Otsego), Allegan ... U 21 ... ×
Acacia, Calhoun ... 40
Ackerson Lake, Jackson ... V 25 ... ×
Acme, Grand Traverse ... L 22 ... 100
Ada, Kent ... S 22 ... 200
Adair, Saint Clair ... S 31 ... 200
Adamsville (r. d. Edwardsburg), Cass ... W 20 ... 300
Addison, Lenawee ... W 26 ... 474
Addisons, Wayne ... ×
Adrian, Lenawee ... W 28 ... 11,201
Advance (r. d. Boyne), Charlevoix ...

[illegible]

Killagors, (R. R. name Killagore Lake) Saint Joseph.........W 23 40
Klink, (r. d. Eaton Rapids) Ingham...T 25 90
Klomann, Menominee H 16 ×
Klondike, (r. d. Hesperia) Oceana.......P 21 10
Klondike, Schoolcraft V 19 ×
Kneeland, Crawford, L 23 ×
Knight, Kalkaska.......... ×
Kosier Lake, Hillsdale V 25 ×
Koppman, Missaukee N 20 ×
Kovic, Newaygo......P 23 ×
Kurelock, (R. R. name Lake Gogebic) Ontonagon.............D 10 ×
Kurth, Leelanau.......... ×
Kose, (r. d. Stephenson) Menominee.......I 15 150
Kreiler, Bay.................. ×
Kullmbach, (r. d. Saginaw) Saginaw.......Q 27 ×

L.

Lamtage, (r. d. Caledonia) Kent.........S 23 100
Labranche, (R. R. name Putnam) Menominee G 17 70
Lacey, (r. d. Assyria) Barry..................U 23 25

Raco, Chippewa.....F 24 ×
Racy, (r. d. Chapin) Saginaw.........R 20 15
Rainbows, Menominee F 11 ×
Raish, Marquette....D 16 ×
Raisin Centre, (r. d. Holloway) Lenawee W 27 ×
Raisinville, (r. d. Dundee) Monroe.......V 28 181
Ralph, Dickinson....G 15 25
Ramona, Newaygo...P 23 50
Ramsey, Gogebic......E 9 150
Rand, Isabella............ ×
Randville, Dickinson, H 15 ×
Rankin, (r. d. Grand Blanc) Genesee.....S 27 41
Ransom, Hillsdale...W 25 200
Ranson, Marquette..D 16 ×
Rapid City, Kalkaska, K 22 400
Rapid River, Delta...G 18 600
Rapson, (r. d. Bad Axe) Huron.............O 30 30
Rathbone, (r. d. Breckenridge) Gratiot...Q 26 ×
Rattle Run, (r. d. Smiths Creek) Saint Clair..S 31 50
Rawsons Switch, Wayne.. ×
Ravenna, Muskegon..R 2 300
Rawsonville, (r. d. Belleville) Wayne...V 28 10
Ray Center, (r. d. New Haven) Macomb...S 30 100
Rea, (r. d. Dundee) Monroe...........W 27 25
Reeds, Marquette ....F 16 ×
Reading, Hillsdale...W 24 1,100
Rosetown, (R. R. name Craigsmere) Ontonagon..............E 12 ×
Rousseau, Huron.....Q 25 ×
Roseville, Macomb...U 30 600
Rosina, (r. d. Lake Odessa) Ionia......T 29 ×
Ross, Kent.............S 21 90
Ross, Oakland........... ×
Ross Siding, Gogebic E 19 ×
Rothbury, Oceana.....Q 19 200
Round Lake Junction, Wexford...........M 22 ×
Rowland, (r. d. Blanchard) Isabella.....Q 23 10
Rowley, Kalkaska....... ×
Roxana, (r. d. Charlotte) Eaton........T 24 150
Royal Oak, Oakland, U 29 1,071
Royalton, (r. d. St. Joseph) Berrien....V 19 1,156
Rubicon, (R. R. name Nesbetts Mill) Ontonagon..............D 11 81
Ruby, (r. d. Atkins) Saint Clair........R 31 115
Rudyard, Chippewa, F 24 100
Rugg, (r. d. Rapid City) Kalkaska.....K 23 40
Rumely, Alger ....E 18 200
Rushton, Livingston..U 27 26
Rusk, (r. d. Zeeland) Ottawa...............S 20 ×
Rust, (r. d. Comins) Montmorency .....K 26 ×
Rutford, (r. d. Morley)

[illegible]

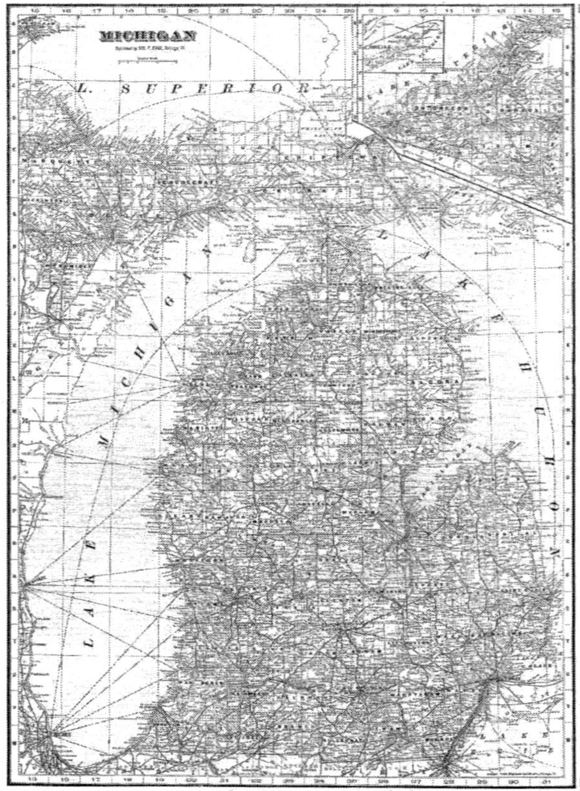
MICHIGAN
L. SUPERIOR
LAKE MICHIGAN
LAKE HURON

The Growth of Our Country

Populations of all Places of 3,000 and over for the Census Years of 1900 and 1910 and Their Elevations above Sea Level.

State	Population 1900	Population 1910
Continental		
United States	75,994,575	91,972,266
Alabama	1,828,697	2,138,093
Arizona	122,931	204,354
Arkansas	1,311,564	1,574,449
California	1,485,053	2,377,549
Colorado	539,700	799,024
Connecticut	908,420	1,114,756
Delaware	184,735	202,322
Dist. of Columbia	278,718	331,069
Florida	528,542	752,619
Georgia	2,216,331	2,609,121
Idaho	161,772	325,594
Illinois	4,821,550	5,638,591
Indiana	2,516,462	2,700,876
Iowa	2,231,853	2,224,771
Kansas	1,470,495	1,690,949
Kentucky	2,147,174	2,289,905
Louisiana	1,381,625	1,656,388
Maine	694,466	742,371
Maryland	1,188,044	1,295,346
Massachusetts	2,805,346	3,366,416
Michigan	2,420,982	2,810,173
Minnesota	1,751,394	2,075,708
Mississippi	1,551,270	1,797,114
Missouri	3,106,665	3,293,335
Montana	243,329	376,053
Nebraska	1,066,300	1,192,214
Nevada	42,335	81,875
N. Hampshire	411,588	430,572
New Jersey	1,883,669	2,537,167
New Mexico	195,310	327,301
New York	7,268,894	9,113,614
North Carolina	1,893,810	2,206,287
North Dakota	319,146	577,056
Ohio	4,157,545	4,767,121
Oklahoma	790,391	1,657,155
Oregon	413,536	672,765
Pennsylvania	6,302,115	7,665,111
Rhode Island	428,556	542,610
South Carolina	1,340,316	1,515,400
South Dakota	401,570	583,888
Tennessee	2,020,616	2,184,789
Texas	3,048,710	3,896,542
Utah	276,749	373,351
Vermont	343,641	355,956
Virginia	1,854,184	2,061,612
Washington	518,103	1,141,990
West Virginia	958,800	1,221,119
Wisconsin	2,069,042	2,333,860
Wyoming	92,531	145,965

United States Possessions

	1900	1910
Alaska	63,592	64,356
Guam Marianas	....	a 11,873
Hawaii	154,001	191,909
Philippine Isl.	....	b 7,635,426
Porto Rico	953,243	1,118,012
Samoan Isl.	....	c 6,663
Mil. and naval	55,608	55,608
		9,983,357

Total population (inclusive of Alaska, Guam, Hawaii, Philippine Islands, Porto Rico and Samoan Islands) 101,055,725

a Census, June 30, 1909.
b Census, 1903.
c Estimated.

ALABAMA

Place	Altitude	1900	1910
Alabama Cy.	...	2,276	4,313
Anniston	811	9,695	12,794
Bessemer	515	6,358	10,864
Birmingham	608	38,415	132,685
Decatur	598	3,114	4,228
Dothan	365	3,275	7,016
Eufaula	290	4,532	4,259
Florence	505	6,478	6,689
Gadsden	321	4,282	10,557
Girard	262	3,840	4,214
Greenville	123	3,162	3,377
Huntsville	625	8,068	7,611
Lanett	694	2,909	3,820
Mobile	57	38,469	51,521
Montgomery	222	30,346	38,136
New Decatur	570	4,437	6,118
Opelika	817	4,245	4,734
Phoenix	...	4,163	4,555
Selma	147	8,713	13,649
Sheffield	481	3,333	4,865
Talladega	553	5,056	5,854
Troy	581	4,097	4,961
Tuscaloosa	230	5,095	8,407
Tuscumbia	468	2,348	3,324
Union Spgs.	318	3,684	4,055

ARIZONA

Place	Altitude	1900	1910
Bisbee	5300	......	9,019
Clifton	3448	......	4,874
Douglas	3955	......	6,437
Globe	3509	1,495	7,083
Nogales	3857	1,761	3,514
Phoenix	1082	5,544	11,134
Prescott	5320	3,559	5,092
Tucson	2389	7,531	13,193

ARKANSAS

Place	Altitude	1900	1910
Argenta	256	.....	11,138
Batesville	272	2,327	3,399
Blytheville	...	302	3,849
Camden	139	2,840	3,995
Eldorado	269	1,069	4,202
Eureka Spgs.	1462	3,572	3,228
Fayetteville	1334	4,061	4,471
Fort Smith	448	11,587	23,975
Helena	189	5,550	8,772
Hope	355	1,644	3,639
Hot Springs	700	9,973	14,434
Jonesboro	345	4,508	7,123
Littl. Rock	239	38,307	45,941
Marianna	256	1,707	4,810
Mena	1140	3,423	3,953
Newport	226	2,860	3,557
Paragould	278	3,324	5,248
Pine Bluff	215	11,496	15,102
Texarkana	304	4,914	5,655
Van Buren	405	3,573	3,878

CALIFORNIA

Place	Altitude	1900	1910
Alameda	12	16,464	23,383
Alhambra	456	.....	5,021
Bakersfield	420	4,836	12,727
Berkeley	153	13,214	40,434
Chico	189	2,640	3,750
Coalinga	662	.....	4,199
Colton	978	.....	3,980
Corona	562	1,434	3,540
Eureka	28	7,327	11,845
Fresno	327	12,470	24,892
Grass Val.	2500	4,719	4,020
Hanford	248	2,929	4,829
Long Beach	47	2,252	17,809
Los Angeles	338	102,479	319,198
Marysville	67	3,497	5,430
Merced	167	1,969	3,102
Modesto	88	2,024	4,034
Monrovia	518	1,205	3,576
Monterey	10	1,748	4,923
Napa	31	4,036	5,791
Oakland	26	66,960	150,174
Ocean Park	71	.....	3,119
Ontario	986	722	4,274
Oroville	265	.....	3,859
Palo Alto	63	1,658	4,486
Pasadena	829	9,117	30,291
Petaluma	19	3,871	5,880
Pomona	861	5,526	10,207
Red Bluff	304	2,750	3,530
Reedley	559	2,846	3,572
Redlands	1335	4,797	10,449
Richmond	10	.....	6,802
Riverside	851	7,973	15,212
Sacramento	30	29,282	44,696
Salinas	44	2,304	3,729
San Ber'dino	1054	6,150	12,779
San Diego	42	17,700	39,578
San Fr'isco	155	342,782	416,912
San Jose	95	21,500	28,946
San Leandro	45	2,253	3,471
San Luis Ob.	201	3,021	5,157
San Mateo	22	1,832	4,384
San Rafael	42	3,879	5,934
Santa Ana	137	4,933	8,429
Santa B'bara	100	6,587	11,659
Santa Clara	88	3,650	4,348
Santa Cruz	15	5,659	11,146
SantaMonica	59	3,057	7,847
Santa Rosa	165	6,673	7,817
So. Pasadena	666	1,001	4,649
Stockton	17	17,506	23,253
Vallejo	37	7,965	11,340
Visalia	348	3,085	4,550
Watsonville	28	3,528	4,446
Whittier	346	1,590	4,550
Woodland	58	2,886	3,187

COLORADO

Place	Altitude	1900	1910
Alamosa	7536	1,141	3,013
Boulder	5350	6,150	9,539
Canon City	6320	3,775	5,162
Colo. City	6077	2,914	4,333
Colo. Sprgs.	6012	21,085	29,078
Cripple Crk.	9591	10,147	6,206
Denver	5270	133,859	213,381
Durango	6563	3,317	4,686
Fort Collins	4984	3,053	8,210
Grand Jcn.	4578	3,503	7,754
Greeley	4664	3,023	8,179
La Junta	4053	2,513	4,154
Leadville	10135	12,455	7,508
Longmont	4980	2,201	4,256
Loveland	4983	1,091	3,651
Montrose	5807	1,217	3,254
Pueblo	4693	28,157	44,395
Rocky Ford	4176	2,018	3,230
Salida	7038	3,722	4,425
Sterling	3932	998	3,044
Trinidad	5985	5,345	10,204
Victor	9771	4,986	3,162

CONNECTICUT

Place	Altitude	1900	1910
Ansonia	21	12,681	15,152
Bethel	377	2,660	3,327
Branford	1907	6,047	6,706
Bridgeport	15	70,996	102,054
Bristol	353	6,268	9,527
Danbury	381	16,537	23,234
Danielson	226	.....	3,225
Derby	16	7,930	8,991
East Hartf'd	39	.....	3,000
East Norw'k	42	.....	3,500
Forestville	212	.....	3,207
Greenwich	28	12,420	3,972
Groton	47	5,962	5,326
Hamden	...	.....	4,682
Hartford	38	79,850	98,915
Litchfield	956	.....	3,300
Manchester	177	.....	3,626
Meriden	150	24,296	27,265
Middletown	79	9,589	11,851
Milford	64	.....	3,683
Mystic	6	.....	3,000
Naugatuck	124	10,541	3,941
New Britain	155	25,998	43,916
New Haven	107	108,027	133,605
New London	45	17,548	19,659
New Milford	283	.....	3,000
Newtown	394	.....	3,276
Norwalk	39	6,125	6,954
Norwich	33	17,251	20,367
Portland	96	3,866	3,386
Putnam	287	6,697	6,637
Rockville	407	7,287	7,977
Seymour	100	.....	3,550
Shelton	...	4,807	4,572
Southington	149	3,411	3,714
So. M'ch'ster	...	.....	6,000
So. Norwalk	42	6,591	8,968
Stamford	34	15,997	25,138
Stratford	21	3,657	3,000
Taftville	...	.....	4,300
Thomaston	378	.....	3,300
Thompsonville	86	.....	4,000
Torrington	592	8,360	15,483
Wallingford	76	6,737	8,690
Waterbury	300	45,859	73,141
Watertown	481	.....	3,100
West Haven	64	3,247	8,513
Willimantic	247	8,937	11,230
Winsted	724	6,804	7,754

DELAWARE

Place	Altitude	1900	1910
Dover	40	3,329	3,720
New Castle	12	3,380	3,351
Wilmington	78	76,508	87,411

DISTRICT OF COLUMBIA

Place	Altitude	1900	1910
Washington	91	218,196	331,069

FLORIDA

Place	Altitude	1900	1910
Apalachicola	...	3,077	3,065
Daytona	...	1,690	3,082
Fernandina	10	3,245	3,482
Gainesville	179	3,633	6,183
Jacksonville	18	28,429	57,699
Key West	38	17,114	19,945
Lake City	201	4,013	5,032
Lakeland	206	1,180	3,719
Live Oak	108	1,659	3,450
Miami	15	1,681	5,471
Ocala	89	3,380	4,370
Orlando	98	2,481	3,894
Palatka	28	3,301	3,779
Pensacola	12	17,747	22,982
Quincy	260	847	3,204
St. Aug'tine	7	4,272	5,494
St. Petersb'g	20	1,575	4,127
Sanford	26	1,450	3,570
Tallahassee	188	2,981	5,018
Tampa	34	15,839	37,782
West Tampa	...	2,355	8,258

GEORGIA

Place	Altitude	1900	1910
Albany	184	4,606	8,190
Americus	369	7,674	8,063
Athens	694	10,245	14,913
Atlanta	1032	89,872	154,839
Augusta	160	39,441	41,040
Bainbridge	110	2,641	4,217
Barnesville	859	3,036	3,036
Brunswick	11	9,081	10,182
Carrollton	...	1,998	3,297
Cartersville	788	3,135	4,067
Cedartown	817	2,823	3,551
Columbus	260	17,614	20,554
Cordele	326	3,473	5,883
Cuthbert	446	2,641	3,210
Dalton	774	4,315	5,324
Dawson	352	2,926	3,827
Douglas	278	617	3,550
Dublin	...	2,987	5,795
East Point	1048	1,315	3,682
Elberton	720	3,834	6,483
Fitzgerald	276	1,817	5,795
Gainesville	1231	4,382	5,925
Griffin	975	6,857	7,478
Hawkinsville	335	2,103	3,420
LaGrange	789	4,274	5,587
Macon	311	23,272	40,665
Marietta	1118	4,446	5,949
Milledgeville	264	4,219	4,385
Monroe	...	1,846	3,029
Moultrie	...	2,221	3,349
Newnan	957	3,654	5,548
Quitman	80	2,781	3,310
Rome	612	7,291	12,099
Savannah	21	54,244	65,064
Summerville	780	3,946	4,881
Thomasville	236	5,322	6,727
Toccoa	1045	2,170	3,120
Valdosta	215	5,613	7,656
Washington	...	3,300	3,046
Waycross	131	5,919	14,485

IDAHO

Place	Altitude	1900	1910
Boise City	2739	5,957	17,358
Caldwell	2367	997	3,543
Coeur d'Alene	2152	508	7,291
Idaho Falls	4629	1,262	4,827
Lewiston	738	2,425	6,043
Moscow	2569	2,484	3,670
Nampa	2483	799	4,205
Pocatello	4483	4,046	9,110
Twin Falls	...	......	5,258
Wallace	2728	2,265	3,000

ILLINOIS

Place	Altitude	1900	1910
Alton	429	14,210	17,528
Aurora	676	24,147	29,807
Batavia	716	3,871	4,436
Beardstown	443	4,827	6,107
Belleville	477	17,484	21,122
Belvidere	783	6,937	7,253
Berwyn	...	......	5,841
Bloomington	781	23,286	25,768
Blue Island	606	6,114	8,043
Cairo	279	12,566	14,548
Canton	659	6,564	10,453
Carbondale	412	3,318	5,411
Carlinville	627	3,502	3,616
Centralia	496	6,721	9,680
Champaign	738	9,098	12,421
Charleston	720	5,488	5,884
Chicago	586	1,698,575	2,185,283
Chgo. Hghts.	684	5,100	14,525
Cicero	...	......	14,557
Clinton	737	4,452	5,165
Collinsville	448	4,021	7,478
Danville	604	16,354	27,871
Decatur	672	20,754	31,140
Dekalb	886	5,904	8,102
Dixon	736	7,917	7,216
Duquoin	458	4,353	5,454
E. St. Louis	415	29,655	58,547
Edwardsville	433	4,157	5,014
Eldorado	385	1,445	3,366
Elgin	715	22,433	25,976
Evanston	601	19,259	24,978
Forest Park	...	4,085	6,594
Freeport	767	13,258	17,567
Galena	601	5,005	4,835
Galesburg	758	18,607	22,089
Geneseo	648	3,256	3,199
Granite	429	3,122	9,903
Greenville	586	2,504	3,178
Harrisburg	368	3,202	5,309
Harvard	...	2,602	3,008
Herrin	420	1,559	6,861
Highland Pk.	691	2,806	4,209
Hillsboro	533	1,937	3,424
Hoopestown	715	3,823	4,698
Jacksonville	600	15,078	15,326
Jerseyville	...	3,517	4,113
Johnston	499	787	3,248
Joliet	584	29,353	34,670
Kankakee	652	13,595	13,986
Kewanee	861	8,382	9,307
LaGrange	643	3,969	5,282
Lake Forest	704	2,215	3,349
Lasalle	517	10,446	11,537
Lawrenceville	405	1,300	3,235
Lincoln	587	8,962	10,892
Litchfield	687	5,918	5,971
Macomb	709	5,375	5,774
Madison	421	1,979	5,046
Marion	423	2,510	7,092
Marseilles	494	2,559	3,291
Mattoon	735	9,622	11,456
Maywood	628	4,532	8,033
Melrose Pk.	620	2,592	4,806
Mendota	750	3,736	3,806
Metropolis	339	4,069	4,655
Moline	573	17,248	24,199
Monmouth	771	7,460	9,128
Morgan Pk.	627	2,329	3,694
Morris	522	4,273	4,563
Mt. Carmel	390	4,311	6,934
Mt. Olive	677	3,935	3,501
Mt. Vernon	483	5,216	8,007
Murphysboro	417	6,463	7,485
Naperville	717	2,629	3,449
Normal	790	3,795	4,024
No. Chicago	...	1,150	3,306
Oak Park	630	......	19,444
Olney	482	4,260	5,011
Ottawa	484	10,588	9,535
Pana	694	5,530	6,055
Paris	698	6,105	7,664
Pekin	495	8,420	9,897
Peoria	464	56,100	66,950
Peru	470	6,863	7,984
Pontiac	648	4,266	6,090
Portland	...	......	3,194
Princeton	700	4,023	4,131
Quincy	360	36,252	36,587
Robinson	500	1,683	3,863
Rock Island	540	19,493	24,335
Rockford	716	31,051	45,401
St. Charles	680	2,675	4,046
Savanna	582	3,325	3,691
Shelbyville	627	3,546	3,880
Sparta	524	2,941	3,081
Spr'g Valley	512	6,214	7,035
Springfield	598	34,159	51,678
Staunton	625	2,786	5,048
Sterling	648	6,309	7,467
Streator	626	14,079	14,253
Sycamore	850	3,653	3,926
Taylorville	625	4,248	5,446
Urbana	725	5,728	8,245
Venice	416	2,450	3,718
Virden	675	2,280	4,000
Waukegan	587	9,426	16,069
W. Ham'ond	...	2,935	4,948
Wheaton	746	2,345	3,423
Wilmette	614	2,300	4,943
Winnetka	639	1,833	3,168
Woodstock	...	2,502	4,331
Zion City	928	....	4,789

INDIANA

Place	Altitude	1900	1910
Alexandria	855	7,221	5,096
Anderson	874	20,178	22,476
Attica	522	3,005	3,335
Auburn	862	3,396	3,919
Aurora	425	3,645	4,416
Bedford	691	6,115	8,716
Bloomington	744	6,460	8,838
Bluffton	827	4,479	4,987
Boonville	395	2,540	3,604
Brazil	637	7,786	9,340
Clinton	490	2,918	6,229
Columbia	832	2,975	3,448
Columbus	621	8,130	8,813
Connersville	825	6,836	7,738
Cra'fordsville	775	6,649	9,371
Decatur	798	4,142	4,471
Dunkirk	946	3,187	3,031
E. Chicago	...	3,411	19,098
Elkhart	764	15,184	19,282
Elwood	859	12,950	11,028
Evansville	378	59,007	69,647
Fort Wayne	780	45,115	63,933
Frankfort	859	7,100	8,634
Franklin	735	4,005	4,502
Garrett	884	3,910	4,149
Gary	...	......	16,802
Gas	...	3,622	3,234
Goshen	756	7,810	8,514
Greencastle	767	3,661	3,790
Greenfield	995	4,489	4,448
Greensburg	941	5,034	5,420
Hammond	597	12,376	20,925
Hartford	888	5,912	6,187
Huntington	741	9,491	10,272
Indianapolis	720	169,164	233,650
Jasonville	628	......	3,295
Jeffers'ville	445	10,774	10,412
Kendallville	979	3,354	4,981
Kokomo	818	10,609	17,010
Lafayette	558	18,116	20,081
Laporte	812	7,113	10,525
Lawrenceb'g	485	4,326	3,930
Lebanon	924	4,465	5,474
Linton	522	3,071	5,906
Logansport	591	16,204	19,050
Madison	450	7,835	6,934
Marion	810	17,337	19,359
Martinsville	599	4,038	4,529
Mich. City	590	14,850	19,027
Mishawaka	720	5,560	11,886
Mitchell	676	1,772	3,438
Mt. Vernon	410	5,132	5,563
Muncie	944	20,942	24,005
New Albany	429	20,628	20,629
New Castle	997	3,406	9,446
Noblesville	772	4,792	5,073
Peru	638	8,463	10,910
Plymouth	790	3,656	3,838
Portland	869	4,798	5,130
Princeton	461	6,041	6,448
Richmond	963	18,226	22,324
Rochester	780	3,421	3,364
Rushville	958	4,541	4,925
Seymour	607	6,445	6,305
Shelbyville	768	7,169	9,500
South Bend	712	35,999	53,684
Sullivan	522	3,118	4,115
Tell	387	2,680	3,369
Terre Haute	496	36,673	58,157
Tipton	864	3,764	4,075
Union	814	2,716	3,209
Valparaiso	798	6,280	6,987
Vincennes	431	10,249	14,895
Wabash	710	8,618	8,687
Warsaw	824	3,987	4,430
Washington	484	8,551	7,854
W. Lafayette	...	2,302	3,867
W. Ter. Haute	...	651	3,083
Whiting	587	3,983	6,587
Winchester	988	3,705	4,266

IOWA

Place	Altitude	1900	1910
Albia	960	3,889	4,969
Ames	922	2,422	4,223
Atlantic	1164	5,046	4,560
Belle Plain	828	3,283	3,121
Boone	1112	8,880	10,347
Burlington	435	23,201	24,324
Carroll	1260	3,823	3,546
Cedar Falls	854	5,319	5,012
Ced. Rapids	738	25,656	32,811
Centerville	1012	5,256	6,936
Chariton	1042	3,989	3,794
Charles	1005	4,227	5,892
Cherokee	1201	3,865	4,884
Clarinda	1009	3,276	3,987
Clinton	593	22,698	25,577
Coun. Bluffs	990	25,802	29,292
Creston	1312	7,752	6,924
Davenport	539	35,254	43,028
Decorah	878	3,246	3,592
Denison	1179	2,771	3,133
Des Moines	861	62,139	86,368
Dubuque	698	36,297	38,494
Eagle Grove	118	3,557	3,387
Esthervillo	1298	3,237	4,404
Fairfield	780	4,689	4,970
Ft. Dodge	1011	12,162	15,543
Ft. Madison	533	9,278	8,900
Glenwood	987	3,040	4,052
Grinnell	1023	3,860	5,036
Independ'ce	921	3,656	3,517
Indianola	969	3,261	3,283
Iowa City	688	7,987	10,091
Keokuk	483	14,641	14,008
Knoxville	910	3,131	3,190
LeMars	1224	4,146	4,157
Maquoketa	688	3,777	3,570
Marion	848	4,102	4,400
Marshallt'n	890	11,544	13,374
Mason	1130	6,746	11,230
Mo. Valley	1008	4,010	3,187
Mt. Pleasant	729	4,109	3,874
Muscatine	551	14,073	16,178
Newton	892	3,682	4,616
Oelwein	1044	5,142	6,028
Oskaloosa	843	9,212	9,466
Ottumwa	649	18,197	22,012
Pella	877	3,023	3,021
Perry	987	3,986	4,630
Red Oak	1077	4,355	4,830
Shenandoah	974	3,573	4,976
Sioux City	1135	33,111	47,828
Spencer	1319	3,095	3,005
Vinton	810	3,499	3,336
Washington	759	4,255	4,380
Waterloo	866	12,580	26,693
Waverly	948	3,177	3,205
Webster	1047	4,613	5,208

KANSAS

Place	Altitude	1900	1910
Abilene	1158	3,507	4,118
Arkansas	1078	6,140	7,508
Atchison	789	15,722	16,429
Beloit	1378	2,353	3,082
Caney	737	887	3,597
Chanute	940	4,208	9,272
Cherryvale	826	3,472	4,304
Clay Center	1200	3,069	3,438
Coffeyville	744	4,953	12,687
Columbus	899	2,310	3,064
Concordia	1398	3,401	4,415
Dodge	2480	1,942	3,214
Eldorado	1284	3,466	3,129
Emporia	1134	8,223	9,058
Fort Scott	800	10,322	10,463
Fredonia	866	1,650	3,040
Frontenac	...	1,805	3,396
Galena	976	10,155	6,096
Garden	2829	1,590	3,171
Great Bend	1843	2,470	4,622
Herington	1324	1,607	3,273
Horton	1128	3,398	3,600
Hutchinson	1529	9,379	16,364
Independ'ce	819	4,851	10,480
Iola	962	5,791	9,032
Junc. City	1078	4,695	5,598
Kansas City	750	51,418	82,331
Lawrence	829	10,862	12,374
Leavenw'th	745	20,735	19,363
McPherson	1488	2,996	3,546
Manhattan	1014	3,438	5,722
Newton	1440	6,208	7,862
Olathe	1036	3,451	3,272
Osawatomie	882	4,127	4,046
Ottawa	975	6,934	7,650
Paola	865	3,144	3,207
Parsons	896	7,682	12,463
Pittsburg	922	10,112	14,755
Pratt	1887	1,315	3,302
Rosedale	792	3,270	5,960
Salina	1227	6,074	9,688
Topeka	998	33,608	43,684
Wellington	1227	4,245	7,034
Wichita	1365	24,671	52,450
Winfield	1124	5,554	6,700

KENTUCKY

Place	Altitude	1900	1910
Ashland	537	6,800	8,688
Bellevue	481	6,332	6,683
Bo'ling Grn.	469	8,226	9,173
Catlettsburg	544	3,081	3,520
Covington	513	42,938	53,270
Cynthiana	725	3,257	3,603
Danville	989	4,285	5,420
Dayton	541	6,104	6,971
Earlington	370	3,012	3,931

Frankfort	560	9,487	10,465
Franklin	691	3,156	3,063
Georgetown	877	3,823	4,533
Harrodsb'g	829	2,876	3,117
Henderson	382	10,272	11,452
Hopkinsville	521	7,280	9,419
Lebanon	779	3,043	3,077
Lexington	989	26,369	35,099
Louisville	525	204,731	223,928
Ludlow	532	3,334	4,163
Madisonville	512	3,628	4,966
Mayfield	...	4,081	5,916
Maysville	448	6,423	6,141
Middlesboro	1158	4,162	7,305
Mt. Sterling	930	3,561	3,932
Newport	598	28,301	30,309
Owensboro	179	13,189	16,011
Paducah	341	19,446	22,760
Paris	847	4,603	5,859
Princeton	455	2,556	3,016
Richmond	926	4,653	5,340
Russellville	534	2,591	3,111
Shelbyville	690	3,016	3,412
Somerset	860	3,384	4,491
Winchester	959	5,964	7,156

LOUISIANA

Place	Altitude	1900	1910
Alexandria	77	5,648	11,213
Baton Rouge	19	11,269	14,897
Crowley	21	4,214	5,099
Don'sonville	32	4,105	4,690
Franklin	10	3,592	3,857
Houma	14	3,212	5,024
Jennings	28	1,539	3,925
Kentwood	200	1,312	2,609
LaFayette	22	3,314	6,392
Lk. Charles	22	6,680	11,449
Minden	181	1,561	3,002
Monroe	82	5,428	10,209
Morgan	6	2,332	5,477
New Iberia	15	6,815	7,499
New Orleans	5	287,104	339,075
Opelousas	68	2,951	4,623
Plaquemine	28	3,590	4,955
Ruston	305	1,324	2,377
Shreveport	204	16,013	28,015
Thibodaux	...	3,253	3,824

MAINE

Place	Altitude	1900	1910
Auburn	183	12,951	15,064
Augusta	47	11,683	13,211
Bangor	24	21,850	24,803
Bath City	7	10,477	9,396
Belfast	7	4,615	4,618
Biddeford	75	16,145	17,079
Brewer	31	4,835	5,667
Bridgton	405	1,862	1,474
Brunswick	68	6,210	6,341
Calais	...	7,655	6,116
Camden	...	2,825	3,015
Caribou	400	4,758	5,377
Chelsea	...	3,092	3,216
Dexter	810	2,941	3,520
Eastport	70	5,311	4,961
Eden	...	4,379	4,441
Ellsworth	112	4,297	3,549
Fairfield	90	3,878	4,435
Farmington	388	3,288	3,219
Ft. Fairfield	398	4,181	4,381
Fort Kent	532	2,528	3,710
Gardiner	32	5,501	5,311
Houlton	357	4,686	5,845
Kennebunk	31	3,228	3,099
Kittery	...	2,872	3,533
Lewiston	185	23,761	26,247
Lisbon	196	3,802	4,116
Lubec	...	3,005	2,363
Madison	257	2,764	3,279
Millinocket	369	....	3,368
Orono	115	3,257	3,556
Old Town	108	5,763	6,317
Portland	26	50,145	58,571
Rockland	...	8,150	8,174
Rumf'dFalls	516	3,595	6,427
Saco	75	6,122	6,583
Sanford	...	6,078	9,049
Skowhegan	...	5,180	5,341
So. Portland	...	6,287	7,471
Van Buren	496	1,878	3,065
Waterville	112	9,477	11,458
Westbrook	...	7,283	8,281

MARYLAND

Place	Altitude	1900	1910
Annapolis	20	8,525	8,609
Baltimore	123	508,957	558,485
Brunswick	248	2,471	3,721
Cambridge	20	5,747	6,407
Crisfield	5	3,165	3,468
Cumberland	650	17,128	21,839
Easton	38	3,074	3,083
Frederick	250	9,296	10,411
Frostburg	2074	5,274	6,028
Hagerstown	550	13,591	16,507
Havre de G.	35	3,423	4,212
Salisbury	23	4,277	6,690
Westm'n'ter	700	3,199	3,295

MASSACHUSETTS

Place	Altitude	1900	1910
Abington	104	4,489	5,455
Adams	799	11,134	13,026
Agawam	...	2,536	3,501
Amesbury	28	9,473	9,894
Amherst	297	5,028	5,112
Andover	85	6,813	7,301
Arlington	46	8,603	11,187
Athol	550	7,061	8,536
Attleboro	129	11,335	16,215
Barnstable	72	4,364	4,676
Belmont	80	3,930	5,542
Beverly	23	13,884	18,650
Blackstone	214	5,721	5,648
Boston	125	560,892	670,585
Braintree	64	5,981	8,066
Bridgewater	82	5,806	7,688
Brockton	125	40,063	56,878
Brookline	43	19,935	27,792
Cambridge	74	91,886	104,839
Canton	113	4,584	4,797
Chelmsford	...	3,984	5,010
Chelsea	11	34,072	32,452
Chicopee	84	19,167	25,401
Clinton	309	13,667	13,075
Concord	139	5,652	6,421
Dalton	1188	3,014	3,568
Danvers	62	8,542	9,407
Dartmouth	...	3,669	4,378
Dedham	115	7,457	9,284
Dracut	...	3,253	3,461
Dudley	...	3,543	4,267
E. Bridgew'r	102	3,025	3,363
East'mpton	169	4,603	5,524
Easton	124	4,837	6,139
Everett	12	24,336	33,484
Fairhaven	17	3,567	5,122
Fall River	200	104,863	119,295
Falmouth	44	3,500	3,144
Fitchburg	550	31,531	37,826
Foxborough	296	3,266	3,863
Framing'am	199	11,302	12,948
Franklin	301	5,017	5,641
Gardner	1030	10,813	14,699
Gloucester	52	26,121	24,398
Grafton	...	4,868	5,705
Gt.Barr'ngt'n	726	5,854	5,926
Greenfield	204	7,927	10,427
Hardwick	40	3,207	3,524
Haverhill	35	37,175	44,115
Hingham	21	5,059	4,965
Holyoke	954	45,712	57,730
Hudson	235	5,454	6,743
Hyde Park	59	13,244	15,507
Ipswich	26	4,658	5,777
Lawrence	51	62,559	85,892
Lee	...	3,596	4,106
Leicester	980	3,416	3,231
Lenox	974	2,942	3,060
Leominster	404	12,392	17,580
Lexington	201	3,831	4,918
Lowell	100	94,969	106,294
Ludlow	239	3,536	4,948
Lynn	26	68,513	89,336
Malden	34	33,664	44,404
Mansfield	169	4,006	5,183
Marblehead	32	7,582	7,338
Marlbo'ugh	375	13,609	14,579
Maynard	176	3,142	6,390
Medfield	188	2,926	3,466
Medford	13	18,244	23,150
Melrose	59	12,962	15,715
Methuen	105	7,512	11,448
Middlebo'gh	110	6,885	8,214
Milford	266	11,376	13,055
Millbury	407	4,460	4,740
Milton	24	6,578	7,924
Monson	420	3,402	4,758
Montague	238	6,150	6,866
Natick	179	9,488	9,866
Needham	169	4,016	5,026
NewBedford	88	62,442	96,652
Newburyport	39	14,478	14,949
Newton	33	33,587	39,806
NorthAdams	406	24,200	22,019
N. Andover	83	4,243	5,529
N.Att'bo'ugh	...	7,253	9,562
N.Brooksfi'ld	807	3,587	3,075
North'mpton	124	18,643	19,431
Northbridge	284	7,036	8,807
Norwood	149	5,480	8,014
Orange	505	5,520	5,282
Oxford	515	2,677	3,361
Palmer	332	7,801	8,610
Peabody	19	11,523	15,721
Pittsfield	1038	21,766	32,121
Plymouth	28	9,592	12,141
Provi'cet'wn	22	4,247	4,369
Quincy	...	23,899	32,642
Randolph	...	3,993	4,301
Reading	107	4,969	5,818
Revere	16	10,395	18,219
Rockland	...	5,327	6,928
Rockport	62	4,592	4,211
Salem	10	35,956	43,697
Saugus	20	5,084	8,047
Somerville	13	61,643	77,236
Southbridge	...	10,025	12,592
SouthHadley	...	4,526	4,894
Spencer	...	7,627	6,740
Springfield	119	62,059	88,926
Stoneham	147	6,197	7,090
Stoughton	229	5,442	6,316
Sutton	346	3,328	3,078
Swampscott	38	4,548	6,204
Taunton	40	31,036	34,259
Templeton	964	3,189	3,756
Tewksbury	115	3,683	3,750
Uxbridge	259	3,599	4,671
Wakefield	107	9,290	11,404
Walpole	177	3,572	4,892
Waltham	105	23,481	27,834
Ware	488	8,263	8,774
Wareham	19	3,433	4,102
Warren	595	4,417	4,188
Watertown	19	9,706	12,875
Webster	440	9,804	11,509
Wellesley	149	5,072	5,413
W. Springf'd	...	7,105	9,224
Westboro'gh	298	5,400	5,446
Westfield	149	12,310	16,044
Weymouth	39	11,324	12,895
Whitman	79	6,155	7,292
Williamst'n	602	5,013	3,708
Winchendon	984	5,001	5,678
Winchester	81	7,248	9,309
Winthrop	...	6,058	10,132
Woburn	98	14,254	15,308
Worcester	479	118,421	145,986

MICHIGAN

Place	Altitude	1900	1910
Adrian	810	9,654	10,763
Albion	930	4,519	5,833
Allegan	628	2,667	3,419
Alpena	592	11,807	12,706
Ann Arbor	811	14,509	14,817
Battle Creek	823	18,563	25,267
Bay City	597	27,628	45,166
Belding	...	3,282	4,119
Benton H'b'r	595	6,562	9,185
Bessemer	1437	3,911	4,583
Big Rapids	923	4,686	4,519
Boyne	...	912	5,218
Cadillac	1293	5,997	8,375
Charlotte	918	4,092	4,886
Cheboygan	604	6,489	6,859
Coldwater	...	6,216	5,945
Crys. Falls	1344	3,231	3,775
Detroit	585	285,704	465,766
Dowagiac	780	4,151	5,088
Escanaba	612	9,549	13,194
Flint	725	13,103	38,550
Gladstone	612	3,380	4,211
G'd Haven	632	4,743	5,856
G'd Rapids	610	87,565	112,571
Greenville	818	3,381	4,045
Hamtramck	...	......	3,559
Hancock	606	4,050	8,981
Hastings	777	3,172	4,383
High'l'd P'k	1002	437	4,120
Hillsdale	1090	4,151	5,001
Holland	612	7,790	10,490
Houghton	668	3,359	5,113
Ionia	648	5,209	5,030
Iron M'nt'n	1160	9,242	9,216
Ironwood	1506	9,705	12,821
Ishpeming	1402	13,255	12,448
Jackson	940	25,180	31,433
Kalamazoo	778	24,404	39,437
Lansing	828	16,485	31,229
Lapeer	827	3,297	3,946
Laurium	1192	5,643	8,537
Ludington	593	7,166	9,132
Manistee	598	14,260	12,381
Manistique	613	4,126	4,722
Marine	583	3,829	3,770
Marquette	628	10,058	11,503
Marshall	906	4,370	4,236
Menominee	594	12,818	10,507
Monroe	590	5,043	6,893
Mt. Clemens	613	6,576	7,707
Mt. Pleas'nt	768	3,662	5,972
Muskegon	593	20,818	24,062
Negaunee	1419	6,935	8,460
Niles	650	4,287	5,156
Norway	846	4,170	4,874
Owosso	737	8,696	9,639
Petoskey	682	5,285	4,778
Pontiac	928	9,769	14,532
Pt. Huron	599	19,158	18,863
Red Jacket	...	4,668	4,211
River Rouge	...	1,748	4,163
Saginaw	590	42,345	50,510
St. Johns	766	3,388	3,151
St. Joseph	591	5,155	5,939
S. St. Marie	614	10,538	12,615
So. Haven	582	4,009	3,577
Sturgis	918	2,465	3,885
Three Riv.	790	3,550	5,072
Traverse	589	9,407	12,115
Wyandotte	549	5,183	8,287
Ypsilanti	718	7,378	6,230

MINNESOTA

Place	Altitude	1900	1910
Albert Lea	1229	4,500	6,192
Alexandria	1391	2,681	3,001
Anoka	879	3,769	3,972
Austin	1195	5,474	6,960
Bemidji	1341	2,183	5,099
Brainerd	1210	7,524	8,526
Chisholm	1504	......	7,684
Cloquet	1189	3,072	7,031
Crookston	863	5,359	7,559
Duluth	603	52,969	78,466
Ely	1417	3,717	3,572
Eveleth	1574	2,752	7,036
Faribault	1003	7,868	9,001
Fergus Fls.	1210	6,072	6,887
Hastings	706	3,811	3,983
Hibbing	1537	2,481	8,832
Lake	688	2,744	3,142
Little Falls	1114	5,774	6,078
Mankato	785	10,599	10,365
Minneapolis	782	202,718	301,408
Montevideo	990	3,146	3,056
Moorhead	935	3,730	4,840
New Ulm	791	5,403	5,648
Northfield	916	3,210	3,265
Owatonna	1145	5,561	5,658
Red Wing	680	7,525	9,048
Rochester	991	6,843	7,844
St. Cloud	1020	8,663	10,600
St. Paul	694	163,065	214,744
St. Peter	711	4,302	4,176
So. St. Paul	...	2,322	4,510
Stillwater	688	12,318	10,198
Thief R. Fls.	...	1,819	3,714
Two Harbors	692	3,278	4,990
Virginia	1449	2,962	10,473
Waseca	1153	3,103	3,054
W. Minneap'ls	...	1,848	3,022
Willmar	1131	3,409	4,135
Winona	666	19,714	18,583

MISSISSIPPI

Place	Altitude	1900	1910
Aberdeen	210	3,424	3,708
B. St. Louis	21	2,872	3,888
Biloxi	24	5,467	8,049
Brookhaven	487	2,678	5,293
Canton	328	3,404	3,929
Clarksdale	173	1,773	4,079
Columbus	250	6,484	8,988
Corinth	460	3,661	5,020
Greenville	125	7,642	9,610
Greenwood	129	3,026	5,836
Gulfport	19	1,060	6,386
Hattiesb'g	132	4,175	11,733
Jackson	288	7,816	21,262
Laurel	243	3,193	8,465
McComb	...	4,477	6,237
Meridian	341	14,050	23,285
Moss Point	...	......	3,054
Natchez	203	12,210	11,791
Pascagoula	...	708	3,379
Tupelo	270	2,118	3,881
Vicksburg	198	14,834	20,814
Water Val.	300	3,813	3,375
W. Point	237	3,193	4,864
Yazoo	117	4,944	6,796

MISSOURI

Place	Altitude	1900	1910
Aurora	1366	6,191	4,148
Boonville	598	4,377	4,252
Brookfield	758	5,484	5,749
Cape Gir'd'u	356	4,815	8,475
Carrollton	665	3,804	3,452
Carterville	976	4,445	4,539
Carthage	972	9,416	9,483
Caruth'ville	...	2,315	3,655
Charleston	327	1,893	3,144
Chillicothe	765	6,905	6,265
Clinton	775	5,061	4,992
Columbia	738	5,651	9,662
De Soto	509	3,611	4,721
Excels'r Sp.	929	1,881	3,900
Flat River	761	......	5,112
Fulton	813	4,883	5,228
Hannibal	524	12,780	18,341
Indep'dence	1050	6,974	9,859
Jeff'son City	437	9,664	11,850
Joplin	1009	26,023	32,073
Kansas City	863	163,752	248,381
Kennett	...	1,509	3,633
Kirksville	966	5,966	6,347
Kirkwood	636	2,836	4,171
Lexington	813	4,190	5,242
Louisiana	474	5,131	4,423
Macon	859	4,068	3,584
Maplewood	...	......	4,976
Marceline	858	2,638	3,920
Marshall	847	5,086	4,869
Maryville	1180	4,577	4,762
Mexico	820	5,099	5,939
Moberly	876	8,012	10,923
Monett	1303	3,116	4,177
Neosho	1011	2,725	3,661
Nevada	860	7,461	7,176
Poplar Bluff	344	4,321	6,916
Richmond	808	3,478	3,664
St. Charles	614	7,982	9,437
St. Joseph	813	102,979	77,403
St. Louis	466	575,238	687,029
Sedalia	919	15,231	17,822
Sikeston	325	1,077	3,327
Slater	861	3,502	3,238
Springfield	1324	23,267	35,201
Trenton	812	5,396	6,656
Warrensb'g	853	4,724	4,689
Washington	491	3,015	3,670
Webb City	986	9,201	11,817
Webst'r G'ves	596	1,896	7,080
Wellston	...	....	7,312

MONTANA

Place	Altitude	1900	1910
Anaconda	5265	9,453	10,134
Billings	3117	3,221	10,031
Bozeman	4784	3,419	5,107
Butte	5484	30,470	39,165
Great Falls	3372	14,930	13,948
Havre	2480	1,033	3,624
Helena	4110	10,770	12,515
Kalispel	2946	2,526	5,549
Livingston	4487	2,778	5,359
Miles City	2357	1,938	4,697
Missoula	3308	4,366	12,869
Red Lodge	5587	2,152	4,360

NEBRASKA

Place	Altitude	1900	1910
Alliance	3963	3,525	3,105
Beatrice	1235	7,875	9,356
Benson	...	510	3,170
Columbus	1442	3,522	5,014
Fairbury	1316	3,140	5,294
Falls	903	3,022	3,255
Fremont	1208	7,241	8,718
Grand Isl'nd	1860	7,554	10,326
Hastings	1932	7,188	9,338
Holdrege	2324	3,007	3,030
Kearney	2146	5,634	6,202
Lincoln	1159	40,169	43,973
McCook	2506	2,445	3,765
Nebraska Cy.	931	7,380	5,488
Norfolk	1532	3,883	6,025
No. Platte	2831	3,640	4,793
Omaha	1123	102,555	124,096
Plattsmouth	979	4,946	4,287
So. Omaha	1107	26,001	26,259
Univ. Place	...	1,120	3,200
York	1642	5,132	6,235

NEVADA.

Place	Altitude	1900	1910
Reno	4484	4,500	10,867

NEW HAMPSHIRE.

Place	Altitude	1900	1910
Berlin City	1018	8,886	11,780
Claremont	514	6,498	7,529
Concord	244	19,632	21,497
Conway	466	3,154	3,413
Derry	278	3,583	5,123
Dover	77	13,207	13,247
Exeter	68	4,922	4,897
Franklin	354	5,846	6,132
Haverhill	617	3,414	3,498
Keene	508	9,165	10,068
Laconia	507	8,042	10,183
Lancaster	887	3,190	3,054
Lebanon	532	4,965	5,718
Littleton	772	....	4,069
Manchester	246	56,987	70,063
Milford	250	3,739	3,939
Nashua	125	23,898	26,005
Newmarket	33	2,892	3,318
Newport	804	3,126	3,765
Pembroke	...	3,183	3,062
Portsmouth	14	10,637	11,269
Rochester	229	8,466	8,868
Somersworth	180	7,023	6,704

NEW JERSEY

Place	Altitude	1900	1910
Asbury Pk.	22	4,148	10,150
Atlantic	52	27,838	46,150
Bayonne	50	32,722	55,545
Bloomfield	120	9,668	15,070
Boontown	412	3,901	4,930
Bordent'wn	16	4,110	4,250
Boundbrook	31	2,622	3,970
Bridgeton	39	13,913	14,209
Burlington	33	7,392	8,336
Camden	31	75,935	94,538
Carlstadt	...	2,574	3,807
Cliffside Pk.	...	868	3,394
Collingsw'd	25	1,633	4,795
Dover	575	5,938	7,468
E. Newark	26	2,590	3,163
E. Orange	173	21,506	34,371
E. Rutherf'd	...	2,640	4,275
Elizabeth	40	52,130	73,409
Englewood	45	6,253	9,924
Fort Lee	314	......	4,472
Freehold	167	2,934	3,233
Garfield	...	3,504	10,213
Glen Ridge	172	1,960	3,260
Gloucester	11	6,840	9,462
Guttenb'g	...	3,825	5,647
Hackensack	14	9,443	14,050
Haddonfield	78	2,776	4,412
Hammonton	80	3,481	5,088
Harrison	33	10,596	14,498
Hawthorne	48	2,096	3,400
Hoboken	7	59,364	70,324
Irvington	...	5,255	11,877
Jersey	31	206,433	267,779
Kearney	...	10,896	18,659
Keyport	33	3,413	3,554
Lamberty'e	61	4,637	4,507
Lodi	28	7,917	4,138
L'ng Branch	28	8,872	13,298
Madison	248	3,754	4,658
Millville	38	10,583	12,451
Montclair	241	13,962	21,550
Morristown	404	11,267	12,507
Newark	56	246,070	347,469
N. Brunsw'k	18	20,006	23,388
Newton	678	4,376	4,467
N. Plainf'ld	...	5,009	6,117
Nutley	99	1,683	6,009
Orange	168	24,141	29,630
Passaic	88	27,777	54,773
Paterson	100	105,171	125,600
P'rth Amb'y	61	17,699	32,121
Phillipsb'g	186	10,052	13,903
Plainfield	100	15,369	20,550
Pleasantv'e	22	2,182	4,350
Princeton	209	3,899	5,136
Rahway	22	7,335	9,337
Raritan	...	3,244	3,672
Redbank	25	5,428	7,398
Ridgewood	139	2,685	5,416
Roosevelt	...	....	5,786
Roselle P'k	...	....	3,138
Rutherford	47	4,411	7,045
Salem	16	5,811	6,614
Secaucus	41	1,626	4,720
Somerville	82	4,843	6,060
So. Amboy	7	6,349	7,007
So. Orange	187	4,608	6,014
So. River	10	2,792	4,772
Summit	370	5,302	7,500
Trenton	60	73,307	96,815
Union	104	15,187	21,023
Vineland	115	4,370	5,282
Wallington	...	1,812	3,448
Washington	462	3,580	3,567
Westfield	128	....	6,420
W. Hoboken	...	23,094	35,403
W. N. York	...	5,267	13,560
W. Orange	...	6,889	10,980
Woodbury	62	4,087	4,642

NEW MEXICO

Place	Altitude	1900	1910
Albuquerque	5008	6,238	11,020
Clovis	....	......	3,255
Las Cruces	3860	......	3,836
Las Vegas	6391	3,552	3,775
Las Vegas	6714	3,797	3,179
Raton	6400	3,540	4,539
Roswell	3567	2,049	6,172
Santa Fe	7013	5,603	5,072
Silver	5851	2,735	3,217

NEW YORK.

Place	Altitude	1900	1910
Albany	18	94,151	100,253
Albion	519	4,477	5,016
Amsterdam	264	20,929	31,267
Auburn	645	30,345	34,668
Baldwinsv'e	389	3,992	3,099
Ballston Spa	320	3,923	4,138
Batavia	950	9,180	11,613
Bath	1103	4,994	3,884
Binghamton	866	39,647	48,443
Brockport	542	3,398	3,579
Buffalo	576	352,387	423,715
Canandaig'a	688	6,151	7,217
Canastota	486	3,030	3,247
Carthage	737	3,896	3,563
Catskill	98	5,484	5,296
Cohoes	159	23,916	24,709
Corning	936	11,061	13,730
Cortland	1130	9,014	11,504
Dansville	1025	3,633	3,938
Depew	680	3,379	3,921
Dobbs Ferry	12	3,858	3,455
Dunkirk	598	11,616	17,221
E. Syracuse	...	3,509	3,274
Ellenville	317	3,879	3,114
Elmira	862	35,672	37,176
Fairport	455	3,489	3,112
Fishkill L'dg	8	3,673	3,902
Ft. Edward	147	3,421	3,762
Frankfort	400	2,984	3,303
Fredonia	767	4,127	5,285
Freeport	23	2,612	4,836
Fulton	352	5,290	10,480
Geneva	451	10,433	12,446
Glens Falls	340	12,613	15,243
Gloversville	860	18,349	20,642
Goshen	431	3,326	3,081
Gouverneur	425	3,589	4,128
Granville	463	3,700	3,920
Green Isl'nd	314	4,770	4,737
Greenport	7	3,368	3,089
Hast.-on-H.	12	2,002	4,552
Haverstraw	103	5,935	5,669
Hempstead	60	3,582	4,964
Herkimer	406	5,555	7,520
Hoosick F'ls	432	5,671	5,532
Hornell	1152	11,918	13,617
Hudson	26	9,528	11,417
Hudson F'ls	...	4,473	5,189
Ilion	408	5,138	6,588
Ithaca	381	13,136	14,802
Jamestown	1328	22,892	31,297
Johnstown	650	10,130	10,447
Kingston	223	24,535	25,908
Lackawanna	...	....	14,549
Lancaster	683	3,750	4,364
Leroy	883	3,144	3,771
Lestershire	847	3,111	3,775
Little Falls	378	10,381	12,273
Lockport	630	16,581	17,970
Lyons	406	4,300	4,460
Malone	810	5,935	5,467
Mamaron'ck	47	....	5,699
Mattewan	119	5,807	6,727
Mech'nicsv'e	81	4,695	6,634
Medina	516	4,716	5,683
Middletown	700	14,522	15,313
Mt. Vernon	114	21,228	30,919
New Roch'le	72	14,720	28,867
New York	54	3,437,202	4,766,883
Boroughs—			
Manhattan	314	1,850,093	2,331,542
Bronx	100	200,507	430,980
Brooklyn	107	1,166,582	1,634,351
Richmond	63	67,021	85,969
Queens	75	152,999	284,041
Newark	456	4,578	6,227
Newburgh	94	24,943	27,805
Niagara F'ls	574	19,457	30,445
N. Tarryt'n	...	4,241	5,421
N. Tonaw'da	580	9,069	11,955
Norwich	1000	5,766	7,422
Nyack	68	4,275	4,619
Ogdensburg	258	12,633	15,933
Olean	1457	9,462	14,743
Oneida	1100	6,364	8,317
Oneonta	1100	7,147	9,491
Ossining	8	7,939	11,480
Oswego	296	22,199	23,368
Owego	816	5,039	4,633
Patchogue	15	2,926	3,824
Peekskill	24	10,358	15,245
Penn Yan	718	4,650	4,597
Perry	1038	3,763	4,338
Plattsburg	120	8,434	11,138
Pt. Chester	34	7,440	12,809
Pt. Jervis	470	9,385	9,564
Potsdam	390	3,843	4,036
Poughk'psie	180	24,029	27,936
Rensselaer	25	7,466	10,711
Rochester	523	162,608	218,149
Rocky'e Cen.	25	1,884	3,667
Rome	445	15,343	20,497
Rye	49	....	3,964
Sag Harbor	8	1,969	3,408
Salamanca	1382	4,251	5,792
Saranac L.	1537	2,594	4,983
Saratoga Sp.	277	12,409	12,693
Saugerties	159	3,697	3,929
Schenect'y	246	31,682	72,826
Seneca F'ls	427	6,519	6,588
Solvay	...	3,493	5,139
Syracuse	404	108,374	137,249
Tarrytown	20	4,770	5,600
Tonawanda	572	7,421	8,290
Troy	35	60,651	76,813
Tupper L'k	1557	....	3,067
Utica	407	56,383	74,419
Walden	358	3,147	4,004
Walton	1233	2,811	3,103
Wapp'g's F'ls	...	3,504	3,195
Warsaw	1322	3,048	3,206
Waterford	33	3,146	3,245
Waterloo	453	4,358	3,931
Watertown	486	21,696	26,730
Watervliet	50	14,321	15,074
Waverly	825	4,465	4,855
Wellsville	1519	3,556	4,382
White P'l'ns	201	7,899	15,949
Whitehall	125	4,377	4,917
Yonkers	19	47,931	79,803

NORTH CAROLINA.

Place	Altitude	1900	1910
Asheville	2250	14,694	18,762
Burlington	663	3,692	4,808
Charlotte	773	18,091	34,014
Concord	608	7,910	8,715
Durham	407	6,679	18,241
Eliz'b'th C'y	8	6,348	8,412
Fayetteville	1?0	4,670	7,045
Gastonia	815	4,610	5,759
Goldsboro	102	5,877	6,107
Greensboro	843	10,035	15,895
Greenville	76	2,565	4,101
Henderson	490	3,746	4,503
Hickory	1164	2,535	3,716
High Points	940	4,163	9,525
Kinston	45	4,106	6,995
Lenoir	1193	1,296	3,364
Lexington	738	1,234	4,163
Monroe	576	2,427	4,082
Mooresville	878	1,532	3,400

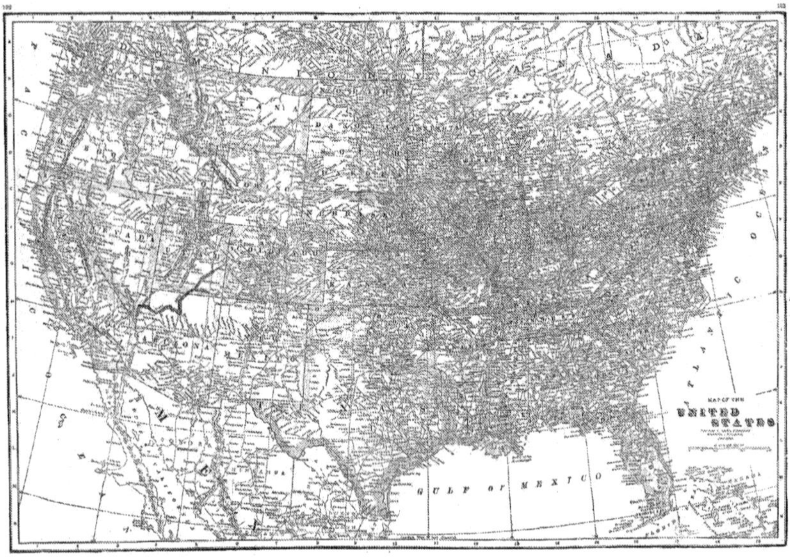
MAP OF THE
UNITED STATES
GULF OF MEXICO

Mount Airy	1014	2,680	3,844
Newbern	18	9,090	9,961
Oxford	451	2,059	3,018
Raleigh	362	13,643	19,218
Reidsville	822	3,262	4,828
Rocky Mt.	129	2,937	8,051
Salem	1006	3,642	5,533
Salisbury	755	6,277	7,153
Shelby	983	1,874	3,127
Statesville	926	3,141	4,599
Tarboro	50	2,499	4,129
Thomasv'e	851	751	3,877
Washington	11	4,842	6,211
Wilmington	19	20,976	25,748
Wilson	128	3,525	6,717
Winston	858	10,008	17,167

NORTH DAKOTA

Place	Altitude	1900	1910
Bismarck	1672	3,319	5,443
Devils Lake	1465	1,729	5,157
Dickinson	2411	2,076	3,678
Fargo	903	9,589	14,331
Grd. Forks	841	7,652	12,478
Jamestown	1395	2,853	4,358
Mandan	1644	1,658	3,873
Minot	1557	1,277	6,188
Valley	1218	2,446	4,606
Williston	1860	763	3,124

OHIO

Place	Altitude	1900	1910
Akron	940	42,728	69,067
Alliance	1068	8,974	15,083
Ashland	1070	4,087	6,795
Ashtabula	580	12,949	18,266
Athens	657	3,066	5,463
Barberton	955	4,354	9,410
Barnesville	1276	3,721	4,233
Bellaire	660	9,912	12,946
Bellefont'ne	1240	6,649	8,238
Bellevue	752	4,101	6,209
Bowling G'n	703	5,067	5,222
Bridgeport	660	3,963	3,974
Bryan	764	3,131	3,641
Bucyrus	1001	6,560	8,122
Byesville	894	1,267	3,156
Cambridge	893	8,241	11,327
Canal Dover	884	5,422	6,621
Canton	1070	30,667	50,217
Carthage	535	2,559	3,613
Celina	863	3,813	3,493
Chillicothe	639	12,976	14,508
Cincinnati	528	325,902	363,591
Circleville	720	6,991	6,744
Cleveland	767	381,768	560,663
Columbus	772	125,560	181,511
Conneaut	652	7,133	8,319
Coshocton	770	6,473	9,603
Crestline	1158	3,282	3,807
Crooksville	...	835	3,028
Cuy'h'a F'ls	1004	3,186	4,020
Dayton	790	85,333	116,577
Defiance	713	7,579	7,327
Delaware	927	7,940	9,076
Delphos	778	4,517	5,038
Dennison	908	3,763	4,008
E. Cleveland	...	2,757	9,179
E. Liverpool	688	16,485	20,387
E. Palestine	1015	2,493	3,537
E. Y'gst'wn	...	...	4,972
Eaton	...	3,155	3,187
Elmwood Pl	...	2,532	3,423
Elyria	755	8,791	14,825
Findlay	782	17,613	14,858
Fostoria	790	7,730	9,597
Fremont	684	8,439	9,939
Galion	1167	7,282	7,214
Gallipolis	561	5,432	5,560
Girard	858	2,630	3,736
Greenfield	...	3,979	4,228
Greenville	1060	5,501	6,237
Hamilton	605	23,914	35,279
Hillsboro	1128	4,535	4,296
Ironton	544	11,868	13,147
Jackson	...	4,672	5,468
Kent	1030	4,541	4,488
Kenton	1015	6,852	7,185
Lakewood	...	3,355	15,181
Lancaster	838	8,991	13,093
Lima	833	21,723	30,508
Lisbon	952	3,330	3,084
Lockland	573	2,695	3,439
Logan	740	3,480	4,850
London	1046	3,511	3,530
Lorain	616	16,028	28,883
Madis'nville	588	3,140	6,192
Mansfield	1154	17,640	20,768
Marietta	599	13,348	12,923
Marion	980	11,862	18,232
Martins F'y	643	7,760	9,133
Marysville	998	3,048	3,576
Massillon	943	11,944	13,879
Miamisburg	702	3,941	4,271
Middleport	584	2,799	3,194
Middletown	654	9,215	13,152
Mingo Jct.	663	2,951	4,049
Mt. Vernon	991	6,633	9,087
Napoleon	680	3,639	4,007
Nelsonville	681	5,421	6,082
New Phila'la	878	6,213	8,542
Newark	832	18,157	25,404
Newburg	910	5,909	5,813
Niles	872	7,468	8,361
Norwalk	719	7,074	7,858
Norwood	612	6,480	16,185
Oberlin	806	4,082	4,365
Orrville	1057	1,901	3,101
Painesville	645	5,024	5,501
Piqua	892	12,172	13,388
Pomeroy	565	4,639	4,029
Pt. Clinton	581	2,450	3,007
Portsm'th	527	17,870	23,481
Ravenna	1138	4,003	5,310
Reading	...	3,076	3,985
Rockport	785	2,039	3,179
St. Bernard	548	3,384	5,002
St. Marys	926	5,359	5,732
Sa[illegible]	...	7,582	8,943
Sandusky	620	19,664	19,989
Shelby	1088	4,683	4,303
Sidney	969	5,688	6,607
Springfield	980	38,253	46,921
Steubenville	682	14,349	22,391
Struthers	833	...	3,370
Tiffin	759	10,989	11,894
Toledo	628	131,822	168,497
Toronto	695	3,526	4,271
Troy	840	5,881	6,122
Uhrichsville	855	4,582	4,751
Up. Sand'ky	880	3,355	3,779
Urbana	1031	6,808	7,739
Van Wert	784	6,422	7,157
Wadsworth	1132	1,764	3,073
Wapakoneta	893	3,915	5,349
Warren	900	8,529	11,081
Wash. C. H.	946	5,751	7,277
Wellston	720	8,045	6,875
Wellsville	684	6,146	7,769
Wilmington	1033	3,613	4,491
Wooster	900	6,063	6,136
Xenia	919	8,696	8,706
Y'ngstown	863	44,885	79,066
Zanesville	704	23,538	28,026

OKLAHOMA

Place	Altitude	1907	1910
Ada	990	3,257	4,349
Altus	1385	1,927	4,821
Ardmore	868	8,759	8,618
Chickasha	1091	7,862	10,320
Durant	645	4,510	5,330
El Reno	1367	6,370	7,872
Enid	1238	10,087	13,799
Frederick	1298	2,088	3,027
Lawton	1111	...	7,788
Mangum	1578	2,672	3,667
McAlester	686	8,144	12,954
Muskogee	585	14,418	25,278
Nowata	696	2,226	3,672
Okla. City	1197	32,452	64,205
Okmulgee	679	2,322	4,176
Sapulpa	718	4,259	8,283
Shawnee	990	10,955	12,474
Sulphur	...	2,555	3,684
Tulsa	687	7,298	18,182

OREGON

Place	Altitude	1900	1910
Albany	224	3,149	4,275
Ashland	1868	2,634	5,020
Astoria	15	8,381	9,599
Baker City	3471	6,663	6,742
Corvallis	227	1,819	4,552
Eugene	455	3,236	9,009
Grants Pass	937	3,290	3,897
LaGrande	2779	2,991	4,843
Medford	1374	1,791	8,840
Oregon	75	3,494	4,287
Pendleton	1123	4,406	4,460
Portland	27	90,426	207,214
Roseburg	403	1,690	4,738
St. Johns	65	...	4,872
Salem	120	4,258	14,094
The Dalles	116	3,542	4,880

PENNSYLVANIA

Place	Altitude	1900	1910
Allentown	321	35,416	51,913
Altoona	1182	38,973	52,127
Ambridge	...	...	5,205
Apollo	...	2,924	3,006
Archbald	894	5,396	7,194
Ashland	885	6,438	6,855
Ashley	642	4,046	5,601
Athens	...	3,749	3,796
Avalon	...	3,130	4,317
Avoca	660	3,487	4,634
Bangor	514	4,106	5,369
Barnesboro	64	1,482	2,535
Beaver	719	2,348	3,456
Beaver F'lls	732	10,054	12,191
Bellefonte	745	4,216	4,145
Bellevue	505	3,416	6,323
Berwick	505	3,916	5,357
Bethlehem	237	7,293	12,837
Blairsville	1012	3,386	3,372
Blakely	...	3,915	5,345
Bloomsburg	484	6,170	7,413
Brack'nridge	...	...	3,134
Braddock	735	15,654	19,357
Bradford	1437	15,029	14,544
Bridgeport	74	3,097	3,860
Bristol	21	7,104	9,256
Brookville	1239	2,472	3,003
Butler	1011	10,853	20,728
Canonsburg	923	2,714	3,891
Carbondale	1069	13,536	17,040
Carlisle	489	9,626	10,303
Carnegie	769	7,330	10,009
Carrick	...	...	6,117
Catasauqua	288	3,963	5,250
Chamb'rsb'g	620	8,864	11,800
Charleroi	764	5,930	9,615
Chester	24	33,988	38,537
Clairton	...	...	3,326
Clearfield	1110	5,081	6,851
Clifton H'ts	109	2,330	3,155
Coaldale	...	...	5,154
Coatesville	376	5,721	11,084
Columbia	261	12,316	11,454
Connellsv'e	880	7,160	12,845
Consh'oh'ken	62	5,762	7,480
Coraopolis	720	2,555	5,252
Corry	1429	5,369	5,991
Coudersport	1650	3,217	3,169
Crafton	877	1,927	4,583
Danville	450	8,042	7,517
Darby	68	3,429	6,305
Dickson C'y	754	4,948	9,331
Donora	...	...	8,174
Dorranceton	...	2,311	4,046
Dowingtown	225	2,133	3,326
Doylestown	341	3,034	3,304
Dubois	1392	9,375	12,623
Dunmore	939	12,583	17,615
Duquesne	...	9,036	15,727
Duryea	555	5,641	7,487
E. Conem'gh	...	2,175	5,046
E. M'ch C'k	551	3,458	3,548
E. Pittsburg	...	2,883	5,615
E. Str'dsb'g	...	2,688	3,320
Easton	325	25,238	28,523
Edwardsv'le	...	5,165	8,407
Ellwood C'y	884	2,243	3,902
Emaus	422	1,468	3,501
Ephrata	381	2,451	3,192
Erie	719	52,733	66,525
Etna	740	5,384	5,830
Exeter	191	1,918	3,537
Ford City	785	2,870	4,850
Forest C'y	1189	4,279	5,749
Frackville	1476	3,594	3,218
Franklin	951	7,317	9,767
Freedom	703	1,783	3,060
Freeland	1825	5,254	6,197
Galeton	1323	3,513	4,027
Gallitzin	2165	2,759	3,504
Gettysburg	520	3,495	4,030
Gilberton	1133	4,373	5,401
Girardville	721	3,666	4,526
Glassport	786	...	5,540
Gr. Punxs't'y	...	6,746	9,058
Greensburg	1110	6,508	13,012
Greenville	945	4,814	5,909
Grove	768	1,509	3,674
Hanover	596	5,302	7,057
Harrisburg	374	50,167	64,186
Hazleton	1624	14,230	25,452
Hollidaysb'g	947	2,998	3,734
Homestead	750	12,554	18,713
Huntingdon	650	6,053	6,861
Indiana	1350	4,142	5,749
Jeannette	...	5,865	8,077
Jermyn	953	2,567	3,158
Jersey Shore	591	3,070	5,381
Johnsonb'g	1452	3,894	4,334
Johnstown	1169	35,936	55,482
Juniata	...	1,709	5,285
Kane	2013	5,296	6,626
Kingston	545	3,846	6,449
Kittanning	804	3,902	4,311
Knoxville	1243	3,511	5,651
Lancaster	418	41,459	47,227
Lansford	...	4,888	8,321
Lansdowne	...	2,630	4,066
Larksville	...	...	9,288
Latrobe	1027	4,614	8,777
Lebanon	468	17,628	19,240
Leechburg	789	2,459	3,824
Lehighton	475	4,629	5,316
Lewisburg	450	3,457	3,071
Lewistown	495	4,451	8,166
Lockhaven	560	7,210	7,772
Luzerne	578	3,817	5,426
McAdoo	1802	2,122	3,389
McKeesport	752	34,227	42,694
McKees R'ks	725	6,352	14,702
M'h'noy C'y	1231	13,504	15,936
Mauch Ch'k	1374	4,036	3,952
Mayfield	...	2,890	3,463
Meadville	1078	10,291	12,780
Mech'nicsb'g	456	3,841	4,469
Media	219	3,075	3,562
Meyersdale	2054	3,024	3,747
Middletown	304	5,608	5,374
Millvale	1088	6,736	7,861
Milton	473	6,175	7,460
Miners M'ls	840	3,234	4,158
Minersville	837	4,815	7,240
Monaca	755	3,008	3,376
Monessen	762	2,197	11,775
Monong'h'la	754	5,173	7,598
Moosic	962	1,227	3,964
Mt. Carmel	1086	13,179	17,532
Mt. Oliver	...	2,295	4,241
Mt. Pleas'nt	1288	4,745	5,812
Mt. Union	598	1,086	3,338
Munhall	761	...	5,185
Nanticoke	546	12,116	18,877
Nazareth	408	2,304	3,978
New Br'ton	750	6,820	8,329
New Castle	808	28,339	36,280
New K'ns't'n	483	4,665	7,707
Norristown	85	22,265	27,875
No. Bradd'ck	...	6,535	11,824
Northamp'n	306	...	8,729
No'th'mb'rl'nd	452	2,748	3,517
Oakmont	764	2,328	3,436
Oil City	1045	13,264	15,657
Old Forge	...	5,630	11,821
Olyphant	768	6,180	8,505
Parsons	581	2,520	4,338
Patton	492	2,651	3,907
Pen Argyl	831	2,784	3,997
Philad'phia	9	1,293,697	1,549,008
Phillipsburg	1432	3,266	3,585
Phoenixv'e	770	9,196	10,743
Pitcairn	...	2,501	4,975
Pittsburg	743	451,512	533,905
Pittston	778	12,556	16,267
Plymouth	538	13,649	16,996
Pottstown	138	13,696	15,599
Pottsville	611	15,710	20,236
Quakert'n	536	3,014	3,801
Rankin	756	3,775	6,042
Reading	250	78,961	96,071
Renovo	672	4,082	4,621
Reynoldsv'e	1372	2,435	3,189
Ridgway	1371	3,515	5,408
Rochester	797	4,688	5,903
Royersford	129	2,607	3,073
St. Clair (Allegheny)	...	...	5,640
St. Clair (Schuylkill)	749	4,638	6,465
St. Marys	1740	4,295	6,346
Sayre	772	5,243	6,426
Sch'yk'l Hav	526	3,654	3,747
Scottdale	1051	4,261	5,456
Scranton	805	102,026	129,867
Sewickley	733	3,568	4,479
Shamokin	750	18,202	19,588
Sharon	852	8,916	15,270
Sharpsburg	733	6,842	8,153
Sharpsville	872	2,970	3,634
Shenandoah	1245	20,321	25,774
Shippensb'g	643	3,228	3,457
Slatington	386	3,773	4,454
S. Bethleh'm	238	13,241	19,973
S. Brownsv'e	...	1,806	4,043
S. Fork	...	2,833	4,592
S. Sharon	...	...	10,190
S. Will'msp't	...	3,326	3,734
Steelton	308	12,086	14,246
Stroudsb'g	426	3,450	4,379
Summit Hill	...	2,986	4,209
Sunbury	456	9,810	13,770
Susquehan'a	916	3,813	3,478
Swissvale	933	1,716	7,381
Swoyersv'le	...	3,254	5,396
Tamaqua	800	7,267	9,462
Tarentum	777	5,472	7,414
Taylor	682	4,215	9,060
Throop	...	2,204	5,133
Titusville	1148	8,244	8,533
Towanda	754	4,663	4,281
Turtle C'k	...	3,262	4,995
Tyrone	909	5,847	7,176
Union City	286	3,104	3,684
Uniontown	981	7,344	13,344
Vandergrift	800	2,076	3,876
V'grift H'ts	...	1,910	3,438
Warren	1187	8,043	11,080
Washingt'n	1029	7,670	18,778
Waynesboro	712	5,396	7,199
Waynesburg	938	3,544	3,615
Wellsboro	1298	2,954	3,183
W. Berwick	...	...	5,512
W. Chester	455	9,524	11,767
W. Hazleton	...	2,816	4,715
W. Hom'st'd	...	...	3,009
W. Pittston	577	5,846	6,848
Wilkes-B're	575	51,721	67,105
Wilkinsb'rg	923	11,886	18,924
Williamsp't	532	28,757	31,860
Wilmerding	...	4,179	6,133
Windber	...	...	8,013
Winton	872	5,426	5,280
Wyoming	567	1,900	3,010
York	386	33,708	44,750

RHODE ISLAND

Place	Altitude	1900	1910
Bristol	58	6,901	8,565
Burrillville	...	6,317	7,878
Central F'ls	83	18,167	22,754
Coventry	365	5,279	5,848
Cranston	84	13,343	21,107
Cumberland	...	8,925	10,107
E. Greenw'h	...	2,775	3,420
E. Prov'd'ce	20	12,138	15,808
Johnston	...	4,305	5,935
Lincoln	...	8,937	9,825
Newport	44	22,441	27,149
N. Kingston	...	4,194	4,048
N. Prov'd'ce	...	3,016	5,407
Pawtucket	79	39,231	51,622
Providence	11	175,597	224,326
Scituate	...	3,161	3,493
S. Kingston	...	4,972	5,176
Tiverton	...	2,977	4,032
Warren	36	5,108	6,585
Warwick	...	21,316	26,629
Westerly	34	7,541	8,696
Woonsocket	165	28,204	38,125

SOUTH CAROLINA

Place	Altitude	1900	1910
Abbeville	520	3,766	4,459
Aiken	490	3,414	3,911
Anderson	784	5,498	9,654
Camden	221	2,441	3,569
Charleston	10	55,807	58,833
Chester	487	4,075	4,754
Clinton	687	1,869	3,272
Columbia	190	21,108	26,319
Darlington	155	3,028	3,789
Florence	138	4,647	7,057
Gaffney	772	3,937	4,767
Georgetown	15	4,138	5,530
Greenville	966	11,860	15,741
Greenwood	671	4,824	6,614
Laurens	589	4,029	4,878
Marion	88	1,821	3,844
Newberry	502	4,607	5,028
Orangeburg	252	4,455	5,906
Rock Hill	661	5,485	7,216
Spartanburg	875	11,395	17,517
Sumter	169	5,673	8,109
Union	578	5,400	5,623

SOUTH DAKOTA

Place	Altitude	1900	1910
Aberdeen	1300	4,087	10,753
Deadwood	4543	3,498	3,653
Huron	1283	2,793	5,791
Lead	5119	6,210	8,392
Madison	1670	2,550	3,137
Mitchell	1297	4,055	6,515
Pierre	1440	2,306	3,656
Rapid	3196	1,342	3,854
Redfield	1299	1,015	3,060
Sioux Falls	1420	10,266	14,094
Watertown	1738	3,352	7,010
Yankton	1233	4,125	3,787

TENNESSEE

Place	Altitude	1900	1910
Bristol	1680	5,271	7,148
Chattanooga	674	30,154	44,604
Clarksville	419	9,431	8,548
Cleveland	884	3,858	5,549
Columbia	656	6,052	5,754
Dyersburg	350	3,647	4,149
Fayetteville	727	2,708	3,439
Harriman	782	3,442	3,061
Humboldt	340	2,866	3,446
Jackson	394	14,511	15,779
Johnson C'y	1651	4,645	8,502
Knoxville	933	32,637	36,346
Lebanon	512	1,956	3,659
Lenoir City	783	...	3,392
Memphis	117	102,320	131,105
Morristown	1258	2,973	4,007
Murfr'sboro	575	3,999	4,679
Nashville	546	80,865	110,364
Paris	474	2,018	3,881
Park City	602	...	6,126
Rockwood	875	2,899	3,660
Tullahoma	1060	2,684	3,049
Union City	328	3,407	4,389

TEXAS

Place	Altitude	1900	1910
Abilene	1738	3,411	9,204
Amarillo	3658	1,442	9,957
Austin	650	22,258	29,860
Ballinger	1850	1,128	3,536
Bay City	55	...	3,156
Beaumont	21	9,427	20,640
Beeville	214	...	3,269
Belton	511	3,700	4,164
Big Sp'ngs	2397	...	4,102
Bonham	566	5,042	4,844
Brenham	350	5,968	4,718
Brownsville	57	6,305	10,517
Brownwood	1342	3,965	6,967
Bryan	367	3,589	4,132
Cameron	390	3,341	3,268
Childress	1877	692	3,818
Cleburne	764	7,493	10,364
Coleman	1820	1,362	3,046
Corpus Ch'ti	35	4,703	8,222
Corsicana	418	9,313	9,749
Crockett	350	2,612	3,947
Cuero	177	3,442	3,109
Dallas	430	42,638	92,104
D'nison	723	11,807	13,632
Denton	620	4,187	4,732
Eagle Pass	725	...	3,536
El Paso	3762	15,906	39,279
Ennis	548	2,513	5,669
Ft. Worth	670	26,688	73,312
Gainesville	738	7,874	7,624
Galveston	5	37,789	36,981
Georgetown	443	2,790	3,096
Gonzales	300	4,297	3,139
Greenville	549	6,860	8,850
Hillsboro	634	5,346	6,115
Houston	53	44,633	78,800
H'ston H'ts	63	908	6,984
Laredo	438	13,429	14,855
Longview	336	3,591	5,155
McKinney	552	4,342	4,714
Marlin	...	3,092	3,878
Marshall	376	7,855	11,452
Min'ral W'ls	...	2,048	3,950
Mt. Pleas'nt	397	...	3,137
Nacogd'ches	282	1,827	3,369
Navasota	215	3,857	3,284
New Br'fels	637	2,097	3,165
Orange	10	3,835	5,527
Palestine	619	8,297	10,482
Paris	598	9,358	11,269
Pt. Arthur	8	900	7,663
Quanah	1568	1,651	3,127
San Angelo	1847	...	10,321
San Antonio	654	53,321	96,614
San Marcos	581	2,292	4,071
Seguin	553	2,421	3,116
Sherman	728	10,243	12,412
Smithville	324	2,577	3,167
Stamford	1603	...	3,902
S'lph'r Sp'gs	503	3,835	5,151
Sweetwater	2164	670	4,176
Taylor	585	4,211	5,314
Teague	...	...	3,288
Temple	630	7,065	10,993
Terrell	530	6,330	7,050
Texarkana	337	5,256	9,790
Tyler	531	8,069	10,400
Uvalde	910	1,889	3,998
Vernon	1206	1,993	3,195
Victoria	187	4,010	3,672
Waco	424	20,686	26,425
Waxahachie	535	4,215	6,205
Weatherford	864	4,786	5,074
Wichita F'ls	946	2,480	8,200
Yoakum	332	3,109	4,657

UTAH

Place	Altitude	1900	1910
Brigham	4306	2,859	3,685
Eureka	6404	3,085	3,416
Logan	4507	5,451	7,522
Murray	4279	...	4,057
Ogden	4307	16,313	25,580
Park	6582	3,759	3,439
Provo	4512	6,185	8,925
Salt L. City	4348	53,531	92,777
Spanish F'k	4570	2,735	3,464
Springville	4558	3,422	3,356

VERMONT

Place	Altitude	1900	1910
Barre	515	8,448	10,734
Bellows F'ls	798	4,337	4,883
Bennington	682	5,656	6,211
Brattleboro	335	5,297	6,517
Burlington	258	18,640	20,468
Hartford	...	3,817	4,179
Montpelier	484	6,266	7,856
Rutland	563	11,499	13,546
St. Albans	383	6,239	6,381
St. Johnsb'y	711	6,666	6,693
Springfield	...	3,040	3,250
W. Rutland	484	2,914	3,427
Winooski	190	3,783	4,520

VIRGINIA

Place	Altitude	1900	1910
Alexandria	47	14,528	15,329
Bristol	1696	4,579	6,247
Buena Vista	...	2,388	3,245
Charlott'sv'e	482	6,449	6,765
Clifton F'ge	1047	2,979	5,748
Covington	1245	2,950	4,881
Danville	413	16,520	19,020
Fred'icksb'g	47	5,068	5,874
Hampton	3	2,764	5,505
Harrisonb'g	1338	3,521	4,879
Lynchburg	631	18,891	29,494
Martinsville	924	2,384	3,368
N'port News	22	19,635	20,205
Norfolk	12	46,624	67,452
Petersburg	74	21,810	24,127
Portsmouth	12	17,427	33,190
Pulaski	1904	2,813	4,807
Radford	1778	3,344	4,202
Richmond	164	85,050	127,628
Roanoke	904	21,495	34,874
Salem	1290	3,412	3,849
S. Boston	318	1,851	3,516
Staunton	1380	7,289	10,604
Suffolk	56	3,827	7,008
Winchester	717	5,161	5,864
Wytheville	2250	3,062	[illegible]

WASHINGTON

Place	Altitude	1900	1910
Aberdeen	19	3,747	13,660
Anacortes	28	1,476	4,168
Bellingham	40	11,062	24,298
Centralia	188	1,600	7,311
Chehalis	186	1,775	4,507
Ellensburg	1510	1,737	4,209
Everett	11	7,838	24,814
Hillyard	...	...	3,276
Hoquiam	10	2,608	8,171
N. Yakima	1067	3,154	14,082
Olympia	17	3,863	6,996
Port T'nsend	...	3,443	4,181
Puyallup	42	1,884	4,544
Roslyn	2218	2,786	3,126
Seattle	12	80,671	237,194
Snohomish	60	2,101	3,244
South Bend	6	711	3,023
Spokane	1891	36,848	104,402
Tacoma	110	37,714	83,743
Vancouver	12	3,126	9,300
Walla Walla	1000	10,049	19,364
Wenatchee	639	451	4,050

WEST VIRGINIA.

Place	Altitude	1900	1910
Benwood	648	4,511	4,976
Bluefield	2563	4,644	11,188
Charleston	602	11,099	22,996
Chester	704	...	3,184
Clarksburg	1034	4,050	9,201
Elkins	1940	2,016	5,260
Fairmont	884	5,655	9,711
Grafton	985	5,650	7,563
Hinton	1372	3,763	3,656
Huntington	565	11,923	31,161
Keyser	802	2,536	3,705
Martinsburg	428	7,564	10,698
Morgantown	821	1,895	9,150
Moundsville	614	5,362	8,918
Parkersburg	628	11,703	17,842
Princeton	2468	...	3,027
Richwood	2189	...	3,061
Wellsburg	635	2,588	4,189
Wheeling	637	38,878	41,641
Williamson	610	...	3,561

WISCONSIN

Place	Altitude	1900	1910
Antigo	1489	5,145	7,196
Appleton	709	15,085	16,773
Ashland	662	13,074	11,594
Baraboo	837	5,751	6,324
Beaver Dam	879	5,128	6,758
Beloit	750	10,436	15,125
Berlin	768	4,489	4,636
Burlington	763	2,526	3,212
Chip'wa F'ls	866	8,094	8,893
Cudahy	...	1,366	3,691
De Pere	594	4,038	4,477
Eau Claire	762	17,517	18,310
Fond du Lac	800	15,110	18,797
Ft. Atkinson	...	3,043	3,877
Gd. Rapids	1016	4,493	6,521
Green Bay	617	18,684	25,236
Janesville	804	13,185	13,894
Kaukauna	...	5,115	4,717
Kenosha	611	11,606	21,371
La Crosse	714	28,895	30,417
Lake Geneva	...	2,585	3,079
Madison	955	19,164	25,531
Manitowoc	616	11,786	13,027
Marinette	600	16,195	14,610
Marshfield	1271	5,240	5,783
Menasha	755	5,589	6,081
Menominee	806	5,655	5,036
Merrill	1288	8,537	8,689
Milwaukee	636	285,315	373,857
Monroe	1066	3,927	4,410
Neenah	753	5,954	5,734
New London	755	2,742	3,383
Oconomowoc	855	2,880	3,054
Oconto	593	5,646	5,629
Oshkosh	744	28,284	33,062
Platteville	932	3,340	4,452
Plymouth	842	2,257	3,094
Pt. Washgtn	717	3,010	3,792
Portage	809	5,459	5,440
Prai. du Chien	630	3,232	3,149
Racine	622	29,102	38,002
Rhinelander	1555	4,998	5,637
Rice Lake	1148	3,002	3,968
Ripon	921	3,818	3,739
Sheboygan	589	22,962	26,398
So. Milw'kee	...	6,392	6,092
Sparta	781	3,555	3,973
Stevens Pt.	1113	9,524	8,692
Stoughton	861	3,431	4,761
Sturg'n Bay	...	3,372	4,262
Superior	628	31,091	40,384
Tomah	960	2,840	3,419
Two Rivers	587	3,784	4,850
Washburn	645	...	3,830
Watertown	825	8,437	8,820
Waukesha	970	7,419	8,740
Waupun	894	3,185	3,362
Wausau	1223	12,354	16,560
Wauwatosa	654	2,842	3,346
West Allis	...	...	6,645
Whitewater	825	3,405	3,224

WYOMING.

Place	Altitude	1900	1910
Cheyenne	6088	14,087	11,320
Laramie	7165	8,207	8,237
Rawlins	6745	2,317	4,256
Rock Sp'gs	6261	4,363	5,778
Sheridan	[illegible]	1,559	8,408

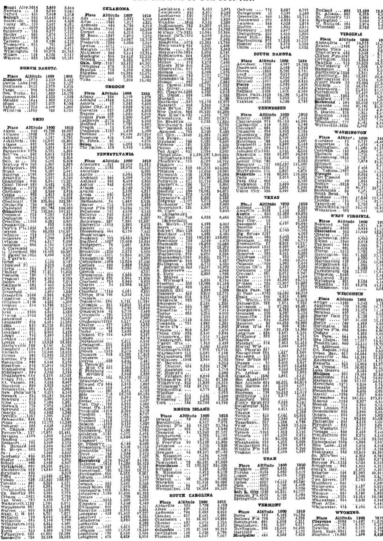

ARMIES OF THE WORLD.

COUNTRIES.	Peace Strength.	Reserves. (a)	Total War Strength.	Available for Duty, Unorganized (b)
Argentina	17,000	223,000	240,000	500,000
Austria-Hungary	367,000	2,217,000	5,117,000	2,000,000
Belgium	90,000	125,000	165,000	240,000
Bolivia	3,000	50,000	53,000	125,000
Brazil	23,000	(k) 25,000	52,000	1,500,000
Bulgaria	52,500	297,500	350,000	100,000
Chile	30,000	122,000	147,000	250,000
China	90,000	100,000	190,000	(i) ....
Colombia	5,000	45,000	50,000	200,000
Denmark	13,000	67,000	76,000	125,000
Ecuador	4,300	40,000	44,300	70,500
France	(c) 609,000	1,600,000	2,100,000	1,000,000
Germany	820,000	2,350,000	1,002,000	2,000,000
Great Britain and Ireland	(d) 257,000	(e) 543,000	800,000	1,700,000
Greece	25,000	25,000	50,000	200,000
Guatemala	7,000	90,000	57,000	90,000
Haiti	6,000	......	6,000	90,000
Italy	325,000	300,000	625,000	1,200,000
Japan	453,000	1,050,000	1,000,000	1,300,000
Mexico	36,800	58,000	34,800	1,000,000
Netherlands	(f) 84,000	68,000	102,000	200,000
Nicaragua	3,000	27,000	30,000	30,000
Norway	18,000	95,000	113,000	100,000
Peru	4,000	46,000	34,000	75,000
Portugal	(g) 30,000	90,000	120,000	300,000
Roumania	70,900	250,000	320,000	175,000
Russia	1,200,000	3,300,000	4,500,000	5,200,000
Salvador	3,000	18,000	21,000	40,000
Servia	35,000	140,000	175,000	90,000
Spain	80,000	420,000	500,000	780,000
Sweden	28,000	300,000	328,000	200,000
Switzerland	(h) 200,000	(h) 54,000	254,000	50,000
Turkey	375,000	350,000	725,000	2,000,000
United States	100,000	121,580	221,580	15,498,125
Uruguay	4,000	36,000	40,000	40,000
Venezuela	5,500	75,000	80,600	300,000

(a) Except as to some of the principal and a few of the minor states, it is doubtful whether the numbers given of the reserves or auxiliary forces could be mobilized and made effective within a considerable period of time. (b) These figures are based on estimated male population of military age, deducting total "war strength." In some states, all men of military age are enrolled in national militia and are partly trained. (c) Exclusive of Colonial troops. (d) Including regular forces at home, in the colonies, and 76,000 men in India and excluding the native Indian army of 160,000. (e) Includes army reserves and territorial force. (f) Exclusive of Colonial army of 36,000. (g) Exclusive of Colonial troops. (h) Trained National militia. (i) National and organized provincial troops; Army being reorganized. (k) National guard.

NAVIES OF THE WORLD.

COUNTRIES.	Modern Battleships.	Older Battleships.	First-class Cruisers.	Second-class Cruisers.	Third-class Cruisers.	Gunboats.	Monitors.	Destroyers.	Torpedo Boats.	Submarines.	Personnel, Officers and Men.
Argentina	3	1	5	..	2	2	..	4	8	..	6,000
Austria-Hungary	9	2	3	..	..	4	..	9	18	..	12,888
Brazil	2	1	1	1	3	5	..	..	..	..	8,000
Chile	2	1	1	3	1	2	..	6	14	..	8,000
China	..	..	1	8	..	..	..	..	..	..	......
Colombia	..	..	..	..	..	7	..	..	..	..	60
Denmark	..	..	..	..	..	3	3	..	23	..	4,000
France	13	10	15	12	21	14	..	83	150	86	66,174
Germany (a)	28	9	13	8	32	47	..	116	70	14	54,067
Great Britain and Ireland (b)	35	23	32	34	34	..	..	182	116	84	138,533
Greece	..	2	..	..	..	8	..	..	12	..	4,000
Italy	7	5	7	3	13	13	..	33	76	19	29,941
Japan (c)	13	4	13	4	18	8	..	58	48	14	46,185
Mexico	..	..	..	..	5	..	..	2	..	..	1,268
Netherlands	9	..	7	..	..	1	1	..	50	1	10,322
Norway	4	..	..	..	..	3	2	..	33	..	1,139
Peru	..	..	..	..	3	6	..	..	..	..	1,000
Portugal	..	..	6	..	..	10	..	2	4	2	6,107
Roumania	..	..	..	..	1	14	..	..	6	..	1,050
Russia	11	6	6	..	2	8	..	87	74	37	60,000
Siam	..	..	..	1	..	21	..	..	..	..	5,132
Spain	3	..	8	..	..	..	..	5	6	..	6,000
Sweden	3	7	1	..	..	5	11	6	51	10	4,705
Turkey	..	3	1	2	2	2	..	4	8	..	35,929
United States (d)	26	9	12	22	6	21	16	40	23	36	53,548

(a) Reserve of 110,000 men. (b) Naval Reserves 46,171. (c) Reserve of 114,000 men. (d) Naval militia 6,201 men.

REGULAR ARMY AND MILITIA OF THE UNITED STATES.

Organized and Unorganized.

STATES. Official Designation of the Organized Militia.	General and General Staff Officers.	Regimental and Company Officers.	Total Commissioned.	Enlisted Men.	Total Commissioned and Enlisted Organized Militia.	Reserve Militia Unorganized.
Alabama—Alabama National Guard	50	190	240	3,134	3,374	350,000
Arizona—National Guard of Arizona	5	43	48	868	916	40,000
Arkansas—Arkansas National Guard	35	101	136	1,534	1,670	275,000
California—National Guard of California	31	168	199	2,777	2,976	309,546
Colorado—National Guard of Colorado	17	59	76	887	963	131,000
Connecticut—Connecticut National Guard	28	152	180	2,441	2,621	124,131
Delaware—Organized Militia of Del'w're	7	37	44	336	380	32,000
District of Col'bia—Nat. Gu'rd of D. C.	30	85	115	1,664	1,779	62,034
Florida—Florida State Troops	25	76	101	1,777	1,878	204,335
Georgia—National Guard of Georgia	34	203	237	2,686	2,923	500,000
Hawaii—National Guard of Hawaii	12	35	47	572	619	8,000
Idaho—National Guard of Idaho	8	49	57	560	617	30,000
Illinois—Illinois National Guard	75	445	520	5,766	6,286	1,032,188
Indiana—Indiana National Guard	32	147	179	2,106	2,285	628,580
Iowa—Iowa National Guard	26	197	223	2,664	2,887	302,000
Kansas—Kansas National Guard	30	153	183	1,745	1,928	350,000
Kentucky—Kentucky State Guard	28	112	140	1,712	1,852	386,000
Louisiana—La. State National Guard	16	111	127	1,692	1,819	400,000
Maine—Nat. Guard of the State of Me.	14	102	116	1,266	1,382	163,375
Maryland—Maryland National Guard	27	130	157	1,944	2,101	180,000
Massachusetts—Mass. Volunteer Militia	93	349	442	5,403	5,845	552,264
Michigan—Michigan National Guard	42	261	303	2,702	3,005	705,000
Minnesota—Minnesota National Guard	42	165	207	2,598	2,805	521,000
Mississippi—Mississippi Nat. Guard	40	101	141	1,422	1,563	325,000
Missouri—National Guard of Missouri	46	208	254	3,362	3,616	650,000
Montana—National Guard of Montana	8	34	42	515	557	37,000
Nebraska—Nebraska National Guard	25	92	117	953	1,070	136,000
Nevada*—Nevada National Guard	....	....	....	......	......	19,000
New Hampshire—N. H. National Guard	21	68	89	1,154	1,243	46,000
New Jersey—Nat. Guard of New Jersey	108	255	363	3,952	4,315	529,458
New Mexico—National Guard of N. M.	11	44	55	711	766	68,000
New York—National Guard of New York	198	786	984	15,395	16,379	1,426,375
North Carolina—N. C. National Guard	41	177	218	2,177	2,395	290,000
North Dakota—N. D. National Guard	11	59	70	678	748	60,000
Ohio—Ohio National Guard	87	430	517	5,776	6,293	1,086,110
Oklahoma—Oklahoma National Guard	11	48	59	898	957	140,000
Oregon—Oregon National Guard	21	91	112	1,411	1,523	180,000
Pennsylvania—National Guard of Penn.	104	618	722	9,558	10,280	1,057,885
Rhode Island—Rhode Island Nat. Guard	25	84	109	939	1,048	110,000
South Carolina—National Guard of S. C.	31	152	183	1,748	1,931	213,274
South Dakota—South Dakota Nat. Gu'rd	16	60	76	690	766	70,000
Tennessee—Nat. Guard of Tennessee	25	106	131	1,409	1,540	425,000
Texas—Texas National Guard	43	177	220	2,804	3,024	500,000
Utah—National Guard of Utah	14	36	50	387	437	30,000
Vermont—Vermont National Guard	7	60	67	850	917	44,300
Virginia—Virginia Volunteers	27	160	187	2,311	2,498	320,000
Washington—National Guard of Wash.	9	69	78	929	1,007	200,000
West Virginia—W. V. National Guard	17	90	107	1,280	1,387	175,000
Wisconsin—Wisconsin National Guard	23	169	192	2,888	3,080	438,172
Wyoming—Wyoming National Guard	7	44	51	665	716	32,000
Total	1606	7638	9133	112447	121580	15498125

*No organized militia.

Alaska has no militia, though provision is made for such if need arises. Guam and Samoa have each a small provisional force, used more for police purposes than for military. The Philippines have a constabulary force which can be used either for police or war purposes, provided the latter is on the islands. Porto Rico has a regiment of eight companies of infantry which is a part of the army. The enlisted men of this regiment are natives of Porto Rico. The reserve militia in the Southern States is assumed to include negroes capable of bearing arms.

GOVERNMENTS OF THE WORLD, DEPENDENCIES AND OFFICIAL HEAD

COUNTRY.	OFFICIAL HEAD.	TITLE.	BORN.	ACCEDED.
Abyssinia	Lij Yasu	Emperor	1896	1909
Afghanistan	Habibullah Khan	Ameer	July 3, 1872	Oct. 3, 1901
Albania		King		
Andorra	Council of Twenty-four			
Argentina	Dr. Victorino de la Plaza	President		Oct. 12, 1916
Austria-Hungary	Franz Josef I.	Emperor	August 18, 1830	Dec. 2, 1848
Belgium	Albert I.	King	April 8, 1875	Dec. 17, 1909
Belgian Kongo	Albert I. (King of the Belgians)	Sovereign	April 8, 1875	Dec. 17, 1909
Bhutan	Sir Ugyen Wangchuk	Maharaja		1907
Bolivia	Dr. Ismael Montes	President		Aug. 13, 1913
Brazil	Wenceslau Braz	President		March 1, 1914
Bulgaria	Ferdinand	King	Feb. 26, 1861	August 14, 1887
Chile	Dr. Ramon Barros Luco	President		Dec. 23, 1910
China	Yuan Shih-K'ai	President	Sept. 16, 1859	October 10, 1913
Colombia	Don Jose Vicente Concha	President		August 7, 1914
Costa Rica	Alfredo Gonzalez	President		May 8, 1914
Cuba	Gen. Mario G. Menocal	President		May 20, 1913
Denmark	Christian X.	King	Sept. 26, 1870	May 14, 1912
Ecuador	Gen. Leonidas Plaza	President		April 1, 1912
France	M. Raymond Poincare	President	1860	Jan. 17, 1913
Algeria	M. C. Lutaud	Governor General		March 22, 1911
Annam	Duy-Tan	King	1899	Oct. .., 1907
Cambodia	Sisowath	King		1904
French Equatorial Africa		Governor General		1912
French Indo-China		Governor General		
Madagascar	M. Albert Picquie	Governor General		1910
Tunis	Sidi Mohamed Bon Nasr	Bey	1855	May 12, 1906
Germany	Wilhelm II.	Emperor	Jan. 27, 1859	June 15, 1888
Alsace-Lorraine	Dr. von Dallwitz	Statthalter		May 1, 1914
Anhalt	Friedrich	Duke	August 19, 1856	Jan. 24, 1904
Baden	Friedrich II	Grand Duke	July 9, 1857	Sept. 28, 1907
Bavaria	Ludwig III	King	Jan. 7, 1845	Nov. 8, 1913
Brunswick	Ernest Augustus	Duke	Nov. 17, 1887	Nov. 1, 1913
Hesse	Ernst Ludwig	Grand Duke	Nov. 25, 1868	March 13, 1892
Lippe	Leopold IV	Prince	May 30, 1871	Sept. 21, 1904
Mecklenburg-Schwerin	Friedrich Franz IV	Grand Duke	April 9, 1882	April 10, 1897
Mecklenburg-Strelitz	Adolf Friedrich VI	Grand Duke	June 17, 1882	June 11, 1914
Oldenburg	Friedrich August	Grand Duke	Nov. 16, 1852	June 13, 1900
Prussia	Wilhelm II.	King	Jan. 27, 1859	June 15, 1888
Reuss (Elder)	Heinrich XXIV	Prince	March 20, 1878	April 19, 1902
Reuss (Younger)	Heinrich XXVII	Prince	Nov. 10, 1858	March 81, 1913
Saxe-Altenburg	Ernst II	Duke	August 31, 1871	Feb. 7, 1908
Saxe-Coburg and Gotha	Charles Edward	Duke	July 19, 1884	July 30, 1900
Saxe-Meiningen	Bernhard	Duke	April 1, 1851	June 25, 1914
Saxony, Grand Duchy	Wilhelm Ernst	Grand Duke	June 10, 1876	Jan. 5, 1901
Saxony, Kingdom	Friedrich August III	King	May 25, 1865	Oct. 15, 1904
Schaumburg-Lippe	Adolf	Prince	Feb. 23, 1883	April 29, 1911
Schwarzburg-Rudolstadt	Gunther	Prince	August 21, 1852	Jan. 19, 1890
Waldeck	Friedrich	Prince	Jan. 20, 1865	May 12, 1893
Wurttemberg	Wilhelm II	King	Feb. 25, 1848	Oct. 6, 1891
Great Britain and Ireland	George V.	King	June 3, 1865	May 6, 1910
Australia	The Rt. Hon. R. C. Munro-Ferguson	Governor General		
Canada	H. R. H. the Duke of Connaught and Strathearn	Governor General		Jan. 30, 1911
India	The Rt. Hon. Baron Hardinge	Governor General		Nov. .., 1910
Newfoundland and Labrador	Walter Edward Davidson	Governor		Oct. .., 1913
New Zealand	The Rt. Hon. the Earl of Liverpool	Governor		
Union of South Africa	The Rt. Hon. Viscount Buxton	Governor General		
Egypt	Hussein Kamil Pasha	Sultan	1854	Dec. 19, 1914
Greece	Konstantinos	King	Aug. 2, 1868	March 18, 1913
Guatemala	Manuel Estrada Cabrera	President	Dec. 24, 1856	March 15, 1911
Haiti	Gen. Orestes Zamor	President		Feb. 8, 1914
Honduras	Dr. Francisco Bertrand	President	1867	March 21, 1913
Italy	Vittorio Emanuele III	King	Nov. 11, 1869	July 29, 1900
Eritrea	Marquis Giuseppe Salvago Raggi	Governor		Jan. .., 1907
Tripoli	Signor Martini			
Japan	Yoshihito, Mikado	Emperor	August 31, 1879	July 30, 1912
Chosen	H. E. Count General Terauchi	Governor General		August 29, 1910
Liberia	Daniel E. Howard	President		Jan. .., 1912
Liechtenstein	John II	Prince	Oct. 5, 1840	Nov. 12, 1858
Luxemburg	Marie Adelaide	Grand Duchess	June 14, 1894	Feb. 25, 1912
Mexico	Gen. Venustiano Carranza	President		Oct. .., 1915
Monaco	Albert	Prince	Nov. 13, 1848	Sept. 10, 1889
Montenegro	Nicholas I	King	Sept. 25, 1841	August 14, 1860
Morocco	Mulai-Yusef	Sultan	1882	Aug. 18, 1912
Nepal	Tribhubana Bir Bikram	Maharaja	June 30, 1906	Dec. 11, 1911
Netherlands	Wilhelmina Helena Pauline Marie	Queen	August 31, 1880	Sept. 6, 1898
Dutch East Indies	A. W. F. Idenburg	Governor General		August 20, 1909
Nicaragua	Adolfo Diaz	President		May 11, 1912
Norway	Haakon VII	King	August 3, 1872	Nov. 18, 1905
Oman	Seyyid Feysil bin Turki	Sultan		Oct. 8, 1913
Panama	Dr. Belisario Porras	President		Oct. 1, 1912
Paraguay	Eduardo Schaerer	President		Aug. 15, 1912
Persia	Sultan Ahmed Shah	Shah	Jan. 20, 1898	July 16, 1909
Peru	Gen. Oscar R. Benavides	Provisional President		May 15, 1914
Portugal	Bernardino Machado	President		Oct. 5, 1915
Roumania	Ferdinand I	King	August 24, 1865	Oct. 11, 1914
Russia	Nicholas II	Emperor	May 18, 1868	Nov. 1, 1894
Bokhara	Sayid Mir-Alim Khan	Amir	Jan. 3, 1880	Jan. 6, 1911
Khiva	Seyid Asfandiar Khan	Khan	1871	August 29, 1910
Salvador	Carlos Melendez	President		March 1, 1915
San Marino	Council of Sixty			
Santo Domingo	Juan Isidro Jimenez	President		Dec. 5, 1914
Servia	Peter I (Karageorgevitch)	King	June 29, 1844	June 2, 1903
Siam	Chowfa Maha Vajiravudh	King	Jan. 1, 1880	Oct. 23, 1910
Spain	Alphonso XIII	King	May 17, 1886	May 17, 1886
Sweden	Gustaf V.	King	June 16, 1858	Dec. 8, 1907
Switzerland	Camille Decoppet	President		Jan. 1, 1916
Turkey	Mohammed V	Sultan	Nov. 3, 1844	April 27, 1909
United States of America	Woodrow Wilson	President	Dec. 28, 1856	March 4, 1913
Uruguay	Dr. Feliciano Viera	President		March 1, 1915
Venezuela	Dr. V. Marquez Bustillos	Provisional President		April 19, 1914

A Table Exhibiting the Difference of Time Between Washington and the Places Named.

When the clock is at 12 noon, at Washington, it is at;

Edinburg, Scot.	4.58 "	Vicksburg, Miss.	11.04 "	Springfield, Ill.	11.09 "	Philadelphia	12.07 p.m.
Lisbon, Port.	4.29 "	New Orleans, La.	11.07 "	Indianapolis, Ind.	11.24 "	Baltimore	12.01 "
Honolulu, Hawaii	6.20 a.m.	Knoxville, Tenn.	11.23 "	Columbus, O.	11.80 "	Wilmington, Del.	12.06 "
Auckland, N. Z.	4.38 "	Memphis, Tenn.	11.08 "	Frankfort, Ky.	11.28 "	Jersey City, N. J.	12.11 "
Sidney, Australia	2.13 "	Louisville, Ky.	11.26 "	Nashville, Tenn.	11.21 "	New York City, N. Y.	12.12 "
Pekin, China	12.54 p.m.	Cleveland, O.	11.40 "	Little Rock, Ark.	10.59 "	Springfield, Mass.	12.18 "
Frankfort, Germany	5.42 "	Fort Wayne, Ind.	11.28 "	Baton Rouge, La.	11.00 "	Newport, R. I.	12.27 "
Berne, Switz.	5.38 "	Chicago, Ill.	11.17 "	Jackson, Miss.	11.07 "	Hartford, Conn.	12.17 "
Rome, Italy	5.58 "	St. Louis, Mo.	11.08 "	Montgomery, Ala.	11.23 "	Burlington, Vt.	12.15 "
Berlin, Ger.	6.02 "	Iowa City, Ia.	11.02 "	Tallahassee, Fla.	11.31 "	Portsmouth, N. H.	12.25 "
Cape of Good Hope	6.22 "	Galveston, Tex.	10.49 "	Columbus, S. C.	11.44 "	Bangor, Me.	12.33 "
St. Petersburg, Rus.	7.10 "	Corpus Christi, Tex.	10.38 "	Raleigh, N. C.	11.53 "	Norfolk, Va.	12.03 "
Jerusalem, Pal.	8.09 "	Salt Lake City, Utah	9.40 "	Richmond, Va.	11.58 "	Augusta, Me.	12.29 "
Calcutta, Ind.	11.03 "	San Francisco, Cal.	8.58 "	Buffalo, N. Y.	11.52 "	Concord, N. H.	12.22 "
Constantinople, Tur.	7.06 "	Portland, Ore.	8.57 "	Rochester, N. Y.	11.58 "	Montpelier, Vt.	12.18 "
Vienna, Aus.-Hun.	6.14 "	Wallawalla, Wash.	9.16 "	Charlottetown, P. E. I.	12.55 p.m.	New Haven, Conn.	12.17 "
Paris, France	5.17 "	Denver, Colo.	10.08 "	Portland, Me.	12.27 "	Providence, R. I.	12.23 "
Dublin, Ireland	4.42 "	Janesville, Wis.	11.12 "	St. John, N. B.	1.36 "	Boston, Mass.	12.24 "
Mexico, Mex.	10.82 a.m.	Milwaukee, Wis.	11.16 "	Halifax, N. S.	12.54 "	Albany, N. Y.	12.15 "
Vera Cruz, Mex.	10.49 "	Detroit, Mich.	11.30 "	Augusta, Ga.	11.40 a.m.	Trenton, N. J.	12.09 "
San Salvador, C. Am.	11.11 "	Lansing, Mich.	11.30 "	Natchez, Miss.	11.01 "	Dover, Del.	12.06 "
Nicaragua, C. Am.	11.26 "	Madison, Wis.	11.12 "	Fredericton, N. F.	2.40 p.m.	Annapolis, Md.	12.03 "
Havana, Cuba	11.38 "	St. Paul, Minn.	10.57 "	Cincinnati, O.	11.30 a.m.	Harrisburg, Pa.	12.01 "
Spanishtown, Jam.	12.00 m	Topeka, Kan.	11.48 "	Quincy, Ill.	11.02 "	Quebec, Que.	12.23 "
Santo Domingo, S. D.	12.28 p.m.	Omaha, Neb.	10.44 "	Toronto, Ont.	11.30 "	Montreal, Que.	12.11 "
Rio Janeiro, Brazil	2.14 "	Olympia, Wash.	8.57 "	Sioux Falls, S. Dak.	10.43 "	Wilmington, N. C.	11.56 a.m.
Cape Horn	12.40 "	Salem, Ore.	8.59 "	Ottawa, Ont.	12.05 p.m.	Charleston, S. C.	11.48 "
Santiago, Chile	12.26 "	Sacramento, Cal.	9.02 "	Sault Ste. Marie, Mich.	11.31 a.m.	Savannah, Ga.	11.44 "
Georgetown, Br. Gui.	1.16 "	Santa Fe, N. M.	10.24 "	Pittsburg, Pa.	11.45 "	St. Augustine, Fla.	11.42 "
Buenos Ayres, Arg.	1.18 "	Austin, Tex.	10.27 "	London, Eng.	5.08 p.m.	Mobile, Ala.	11.18 "
Lima, Peru	11.59 a.m.	Des Moines, Ia.	10.53 "				
Panama	11.50 "	Jefferson City, Mo.	10.50 "				

ORGANIZATION OF THE UNITED STATES ARMY.

The army in active service as now organized under the acts of Congress of February 2, 1901, January 25, 1907, and April 23, 1908, comprises 15 regiments of cavalry, 705 officers and 12,775 enlisted men; 6 regiments of field artillery, 236 officers and 5,220 enlisted men; a coast artillery corps, 170 companies, 672 officers and 19,321 enlisted men; 30 regiments of infantry; 1,530 officers and 26,231 enlisted men; 3 battalions of engineers, 2,002 enlisted men, commanded by officers detailed from the corps of engineers; the Porto Rico Regiment of Infantry, 32 officers and 576 enlisted men; staff corps. Service School detachments, Military Academy, Indian scouts, recruits, etc., 11,777 enlisted men, and a provisional force of 52 companies of native scouts in the Philippines, 180 officers and 5,732 enlisted men. The total number of commissioned officers, staff and line, on the active list is 4,453 (including 103 first lieutenants, Medical Reserve Corps on active duty), and the total enlisted strength, staff and line, is 76,011, exclusive of the provisional force and the hospital corps. The law provides that the total enlisted strength of the army shall not exceed at any one time 100,000.

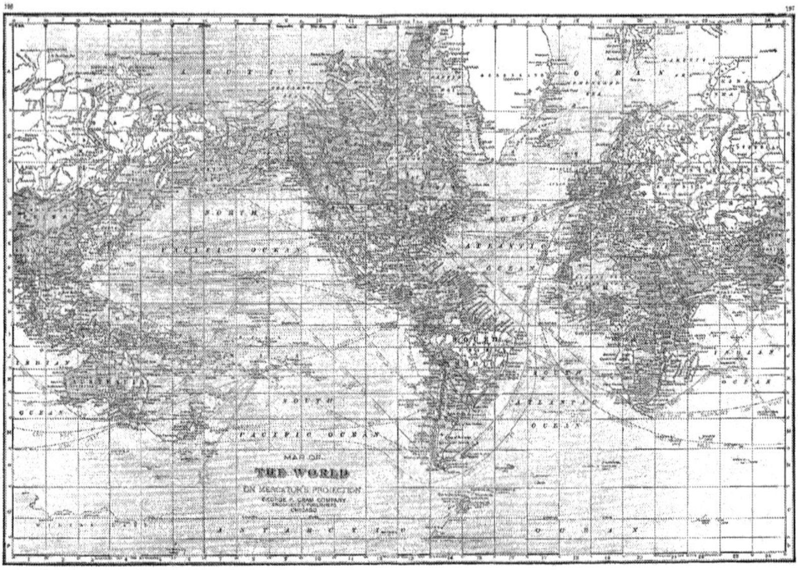
ARCTIC
NORTH
PACIFIC OCEAN
NORTH
ATLANTIC
OCEAN
SOUTH
PACIFIC OCEAN
SOUTH
ATLANTIC
OCEAN
INDIAN
OCEAN
MAP OF
THE WORLD
ON MERCATOR'S PROJECTION
GEORGE F. CRAM COMPANY
CHICAGO
ANTARCTIC
OCEAN

Geographical Tables

Also Tables of Temperature and Rainfall for United States and Foreign Cities

Dimensions of the Earth.

	Miles.
Equatorial Diameter	7,926.6
Earth's Axis	7,899.6
Circumference at Equator	24,899.2

Areas of the Earth.

	Sq. Miles.
Land Surface	55,441,763
Water Surface	143,317,388
Total	198,758,951

Continents.

	Sq. Miles.		Sq. Miles.
Africa	11,512,979	Australasia	3,456,290
America, N.	8,083,714	Europe	3,756,262
America, S.	6,861,496	Polar Regions	4,970,285
Asia	17,057,666	Total	55,541,102

Oceans.

	Sq. Miles.		Sq. Miles.
Pacific	71,000,000	Antarctic	8,500,000
Atlantic	35,000,000	Arctic	4,000,000
Indian	28,000,000		

Seas.

	Sq. Miles.		Sq. Miles.
China Sea, Asia	1,257,000	Gulf of Mexico, N. Am.	716,000
Caribbean Sea, N. & S. Am.	1,163,000	Baltic Sea, Europe	158,000
Bering Sea, N. Am.	878,000	Red Sea, Africa, Asia	180,000
Mediterranean, Afr., Eur., Asia	813,000	Black Sea, Europe, Asia	170,000

Principal Salt Lakes.

Lake or Sea.	Country.	Area, Sq. Miles.	Elevation, Feet.	
Caspian Sea	Asia	180,000	84	below sea
Sea of Aral	Asia	26,000	26	above sea
Balkash	Asia	12,500	700	" "
Maracaibo	South America	8,000	100	" "
Eyre	Australia	4,300	70	" "
Titicaca	South America	3,200	12,847	" "
Issik-Kul	Asia	2,300	5,300	" "
Koko-nor	Asia	2,000	270	" "
Van	Asia	2,000	5,360	" "
Great Salt Lake	North America	1,875	4,200	" "
Urumiah	Asia	1,700	4,000	" "
Dead Sea	Asia	445	1,312	below sea
Ngami	Africa	300	2,500	above sea
Salton	North America	400	263	below sea

Principal Freshwater Lakes.

Lake or Sea.	Country.	Area, Sq. Miles.	Elevation, Feet.	
Superior	N. America	32,000	602	above sea
Victoria Nyanza	Africa	26,000	3,800	" "
Michigan	N. America	23,000	590	" "
Huron	N. America	22,000	578	" "
Tanganyika	Africa	15,000	2,750	" "
Baikal	Asia	13,000	1,820	" "
Great Bear	N. America	14,000	230	" "
Nyassa	Africa	12,000	1,570	" "
Tchad	Africa	11,000	1,150	" "
Great Slave	N. America	10,400	400	" "
Bangweolo	Africa	10,200	3,690	" "
Winnipeg	N. America	8,500	628	" "
Erie	N. America	9,900	565	" "
Lake of the Woods	N. America	7,850	.....	" "
Albert Nyanza	Africa	7,500	2,350	" "
Ladoga	Europe	7,100	49	" "
Ontario	N. America	6,000	242	" "
Athabasca	N. America	4,000	.....	" "
Nicaragua	N. America	3,800	128	" "
Onega	Europe	3,800	237	" "
Tungting	Asia	2,500	300	" "
Wener	Europe	2,100	148	" "
Champlain	N. America	1,300	.....	" "
Dembea	Africa	1,200	6,125	" "
Wetter	Europe	830	288	" "
Managua	N. America	480	136	" "
Balaton, (Platten See)	Europe	300	300	" "
Geneva, (or Leman)	Europe	240	1,230	" "
Constance, (or Boden See)	Europe	208	1,283	" "
Garda	Europe	183	320	" "
Maggiore	Europe	102	678	" "
Neufchatel	Europe	115	1,427	" "
George	N. America	110	.....	" "
Cayuga	N. America	104	.....	" "
Lucerne, (or Lake of 4 Cantons)	Europe	99	1,420	" "
Zurich	Europe	76	1,332	" "
Como	Europe	66	661	" "

Longest Rivers.

Names.	Countries.	Length Miles.	Aver. Breadth. Ft.	Dis. Nav. Miles.	Approx. Area of Basin Sq. Miles.
Mississippi-Missouri	United States	4,200	1,900	16,500	1,250,000
Nile	Egypt	3,540	800	720	1,520,000
Amazon-Maranon	Brazil	3,270	10,000	.....	2,600,000
Yangtse-Kiang	China	2,880	1,300	1,500	747,000
Kongo	Central Africa	3,034	880	286	1,200,000
Ob	Russia in Asia	2,700	310	.....	1,500,000
Hoangho	China	2,600	.....	.....	537,000
Lena	Russia in Asia	2,500	.....	.....	581,000
Niger	West Africa	2,900	1,900	250	900,000
Yenesei	Russia in Asia	2,400	.....	.....	1,150,000
Plata-Parana	Argentine & Brazil	2,300	.....	.....	1,243,000
Mackenzie	Canada	2,300	.....	2,000	442,000
Amur	Russia in Asia	2,700	.....	.....	766,000
Volga	Russia in Europe	2,200	1,000	320	627,000
St. Lawrence	United States & Can.	2,200	10,500	780	505,516
Yukon	Alaska	2,044	10,000	1,300	260,000
Arkansas	United States	2,000	.....	.....	....
Zambesi	East Africa	1,800	.....	.....	600,000
Indus	India	1,800	.....	.....	372,000
Brahmaputra-Sanpo	India	1,800	.....	.....	361,000
Rio Grande del Norte	U.S. States & Mex.	1,800	.....	.....	245,000
Danube	Austria-Hungary	1,750	2,000	8.5	300,000
Mekong	Indo-China	1,700	.....	.....	736,000
Saskatchewan-Nelson	Canada	1,700	.....	.....	412,000
Euphrates	Turkey in Asia	1,700	.....	.....	259,000
Orinoco	Colombia & Ven.	1,600	.....	.....	252,000
Colorado	United States	1,500	650	600	257,000
Ganges	India	1,500	7,500	900	432,000
Amu	Turkestan	1,500	.....	.....	30,964
San Francisco	Brazil	1,400	.....	.....	187,000
Sir-Daria	Turkestan	1,300	.....	.....	375,000
Irawaddy	India	1,200	.....	.....	200,000
Columbia	United States	1,300	550	165	298,000
Dnieper	Russia in Europe	1,200	.....	.....	190,000
Para, or Tocantins	Brazil	1,120	.....	.....	284,000
Darling	Australia	1,100	.....	.....	199,000
Don	Russia in Europe	1,100	.....	.....	166,000
Tigris	Turkey in Asia	1,150	.....	.....	....
Murray	Australia	1,000	.....	.....	150,000
Orange, or Gariep	South'rn Africa	1,000	.....	.....	400,000
Senegal	West Africa	1,000	.....	.....	98,000
Ural, or Jaik	Russia in Europe	1,000	.....	.....	88,200
Gambia	West Africa	1,000	.....	.....	80,000
Rhine	Germany	800	.....	.....	63,000
Ohio	United States	950	.....	.....	214,000
Churchill, or Missinnippi	Canada	800	.....	.....	72,000
Magdalena	Colombia	830	.....	.....	77,000
Parnahiba	Brazil	788	.....	.....	115,200
Fraser	Canada	670	.....	.....	100,000
Loire	France	645	.....	.....	50,000
Elbe	Germany	550	.....	.....	51,000
Oder	Germany	550	.....	.....	50,000
Rhone	France	550	.....	.....	38,000
Tagus	Portugal	540	.....	.....	31,000
Vistula	Germany	530	.....	.....	56,000
Seine	France	470	.....	.....	33,000
Susquehanna	United States	478	.....	.....	....
Potomac	United States	450	200	110	....
Garonne	France	380	.....	.....	21,450
Guadiana	Spain	380	.....	.....	18,000
Sacramento	United States	370	.....	.....	30,000
Po	Italy	360	.....	.....	28,100
Ebro	Spain	340	.....	.....	33,100
Neva	Russia in Europe	300	.....	.....	61,200
Thames	England	215	.....	.....	6,160
Hudson	United States	310	.....	.....	7,000

Principal Mountains.

Mountains.	Countries.	Elev. Ft.	Mountains.	Countries.	Elev. Ft.
Mount Everest (Gaurisankar)	Asia	29,002	Mount Morrison	Asia	12,800
Dapsang, (Karakoram)	Asia	28,278	Mount Katmak	Asia	12,790
Mount Godwin Austen	Asia	28,250	Colima	N. Am	12,750
Mount Kanchinjanga	Asia	28,176	San Francisco Mts	N. Am	12,611
Dhawalagiri Peak	Asia	26,826	Mount Albert Edward	Oceania	12,590
Jamnotri	Asia	25,500	Ajusco	N. Am	12,500
Nanda devi	Asia	25,660	Pass of Quindiu	S. Am	12,500
Junno	Asia	25,304	Erebus	Antarctica	12,400
Gwalagiri	Asia	24,000	Mount Lamington	Oceania	12,215
Chumalari	Asia	23,730	Mount Cook	Oceania	12,349
Mount Kailas	Asia	21,615	Volcano de Agua	N. Am	12,160
Mount Chamalhari	Asia	23,914	Mount Ama	Oceania	12,250
Donkiakhan	Asia	23,190	Wetterhorn	Europe	12,210
Aconcagua	S. Am	22,860	Hyndman Peak	N. Am	12,078
Kidarnath Peak	Asia	22,780	Mount Semeru	Oceania	12,040
[illegible]	Asia	22,600	Yue-lo	Asia	12,000
St. Patrick	Asia	22,000	Mulahacen	Europe	11,658
Sahama	S. Am	22,350	Khawak Pass	Asia	11,600
Mercedario	S. Am	21,855	Mont [illegible]	Europe	11,400
St. George	Asia	22,210	Volcano de Colima	N. Am	11,400
Leopergyal	Asia	21,327	James Peak	N. Am	11,200
Parinacotta	S. Am	22,030	Mount Douglas	N. Am	11,300
Kuenlun	Asia	21,000	Lalamber Pass	Asia	11,280
Sirimo	S. Am	21,490	Mount [illegible]	Oceania	11,247
Gualatieri	S. Am	21,960	Mount Hood	N. Am	11,225
Mount Honda	Asia	21,712	Mount Herbstatter	Oceania	11,200
Nevado de Sorata	S. Am	21,286	Pic de Nethou	Europe	11,170
Illimani	S. Am	21,200	Mount [illegible]	Africa	11,000
Nevado de Chuquibamba	S. Am	21,000	Tapalpa	N. Am	11,000
Tengri Tagh	Asia	21,000	Spanish Peak	N. Am	11,000
Pyramid	Asia	20,956	Mount Perdu	Europe	10,997
Chimborazo	S. Am	20,498	Mount Lary Pass	Oceania	10,922
Lomas	S. Am	20,145	St. Theodule Pass, (or Matterjoch)	Europe	10,899
Arequipa, or Misti	S. Am	20,320	Mount Aetna	Europe	10,886
Mount McKinley	N. Am	20,300	Peak	Oceania	10,686
Tupungato	S. Am	20,286	Vignemale	Europe	10,820
San Jose	S. Am	20,020	Kronotzkaia	Asia	10,838
Tsar Liberator Mount	Asia	20,000	Schiveluch	Asia	10,551
Copiapo	S. Am	19,700	Sierra de Gredos	Europe	10,522
Mount Kilimanjaro	Africa	19,700	Maravaca	S. Am	10,500
Cotopaxi	S. Am	19,613	Mount Baker	N. Am	10,500
Cayambe Urcu	S. Am	19,531	Cathkin Peak	Africa	10,800
Mount Logan	N. Am	19,500	Mount Apo	Oceania	10,280
Antisana	S. Am	19,335	Monte Corno	Europe	10,306
Horqueta	S. Am	19,152	Piton des Neiges	Oceania	10,069
Carihuairazo	S. Am	19,188	Mount Tian	Oceania	10,046
Mount Kenia	Africa	18,620	Bulghardagh	Asia	10,000
Mount Elbrus	Europe	18,471	Buska Jovana	Europe	9,912
Mount Demavend	Asia	18,464	Mount Char Dagh	Europe	9,810
Tolima	S. Am	18,325	Mount St. Helens	N. Am	9,750
Orizaba, (or Citlaltepetl)	N. Am	18,205	Mount Olympus, (or Lacha)	Europe	9,749
Mount St. Elias	N. Am	18,024	Butschetje	Europe	9,528
Koh-i-Baba, (Hindu Kush)	Asia	18,000	Monte Stelvio Pass	Europe	9,172
Mount [illegible]	Asia	18,000	Ruapehu	Oceania	9,100
Maipo	S. Am	17,670	Mount Brown	N. Am	9,050
Popocatepetl	N. Am	17,540	Tomboro	Oceania	9,040
Knot of Cusco, (Vilcanota)	S. Am	17,820	Mount Tatra, (Lomnitz)	Europe	8,780
Mount Wrangell	N. Am	17,500	Dodabetta, (Nilgiri Hills)	Asia	8,760
Ylimani	S. Am	17,374	El Capitan	N. Am	8,690
Mount Ararat, (Agri-dagh)	Asia	17,160	Cibao	N. Am	8,600
Nevado de Chachani	S. Am	16,906	Hassan	Asia	8,490
Nevada de Toluca	N. Am	16,610	[illegible]	Europe	8,288
Ruwenzori	Africa	16,600	Great St. Bernard Pass	Europe	8,131
Tungaragua	S. Am	16,570	[illegible], (Norway)	Europe	8,100
Mount Kazbek	Europe	16,546	Karadagh	Asia	8,160
Cerro de Potosi	S. Am	16,037	Nanling	Asia	8,100
Villa Rica	S. Am	16,000	Furka Pass	Europe	7,992
Nevado de [illegible]	S. Am	15,986	Pass of Dariel	Europe	7,977
La Viuda	S. Am	15,968	Bernina Pass	Europe	7,658
Pichincha	S. Am	15,918	Pass of Savern	Europe	7,624
Mount Crillon	N. Am	15,900	Sneehatten, (Dovrefeld)	Europe	7,620
Ras Detchen	Africa	15,986	Gemmi Pass	Europe	7,582
Kliutschew	Asia	15,863	Duida	S. Am	7,150
Mount Murchison	N. Am	15,780	Julier Pass	Europe	7,140
Mont Blanc	Europe	15,781	Harney Peak	N. Am	7,216
Iztaccihuatl	N. Am	15,705	Little St. Bernard Pass	Europe	7,212
Mount Hooker	N. Am	15,700	Pike's Mts	N. Am	7,130
Cumbal	S. Am	15,624	Grimsel Pass	Europe	7,103
Overo	S. Am	15,500	Bernardin Pass	Europe	7,086
Mount Fairweather	N. Am	15,300	Pico de Turquino	N. Am	7,400
Pass of Ascasy	S. Am	15,500	Pacaraima	S. Am	7,000
Sierra Nevada	S. Am	15,420	Splugen Pass	Europe	6,946
[illegible]	N. Am	15,211	St. Gothard Pass	Europe	6,936
Monte Rosa	Europe	15,217	Mont Cenis Pass	Europe	6,772
Bismarck Mts	Oceania	15,000	Mitchell's Peak	N. Am	6,711
Abba Yared	Africa	15,000	Mount Guyot	N. Am	6,636
Kawasambo	Oceania	15,000	Simplon Pass	Europe	6,628
Mount Gordon Bennett	Africa	15,000	Mount Lecomte	N. Am	6,612
Weisshorn	Europe	14,804	Monte Santo, (Athos)	Europe	6,349
Mount [illegible]	Europe	14,782	Mount Washington	N. Am	6,290
Matterhorn, (Mount Cervino)	Europe	14,705	Mont Genevre Pass	Europe	6,155
Mount Meru	Africa	14,860	[illegible], (Riesen)	Europe	6,152
Mount Whitney	N. Am	14,501	Mount Dore, (Auvergne)	Europe	6,187
Mount Harvard	N. Am	14,375	Col di Tenda Pass	Europe	6,000
Blanca Peak	N. Am	14,464	Plomb du Cantal, (Auvergne)	Europe	6,093
Mount Shasta	N. Am	14,440	Maloja Pass	Europe	5,941
Mount Elbert	N. Am	14,436	Mount Adams	N. Am	5,805
Mount Rainier (Tacoma)	N. Am	14,363	Bolan Pass	Asia	5,793
Longs Peak	N. Am	14,271	Kazdagh, (Ida)	Asia	5,748
Pikes Peak	N. Am	14,108	Mount Rogers	N. Am	5,719
Fusi Yama	Asia	14,100	Toll Pass	Europe	5,633
Finster Aarhorn	Europe	14,026	Yaman	Europe	5,400
Mount Gunu	Africa	13,872	Koschkovrikh	Europe	5,397
Mauna Kea	Oceania	13,953	Mount Marcy	N. Am	5,344
Mount Ophir	Oceania	13,642	Mount Katahdin	N. Am	5,268
Fremont's Peak	N. Am	13,790	Hecla	Europe	5,115
Mount Gannett	N. Am	13,785	Schneekoppe, (Riesengeb.)	Europe	5,100
Jungfrau	Europe	13,671	Mont Mezenc, (Cevennes)	Europe	4,884
[illegible]	Africa	13,760	Ballon de Sulz, (Vosges)	Europe	4,678
Mauna Loa	Oceania	13,760	Feldberg, (Black Forest)	Europe	4,675
Kinabalu	Oceania	13,698	Brenner Pass	Europe	4,460
Mount Pelvoux	Europe	13,460	Ben Nevis	Europe	4,406
Mount Alaghez	Europe	13,436	Mount Vesuvius	Europe	4,260
Mount Emmons	N. Am	13,428	Ben Attow	Europe	4,000
[illegible]	N. Am	13,416	Table Mountain	Africa	3,816
Schreckhorn	Europe	13,386	Brocken	Europe	3,658
Mount Lyell	N. Am	13,190	Snowdon	Europe	3,560
Volcano de Fuego	N. Am	13,120	Carn Tual	Europe	3,404
Mount Argaeus	Asia	13,100	Khyber Pass	Asia	3,373
Wheeler Peak	N. Am	13,058	Scaw Fell Pikes	Europe	3,229
Eiger	Europe	13,042	Semmering Pass	Europe	3,160
Kamerun	Africa	13,000	Cross Fell	Europe	2,927
Mount Dana	N. Am	13,050			
Granite Peak	N. Am	12,834			

Elevations of the United States,

showing the Highest Point in Each State.

State. Place.	Feet.	State. Place.	Feet.
Alabama, Cheaha Mt.	2,407	Montana, Granite Peak	12,834
Alaska, Mount McKinley	20,300	Nebraska, Plains in southw'n corner	5,300
Arizona, San Francisco Peak	12,611	Nevada, Wheeler Peak	13,058
Arkansas, Magazine Mountain	2,800	New Hampshire, Mt. Washing'n	6,290
California, Mount Whitney	14,501	New Jersey, High Point	1,809
Colorado, Mount Elbert	14,436	New Mexico, peak near Truchas Peak	13,306
Connecticut, Bear Mountain	2,355	New York, Mount Marcy	5,344
Delaware, near Brandywine	440	North Carolina, Mt. Mitchell	6,711
District of Columbia, Ft. Reno	420	North Dakota, south part of Bowman County	3,500
Florida, near Mt. Pleasant Sta.	301	Ohio, 2½ miles east of Bellefontaine	1,550
Georgia, Brasstown Bald Mt.	4,768	Oklahoma, near Kenton	4,500
Idaho, Hyndman Peak	12,078	Oregon, Mount Hood	11,225
Illinois, Chas. M'd, Jo Daviess Co.	1,241	Pennsylvania, Blue Knob	3,136
Indiana, near Summit, Randolph County	1,285	Rhode Island, Durfee Hill	805
Iowa, five m. northeast of Sibley	1,670	South Carolina, Sassafras Mt.	3,548
Kansas, west boundary north of Arkansas River	4,135	South Dakota, Harney Peak	7,240
Kentucky, The Double, Harlan County	4,100	Tennessee, Mount Guyot	6,636
Louisiana, Sonumite in western Parishes	400	Texas, El Capitan, Guadalupe Mountain	8,690
Maine, Mount Katahdin (west)	5,268	Utah, Mount Emmons	13,428
Maryland, Backbone Mountain	3,400	Vermont, Mount Mansfield	4,406
Massachusetts, Mt. Greylock	3,505	Virginia, Mount Rogers	5,719
Michigan, Porcupine Mountains	2,023	Washington, Mount Rainier	14,363
Minnesota, Misquah Hills, Cook County	2,230	West Virginia, Spruce Knob	4,860
Mississippi, near Holly Springs	602	Wisconsin, Rib Hill, Marathon Co.	1,940
Missouri, Tom Sauk Mountain	1,800	Wyoming, Mount Gannett	13,785

Temperature and Rainfall, United States.

Stations.	Temperature. Mean. January.	July.	Extremes. Highest.	Lowest.	Mean Annual Precipitation. Rain and Melted Snow (inches).
Birmingham, Ala.	45	82	106	−10	49.5
Mobile, Ala.	50	81	102	−1	62.0
Montgomery, Ala.	48	82	107	−5	51.2
Flagstaff, Ariz.	27	65	92	−21	23.9
Phoenix, Ariz.	50	90	119	12	7.5
Yuma, Ariz.	55	91	118	22	3.1
Fort Smith, Ark.	38	81	108	−15	41.8
Little Rock, Ark.	41	81	108	−12	49.9
Fresno, Cal.	45	82	115	20	9.7
Los Angeles, Cal.	53	67	109	28	15.4
Red Bluff, Cal.	45	82	115	18	25.6
Sacramento, Cal.	46	72	110	19	20.1
San Diego, Cal.	54	67	101	32	10.0
San Francisco, Cal.	50	57	101	29	22.3
Denver, Colo.	28	72	105	−29	14.0
Grand Junction, Colo.	25	79	104	−16	8.8
Pueblo, Colo.	29	71	104	−31	12.6
New Haven, Conn.	27	72	100	−14	47.3
Washington, D. C.	33	77	104	−15	43.5
Jacksonville, Fla.	54	81	104	10	53.2
Jupiter, Fla.	64	81	96	24	60.2
Key West, Fla.	69	84	100	41	38.7
Pensacola, Fla.	53	81	103	7	56.3
Tampa, Fla.	57	80	96	19	53.1
Atlanta, Ga.	43	78	100	−8	49.4
Augusta, Ga.	46	80	105	3	47.9
Savannah, Ga.	50	80	105	8	51.8
Boise, Idaho	29	73	111	−28	13.7
Pocatello, Idaho	25	71	102	−20	13.9
Cairo, Ill.	35	79	106	−16	41.1
Chicago, Ill.	24	72	103	−23	33.3
Springfield, Ill.	26	76	107	−24	37.6
Indianapolis, Ind.	28	76	106	−25	41.5
Des Moines, Iowa	20	76	109	−30	32.4
Dubuque, Iowa	19	75	106	−32	31.9
Keokuk, Iowa	24	77	108	−27	35.1
Concordia, Kans.	24	78	108	−25	27.1
Dodge, Kans.	27	74	108	−26	21.5
Wichita, Kans.	30	79	106	−22	30.6
Louisville, Ky.	34	79	107	−20	44.8
New Orleans, La.	53	81	102	7	57.4
Shreveport, La.	46	83	110	−5	47.3
Eastport, Me.	20	60	93	−21	45.8
Portland, Me.	22	68	98	−17	42.0
Baltimore, Md.	33	77	105	−7	43.2
Boston, Mass.	27	71	103	−13	44.1
Alpena, Mich.	19	66	98	−27	32.2
Detroit, Mich.	24	72	101	−24	32.1
Marquette, Mich.	16	66	108	−27	32.6
Port Huron, Mich.	22	69	98	−25	30.6
Duluth, Minn.	10	66	99	−41	29.9
Moorhead, Minn.	3	68	103	−48	23.5
St. Paul, Minn.	12	72	104	−41	29.3
Vicksburg, Miss.	47	80	103	−1	52.7
Kansas City, Mo.	26	78	106	−22	37.2
St. Louis, Mo.	31	79	107	−22	37.2
Springfield, Mo.	31	76	106	−29	44.6
Havre, Mont.	14	69	108	−50	13.5
Helena, Mont.	20	67	103	−42	12.6
Kalispell, Mont.	23	64	96	−34	16.2
Miles City, Mont.	14	73	111	−49	13.8
North Platte, Nebr.	21	75	107	−35	18.9
Omaha, Nebr.	20	76	102	−32	30.1
Valentine, Nebr.	18	73	106	−38	22.8
Winnemucca, Nev.	29	72	104	−28	8.4
Concord, N. H.	21	69	100	−35	40.1
Atlantic City, N. J.	32	72	99	−7	40.8
Cape May, N. J.	33	73	96	−7	40.5
Roswell, N. Mex.	37	79	110	−29	15.5
Santa Fe, N. Mex.	28	65	97	−13	14.5
Albany, N. Y.	22	72	100	−24	36.4
Binghamton, N. Y.	23	70	96	−28	32.9
Buffalo, N. Y.	23	70	96	−14	37.3
New York City, N. Y.	30	74	100	−6	44.6
Oswego, N. Y.	24	70	100	−23	36.2
Charlotte, N. Car.	40	79	102	−5	48.8
Hatteras, N. Car.	46	79	93	8	60.8
Wilmington, N. Car.	46	79	103	5	51.0
Bismarck, N. Dak.	7	70	106	−45	17.8
Williston, N. Dak.	5	69	107	−49	15.1
Cincinnati, Ohio	32	78	105	−17	37.3
Columbus, Ohio	28	73	104	−20	36.9
Toledo, Ohio	24	72	103	−16	30.6
Oklahoma, Okla.	36	80	104	−17	31.7
Portland, Ore.	39	66	102	−2	45.1
Roseburg, Ore.	41	66	104	−6	31.4
Erie, Pa.	26	72	94	−16	36.6
Philadelphia, Pa.	32	76	103	−6	41.0
Pittsburgh, Pa.	31	75	103	−20	36.4
Block Island, R. I.	31	68	92	−4	44.4
Charleston, S. Car.	49	81	104	7	52.1
Huron, S. Dak.	12	72	108	−43	21.1
Pierre, S. Dak.	14	75	110	−40	16.6
Yankton, S. Dak.	16	75	107	−35	24.4
Chattanooga, Tenn.	41	78	101	−10	50.7
Memphis, Tenn.	40	81	104	−9	50.9
Nashville, Tenn.	39	79	104	−13	48.0
Abilene, Tex.	43	82	110	−6	24.7
Amarillo, Tex.	34	75	108	−16	22.6
El Paso, Tex.	44	80	113	−5	9.8
Galveston, Tex.	53	83	98	8	47.1
Palestine, Tex.	46	82	108	−6	42.0
San Antonio, Tex.	51	82	108	4	25.6
Salt Lake City, Utah	29	76	102	−20	16.0
Burlington, Vt.	16	68	97	−27	31.6
Northfield, Vt.	15	67	98	−35	32.9
Lynchburg, Va.	36	75	102	−6	48.4
Norfolk, Va.	40	78	102	2	49.5
Seattle, Wash.	39	64	96	11	36.2
Spokane, Wash.	27	69	104	−30	18.3
Walla Walla, Wash.	33	74	113	−17	17.7
Elkins, W. Va.	29	70	94	−21	42.6
Parkersburg, W. Va.	31	76	102	−27	40.2
La Crosse, Wis.	15	73	104	−43	31.2
Milwaukee, Wis.	20	70	100	−25	31.4
Cheyenne, Wyo.	26	67	100	−38	13.6
Lander, Wyo.	17	68	100	−34	13.9
Washakie, Wyo.	17	68	100	−54	13.9

The minus (—) sign indicates temperature below zero.

Temperature and Rainfall, Foreign Cities.

Cities.	Mean Annual Temp.	Annual Aver. Rainf'll Inches.	Cities.	Mean Annual Temp.	Annual Aver. Rainf'll Inches.
Alexandria, Egypt	69.5	10	London, England	50.8	25
Berlin, Germany	48.2	24	Madrid, Spain	58.2	9
Bermuda	72.0	55	Manila, Philippine Isls.	78.4	...
Bern, Switzerland	46.0	46	Maranhao, Brazil	...	277
Bordeaux, France	57.0	30	Marseilles, France	58.3	20
Brussels, Belgium	50.4	29	Melbourne, Australia	57.5	26
Budapest, Austria-Hun.	51.9	17	Mexico, Mexico	60.0	...
Buenos Ayres, Argentina	62.8	...	Montevideo, Uruguay	62.6	44
Calcutta, India	82.4	76	Montreal, Quebec	44.6	...
Canton, China	71.0	68	Nice, France	58.0	29
Capetown, Cape Colony	62.0	25	Para, Brazil	81.0	71
Cayenne, Fr. Guiana	...	116	Paris, France	51.3	22
Cherrapongee, India	...	610	Pekin, China	53.5	27
Constantinople, Turkey	56.5	...	Prague, Austria-Hun.	50.2	14
Copenhagen, Denmark	46.6	19	Quito, Ecuador	55.0	...
Dublin, Ireland	50.1	29	Rio de Janeiro, Brazil	77.2	44
Edinburgh, Scotland	47.1	38	Rome, Italy	59.5	31
Florence, Italy	59.2	41	Smyrna, Turkey in Asia	63.9	23
Geneva, Switzerland	52.7	32	St. Petersburg, Russia	38.6	17
Genoa, Italy	61.1	47	Stockholm, Sweden	42.3	20
Havana, Cuba	79.1	52	Sydney, Australia	63.8	49
[illegible]	62.2	20	The Hague, Netherlands	51.0	...
Jerusalem, Palestine	62.6	16	Valdivia, Chile	52.0	106
Lima, Peru	[illegible]	...	Valparaiso, Chile	54.0	...
Lisbon, Portugal	61.3	27	Venice, Italy	55.4	...
			Vienna, Austria-Hun.	51.0	19

www.ingramcontent.com/pod-product-compliance
Lightning Source LLC
LaVergne TN
LVHW022228200125
801702LV00040B/748